CHRISTIAN LEADERS

OF

THE EIGHTEENTH CENTURY

J. C. RYLE

THE BANNER OF TRUTH TRUST

THE BANNER OF TRUTH TRUST
3 Murrayfield Road, Edinburgh EH12 6EL
PO Box 621, Carlisle, Pennsylvania 17013, USA

*

First published 1885
Reprinted by Banner of Truth Trust 1978
Reprinted 1990
Reprinted 1997
Reprinted 2002
ISBN 0 85151 268 2

*

Printed and bound in Finland
by WS Bookwell

Preface

HE volume now in the reader's hands requires a few prefatory sentences of explanation. I should be sorry if there was any mistake as to its nature and intention.

It consists of a series of biographical papers, contributed to a well-known and most valuable monthly periodical during the years 866 and 1867.* My object in drawing up these papers was o bring before the public in a comprehensive form the lives, characters, and work of the leading ministers by whose agency God was pleased to revive Christianity in England a hundred years ago. I had long felt that these great men were not sufficiently known, and their merit in consequence not sufficiently recognized. I thought that the Church and the world ought to know something more than they seem to know about such men as Whitefield, Wesley, Romaine, Rowlands, Grimshaw, Berridge, Venn, Toplady, Hervey, Walker, and Fletcher. For twenty years I waited anxiously for some worthy account of these mighty spiritual heroes. At last I became weary of waiting, and resolved to take the pen in my own hand, and do what I could in the pages of a periodical. These papers, in compliance with the wishes of friends, are now brought together in a portable form.

How far my attempt has been successful, I must now leave

* The *Family Treasury*.

the public to judge. To literary merits the volume can lay no claim. Its chapters were written from month to month in the midst of many ministerial engagements, under a pressure which none can understand but those who write for periodicals. To expect such a volume to be a model of finished composition would be absurd. I only lay claim to a tolerable degree of accuracy about historical facts. I have been careful to make no statement for which I could not find some authority.

The reader will soon discover that I am an enthusiastic admirer of the men whose pictures I have sketched in this volume. I confess it honestly. I am a thorough enthusiast about them. I believe firmly that, excepting Luther and his Continental contemporaries and our own martyred Reformers, the world has seen no such men since the days of the apostles. I believe there have been none who have preached so much clear scriptural truth, none who have lived such lives, none who have shown such courage in Christ's service, none who have suffered so much for the truth, none who have done so much good. If any one can name better men, he knows more than I do.

I now send forth this volume with an earnest prayer that God may pardon all its defects, use it for his own glory, and raise up in his Church men like those who are here described. Surely, when we look at the state of England, we may well say, " Where is the Lord God of Whitefield and of Rowlands, of Grimshaw and of Venn ? O Lord, revive thy work ! "

J. C. RYLE.

STRADBROKE VICARAGE, *August* 10, 1868.

P.S.—I think it right to say that the chief substance of the biography of " Whitefield," in this volume, was originally delivered as a lecture in London in 1852. It now appears remoulded and enlarged. The other ten biographies were prepared expressly for the *Family Treasury.*

CONTENTS.

———o———

I.

The Religious and Moral Condition of England

AT THE BEGINNING OF THE EIGHTEENTH CENTURY.

II.

The Agency by which Christianity was Revived in England

IN THE MIDDLE OF THE EIGHTEENTH CENTURY.

III.

George Whitefield and his Ministry.

CHAPTER I.

IV.

John Wesley and his Ministry.

V.

William Grimshaw of Haworth, and his Ministry.

VI.

𝔚illiam 𝔯omaine and his 𝔐inistry.

CHAPTER I.

CHAPTER II.

VII.

𝔇aniel 𝔯owlands and his 𝔐inistry.

CHAPTER I.

CHAPTER II.

VIII.

𝔍ohn 𝔅erridge and his 𝔐inistry.

CHAPTER I.

ENGLAND A HUNDRED YEARS AGO.

I.

𝕿𝖍𝖊 𝕽𝖊𝖑𝖎𝖌𝖎𝖔𝖚𝖘 𝖆𝖓𝖉 𝕸𝖔𝖗𝖆𝖑 𝕮𝖔𝖓𝖉𝖎𝖙𝖎𝖔𝖓 𝖔𝖋 𝕰𝖓𝖌𝖑𝖆𝖓𝖉

AT THE BEGINNING OF THE EIGHTEENTH CENTURY.

Importance of the History of the Eighteenth Century—Political and Financial Position of England—Low State of Religion both in Churches and Chapels—Testimonies on the subject—Defects of Bishops and Clergy—Poverty of the Printed Theology—Wretched Condition of the Country as to Education, Morals, and popular Literature—The "Good Old Times" a mere Myth.

HE subject I propose to handle in this volume is partly historical and partly biographical. If any reader expects from the title a fictitious tale, or something partly drawn from my imagination, I fear he will be disappointed. Such writing is not in my province, and I have no leisure for it if it was. Facts, naked facts, and the stern realities of life, absorb all the time that I can spare for the press.

I trust, however, that with most readers the subject I have chosen is one that needs no apology. The man who feels no interest in the history and biography of his own country is surely a poor patriot and a worse philosopher.

"Patriot" he cannot be called. True patriotism will make an Englishman care for everything that concerns England. A true patriot will like to know something about every one who has left his mark on English character, from the Venerable Bede down to Hugh Stowell, from Alfred the Great down to Pounds, the originator of Ragged Schools.

"Philosopher" he certainly is not. What is philosophy but history teaching by examples? To know the steps by which England has reached her present position is essential to a right understanding both of our national privileges and our national dangers. To know the men whom God raised up to do his work in days gone by, will guide us in looking about for standard-bearers in our own days and days to come.

I venture to think that there is no period of English history which is so thoroughly instructive to a Christian as the middle of last century. It is the period of which we are feeling the influence at this very day. It is the period with which our grandfathers and great-grandfathers were immediately connected. It is a period, not least, from which we may draw most useful lessons for our own times.

Let me begin by trying to describe the actual condition of England a hundred years ago. A few simple facts will suffice to make this plain.

The reader will remember that I am not going to speak of our *political* condition. I might easily tell him that, in the days of Sir Robert Walpole, the Duke of Newcastle, and the elder Pitt, the position of England was very different from what it is now. Great statesmen and orators there were among us, no doubt. But our standing among the nations of the earth was comparatively poor, weak, and low. Our voice among the nations of the earth carried far less weight than it has since obtained. The foundation of our Indian Empire had hardly been laid. Our Australian possessions were a part of the world only just discovered, but not colonized. At home there was a strong party in the country which still longed for the restoration of the Stuarts. In 1745 the Pretender and a Highland army marched from Scotland to invade England, and got as far as

Derby. Corruption, jobbing, and mismanagement in high places were the rule, and purity the exception. Civil and religious disabilities still abounded. The test and corporation Acts were still unrepealed. To be a Dissenter was to be regarded as only one degree better than being seditious and a rebel. Rotten boroughs flourished. Bribery among all classes was open, unblushing, and profuse. Such was England politically a hundred years ago.

The reader will remember, furthermore, that I am not going to speak of our condition in a *financial and economical* point of view. Our vast cotton, silk, and linen manufactures had hardly begun to exist. Our enormous mineral treasures of coal and iron were scarcely touched. We had no steam-boats, no locomotive engines, no railways, no gas, no electric telegraph, no penny post, no scientific farming, no macadamized roads, no free-trade, no sanitary arrangements, and no police deserving the name. Let any Englishman imagine, if he can, his country without any of the things that I have just mentioned, and he will have some faint idea of the economical and financial condition of England a hundred years ago.

But I leave these things to the political economists and historians of this world. Interesting as they are, no doubt, they form no part of the subject that I want to dwell upon. I wish to treat that subject as a minister of Christ's gospel. It is the *religious and moral* condition of England a hundred years ago to which I shall confine my attention. Here is the point to which I wish to direct the reader's eye.

The state of this country in a religious and moral point of view in the middle of last century was so painfully unsatisfactory that it is difficult to convey any adequate idea of it. English people of the present day who have never been led to inquire into the subject, can have no conception of the darkness that prevailed. From the year 1700 till about the era of the French Revolution, England seemed barren of all that is really good. How such a state of things can have arisen in a land of free Bibles and professing Protestantism is almost past comprehension. Christianity seemed to lie as one dead, insomuch that you might have said " she is dead." Morality, however much exalted in pulpits, was thoroughly trampled under foot in the streets. There was darkness in high places and darkness in low places—darkness in the court, the camp, the Parliament, and the bar—darkness in country, and darkness in town—darkness among rich and darkness among poor—a gross, thick, religious and moral darkness—a darkness that might be felt.

Does any one ask what the churches were doing a hundred years ago? The answer is soon given. The Church of England existed in those days, with her admirable articles, her time-honoured liturgy, her parochial system, her Sunday services, and her ten thousand clergy. The Nonconformist body existed, with its hardly won liberty and its free pulpit. But one account unhappily may be given of both parties. They existed, but they could hardly be said to have lived. They did nothing ; they were sound asleep. The curse of the Uniformity Act seemed to rest on the Church of England. The blight of ease and freedom from persecution seemed to rest upon the Dissenters. Natural theology, without a single distinctive doctrine of Christianity, cold morality, or barren orthodoxy, formed the staple teaching both in church and chapel. Sermons everywhere were little better than miserable moral essays, utterly devoid of anything likely to awaken, convert, or save souls. Both parties seemed at last agreed on one point, and that was to let the devil alone, and to do nothing for hearts and souls. And as for the weighty truths for which Hooper and Latimer had gone to the stake, and Baxter and scores of Puritans had gone to jail, they seemed clean forgotten and laid on the shelf.

When such was the state of things in churches and chapels,

it can surprise no one to learn that the land was deluged with infidelity and scepticism. The prince of this world made good use of his opportunity. His agents were active and zealous in promulgating every kind of strange and blasphemous opinion. Collins and Tindal denounced Christianity as priestcraft. Whiston pronounced the miracles of the Bible to be grand impositions. Woolston declared them to be allegories. Arianism and Socinianism were openly taught by Clark and Priestly, and became fashionable among the intellectual part of the community. Of the utter incapacity of the pulpit to stem the progress of all this flood of evil, one single fact will give us some idea. The celebrated lawyer, Blackstone, had the curiosity, early in the reign of George III., to go from church to church and hear every clergyman of note in London. He says that he did not hear a single discourse which had more Christianity in it than the writings of Cicero, and that it would have been impossible for him to discover, from what he heard, whether the preacher were a follower of Confucius, of Mahomet, or of Christ!

Evidence about this painful subject is, unhappily, only too abundant. My difficulty is not so much to discover witnesses, as to select them. This was the period at which Archbishop Secker said, in one of his charges, " In this we cannot be mistaken, that an open and professed disregard of religion is become, through a variety of unhappy causes, the distinguishing character of the age. Such are the dissoluteness and contempt of principle in the higher part of the world, and the profligacy, intemperance, and fearlessness of committing crimes in the lower part, as must, if the torrent of impiety stop not, become absolutely fatal. Christianity is ridiculed and railed at with very little reserve ; and the teachers of it without any at all." This was the period when Bishop Butler, in his preface to the " Analogy," used the following remarkable words: " It has come to be taken for granted that Christianity is no longer a subject of inquiry ; but that it is now at length discovered to be fictitious. And accordingly it is treated as if, in the present age, this were an agreed point among all persons of discernment, and nothing remained but to set it up as a principal subject for mirth and ridicule." Nor were such complaints as these confined to Churchmen. Dr. Watts declares that in his day " there was a general decay of vital religion in the hearts and lives of men, and that it was a general matter of mournful observation among all who lay the cause of God to heart." Dr. Guyse, another most respectable Nonconformist, says, " The religion of nature makes up the darling topic of our age ; and the religion of Jesus is valued only for the sake of that, and only so far as it carries on the light of nature, and is a bare improvement of that kind of light. All that is distinctively Christian, or that is peculiar to Christ, everything concerning him that has not its apparent foundation in natural light, or that goes beyond its principles, is waived, and banished and despised." Testimony like this might easily be multiplied tenfold. But I spare the reader. Enough probably has been adduced to prove that when I speak of the moral and religious condition of England at the beginning of the eighteenth century as painfully unsatisfactory, I do not use the language of exaggeration.

What were the bishops of those days ? Some of them were undoubtedly men of powerful intellect and learning, and of un blamable lives. But the best of them, like Secker, and Butler, and Gibson, and Lowth, and Horn, seemed unable to do more than deplore the existence of evils which they saw but knew not how to remedy. Others, like Lavington and Warburton, fulminated fierce charges against enthusiasm and fanaticism, and appeared afraid of England becoming too religious ! The majority of the bishops, to say the truth, were mere men of the world. They were unfit for their position. The prevailing tone of the Episcopal body may be estimated by the fact, that Archbishop Cornwallis gave balls and routs at Lambeth Palace until the king himself interfered by letter and requested him to desist.* Let me also add, that when the occupants of the Episcopal bench were troubled by the rapid spread of Whitefield's influence, it was gravely suggested in high quarters that the best way to stop his influence was to make him a bishop.

What were the parochial clergy of those days? The vast majority of them were sunk in worldliness, and neither knew nor cared anything about their profession. They neither did good themselves, nor liked any one else to do it for them. They hunted, they shot, they farmed, they swore, they drank, they gambled. They seemed determined to know everything except Jesus Christ and him crucified. When they assembled it was generally to toast "Church and King," and to build one another up in earthly-mindedness, prejudice, ignorance, and formality. When they retired to their own homes, it was to do as little and preach as seldom as possible. And when they did preach, their sermons were so unspeakably and indescribably bad, that it is comforting to reflect they were generally preached to empty benches.

What sort of theological literature was a hundred years ago bequeathed to us? The poorest and weakest in the English language. This is the age to which we owe such divinity as that of the "Whole Duty of Man," and the sermons of Tillotson

* The king's letter on this occasion is so curious, that I give it in its entirety, as I find it in that interesting though ill-arranged book, "The Life and Times of Lady Huntingdon." The letter was evidently written in consequence of an interview which Lady Huntingdon had with the king. A critical reader will remember that the king was probably more familiar with the German than the English language.

"MY GOOD LORD PRELATE,—I could not delay giving you the notification of the grief and concern with which my breast was affected at receiving authentic information that routs have made their way into your palace. At the same time, I must signify to you my sentiments on this subject, which hold these levities and vain dissipations as utterly inexpedient, if not unlawful, to pass in a residence for many centuries devoted to divine studies, religious retirement, and the extensive exercise of charity and benevolence; I add, in a place where so many of your predecessors have led their lives in such sanctity as has thrown lustre on the pure religion they professed and adorned. From the dissatisfaction with which you must perceive I behold these improprieties, not to speak in harsher terms, and on still more pious principles, I trust you will suppress them immediately; so that I may not have occasion to show any further marks of my displeasure, or to interpose in a different manner. May God take your grace into his almighty protection!—I remain, my Lord Primate, your gracious friend,   G. R."

and Blair. Inquire at any old bookseller's shop, and you will find there is no theology so unsaleable as the sermons published about the middle and latter part of last century.

What sort of education had the lower orders a hundred years ago? In the greater part of parishes, and especially in rural districts, they had no education at all. Nearly all our rural schools have been built since 1800. So extreme was the ignorance, that a Methodist preacher in Somersetshire was charged before the magistrates with swearing, because in preaching he quoted the text, " He that believeth not shall be damned !" While, not to be behind Somersetshire, Yorkshire furnished a constable who brought Charles Wesley before the magistrates as a favourer of the Pretender, because in public prayer he asked the Lord to " bring back his banished ones !" To cap all, the vice-chancellor of Oxford actually expelled six students from the University because " they held Methodistic tenets, and took on them to pray, read, and expound Scripture in private houses." To swear extempore, it was remarked by some, brought an Oxford student into no trouble ; but to pray extempore was an offence not to be borne !

What were the morals of a hundred years ago? It may suffice to say that duelling, adultery, fornication, gambling, swearing, Sabbath-breaking and drunkenness were hardly regarded as vices at all. They were the fashionable practices of people in the highest ranks of society, and no one was thought the worse of for indulging in them. The best evidence of this point is to be found in Hogarth's pictures.

What was the popular literature of a hundred years ago? I pass over the fact that Bolingbroke, and Gibbon, and Hume the historian, were all deeply dyed with scepticism. I speak of the light reading which was most in vogue. Turn to the pages of Fielding, Smollett, Swift, and Sterne, and you have the answer. The cleverness of these writers is undeniable ; but the indecency of many of their writings is so glaring and gross, that few people now-a-days would like to allow their works to be seen on their drawing-room table.

My picture, I fear, is a very dark and gloomy one. I wish it were in my power to throw a little more light into it. But facts are stubborn things, and specially facts about literature. The best literature of a hundred years ago is to be found in the moral writings of Addison, Johnson, and Steele. But the effects of such literature on the general public, it may be feared, was infinitesimally small. In fact, I believe that Johnson and the essayists had no more influence on the religion and morality of the masses than the broom of the renowned Mrs. Partington had on the waves of the Atlantic Ocean.

To sum up all, and bring this part of my subject to a conclusion, I ask my readers to remember that the good works with which every one is now familiar did not exist one hundred years ago. Wilberforce had not yet attacked the slave trade. Howard had not yet reformed prisons. Raikes had not established Sunday schools. We had no Bible Societies, no ragged schools, no city missions, no pastoral aid societies, no missions to the heathen. The spirit of slumber was over the land. In a religious and moral point of view, England was sound asleep.

I cannot help remarking, as I draw this chapter to a conclusion, that we ought to be more thankful for the times in which we live. I fear we are far too apt to look at the evils we see around us, and to forget how much worse things were a hundred years ago. I have no faith, for my part, and I boldly avow it, in those "good old times" of which some delight to speak. I regard them as a mere fable and a myth. I believe that our own times are the best times that England has ever seen. I do not say this boastfully. I know we have many things to deplore; but I do say that we might be worse. I do say that we were much worse a hundred years ago. The general standard of religion and morality is undoubtedly far higher. At all events, in 1868, we are awake. We see and feel evils to which, a hundred years ago, men were insensible. We struggle to be free from these evils; we desire to amend. This is a vast improvement. With all our many faults we are not sound asleep. On every side there is stir, activity, movement, progress, and not stagnation. Bad as we are, we confess our badness; weak as we are, we acknowledge our failings; feeble as our efforts are, we strive to amend; little as we do for Christ, we do try to do something. Let us thank God for this! Things might be worse. Comparing our own days with the middle of last century, we have reason to thank God and take courage. England is in a better state than it was a hundred years ago.

The Agency by which Christianity was revived in England

IN THE MIDDLE OF THE EIGHTEENTH CENTURY.

Improvement of England since middle of Eighteenth Century an undeniable Fact—Agents in effecting the Change a few isolated and humble Clergymen—Preaching the chief Instrument they employed—The Manner of their Preaching—The Substance of their Preaching.

THAT a great change for the better has come over England in the last hundred years is a fact which I suppose no well-informed person would ever attempt to deny. You might as well attempt to deny that there was a Protestant Reformation in the days of Luther, a Long Parliament in the time of Cromwell, or a French republic at the end of the last century. There has been a vast change for the better. Both in religion and morality the country has gone through a complete revolution. People neither think, nor talk, nor act as they did in 1750. It is a great fact, which the children of this world cannot deny, however they may attempt to explain it. They might as well try to persuade us that high-water and low-water at London Bridge are one and the same thing.

But by what agency was this great change effected? To whom are we indebted for the immense improvement in religion and morality which undoubtedly has come over the land? Who, in a word, were the instruments that God employed in bringing about the great English Reformation of the eighteenth century?

This is the one point that I wish to examine generally in the present chapter. The names and biographies of the principal agents I shall reserve for future chapters.

The government of the country can lay no claim to the credit of the change. Morality cannot be called into being by penal enactments and statutes. People were never yet made religious by Acts of Parliament. At any rate, the Parliaments and administrations of last century did as little for religion and morality as any that ever existed in England.

Nor yet did the change come from the Church of England, as a body. The leaders of that venerable communion were utterly unequal to the times. Left to herself, the Church of England would probably have died of dignity, and sunk at her anchors.

Nor yet did the change come from the Dissenters. Content with their hardly-won triumphs, that worthy body of men seemed to rest upon their oars. In the plenary enjoyment of their rights of conscience, they forgot the great vital principles of their forefathers, and their own duties and responsibilities.

Who, then, were the reformers of the last century? To whom are we indebted, under God, for the change which took place?

The men who wrought deliverance for us, a hundred years ago, were a few individuals, most of them clergymen of the Established Church, whose hearts God touched about the same time in various parts of the country. They were not wealthy or highly connected. They had neither money to buy adherents, nor family influence to command attention and respect. They were not put forward by any Church, party, society, or institution. They were simply men whom God stirred up and brought out to do his work, without previous concert, scheme, or plan. They did his work in the old apostolic way, by becoming the evangelists of their day. They taught one set of truths. They taught them in the same way, with fire, reality, earnestness, as men fully convinced of what they taught. They taught them in the same spirit, always loving, compassionate, and, like Paul, even weeping, but always bold, unflinching, and not fearing the face of man. And they taught them on the same plan, always acting on the aggressive; not waiting for sinners to come to them, but going after, and seeking sinners; not sitting idle till sinners offered to repent, but assaulting the high places of ungodliness like men storming a breach, and giving sinners no rest so long as they stuck to their sins.

The movement of these gallant evangelists shook England from one end to another. At first people in high places affected to despise them. The men of letters sneered at them as fanatics; the wits cut jokes, and invented smart names for them; the Church shut her doors on them; the Dissenters turned the cold shoulder on them; the ignorant mob persecuted them. But the movement of these few evangelists went on, and made itself felt in every part of the land. Many were aroused and awakened to think about religion; many were shamed out of their sins; many were restrained and frightened at their own ungodliness; many were gathered together and induced to profess a decided hearty religion; many were converted; many who affected to dislike the movement were secretly provoked to emulation. The little sapling became a strong tree; the little rill became a deep, broad stream; the little spark became a steady burning flame. A candle was lighted, of which we are now enjoying the benefit. The feeling of all classes in the land about religion and morality gradually assumed a totally different complexion. And all this, under God, was effected by a few unpatronized, unpaid adventurers! When God takes a work in hand, nothing can stop it. When God is for us, none can be against us.

The instrumentality by which the spiritual reformers of the last century carried on their operations was of the simplest description. It was neither more nor less than the old apostolic weapon of *preaching*. The sword which St. Paul wielded with

such mighty effect, when he assaulted the strongholds of heathenism eighteen hundred years ago, was the same sword by
which they won their victories.   To say, as some have done,
that they neglected education and schools, is totally incorrect.
Wherever they gathered congregations, they cared for the children.   To say, as others have done, that they neglected the
sacraments, is simply false.   Those who make that assertion
only expose their entire ignorance of the religious history of
England a hundred years ago.   It would be easy to name men
among the leading reformers of the last century whose communicants might be reckoned by hundreds, and who honoured
the Lord's Supper more than forty-nine out of fifty clergymen
in their day.   But beyond doubt preaching was their favourite
weapon.   They wisely went back to first principles, and took
up apostolic plans.   They held, with St. Paul, that a minister's
first work is " to preach the gospel."

They preached *everywhere*.   If the pulpit of a parish church
was open to them, they gladly availed themselves of it.   If it
could not be obtained, they were equally ready to preach in a
barn.   No place came amiss to them.   In the field or by the
road-side, on the village-green or in a market-place, in lanes or
in alleys, in cellars or in garrets, on a tub or on a table, on a
bench or on a horse-block, wherever hearers could be gathered,
the spiritual reformers of the last century were ready to speak
to them about their souls.   They were instant in season and
out of season in doing the fisherman's work, and compassed sea
and land in carrying forward their Father's business.   Now, all
this was a new thing.   Can we wonder that it produced a great
effect?

They preached *simply*.   They rightly concluded that the very
first qualification to be aimed at in a sermon is to be understood.   They saw clearly that thousands of able and well-com-
posed sermons are utterly useless, because they are above the
heads of the hearers.   They strove to come down to the level

of the people, and to speak what the poor could understand. To attain this they were not ashamed to crucify their style, and to sacrifice their reputation for learning. To attain this they used illustrations and anecdotes in abundance, and, like their divine Master, borrowed lessons from every object in nature. They carried out the maxim of Augustine,—" A wooden key is not so beautiful as a golden one, but if it can open the door when the golden one cannot, it is far more useful." They re· vived the style of sermons in which Luther and Latimer used to be so eminently successful. In short, they saw the truth of what the great German reformer meant when he said, " No one can be a good preacher to the people who is not willing to preach in a manner that seems childish and vulgar to some." Now, all this again was quite new a hundred years ago.

They preached *fervently and directly.* They cast aside that dull, cold, heavy, lifeless mode of delivery, which had long made sermons a very proverb for dulness. They proclaimed the words of faith with faith, and the story of life with life. They spoke with fiery zeal, like men who were thoroughly persuaded that what they said was true, and that it was of the utmost importance to your eternal interest to hear it. They spoke like men who had got a message from God to you, and must deliver it, and must have your attention while they delivered it. They threw heart and soul and feeling into their sermons, and sent their hearers home convinced, at any rate, that the preacher was sincere and wished them well. They believed that you must speak *from* the heart if you wish to speak *to* the heart, and that there must be unmistakable faith and conviction within the pulpit if there is to be faith and conviction among the pews. All this, I repeat, was a thing that had become almost obsolete a hundred years ago. Can we wonder that it took people by storm, and produced an immense effect ?

But what was the substance and subject-matter of the preach· ing which produced such wonderful effect a hundred years ago ?

I will not insult my readers' common sense by only saying that it was "simple, earnest, fervent, real, genial, brave, life-like," and so forth; I would have it understood that it was eminently doctrinal, positive, dogmatical, and distinct. The strongholds of the last century's sins would never have been cast down by mere earnestness and negative teaching. The trumpets which blew down the walls of Jericho were trumpets which gave no uncertain sound. The English evangelists of last century were not men of an uncertain creed. But what was it that they proclaimed? A little information on this point may not be without use.

For one thing, then, the spiritual reformers of the last century taught constantly *the sufficiency and supremacy of Holy Scripture.* The Bible, whole and unmutilated, was their sole rule of faith and practice. They accepted all its statements without question or dispute. They knew nothing of any part of Scripture being uninspired. They never allowed that man has any "verifying faculty" within him, by which Scripture statements may be weighed, rejected, or received. They never flinched from asserting that there can be no error in the Word of God; and that when we cannot understand or reconcile some part of its contents, the fault is in the interpreter and not in the text. In all their preaching they were eminently men of one book. To that book they were content to pin their faith, and by it to stand or fall. This was one grand characteristic of their preaching. They honoured, they loved, they reverenced the Bible.

Furthermore, the reformers of the last century taught constantly the *total corruption of human nature.* They knew nothing of the modern notion that Christ is in every man, and that all possess something good within, which they have only to stir up and use in order to be saved. They never flattered men and women in this fashion. They told them plainly that they were dead, and must be made alive again; that they were guilty, lost, helpless, and hopeless, and in imminent danger of eternal ruin. Strange and paradoxical as it may seem to some, their first step towards making men good was to show them that they were utterly bad; and their primary argument in persuading men to do something for their souls was to convince them that they could do nothing at all.

Furthermore, the reformers of the last century taught constantly that *Christ's death upon the cross was the only satisfaction for man's sin;* and that, when Christ died, he died as our substitute—" the just for the unjust." This, in fact, was the cardinal point in almost all their sermons. They never taught the modern doctrine that Christ's death was only a great example of self-sacrifice. They saw in it something far higher, greater, deeper than this. They saw in it the payment of man's mighty debt to God. They loved Christ's person; they rejoiced in Christ's promises; they urged men to walk after Christ's example. But the one subject, above all others, concerning Christ, which they delighted to dwell on, was the atoning blood which Christ shed for us on the cross.

Furthermore, the reformers of the last century taught constantly the great doctrine of *justification by faith.* They told men that faith was the one thing needful in order to obtain an interest in Christ's work for their souls; that before we believe, we are dead, and have no interest in Christ; and that the moment we do believe, we live, and have a plenary title to all Christ's benefits. Justification by virtue of church membership—justification without believing or trusting—were notions to which they gave no countenance. Everything, if you will believe, and the moment you believe; nothing, if you do not believe,—was the very marrow of their preaching.

Furthermore, the reformers of the last century taught constantly the *universal necessity* of heart conversion and a new creation by the Holy Spirit. They proclaimed everywhere to the crowds whom they addressed, " Ye must be born again." Sonship to God by baptism—sonship to God while we do the will of the devil—such sonship they never admitted. The regeneration which they preached was no dormant, torpid, motionless thing. It was something that could be seen, discerned, and known by its effects.

Furthermore, the reformers of the last century taught constantly the inseparable *connection between true faith and personal holiness.* They never allowed for a moment that any church membership or religious profession was the least proof of a man being a true Christian if he lived an ungodly life. A true Christian, they maintained, must always be known by his fruits; and these fruits must be plainly manifest and unmistakable in all the relations of life. " No fruits, no grace," was the unvarying tenor of their preaching.

Finally, the reformers of the last century taught constantly, as doctrines both equally true, *God's eternal hatred against sin, and God's love towards sinners.* They knew nothing of a " love lower than hell," and a heaven where holy and unholy are all at length to find admission. Both about heaven and hell they used the utmost plainness of speech. They never shrunk from declaring, in plainest terms, the certainty of God's judgment and of wrath to come, if men persisted in impenitence and unbelief; and yet they never ceased to magnify the riches of God's kindness and compassion, and to entreat all sinners to repent and turn to God before it was too late.

Such were the main truths which the English evangelists of last century were constantly preaching. These were the principal doctrines which they were always proclaiming, whether in town or in country, whether in church or in the open air, whether among rich or among poor. These were the doctrines by which they turned England upside down, made ploughmen and colliers weep till their dirty faces were seamed with tears, arrested the attention of peers and philosophers, stormed the strongholds of Satan, plucked thousands like brands from the burning, and altered the character of the age. Call them simple and elementary doctrines if you will. Say, if you please, that you see nothing grand, striking, new, peculiar about this list of truths. But the fact is undeniable, that God blessed these truths to the reformation of England a hundred years ago What God has blessed it ill becomes man to despise.

III.

George Whitefield and his Ministry.

CHAPTER I.

Whitefield's Birth-place and Parentage—Educated at Gloucester Grammar School—Enters Pembroke College, Oxford—Season of Spiritual Conflict—Books which were made useful to him—Ordained by Bishop Benson—First Sermon—Preaches in London— Curate of Dummer, Hants—Goes to America—Returns in a Year—Preaches in the open air—Is excluded from most London Pulpits—Extent of his Labours for thirty-one years—Dies at Newbury Port, America, in 1770—Interesting circumstances of his Death.

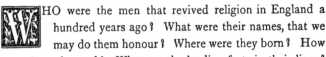WHO were the men that revived religion in England a hundred years ago? What were their names, that we may do them honour? Where were they born? How were they educated? What are the leading facts in their lives? What was their special department of labour? To these questions I wish to supply some answers in the present and future chapters.

I pity the man who takes no interest in such inquiries. The instruments that God employs to do his work in the world deserve a close inspection. The man who did not care to look at the rams' horns that blew down Jericho, the hammer and nail that slew Sisera, the lamps and trumpets of Gideon, the sling and stone of David, might fairly be set down as a cold and heartless person. I trust that all who read this volume will like to know something about the English evangelists of the eighteenth century.

The first and foremost whom I will name is the well-known George Whitefield. Though not the first in order, if we look at the date of his birth, I place him first in the order of merit, without any hesitation. Of all the spiritual heroes of a hundred years ago none saw so soon as Whitefield what the times demanded, and none were so forward in the great work of spiritual aggression. I should think I committed an act of injustice if I placed any name before his.

Whitefield was born at Gloucester in the year 1714. That venerable county-town, which was his birth-place, is connected with more than one name which ought to be dear to every lover of Protestant truth. Tyndal, one of the first and ablest translators of the English Bible, was a Gloucestershire man. Hooper, one of the greatest and best of our English reformers, was Bishop of Gloucester, and was burned at the stake for Christ's truth, within view of his own cathedral, in Queen Mary's reign. In the next century Miles Smith, Bishop of Gloucester, was one of the first to protest against the Romanizing proceedings of Laud, who was then Dean of Gloucester. In fact, he carried his Protestant feeling so far that, when Laud moved the communion-table in the cathedral to the east end, and placed it for the first time " altar-wise," in 1616, Bishop Smith was so much offended that he refused to enter the walls of the cathedral from that day till his death. Places like Gloucester, we need not doubt, have a rich entailed inheritance of many prayers. The city where Hooper preached and prayed, and where the zealous Miles Smith protested, was the place where the greatest preacher of the gospel England has ever seen was born.

Like many other famous men, Whitefield was of humble origin, and had no rich or noble connections to help him forward in the world. His mother kept the Bell Inn at Gloucester, and appears not to have prospered in business; at any rate, she never seems to have been able to do anything for Whitefield's advancement in life. The inn itself is still standing, and is reputed to be the birth-place, not only of our greatest

English preacher, but also of a well-known English prelate —
Henry Philpot, Bishop of Exeter.

Whitefield's early life, according to his own account, was
anything but religious ; though, like many boys, he had occasional prickings of conscience and spasmodic fits of devout
feeling.   But habits and general tastes are the only true test of
young people's characters. He confesses that he was " addicted
to lying, filthy talking, and foolish jesting," and that he was
a " Sabbath-breaker, a theatre-goer, a card-player, and a
romance-reader."   All this, he says, went on till he was fifteen
years old.

Poor as he was, his residence at Gloucester procured him the
advantage of a good education at the Free Grammar School of
that city.   Here he was a day-scholar until he was fifteen.
Nothing is known of his progress there.   He can hardly, however, have been quite idle, or else he would not have been
ready to enter an University afterwards at the age of eighteen.
His letters, moreover, show an acquaintance with Latin, in the
shape of frequent quotations, which is seldom acquired, if not
picked up at school.   The only known fact about his school-
days is this curious one, that even then he was remarkable for
his good elocution and memory, and was selected to recite
speeches before the Corporation of Gloucester at their annual
visitation of the Grammar School.

At the age of fifteen Whitefield appears to have left school,
and to have given up Latin and Greek for a season.   In all
probability, his mother's straitened circumstances made it absolutely necessary for him to do something to assist her in business and to get his own living.   He began, therefore, to help
her in the daily work of the Bell Inn.   " At length," he
says, " I put on my blue apron, washed cups, cleaned rooms,
and, in one word, became a professed common drawer for nigh
a year and a half."

This state of things, however, did not last long.   His mother's business at the Bell did not flourish, and she finally retired from it altogether. An old school-fellow revived in his mind the idea of going to Oxford, and he went back to the Grammar School and renewed his studies. Friends were raised up who made interest for him at Pembroke College, Oxford, where the Grammar School of Gloucester held two exhibitions. And at length, after several providential circumstances had smoothed the way, he entered Oxford as a servitor at Pembroke at the age of eighteen.*

Whitefield's residence at Oxford was the great turning-point in his life. For two or three years before he went to the University his journal tells us that he had not been without religious convictions. But from the time of his entering Pembroke College these convictions fast ripened into decided Christianity. He diligently attended all means of grace within his reach. He spent his leisure time in visiting the city prison, reading to the prisoners, and trying to do good. He became acquainted with the famous John Wesley and his brother Charles, and a little band of like-minded young men, including the well-known author of " Theron and Aspasio," James Hervey. These were the devoted party to whom the name " Methodists " was first applied, on account of their strict " method " of living. At one time he seems to have greedily devoured such books as " Thomas à Kempis," and " Castanuza's Spiritual Combat," and to have been in danger of becoming a semi-papist, an ascetic, or a mystic, and of placing the whole of religion in self-denial. He says in his Journal, " I always chose the worst sort of food. I fasted twice a week. My apparel was mean. I thought it unbecoming a penitent to have his hair powdered. I wore woollen gloves, a patched gown, and dirty shoes ; and though I was convinced

* Happening to be at Oxford in June 1865, I went to Pembroke College, and asked whether any one knew the rooms which Whitefield occupied when he was at Oxford. The porter informed me that nothing whatever was known about them. The rooms which the famous Dr. Johnson occupied at Pembroke are still pointed out. Johnson left Oxford just before Whitefield went up.

that the kingdom of God did not consist in meat and drink, yet I resolutely persisted in these voluntary acts of self-denial, because I found in them great promotion of the spiritual life." Out of all this darkness he was gradually delivered, partly by the advice of one or two experienced Christians, and partly by reading such books as Scougal's "Life of God in the Heart of Man," Law's "Serious Call," Baxter's "Call to the Unconverted," Alleine's "Alarm to Unconverted Sinners," and Matthew Henry's "Commentary." "Above all," he says, "my mind being now more opened and enlarged, I began to read the Holy Scriptures upon my knees, laying aside all other books, and praying over, if possible, every line and word. This proved meat indeed and drink indeed to my soul. I daily received fresh life, light, and power from above. I got more true knowledge from reading the book of God in one month than I could ever have acquired from all the writings of men." Once taught to understand the glorious liberty of Christ's gospel, Whitefield never turned again to asceticism, legalism, mysticism, or strange views of Christian perfection. The experience received by bitter conflict was most valuable to him. The doctrines of free grace, once thoroughly grasped, took deep root in his heart, and became, as it were, bone of his bone and flesh of his flesh. Of all the little band of Oxford methodists, none seem to have got hold so soon of clear views of Christ's gospel as he did, and none kept it so unwaveringly to the end.

At the early age of twenty-two Whitefield was admitted to holy orders by Bishop Benson of Gloucester, on Trinity Sunday, 1736. His ordination was not of his own seeking. The bishop heard of his character from Lady Selwyn and others, sent for him, gave him five guineas to buy books, and offered to ordain him, though only twenty-two years old, whenever he wished. This unexpected offer came to him when he was full of scruples about his own fitness for the ministry. It cut the knot and brought him to the point of decision. "I began to think."

he says, " that if I held out longer I should fight against God."

Whitefield's first sermon was preached in the very town where he was born, at the church of St. Mary-le-Crypt, Gloucester. His own description of it is the best account that can be given: —" Last Sunday, in the afternoon, I preached my first sermon in the church of St. Mary-le-Crypt, where I was baptized, and also first received the sacrament of the Lord's Supper. Curiosity, as you may easily guess, drew a large congregation together upon this occasion. The sight at first a little awed me. But I was comforted with a heartfelt sense of the divine presence, and soon found the unspeakable advantage of having been accustomed to public speaking when a boy at school, and of exhorting the prisoners and poor people at their private houses while at the university. By these means I was kept from being daunted overmuch. As I proceeded I perceived the fire kindled, till at last, though so young and amidst a crowd of those who knew me in my childish days, I trust I was enabled to speak with some degree of gospel authority. Some few mocked, but most seemed for the present struck ; and I have since heard that a complaint was made to the bishop that I drove fifteen mad the first sermon ! The worthy prelate wished that the madness might not be forgotten before next Sunday."

Almost immediately after his ordination, Whitefield went to Oxford and took his degree as Bachelor of Arts. He then commenced his regular ministerial life by undertaking temporary duty at the Tower Chapel, London, for two months. While engaged there he preached continually in many London churches; and among others, in the parish churches of Islington, Bishopsgate, St. Dunstan's, St. Margaret's, Westminster, and Bow, Cheapside. From the very first he obtained a degree of popularity such as no preacher, before or since, has probably ever reached. Whether on week-days or Sundays, wherever he preached, the churches were crowded, and an immense sensation was produced. The plain truth is, that a really eloquent, extempore preacher, preaching the pure gospel with most uncommon gifts of voice and manner, was at that time an entire novelty in London. The congregations were taken by surprise and carried by storm.

From London he removed for two months to Dummer, a little rural parish in Hampshire, near Basingstoke. This was a totally new sphere of action, and he seemed like a man buried alive among poor illiterate people. But he was soon reconciled to it, and thought afterwards that he reaped much profit by conversing with the poor. From Dummer he accepted an invitation, which had been much pressed on him by the Wesleys, to visit the colony of Georgia in North America, and assist in the care of an Orphan House which had been set up near Savannah for the children of colonists. After preaching for a few months in Gloucestershire, and especially at Bristol and Stonehouse, he sailed for America in the latter part of 1737, and continued there about a year. The affairs of this Orphan House, it may be remarked, occupied much of his attention from this period of his life till he died. Though well-meant, it seems to have been a design of very questionable wisdom, and certainly entailed on Whitefield a world of anxiety and responsibility to the end of his days.

Whitefield returned from Georgia at the latter part of the year 1738, partly to obtain priest's orders, which were conferred on him by his old friend Bishop Benson, and partly on business connected with the Orphan House. He soon, however, discovered that his position was no longer what it was before he sailed for Georgia. The bulk of the clergy were no longer favourable to him, and regarded him with suspicion as an enthusiast and a fanatic. They were especially scandalized by his preaching the doctrine of regeneration or the new birth, as a thing which many baptized persons greatly needed! The number of pulpits to which he had access rapidly diminished.

Churchwardens, who had no eyes for drunkenness and impurity. were filled with intense indignation about what they called "breaches of order." Bishops who could tolerate Arianism, Socinianism, and Deism, were filled with indignation at a man who declared fully the atonement of Christ and the work of the Holy Ghost, and began to denounce him openly. In short, from this period of his life, Whitefield's field of usefulness within the Church of England narrowed rapidly on every side.

The step which at this juncture gave a turn to the whole current of Whitefield's ministry was his adoption of the system of open-air preaching. Seeing that thousands everywhere would attend no place of worship, spent their Sundays in idleness or sin, and were not to be reached by sermons within walls, he resolved, in the spirit of holy aggression, to go out after them "into the highways and hedges," on his Master's principle, and "compel them to come in." His first attempt to do this was among the colliers at Kingswood near Bristol, in February 1739. After much prayer he one day went to Hannam Mount, and standing upon a hill began to preach to about a hundred colliers upon Matt. v. 1–3. The thing soon became known. The number of hearers rapidly increased, till the congregation amounted to many thousands. His own account of the behaviour of these neglected colliers, who had never been in a church in their lives, is deeply affecting :—" Having," he writes to a friend, "no righteousness of their own to renounce, they were glad to hear of a Jesus who was a friend to publicans, and came not to call the righteous but sinners to repentance. The first discovery of their being affected was the sight of the white gutters made by their tears, which plentifully fell down their black cheeks as they came out of their coal-pits. Hundreds of them were soon brought under deep conviction, which, as the event proved, happily ended in a sound and thorough conversion. The change was visible to all, though numbers chose to impute it to anything rather than the finger of God. As the

scene was quite new, it often occasioned many inward conflicts.
Sometimes, when twenty thousand people were before me, I had
not in my own apprehension a word to say either to God or
them.   But I was never totally deserted, and frequently (for to
deny it would be lying against God) was so assisted that I knew
by happy experience what our Lord meant by saying, ' Out of
his belly shall flow rivers of living water.'   The open firmament
above me, the prospect of the adjacent fields, with the sight of
thousands, some in coaches, some on horseback, and some in
the trees, and at times all affected and in tears, was almost too
much for, and quite overcame me."

Two months after this Whitefield began the practice of open-
air preaching in London, on April 27, 1739.   The circumstances
under which this happened were curious.   He had gone to
Islington to preach for the vicar, his friend Mr. Stonehouse.
In the midst of the prayer the churchwardens came to him and
demanded his license for preaching in the diocese of London.
Whitefield, of course, had not got this license any more than
any clergyman not regularly officiating in the diocese has at
this day.   The upshot of the matter was, that being forbidden
by the churchwardens to preach in the pulpit, he went outside
after the communion-service, and preached in the churchyard.
" And," says he, " God was pleased so to assist me in preaching,
and so wonderfully to affect the hearers, that I believe we could
have gone singing hymns to prison.   Let not the adversaries
say, I have thrust myself out of their synagogues.   No ; they
have thrust me out."

From that day forward he became a constant field-preacher,
whenever weather and the season of the year made it possible.
Two days afterwards, on Sunday, April 29, he records :—" I
preached in Moorfields to an exceeding great multitude.   Being
weakened by my morning's preaching, I refreshed myself in
the afternoon by a little sleep, and at five went and preached
at Kennington Common, about two miles from London, when

no less than thirty thousand people were supposed to be present." Henceforth, wherever there were large open spaces round London, wherever there were large bands of idle, godless, Sabbath-breaking people gathered together, in Hackney Fields, Mary-le-bonne Fields, May Fair, Smithfield, Blackheath, Moorfields, and Kennington Common, there went Whitefield and lifted up his voice for Christ.* The gospel so proclaimed was listened to and greedily received by hundreds who never dreamed of going to a place of worship. The cause of pure religion was advanced, and souls were plucked from the hand of Satan, like brands from the burning. But it was going much too fast for the Church of those days. The clergy, with a few honourable exceptions, refused entirely to countenance this strange preacher. In the true spirit of the dog in the manger, they neither liked to go after the semi-heathen masses of population themselves, nor liked any one else to do the work for them. The consequence was, that the ministrations of Whitefield in the pulpits of the Church of England from this time almost entirely ceased. He loved the Church in which he had been ordained ; he gloried in her Articles ; he used her Prayerbook with pleasure. But the Church did not love him, and so lost the use of his services. The plain truth is, that the Church of England of that day was not ready for a man like Whitefield The Church was too much asleep to understand him, and was vexed at a man who would not keep still and let the devil alone.

The facts of Whitefield's history from this period to the day of his death are almost entirely of one complexion. One year was just like another ; and to attempt to follow him would be only going repeatedly over the same ground. From 1739 to the year of his death, 1770, a period of thirty-one years, his life was one uniform employment. He was eminently a man of one thing,

* The reader will remember that all this happened a hundred years ago, when London was comparatively a small place. Most of the open places where Whitefield preached are now covered with buildings. Kennington Oval and Blackheath alone remain open at this day.

and always about his Master's business. From Sunday mornings to Saturday nights, from the 1st of January to the 31st of December, excepting when laid aside by illness, he was almost incessantly preaching Christ, and going about the world entreating men to repent and come to Christ and be saved. There was hardly a considerable town in England, Scotland, or Wales, that he did not visit as an evangelist. When churches were opened to him he gladly preached in churches ; when only chapels could be obtained, he cheerfully preached in chapels. When churches and chapels alike were closed, or were too small to contain his hearers, he was ready and willing to preach in the open air. For thirty-one years he laboured in this way, always proclaiming the same glorious gospel, and always, as far as man's eye can judge, with immense effect. In one single Whitsuntide week, after preaching in Moorfields, he received one thousand letters from people under spiritual concern, and admitted to the Lord's table three hundred and fifty persons. In the thirty-four years of his ministry it is reckoned that he preached publicly eighteen thousand times.

His journeyings were prodigious, when the roads and conveyances of his time are considered. He was familiar with " perils in the wilderness and perils in the seas," if ever man was in modern times. He visited Scotland fourteen times, and was nowhere more acceptable or useful than he was in that Bible-loving country. He crossed the Atlantic seven times, backward and forward, in miserable slow sailing ships, and arrested the attention of thousands in Boston, New York, and Philadelphia. He went over to Ireland twice, and on one occasion was almost murdered by an ignorant Popish mob in Dublin. As to England and Wales, he traversed every county in them, from the Isle of Wight to Berwick-on-Tweed, and from the Land's End to the North Foreland.

His regular ministerial work in London for the winter season, when field-preaching was necessarily suspended, was something prodigious. His weekly engagements at the Tabernacle in Tottenham Court Road, which was built for him when the pulpits of the Established Church were closed, comprised the following work :—Every Sunday morning he administered the Lord's Supper to several hundred communicants at half-past six. After this he read prayers, and preached both morning and afternoon. Then he preached again in the evening at half-past five, and concluded by addressing a large society of widows, married people, young men and spinsters, all sitting separately in the area of the Tabernacle, with exhortations suitable to their respective stations. On Monday, Tuesday, Wednesday, and Thursday mornings, he preached regularly at six. On Monday, Tuesday, Wednesday, Thursday, and Saturday evenings, he delivered lectures. This, it will be observed, made thirteen sermons a week ! And all this time he was carrying on a large correspondence with people in almost every part of the world.

That any human frame could so long endure the labours that Whitefield went through does indeed seem wonderful. That his life was not cut short by violence, to which he was frequently exposed, is no less wonderful. But he was immortal till his work was done. He died at last very suddenly at Newbury Port, in North America, on Sunday, September the 29th, 1770, at the comparatively early age of fifty-six. He was once married to a widow named James, of Abergavenny, who died before him. If we may judge from the little mention made of his wife in his letters, the marriage does not seem to have contributed much to his happiness. He left no children, but he left a name far better than that of sons and daughters. Never perhaps was there a man of whom it could be so truly said that he spent and was spent for Christ than George Whitefield.

The circumstances and particulars of this great evangelist's end are so deeply interesting, that I shall make no excuse for dwelling on them. It was an end in striking harmony with the tenor of his life. As he had lived for more than thirty years, so he died, preaching to the very last. He literally almost died in harness. "Sudden death," he had often said, "is sudden glory. Whether right or not, I cannot help wishing that I may go off in the same manner. To me it would be worse than death to live to be nursed, and to see friends weeping about me." He had the desire of his heart granted. He was cut down in a single night by a spasmodic fit of asthma, almost before his friends knew that he was ill.

On the morning of Saturday the 29th of September, the day before he died, Whitefield set out on horseback from Portsmouth in New Hampshire, in order to fulfil an engagement to preach at Newbury Port on Sunday. On the way, unfortunately, he was earnestly importuned to preach at a place called Exeter, and though feeling very ill, he had not the heart to refuse. A friend remarked before he preached that he looked more uneasy than usual, and said to him, " Sir, you are more fit to go to bed than to preach." To this Whitefield replied: " True, sir ;" and then turning aside, he clasped his hands together, and looking up, said : " Lord Jesus, I am weary in thy work, but not of thy work. If I have not yet finished my course, let me go and speak for thee once more in the fields, seal thy truth, and come home and die." He then went and preached to a very great multitude in the fields from the text 2 Cor. xiii. 5, for the space of nearly two hours. It was his last sermon, and a fitting conclusion to his whole career.

An eye-witness has given the following striking account of this closing scene of Whitefield's life :—" He rose from his seat, and stood erect. His appearance alone was a powerful sermon. The thinness of his visage, the paleness of his countenance, the evident struggling of the heavenly spark in a decayed body for utterance, were all deeply interesting ; the spirit was willing, but the flesh was dying. In this situation he remained several minutes, unable to speak. He then said : ' I will wait for the gracious assistance of God, for he will, I am certain, assist me once more to speak in his name.' He then delivered perhaps one of his best sermons. The latter part contained the following passage : ' I go; I go to a rest prepared : my sun has given light to many, but now it is about to set—no, to rise to the zenith of immortal glory. I have outlived many on earth, but they cannot outlive me in heaven. Many shall outlive me on earth and live when this body is no more, but there—oh, thought divine !—I shall be in a world where time, age, sickness, and sorrow are unknown. My body fails, but my spirit expands. How willingly would I live for ever to preach Christ. But I die to be with him. How brief—comparatively brief—has been my life compared to the vast labours which I see before me yet to be accomplished. But if I leave now, while so few care about heavenly things, the God of peace will surely visit you."

After the sermon was over, Whitefield dined with a friend, and then rode on to Newbury Port, though greatly fatigued. On arriving there he supped early, and retired to bed. Tradition says, that as he went up-stairs, with a lighted candle in his hand, he could not resist the inclination to turn round at the head of the stair, and speak to the friends who were assembled to meet him. As he spoke the fire kindled within him, and before he could conclude, the candle which he held in his hand had actually burned down to the socket. He retired to his bedroom, to come out no more alive. A violent fit of spasmodic asthma seized him soon after he got into bed, and before six o'clock the next morning the great preacher was dead. If ever man was ready for his change, Whitefield was that man. When his time came, he had nothing to do but to die. Where he died there he was buried, in a vault beneath the pulpit of the church where he had engaged to preach. His sepulchre is shown to this very day ; and nothing makes the little town where he died so famous as the fact that it contains the bones of George Whitefield

Such are the leading facts in the life of the prince of English evangelists of a hundred years ago. His personal character, the real extent of his usefulness, and some account of his style of preaching, are subjects which I must reserve for another chapter.

CHAPTER II.

Estimate of good that Whitefield did—Testimonies to his direct Usefulness—Indirect good that he did—Peculiar character of his Preaching—Witnesses to his real power as a Preacher—Analysis of his seventy-five published Sermons—Simplicity, Directness, Power of Description, Earnestness, Pathos, Action, Voice, and Fluency, his leading Excellences—Inner Life, Humility, Love to Christ, Laboriousness, Self-denial, Disinterestedness, Cheerfulness, Catholicity—Specimen of his Preaching.

GEORGE WHITEFIELD, in my judgment, was so entirely chief and first among the English Reformers of the last century, that I make no apology for offering some further information about him. The real amount of good he did, the peculiar character of his preaching, the private character of the man, are all points that deserve consideration. They are points, I may add, about which there is a vast amount of misconception.

This misconception perhaps is unavoidable, and ought not to surprise us. The materials for forming a correct opinion about such a man as Whitefield are necessarily very scanty. He wrote no book for the million, of world-wide fame, like Bunyan's "Pilgrim's Progress." He headed no crusade against an apostate Church, with a nation at his back, and princes on his side, like Martin Luther. He founded no religious denomination, which pinned its faith on his writings and carefully embalmed his best acts and words, like John Wesley. There are Lutherans and Wesleyans in the present day, but there are no Whitefieldites. No! The great evangelist of last century was a simple, guileless man, who lived for one thing only, and that was to preach Christ. If he did that, he cared for nothing else. The records of such a man are large and full in heaven, I have no doubt. But they are few and scanty upon earth.

We must not forget, beside this, that the many in every age see nothing in a man like Whitefield but fanaticism and enthusiasm. They abhor everything like "zeal" in religion. They dislike every one who turns the world upside down, and departs from old traditional ways, and will not let the devil alone. Such persons, no doubt, would tell us that the ministry of Whitefield only produced temporary excitement, that his preaching was common-place rant, and that his character had nothing about it to be specially admired. It may be feared that eighteen hundred years ago they would have said much the same of St. Paul.

The question, "What good did Whitefield do?" is one which I answer without the least hesitation. I believe that the *direct good* which he did to immortal souls was enormous. I will go further,—I believe it is incalculable. Credible witnesses in England, Scotland, and America, have placed on record their conviction that he was the means of converting thousands of people. Many, wherever he preached, were not merely pleased, excited, and arrested, but positively turned from sin, and made thorough servants of God. "Numbering the people," I do not forget, is at all times an objectionable practice. God alone can read hearts and discern the wheat from the tares. Many, no doubt, in days of religious excitement, are set down as converted who are not converted at all. But I wish my readers to understand that my high estimate of Whitefield's usefulness is based on a solid foundation. I ask them to mark well what Whitefield's cotemporaries thought of the value of his labours.

Franklin, the well-known American philosopher, was a cold-blooded, calculating man, a Quaker by profession, and not likely to form too high an estimate of any minister's work. Yet even he confessed that "it was wonderful to see the change soon made by his preaching in the manners of the inhabitants of Philadelphia. From being thoughtless or indifferent about religion, it seemed as if all the world were growing religious."

Franklin himself, it may be remarked, was the leading printer of religious works at Philadelphia; and his readiness to print Whitefield's sermons and journals shows his judgment of the hold that he had on the American mind.

Maclaurin, Willison, and Macculloch, were Scotch ministers whose names are well known north of the Tweed, and the two former of whom deservedly rank high as theological writers. All these have repeatedly testified that Whitefield was made an instrument of doing immense good in Scotland. Willison in particular says, " that God honoured him with surprising success among sinners of all ranks and persuasions."

Old Henry Venn, of Huddersfield and Yelling, was a man of strong good sense, as well as of great grace. His opinion was, that "if the greatness, extent, success, and disinterestedness of a man's labours can give him distinction among the children of Christ, then we are warranted to affirm that scarce any one has equalled Mr. Whitefield." Again he says : " He was abundantly successful in his vast labours. The seals of his ministry, from first to last, I am persuaded, were more than could be credited could the number be fixed. This is certain, his amazing popularity was only from his usefulness; for he no sooner opened his mouth as a preacher, than God commanded an extraordinary blessing upon his word."

John Newton was a shrewd man, as well as an eminent minister of the gospel. His testimony is : " That which finished Mr. Whitefield's character as a shining light, and is now his crown of rejoicing, was the singular success which the Lord was pleased to give him in winning souls. It seemed as if he never preached in vain. Perhaps there is hardly a place in all the extensive compass of his labours where some may not yet be found who thankfully acknowledge him as their spiritual father."

John Wesley did not agree with Whitefield on several theological points of no small importance. But when he preached his funeral sermon, he said : " Have we read or heard of any person who called so many thousands, so many myriads of sinners to repentance ? Above all, have we read or heard of any one who has been the blessed instrument of bringing so many sinners from darkness to light, and from the power of Satan unto God ? "

Valuable as these testimonies undoubtedly are, there is one point which they leave totally untouched. That point is the quantity of *indirect good* that Whitefield did. Great as the direct effects of his labours were, I believe firmly that the indirect effects were even greater. His ministry was made a blessing to thousands who never perhaps either saw or heard him.

He was among the first in the eighteenth century who revived attention to the old truths which produced the Protestant Reformation. His constant assertion of the doctrines taught by the Reformers, his repeated reference to the Articles and Homilies, and the divinity of the best English theologians, obliged many to think, and roused them to examine their own principles. If the whole truth was known, I believe it would prove that the rise and progress of the Evangelical body in the Church of England received a mighty impulse from George Whitefield.

But this is not the only indirect good that Whitefield did in his day. He was among the first to show the right way to meet the attacks of infidels and sceptics on Christianity. He saw clearly that the most powerful weapon against such men is not cold, metaphysical reasoning and dry critical disquisition, but preaching the whole gospel—living the whole gospel—and spreading the whole gospel. It was not the writings of Leland, and the younger Sherlock, and Waterland, and Leslie, that rolled back the flood of infidelity one half so much as the preaching of Whitefield and his companions. They were the men who were the true champions of Christianity. Infidels are

seldom shaken by mere abstract reasoning. The surest arguments against them are gospel truth and gospel life.

Above all, he was the very first Englishman who seems to
have thoroughly understood what Dr. Chalmers aptly called
the *aggressive* system. He was the first to see that Christ's
ministers must do the work of fishermen. They must not wait
for souls to come to them, but must go after souls, and " compel
them to come in." He did not sit tamely by his fireside, like
a cat in a rainy day, mourning over the wickedness of the land.
He went forth to beard the devil in his high places. He
attacked sin and wickedness face to face, and gave them no
peace. He dived into holes and corners after sinners. He
hunted out ignorance and vice wherever they could be found.
In short, he set on foot a system of action which, up to his
time, had been comparatively unknown in this country, but a
system which, once commenced, has never ceased to be employed down to the present day. City missions, town missions,
district visiting societies, open-air preachings, home missions,
special services, theatre preachings, are all evidences that the
value of the "aggressive system" is now thoroughly recognized
by all the Churches. We understand better how to go to work
now than we did a hundred years ago. But let us never forget
that the first man to commence operations of this kind was
George Whitefield, and let us give him the credit he deserves.

The peculiar *character of Whitefield's preaching* is the subject
which next demands some consideration. Men naturally wish
to know what was the secret of his unparalleled success. The
subject is one surrounded with considerable difficulty, and it is
no easy matter to form a correct judgment about it. The
common idea of many people, that he was a mere common-
place ranting Methodist, remarkable for nothing but great
fluency, strong doctrine, and a loud voice, will not bear a
moment's investigation. Dr. Johnson was foolish enough to
say, that " he vociferated and made an impression, but never

drew as much attention as a mountebank does; and that he did not draw attention by doing better than others, but by doing what was strange." But Johnson was anything but infallible when he began to talk about ministers and religion. Such a theory will not hold water. It is contradictory to undeniable facts.

It is a fact that no preacher in England has ever succeeded in arresting the attention of such crowds as Whitefield constantly addressed around London. No preacher has ever been so universally popular in every country that he visited, in England, Scotland, and America. No preacher has ever retained his hold on his hearers so entirely as he did for thirty-four years. His popularity never waned. It was as great at the end of his day as it was at the beginning. Wherever he preached, men would leave their workshops and employments to gather round him, and hear like those who heard for eternity. This of itself is a great fact. To command the ear of " the masses " for a quarter of a century, and to be preaching incessantly the whole time, is an evidence of no common power.

It is another fact that Whitefield's preaching produced a powerful effect on people in every rank of life. He won the admiration of high as well as low, of rich as well as poor, of learned as well as unlearned. If his preaching had been popular with none but the uneducated and the poor, we might have thought it possible that there was little in it but declamation and noise. But, so far from this being the case, he seems to have been acceptable to numbers of the nobility and gentry. The Marquis of Lothian, the Earl of Leven, the Earl of Buchan, Lord Rae, Lord Dartmouth, Lord James A. Gordon, might be named among his warmest admirers, beside Lady Huntingdon and a host of ladies.

It is a fact that eminent critics and literary men, like Lord Bolingbroke and Lord Chesterfield, were frequently his delighted hearers. Even the cold artificial Chesterfield was known to warm under Whitefield's eloquence. Bolingbroke said, "He is the most extraordinary man in our times. He has the most commanding eloquence I ever heard in any person." Franklin the philosopher spoke in no measured terms of his preaching powers. Hume the historian declared that it was worth going twenty miles to hear him.

Now, facts like these can never be explained away. They completely upset the theory that Whitefield's preaching was nothing but noise and rant. Bolingbroke, Chesterfield, Hume, and Franklin, were not men to be easily deceived. They were no mean judges of eloquence. They were probably among the best qualified critics of their day. Their unbought and un-biassed opinions appear to me to supply unanswerable proof that there must have been something very extraordinary about Whitefield's preaching. But still, after all, the question remains to be answered, What was the secret of Whitefield's unrivalled popularity and effectiveness? And I frankly admit that, with the scanty materials we possess for forming our judgment, the question is a very hard one to answer.

The man who turns to the seventy-five sermons published under Whitefield's name will probably be much disappointed. He will see in them no commanding intellect or grasp of mind. He will find in them no deep philosophy, and no very striking thoughts. It is only fair, however, to say, that by far the greater part of these sermons were taken down in shorthand by reporters, and published without correction. These worthy men appear to have done their work very indifferently, and were evidently ignorant alike of stopping and paragraphing, of grammar and of gospel. The consequence is, that many passages in these seventy-five sermons are what Bishop Latimer would have called a "mingle-mangle," and what we should call in this day "a complete mess." No wonder that poor White-field says, in one of his last letters, dated September 26, 1769, "I wish you had advertised against the publication of my last sermon. It is not verbatim as I delivered it. It some places it makes me speak false concord, and even nonsense. In others the sense and connection are destroyed by injudicious, disjointed paragraphs, and the whole is entirely unfit for the public review."

I venture, however, to say boldly that, with all their faults, Whitefield's printed sermons will well repay a candid perusal. The reader must recollect that they were not carefully prepared for the press, like the sermons of Melville or Bradley, but wretchedly reported, paragraphed, and stopped, and he must read with this continually before his mind. Moreover, he must remember that English composition for speaking to hearers, and English composition for private reading, are almost like two different languages, so that sermons which "preach" well " read " badly. Let him, I say, remember these two things, and judge accordingly, and I am much mistaken if he does not find much to admire in many of Whitefield's sermons. For my own part, I must plainly say that I think they are greatly under-rated.

Let me now point out what appear to have been the distinctive characteristics of Whitefield's preaching.

For one thing, Whitefield preached a *singularly pure gospel*. Few men, perhaps, ever gave their hearers so much wheat and so little chaff. He did not get up to talk about his party, his cause, his interest or his office. He was perpetually telling you about your sins, your heart, Jesus Christ, the Holy Ghost, the absolute need of repentance, faith, and holiness, in the way that the Bible presents these mighty subjects. "Oh, the righteousness of Jesus Christ!" he would often say; "I must be excused if I mention it in almost all my sermons." Preaching of this kind is the preaching that God delights to honour. It must be pre-eminently a *manifestation of truth*.

For another thing, Whitefield's preaching was *singularly lucid and simple*. His hearers, whatever they might think of his doctrine, could never fail to understand what he meant. His style of speaking was easy, plain, and conversational. He seemed to abhor long and involved sentences. He always saw his mark, and went directly at it. He seldom troubled his hearers with abstruse argument and intricate reasoning. Simple Bible statements, apt illustrations, and pertinent anecdotes, were the more common weapons that he used. The consequence was that his hearers always understood him. He never shot above their heads. Here again is one grand element of a preacher's success. He must labour by all means to be understood. It was a wise saying of Archbishop Usher, "To make easy things seem hard is every man's work ; but to make hard things easy is the work of a great preacher."

For another thing, Whitefield was a singularly *bold and direct preacher.* He never used that indefinite expression "we," which seems so peculiar to English pulpit oratory, and which only leaves a hearer's mind in a state of misty confusion. He met men face to face, like one who had a message from God to them, "I have come here to speak to you about your soul." The result was that many of his hearers used often to think that his sermons were specially meant for themselves. He was not content, as many, with sticking on a meagre tail-piece of application at the end of a long discourse. On the contrary, a constant vein of application ran through all his sermons. "This is for you, and this is for you." His hearers were never let alone.

Another striking feature in Whitefield's preaching was *his singular power of description.* The Arabians have a proverb which says, "He is the best orator who can turn men's ears into eyes." Whitefield seems to have had a peculiar faculty of doing this. He dramatized his subject so thoroughly that it seemed to move and walk before your eyes. He used to draw such vivid pictures of the things he was handling, that his hearers could believe they actually saw and heard them. "On one occasion," says one of his biographers, "Lord Chesterfield was among his hearers. The great preacher, in describing the miserable condition of an unconverted sinner, illustrated the subject by describing a blind beggar. The night was dark, and the road dangerous. The poor mendicant was deserted by his dog near the edge of a precipice, and had nothing to aid him in groping his way but his staff. Whitefield so warmed with his subject, and enforced it with such graphic power, that the whole auditory was kept in breathless silence, as if it saw the movements of the poor old man ; and at length, when the beggar was about to take the fatal step which would have hurled him down the precipice to certain destruction, Lord Chesterfield actually made a rush forward to save him, exclaiming aloud, ' He is gone ! he is gone ! ' The noble lord had been so entirely carried away by the preacher, that he forgot the whole was a picture."

Another leading characteristic of Whitefield's preaching was his *tremendous earnestness.* One poor uneducated man said of him, that " he preached like a lion." He succeeded in showing people that he at least believed all he was saying, and that his heart, and soul, and mind, and strength, were bent on making them believe it too. His sermons were not like the morning and evening gun at Portsmouth, a kind of formal discharge, fired off as a matter of course, that disturbs nobody. They were all life and fire. There was no getting away from them. Sleep was next to impossible. You must listen whether you liked it or not. There was a holy violence about him which firmly took your attention by storm. You were fairly carried off your legs by his energy before you had time to consider what you would do. This, we may be sure, was one secret of his success. We must convince men that we are in earnest ourselves, if we want to be believed. The difference between one preacher and another, is often not so much in the things said, as in the manner in which they are said.

It is recorded by one of his biographers that an American

gentleman once went to hear him, for the first time, in consequence of the report he heard of his preaching powers. The day was rainy, the congregation comparatively thin, and the beginning of the sermon rather heavy. Our American friend began to say to himself, " This man is no great wonder after all." He looked round, and saw the congregation as little interested as himself. One old man, in front of the pulpit, had fallen asleep. But all at once Whitefield stopped short. His countenance changed. And then he suddenly broke forth in an altered tone : " If I had come to speak to you in my own name, you might well rest your elbows on your knees, and your heads on your hands, and sleep ; and once in a while look up, and say, What is this babbler talking of ?   But I have not come to you in my own name. No ! I have come to you in the name of the Lord of Hosts" (here he brought down his hand and foot with a force that made the building ring), " and I must and will be heard." The congregation started. The old man woke up at once. " Ay, ay !" cried Whitefield, fixing his eyes on him, " I have waked you up, have I ? I meant to do it. I am not come here to preach to stocks and stones : I have come to you in the name of the Lord God of Hosts, and I must, and will, have an audience." The hearers were stripped of their apathy at once. Every word of the sermon after this was heard with deep attention, and the American gentleman never forgot it.

One more feature in Whitefield's preaching deserves special notice ; and that is, the *immense amount of pathos and feeling* which it always contained. It was no uncommon thing with him to weep profusely in the pulpit. Cornelius Winter, who often accompanied him in his latter journeys, went so far as to say that he hardly ever knew him get through a sermon without some tears. There seems to have been nothing of affectation in this. He felt intensely for the souls before him, and his feelings found an outlet in tears. Of all the ingredients of his success in preaching, none, I suspect, were so powerful as this. It awakened affections and touched secret springs in men, which no amount of reasoning and demonstration could have moved. It smoothed down the prejudices which many had conceived against him. They could not hate the man who wept so much over their souls. " I came to hear you," said one to him, " with my pocket full of stones, intending to break your head ; but your sermon got the better of me, and broke my heart." Once become satisfied that a man loves you, and you will listen gladly to anything he has to say.

I will now ask the reader to add to this analysis of White-field's preaching, that even by nature he possessed several of the rarest gifts which fit a man to be an orator. His *action* was perfect—so perfect that even Garrick, the famous actor, gave it unqualified praise. His *voice* was as wonderful as his action — so powerful that he could make thirty thousand people hear him at once, and yet so musical and well toned that some said he could raise tears by his pronunciation of the word " Meso-potamia." His *manner* in the pulpit was so curiously graceful and fascinating that it was said that no one could hear him for five minutes without forgetting that he squinted. His *fluency* and command of appropriate language were of the highest order, prompting him always to use the right word and to put it in the right place. Add, I repeat, these gifts to the things already mentioned, and then consider whether there is not sufficient in our hands to account for his power and popularity as a preacher.

For my own part, I have no hesitation in saying that I believe no English preacher has ever possessed such a combination of excellent qualifications as Whitefield. Some, no doubt, have surpassed him in some of his gifts ; others, perhaps, have equalled him in others. But for a well-balanced combination of some of the finest gifts that a preacher can possess, united with an unrivalled voice, manner, delivery, action, and command of words, Whitefield, I repeat my opinion, stands alone. No Englishman, I believe, dead or alive, has ever equalled him. And I suspect we shall always find that, just in proportion as preachers have approached that curious combination of rare gifts which Whitefield possessed, just in that very proportion have they attained what Clarendon defines true eloquence to be—" a strange power of making themselves believed."

The inner life and personal character of this great spiritual hero of the last century are a branch of my subject on which I shall not dwell at any length. In fact, there is no necessity for my doing so. He was a singularly transparent man. There was nothing about him requiring apology or explanation. His faults and good qualities were both clear and plain as noon-day. I shall therefore content myself with simply pointing out the prominent features of his character, so far as they can be gathered from his letters and the accounts of his contemporaries, and then bring my sketch of him to a conclusion.

He was a man of *deep and unfeigned humility.* No one can read the fourteen hundred letters of his, published by Dr. Gillies, without observing this. Again and again, in the very zenith of his popularity, we find him speaking of himself and his works in the lowliest terms. " God be merciful to me a sinner," he writes on September 11, 1753, " and give me, for his infinite mercy's sake, an humble, thankful, and resigned heart. Truly I am viler than the vilest, and stand amazed at his employing such a wretch as I am." " Let none of my friends," he writes on December 27, 1753, " cry to such a sluggish, lukewarm, unprofitable worm, Spare thyself. Rather spur me on, I pray you, with an Awake, thou sleeper, and begin to do something for thy God." Language like this, no doubt, seems foolishness and affectation to the world ; but the well-instructed Bible reader will see in it the heartfelt experience of all the brightest saints. It is the language of men like Baxter, and Brainerd, and M'Cheyne. It is the same mind that was in the inspired Apostle Paul. Those that have most light and grace are always the humblest men.

He was a man of burning *love to our Lord Jesus Christ.* That name which is "above every name" stands out incessantly in all his correspondence. Like fragrant ointment, it gives a savour to all his communications. He seems never weary of saying something about Jesus. "My Master," as George Herbert said, is never long out of his mind. His love, his atonement, his precious blood, his righteousness, his readiness to receive sinners, his patience and tender dealing with saints, are themes which appear ever fresh before his eyes. In this respect, at least, there is a curious likeness between him and that glorious Scotch divine, Samuel Rutherford.

He was a man of *unwearied diligence and laboriousness* about his Master's business. It would be difficult, perhaps, to name any one in the annals of the Churches who worked so hard for Christ, and so thoroughly spent himself in his service. Henry Venn, in a funeral sermon for him, preached at Bath, bore the following testimony :—" What a sign and wonder was this man of God in the greatness of his labours ! One cannot but stand amazed that his mortal frame could, for the space of near thirty years, without interruption, sustain the weight of them ; for what so trying to the human frame, in youth especially, as long-continued, frequent, and violent straining of the lungs ? Who that knows their structure would think it possible that a person little above the age of manhood could speak in a single week, and that for years—in general forty hours, and in very many weeks sixty—and that to thousands ; and after this labour, instead of taking any rest, could be offering up prayers and intercessions, with hymns and spiritual songs, as his manner was, in every house to which he was invited ? The truth is, that in point of labour this extraordinary servant of God did as much in a few weeks as most of those who exert themselves are able to do in the space of a year."

He was to the end a man of *eminent self-denial*. His style of living was most simple. He was remarkable to a proverb for moderation in eating and drinking. All through life he was an early riser. His usual hour for getting up was four o'clock, both in summer and winter ; and equally punctual was he in retiring about ten at night. A man of prayerful habits, he frequently spent whole nights in reading and devotion. Cornelius Winter, who often slept in the same room, says that he would sometimes rise during the night for this purpose. He cared little for money, except as a help to the cause of Christ, and refused it, when pressed upon him for his own use, once to the amount of £7000. He amassed no fortune, and founded no wealthy family. The little money he left behind him at his death arose entirely from the legacies of friends. The Pope's coarse saying about Luther, " This German beast does not love gold," might have been equally applied to Whitefield.

He was a man of remarkable *disinterestedness and singleness of eye*. He seemed to live only for two objects—the glory of God and the salvation of souls. Of secondary and covert objects he knew nothing at all. He raised no party of followers who took his name. He established no denominational system, of which his own writings should be cardinal elements. A favourite expression of his is most characteristic of the man : " Let the name of George Whitefield perish, so long as Christ is exalted."

He was a man of a singularly *happy and cheerful spirit*. No one who saw him could ever doubt that he enjoyed his religion. Tried as he was in many ways throughout his ministry — slandered by some, despised by others, misrepresented by false brethren, opposed everywhere by the ignorant clergy of his time, worried by incessant controversy — his elasticity never failed him. He was eminently a rejoicing Christian, whose very demeanour recommended his Master's service. A venerable lady of New York, after his death, when speaking of the influences by which the Spirit won her heart to God, used these remarkable words,—" Mr. Whitefield was *so cheerful* that it tempted me to become a Christian."

Last, but not least, he was a man of extraordinary *charity, catholicity, and liberality* in his religion. He knew nothing of that narrow-minded feeling which makes some men fancy that everything must be barren outside their own camps, and that their own party has got a complete monopoly of truth and heaven. He loved all who loved the Lord Jesus Christ in sincerity. He measured all by the measure which the angels use,—" Did they profess repentance towards God, faith towards our Lord Jesus Christ, and holiness of conversation ?" If they did, they were as his brethren. His soul was with such men, by whatever name they were called. Minor differences were wood, hay, and stubble to him. The marks of the Lord Jesus were the only marks he cared for. This catholicity is the more remarkable when the spirit of the times he lived in is considered. Even the Erskines, in Scotland, wanted him to preach for no other denomination but their own—viz., the Secession Church. He asked them, " Why only for them ?"— and received the notable answer that " they were the Lord's people." This was more than Whitefield could stand. He asked " if there were no other Lord's people but themselves ;" he told them, " if all others were the devil's people, they certainly had more need to be preached to ;" and he wound up by informing them, that " if the Pope himself would lend him his pulpit, he would gladly proclaim the righteousness of Christ in it." To this catholicity of spirit he adhered all his days. If other Christians misrepresented him, he forgave them ; and if they refused to work with him, he still loved them. Nothing could be a more weighty testimony against narrow-mindedness than his request, made shortly before his death, that, when he did die, John Wesley should be asked to preach his funeral sermon. Wesley and he had long ceased to agree about Calvinistic points ; but Whitefield, to the very last, was determined to forget minor differences, and to regard Wesley as Calvin did Luther, " only as a good servant of Jesus Christ." On another occasion a censorious professor of religion asked him " whether he thought they would see John Wesley in heaven?" " No, sir," was the striking answer ; " I fear not. He will be so near the throne, and we shall be at such a distance, that we shall hardly get a sight of him."

Far be it from me to say that the subject of this chapter was a man without faults. Like all God's saints, he was an imperfect creature. He sometimes erred in judgment. He often drew rash conclusions about Providence, and mistook his own inclination for God's leadings. He was frequently hasty both with his tongue and his pen. He had no business to say that "Archbishop Tillotson knew no more of the gospel than Mahomet." He was wrong to set down some people as the Lord's enemies, and others as the Lord's friends so precipitately and positively as he sometimes did. He was to blame for denouncing many of the clergy as "letter-learned Pharisees," because they could not receive the doctrine of the new birth. But still, after all this has been said, there can be no doubt that in the main he was an eminently holy, self-denying, and consistent man. "The faults of his character," says an American writer, "were like spots on the sun—detected without much difficulty by any cool and careful observer who takes pains to look for them, but to all practical purposes lost in one general and genial effulgence." Well indeed would it be for the Churches of our day, if God was to give them more ministers like the great evangelist of England a hundred years ago !

It only remains to say that those who wish to know more about Whitefield would do well to peruse the seven volumes of his letters and other publications, which Dr. Gillies edited in 1770. I am much mistaken if they are not agreeably surprised at their contents. To me it is matter of astonishment that, amidst the many reprints of the nineteenth century, no publisher has yet attempted a complete reprint of the works of George Whitefield.

A short extract from the conclusion of a sermon preached by Whitefield on Kennington Common, may be interesting to some readers, and may serve to give them some faint idea of the great preacher's style. It was a sermon on the text, "What think ye of Christ?" (Matt. xxii. 42.)

"O my brethren, my heart is enlarged towards you. I trust I feel something of that hidden but powerful presence of Christ, whilst I am preaching to you. Indeed it is sweet—it is exceedingly comfortable. All the harm I wish you who without cause are my enemies, is that you felt the like. Believe me, though it would be hell to my soul to return to a natural state again, yet I would willingly change states with you for a little while, that you might know what it is to have Christ dwelling in your hearts by faith. Do not turn your backs. Do not let the devil hurry you away. Be not afraid of convictions. Do not think worse of the doctrine because preached without the church walls. Our Lord, in the days of his flesh, preached on a mount, in a ship, and a field; and I am persuaded many have felt his gracious presence here. Indeed, we speak what we know. Do not therefore reject the kingdom of God against yourselves. Be so wise as to receive our witness.

"I cannot, I will not let you go. Stay a little, and let us reason together. However lightly you may esteem your souls, I know our Lord has set an unspeakable value on them. He thought them worthy of his most precious blood. I beseech you, therefore, O sinners, be ye reconciled to God. I hope you do not fear being accepted in the Beloved. Behold, he calleth you. Behold, he prevents, and follows you with his mercy, and hath sent forth his servants into the highways and hedges to compel you to come in.

"Remember, then, that at such an hour of such a day, in such a year, in this place, you were all told what you ought to think concerning Jesus Christ. If you now perish, it will not be from lack of knowledge. I am free from the blood of you all. You cannot say I have been preaching damnation to you. You cannot say I have, like legal preachers, been requiring you to make bricks without straw. I have not bidden you to make yourselves saints and then come to God. I have offered you salvation on as cheap terms as you can desire. I have offered you Christ's whole wisdom, Christ's whole righteousness, Christ's whole sanctification and eternal redemption, if you will but believe on him. If you say you cannot believe, you say right; for faith, as well as every other blessing, is the gift of God. But then wait upon God, and who knows but he may have mercy on thee.

"Why do we not entertain more loving thoughts of Christ? Do you think he will have mercy on others and not on you? Are you not sinners? Did not Jesus Christ come into the world to save sinners?

"If you say you are the chief of sinners, I answer that will be no hindrance to your salvation. Indeed it will not, if you lay hold on Christ by faith. Read the Evangelists, and see how kindly he behaved to his disciples, who had fled from and denied him. 'Go, tell my *brethren*,' says he. He did not say, 'Go, tell those traitors,' but, 'Go, tell my brethren and *Peter*.' It is as though he had said, 'Go, tell my brethren in general, and Peter in particular, that I am risen. Oh, comfort his poor drooping heart. Tell him I am reconciled to him. Bid him weep no more so bitterly. For though with oaths and curses he thrice denied me, yet I have died for his sins; I have risen again for his justification : I freely forgive him all." Thus slow to anger and of great kindness, was our all-merciful High Priest. And do you think he has changed his nature and forgets poor sinners, now he is exalted to the right hand of God? No; he is the same yesterday, to-day, and for ever; and sitteth there only to make intercession for us.

"Come, then, ye harlots; come, ye publicans; come, ye most abandoned sinners, come and believe on Jesus Christ. Though the whole world despise you and cast you out, yet he will not disdain to take you up. Oh amazing, oh infinitely condescending love! even you he will not be ashamed to call his brethren. How will you escape if you neglect such a glorious offer of salvation? What would the damned spirits now in the prison of hell give if Christ was so freely offered to them? And why are we not lifting up our eyes in torments? Does any one out of this great multitude dare say he does not *deserve* damnation? Why are we left, and others taken away by death? What is this but an instance of God's free grace, and a sign of his good-will toward us? Let God's goodness lead us to repentance. Oh, let there be joy in heaven over some of you repenting!"

IV.

John Wesley and his Ministry.

CHAPTER I.

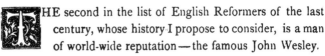 HE second in the list of English Reformers of the last century, whose history I propose to consider, is a man of world-wide reputation — the famous John Wesley.

The name of this great evangelist is perhaps better known than that of any of his fellow-labourers a hundred years ago. This, however, is easily accounted for. He lived to the ripe old age of eighty-eight. For sixty-five years he was continually before the eyes of the public, and doing his Master's work in every part of England. He founded a new religious denomination, remarkable to this very day for its numbers, laboriousness, and success, and justly proud of its great founder. His life has been repeatedly written by his friends and followers, his works constantly reprinted, his precepts and maxims reverentially treasured up and embalmed, like Joseph's bones. In fact, if ever a good Protestant has been practically *canonized*, it has been John Wesley! It would be strange indeed if his name was not well known.

Of such a man as this I cannot pretend to give more than a brief account in the short space of a few pages. The leading facts of his long and well-spent life, and the leading features of his peculiar character, are all that I can possibly compress into the limits of this memoir. Those who want more must look elsewhere.*

John Wesley was born on the 17th of June 1703, at Epworth, in North Lincolnshire, of which parish his father was rector. He was the ninth of a family of at least thirteen children, comprising three sons and ten daughters. Of the daughters, those who grew up made singularly foolish and unhappy marriages. Of the sons, the eldest, Samuel, was for some years usher of Westminster School, and an intimate friend of the famous Bishop Atterbury, and finally died head-master of Tiverton School. The second, John, was founder of the Methodist communion; and the third, Charles, was almost throughout life John's companion and fellow-labourer.

John Wesley's father was a man of considerable learning and great activity of mind. As a writer, he was always bringing out something either in prose or in verse, but nothing, unhappily for his pocket, which was ever acceptable to the reading public, or is much cared for in the present day. As a politician, he was a zealous supporter of the Revolution which brought into England the House of Orange; and it was on this account that Queen Mary presented him to the Crown living of Epworth. As a clergyman, he seems to have been a diligent pastor and preacher, of the theological school of Archbishop Tillotson. As a manager of his worldly affairs, he appears to have been most unsuccessful. Though rector of a living now valued at £1000 a-year, he was always in pecuniary difficulties, was once

---

* The principal lives of Wesley by Methodist hands are those of Whitehead, Moore, and Watson. Southey's well-known life of Wesley is not a fair book, and the unfavourable animus of the writer throughout is painfully manifest. The best, most impartial, and most complete account of Wesley is one published by Seeley in 1856, by an anonymous writer.

in prison for debt, and finally left his widow and children almost destitute.   When I add to this that he was not on good terms with his parishioners, and, poor as he was, insisted on going up to London every year to attend the very unprofitable meetings of Convocation for months at a time, the reader will probably agree with me that, like too many, he was a man of more book-learning and cleverness than good sense.

The mother of John Wesley was evidently a woman of extra-ordinary power of mind.   She was the daughter of Dr. Annesley, a man well known to readers of Puritan theology as one of the chief promoters of the Morning Exercises, and ejected from St. Giles', Cripplegate, in 1662.   From him she seems to have inherited the masculine sense and strong decided judgment which distinguished her character.   To the influence of his mother's early training and example, John Wesley, doubtless, was indebted for many of his peculiar habits of mind and qualifications.

Her own account of the way in which she educated all her children, in one of her letters to her son John, is enough to show that she was no common woman, and that her sons were not likely to turn out common men.   She says, " None of them was taught to read till five years old, except Keziah, in whose case I was over-ruled ; and she was more years in learning than any of the rest had been months.   The way of teaching was this : the day before a child began to learn, the house was set in order, every one's work appointed them, and a charge given that none should come into the room from nine to twelve, or from two to five, which were our school hours.   One day was allowed the child wherein to learn its letters, and each of them did in that time know all its letters, great and small, except Molly and Nancy, who were a day and a half before they knew them perfectly, for which I then thought them very dull ; but the reason why I thought them so was because the rest learned so readily, and your brother Samuel, who was the first child I ever taught, learnt the alphabet in a few hours. He was five years old on the 10th of February; the next day he began to learn, and as soon as he knew the letters, began at the first chapter of Genesis. He was taught to spell the first verse, then to read it over and over till he could read it off-hand without any hesitation; so on to the second, &c., till he took ten verses for a lesson, which he quickly did. Easter fell low that year, and by Whitsuntide he could read a chapter very well, for he read continually, and had such a prodigious memory that I cannot remember ever to have told him the same word twice. What was stranger, any word he had learnt in his lesson he knew wherever he saw it, either in his Bible or any other book, by which means he learned very soon to read an English author well."

Her energetic and decided conduct, as wife of a parish clergyman, is strikingly illustrated by a correspondence still extant between herself and her husband on a curious occasion. It appears that during Mr. Wesley's long-protracted absences from home in attending Convocation, Mrs. Wesley, dissatisfied with the state of things at Epworth, began the habit of gathering a few parishioners at the rectory on Sunday evenings and reading to them. As might naturally have been expected, the attendance soon became so large that her husband took alarm at the report he heard, and made some objections to the practice. The letters of Mrs. Wesley on this occasion are a model of strong, hard-headed, Christian good sense, and deserve the perusal of many timid believers in the present day. After defending what she had done by many wise and unanswerable arguments, and beseeching her husband to consider seriously the bad consequences of stopping the meeting, she winds up all with the following remarkable paragraph :—" If you do, after all, think fit to dissolve this assembly, do not tell me that you desire me to do it, for that will not satisfy my conscience. But send me your positive *command* in such full and express terms as may absolve me from all guilt and punishment for neglecting the opportunity of doing good, when you and I shall appear before the great and awful tribunal of our Lord Jesus Christ."

A mother of this stamp was just the person to leave deep marks and impressions on the minds of her children. Of the old rector of Epworth we can trace little in his sons John and Charles, except, perhaps, their poetical genius. But there is much in John's career and character throughout life which shows the hand of his mother.

The early years of John Wesley's life appear to have passed quietly away in his Lincolnshire home. The only remarkable event recorded by his biographers is his marvellous escape from being burnt alive, when Epworth rectory was burned down. This happened in 1709, when he was six years old, and seems to have been vividly impressed on his mind. He was pulled through the bedroom window, at the last moment, by a man who, for want of a ladder, stood on another man's shoulders. Just at that moment the roof of the house fell in, but happily fell inward, and the boy and his deliverer escaped unhurt. He says himself, in his description of the event, "When they brought me to the house where my father was, he cried out, 'Come, neighbours, let us kneel down! let us give thanks to God! He has given me all my eight children; let the house go, I am rich enough.'"

In the year 1714, at the age of eleven, John Wesley was placed at the Charter-house School in London. That mighty plunge in life—a boy's first entrance at a public school—seems to have done him no harm. He had probably been well grounded at his father's house in all the rudiments of a classical education, and soon became distinguished for his diligence and progress at school. At the age of sixteen his elder brother, then an usher at Westminster, describes him as "a brave boy, learning Hebrew as fast as he can."

In the year 1720, at the age of seventeen, John Wesley went up to Oxford as an undergraduate, having been elected to

Christ Church. Little is known of the first three or four years of his university life, except that he was steady, studious, and remarkable for his classical knowledge and genius for composition. It is evident, however, that he made the best use of his time at college, and picked up as much as he could in a day when honorary class-lists were unknown, and incitements to study were very few. Like most great divines, he found the advantage of university education all his life long. Men might dislike his theology, but they could never say that he was a fool, and had no right to be heard.

In the beginning of 1725, at the age of twenty-two, he seems to have gone through much exercise of mind as to the choice of a profession. Naturally enough, he thought of taking orders, but was somewhat daunted by serious reflection on the solemnity of the step. This very reflection, however, appears to have been most useful to him, and to have produced in his mind deeper thoughts about God, his soul, and religion generally, than he had ever entertained before. He began to study divinity, and to go through a regular course of reading for the ministry. He had, probably, no very trustworthy guide in his choice of religious literature at this period. The books which apparently had the greatest influence on him were Jeremy Taylor's "Holy Living and Dying," and Thomas à Kempis's "Imitation of Christ." Devout and well-meaning as these authors are, they certainly were not likely to give him very clear views of scriptural Christianity, or very cheerful and happy views of Christ's service. In short, though they did him good by making him feel that true religion was a serious business, and a concern of the heart, they evidently left him in much darkness and perplexity.

At this stage of John Wesley's life, his correspondence with his father and mother is peculiarly interesting, and highly creditable both to the parents and the son. He evidently opened his mind to them, and told them all his mental and spiritual difficulties.   His letters and their replies are well worth reading.   They all show more or less absence of spiritual light and clear views of the gospel.   But a singular vein of honesty and conscientiousness runs throughout.   One feels " This is just the spirit that God will bless.   This is the single eye to which will be given more light."

Let us hear what his father says about the question, " Which is the best commentary on the Bible?"   " I answer, the Bible itself.   For the several paraphrases and translations of it in the Polyglot, compared with the original and with one another, are in my opinion, to an honest, devout, industrious, and humble man, infinitely preferable to any comment I ever saw."

Let us hear what his mother says on the point of taking holy orders :—" The alteration of your temper has occasioned me much speculation.   I, who am apt to be sanguine, hope it may proceed from the operation of God's Holy Spirit, that by taking off your relish for earthly enjoyments he may prepare and dispose your mind for a more serious and close application to things of a more sublime and spiritual nature.   If it be so, happy are you if you cherish those dispositions.   And now in good earnest resolve to make religion the business of your life ; for, after all, that is the one thing that, strictly speaking, is necessary : all things beside are comparatively little to the purposes of life.   I heartily wish you would now enter upon a strict examination of yourself, that you may know whether you have a reasonable hope of salvation by Jesus Christ.   If you have the satisfaction of knowing, it will abundantly reward your pains ; if you have not, you will find a more reasonable occasion for tears than can be met with in a tragedy.   This matter deserves great consideration by all, but especially by those designed for the ministry, who ought above all things to make their own calling and election sure, lest, after they have preached to others, they themselves should be cast away."

Let us hear what his mother says about Thomas à Kempis's

opinion, that all mirth or pleasure is useless, if not sinful. She observes :—" I take Kempis to have been an honest, weak man, that had more zeal than knowledge, by his condemning all mirth or pleasure as sinful or useless, in opposition to so many direct and plain texts of Scripture. Would you judge of the lawfulness or unlawfulness of pleasures? of the innocence or malignity of actions? take this rule,—whatever weakens your reason, impairs the tenderness of your conscience, obscures your sense of God, or takes off the relish of spiritual things ; in short, whatever increases the strength and authority of your body over your mind, that thing is sin to you, however innocent it may be in itself."

Let us hear what John Wesley himself says in a letter on the opinion of Jeremy Taylor—" Whether God has forgiven us or no, we know not ; therefore let us be sorrowful for ever having sinned." He remarks—" Surely the graces of the Holy Ghost are not of so little force as that we cannot perceive whether we have them or not. If we dwell in Christ, and Christ in us, which He will not do unless we be regenerate, certainly we must be sensible of it. If we never can have any certainty of being in a state of salvation, good reason is it that every moment should be spent, not in joy, but in fear and trembling ; and then, undoubtedly, in this life we are of all men most miserable. God deliver us from such a fearful expectation as this."

Correspondence of this style could hardly fail to do good to a young man in John Wesley's frame of mind. It led him no doubt to closer study of the Scriptures, deeper self-examination, and more fervent prayer. Whatever scruples he may have had were finally removed, and he was at length ordained deacon on September the 19th, 1725, by Dr. Potter, then Bishop of Oxford, and afterwards Archbishop of Canterbury.

In the year 1726 John Wesley was elected Fellow of Lincoln College, after a contest of more than ordinary severity. His recently adopted seriousness of deportment and general reli-

giousness were used as a handle against him by his adversaries.
But his high character carried him triumphantly through all
opposition, to the great delight of his father. Tried as he apparently was at the time in his temporal circumstances, he
wrote: " Whatever will be my own fate before the summer is
over God knows; but, wherever I am, my Jack is Fellow of
Lincoln."

The eight years following John Wesley's election to his fellowship of Lincoln—from 1726 to 1734—form a remarkable
epoch in his life, and certainly gave a tone and colour to all
his future history. During the whole of these years he was
resident at Oxford, and for some time at any rate acted as tutor
and lecturer in his college. Gradually, however, he seems to
have laid himself out more and more to try to do good to
others, and latterly was entirely taken up with it.

His mode of action was in the highest degree simple and
unpretending. Assisted by his brother Charles, then a student
of Christ Church, he gathered a small society of like-minded
young men, in order to spend some evenings in a week together
in the study of the Greek Testament. This was in November
1729. The members of this society were at first four in number; namely, John Wesley, Charles Wesley, Mr. Morgan of
Christ Church, and Mr. Kirkman of Merton. At a somewhat
later period they were joined by Mr. Ingham of Queen's, Mr.
Broughton of Exeter, Mr. Clayton of Brazenose, the famous
George Whitefield of Pembroke, and the well-known James
Hervey of Lincoln.

This little band of witnesses, as might reasonably have been
expected, soon began to think of doing good to others, as well as
getting good themselves. In the summer of 1730 they began
to visit prisoners in the castle and poor people in the town, to
send neglected children to school, to give temporal aid to the
sick and needy, and to distribute Bibles and Prayer-books
among those who had not got them. Their first steps were

taken very cautiously, and with frequent reference to John Wesley's father for advice. Acting by his advice, they laid all their operations before the Bishop of Oxford and his chaplain, and did nothing without full ecclesiastical sanction.

Cautious, and almost childish, however, as the proceedings of these young men may appear to us in the present day, they were too far in advance of the times to escape notice, hatred, and opposition. A kind of persecution and clamour was raised against Wesley and his companions as enthusiasts, fanatics, and troublers of Israel. They were nicknamed the " Methodists" or " Holy Club," and assailed with a storm of ridicule and abuse. Through this, however, they manfully persevered, and held on their way, being greatly encouraged by the letters of the old Rector of Epworth. In one of them he says, " I hear my son John has the honour of being styled the Father of the Holy Club. If it be so, I am sure I must be the grand-father of it, and I need not say that I had rather any of my sons should be so dignified and distinguished than have the title His Holiness."

The real amount of spiritual good that John Wesley did during these eight years of residence at Oxford is a point that cannot easily be ascertained. With all his devotedness, asceti-cism, and self-denial, it must be remembered that at this time he knew very little of the pure gospel of Christ. His views of religious truth, to say the least, were very dim, misty, defective, and indistinct. No one was more sensible of this than he afterwards was himself, and no one could be more ready and willing to confess it. Such books as " Law's Serious Call," " Law's Christian Perfection," " Theologia Germanica," and mystical writers, were about the highest pitch of divinity that he had yet attained. But we need not doubt that he learned experience at this period which he found useful in after-life. At any rate he became thoroughly trained in habits of labo-riousness, time redemption, and self-mortification, which he carried with him to the day of his death. God has his own way of tempering and preparing instruments for his work, and, whatever we may think, we may be sure his way is best.

In the year 1734 John Wesley's father died, and the family home was broken up. Just at this time the providence of God opened up to him a new sphere of duty, the acceptance of which had a most important effect on his whole spiritual history. This sphere was the colony of Georgia, in North America. The trustees of that infant settlement were greatly in want of proper clergymen to send out, both to preach the gospel to the Indians and to provide means of grace for the colonists. At this juncture John Wesley and his friends were suggested to their notice, as the most suitable persons they could find, on account of their high character for regular behaviour, attention to religious duties, and readiness to endure hardships. The upshot of the matter was, that an offer was made to John Wesley, and, after conferring with Mr. Law, his mother, his elder brother, and other friends, he accepted the proposal of the trustees, and, in company with his brother Charles and their common friend Mr. Ingham, set sail for Georgia.

Wesley landed in Georgia on the 6th of February 1736, after a long stormy voyage of four months, and remained in the colony two years. I shall not take up the reader's time by any detailed account of his proceedings there. It may suffice to say, that, for any good he seems to have done, his mission was almost useless. Partly from the inherent difficulties of an English clergyman's position in a colony—partly from the confused and disorderly condition of the infant settlement where he was stationed—partly from a singular want of tact and discretion in dealing with men and things—partly, above all, from his own very imperfect views of the gospel, Wesley's expedition to Georgia appears to have been a great failure, and he was evidently glad to get away.

The ways of God, however, are not as man's ways. There

was a "need be" for the two years' absence in America, just as there was for Philip's journey down the desert road to Gaza, and Paul's sojourn in prison at Cæsarea. If Wesley did nothing in Georgia, he certainly gained a great deal. If he taught little to others, he undoubtedly learned much. On the outward voyage he became acquainted with some Moravians on board, and was deeply struck by their deliverance from "the fear of death" in a storm. After landing in Georgia he continued his intercourse with them, and discovered to his astonishment that there was such a thing as personal assurance of forgiveness. These things, combined with the peculiar trials, difficulties, and disappointments of his colonial ministry, worked mightily on his mind, and showed him more of himself and the gospel than he had ever learned before. The result was that he landed at Deal on the 1st of February 1738, a very much humbler, but a much wiser man than he had ever been before. In plain words, he had become the subject of a real inward work of the Holy Ghost.

Wesley's own accounts of his spiritual experience during these two years of his life are deeply interesting. I will transcribe one or two of them.

On February the 7th, 1736, he records :—"On landing in Georgia I asked the advice of Mr. Spangenberg, one of the German pastors, with regard to my own conduct. He said in reply, ' My brother, I must first ask you one or two questions. Have you the witness within yourself ? Does the Spirit of God bear witness with your spirit that you are a child of God ?'—I was surprised, and knew not what to answer. He observed it, and asked, ' Do you know Jesus Christ ?'—I paused, and said, ' I know he is the Saviour of the world.'—' True,' replied he ; ' but do you know he has saved you ?'—I answered, ' I hope he has died to save me.'—He only added, ' Do you know yourself ?' —I said, ' I do.' But I fear they were vain words."

On January 24th, 1738, on board ship on his homeward

voyage, he makes the following record :—' I went to America to convert the Indians ; but oh, who shall convert me ? Who, what is he that will deliver me from this evil heart of unbelief ? I have a fair summer religion ; I can talk well ; nay, and believe myself, while no danger is near. But let death look me in the face, and my spirit is troubled, nor can I say to die is gain."

On February the 1st, 1738, the day that he landed in England, he says : " It is now two years and almost four months since I left my native country in order to teach the Georgian Indians the nature of Christianity ; but what have I learned of myself in the meantime ? Why, what I least suspected, that I, who went to America to convert others, was myself never converted to God ! I am not mad, though I thus speak ; but I speak the words of truth and soberness."

" If it be said that I have faith—for many such things have I heard from miserable comforters—I answer, so have the devils a sort of faith ; but still they are strangers to the covenant of promise. . . . The faith I want is a sure trust and confidence in God that through the merits of Christ my sins are forgiven, and I reconciled to the favour of God. I want that faith which St. Paul recommends to all the world, especially in his Epistle to the Romans ; that faith which makes every one that hath it to cry, ' I live, yet not I, but Christ liveth in me ; and the life which I now live in the flesh, I live by the faith of the Son of God, who loved me, and gave himself for me.' I want that faith which none can have without knowing that he hath it."

Records like these are deeply instructive. They teach that important lesson which man is so slow to learn—that we may have a great deal of earnestness and religiousness without any true soul-saving and soul-comforting religion—that we may be diligent in the use of fasting, prayers, forms, ordinances, and the sacrament of the Lord's Supper, without knowing anything of inward joy, peace, or communion with God—and above all, that we may be moral in life, and laborious in good works, without being true believers in Christ, or fit to die and meet God. Well would it be for the churches if truths like these were proclaimed from every pulpit, and pressed on every congregation! Thousands, for lack of such truths, are walking in a vain shadow, and totally ignorant that they are yet dead in sins. If any one wants to know how far a man may go in outward goodness, and yet not be a true Christian, let him carefully study the experience of John Wesley. I am bold to say that it is eminently truth for the times.

A man hungering and thirsting after righteousness, as Wesley was now, was not left long without more light. The good work which the Holy Ghost had begun within him was carried on rapidly after he landed in England, until the sun rose on his mind, and the shadows passed away. Partly by conference with Peter Bohler, a Moravian, and other Moravians in London, partly by study of the Scriptures, partly by special prayer for living, saving, justifying faith as the gift of God, he was brought to a clear view of the gospel, and found out the meaning of joy and peace in simply believing. Let me add—as an act of justice to one of whom the world was not worthy—that at this period he was, by his own confession, much helped by Martin Luther's preface to the Epistle to the Romans.

This year, 1738, was beyond doubt the turning-point in Wesley's spiritual history, and gave a direction to all his subsequent life. It was in the spring of this year that he began a religious society at the Moravian Chapel in Fetter Lane, London, which was the rough type and pattern of all Methodist societies formed afterwards. The rules of this little society are extant still, and with some additions, modifications, and improvements, contain the inward organization of Methodism in the present day. It was at this period also that he began preaching the new truths he had learned, in many of the pulpits in London, and soon found, like Whitefield, that the proclamation of salvation by grace, and justification by faith, was seldom allowed a second time. It was in the winter of this year, after returning from a visit to the Moravian settlement in Germany, that he began aggressive measures on home heathenism, and in the neighbourhood of Bristol followed Whitefield's example by preaching in the open air, in rooms, or wherever men could be brought together.

We have now reached a point at which John Wesley's history, like that of his great contemporary Whitefield, becomes one undeviating uniform narrative up to the time of his death. It would be useless to dwell on one year more than another. He was always occupied in one and the same business, always going up and down the land preaching, and always conducting evangelistic measures of some kind and description. For fifty-three years—from 1738 to 1791—he held on his course, always busy, and always busy about one thing—attacking sin and ignorance everywhere, preaching repentance toward God and faith toward our Lord Jesus Christ everywhere—awakening open sinners, leading on inquirers, building up saints—never wearied, never swerving from the path he had marked out, and never doubting of success. Those only who read the Journals he kept for fifty years can have any idea of the immense amount of work that he got through. Never perhaps did any man have so many irons in the fire at one time, and yet succeed in keeping so many hot.

Like Whitefield, he justly regarded preaching as God's chosen instrument for doing good to souls, and hence, wherever he went, his first step was to preach. Like him, too, he was ready to preach anywhere or at any hour—early in the morning or late at night, in church, in chapel, or in room—in streets, in fields, or on commons and greens. Like him, too, he was always preaching more or less the same great truths—sin, Christ, and holiness—ruin, redemption, and regeneration—the blood of Christ and the work of the Spirit—faith, repentance, and conversion—from one end of the year to the other.

Wesley, however, was very unlike Whitefield in one important respect. He did not forget to organize as well as to preach. He was not content with reaping the fields which he found ripe for the harvest. He took care to bind up his sheaves and gather them into the barn. He was as far superior to Whitefield as an administrator and man of method, as he was inferior to him as a mere preacher.* Shut out from the Church of England by the folly of its rulers, he laid the foundation of a new denomination with matchless skill, and with a rare discernment of the wants of human nature. To unite his people as one body—to give every one something to do—to make each one consider his neighbour and seek his edification—to call forth latent talent and utilize it in some direction—to keep " all at it and always at it " (to adopt his quaint saying),—these were his aims and objects. The machinery he called into existence was admirably well adapted to carry out his purposes. His preachers, lay-preachers, class-leaders, band-leaders, circuits, classes, bands, love-feasts, and watch-nights, made up a spiritual engine which stands to this day, and in its own way can hardly be improved. If one thing more than another has given permanence and solidity to Methodism, it was its founder's masterly talent for organization.

It is needless to tell a Christian reader that Wesley had constantly to fight with opposition. The prince of this world will

* A writer in the *North British Review* has well and forcibly described the difference between the two great English evangelists of the last century. " Whitefield was soul, and Wesley was system. Whitefield was the summer cloud which burst at morning or noon a fragrant exhalation over an ample track, and took the rest of the day to gather again ; Wesley was the polished conduit in the midst of the garden, through which the living water glided in pearly brightness and perennial music, the same vivid stream from day to day. All force and impetus, Whitefield was the powder-blast in the quarry, and by one explosive sermon would shake a district, and detach materials for other men's long work ; deft, neat, and painstaking, Wesley loved to split and trim each fragment into uniform plinths and polished stones. Whitefield was the bargeman or the waggoner who brought the timber of the house, and Wesley was the architect who set it up. Whitefield had no patience for ecclesiastical polity, no aptitude for pastoral details ; Wesley, with a leader-like propensity for building, was always constructing societies, and with a king-like craft of ruling, was most at home when presiding over a class or a conference. It was their infelicity that they did not always work together ; it was the happiness of the age, and the furtherance of the gospel, that they lived alongside of one another."

never allow his captives to be rescued from him without a struggle. Sometimes he was in danger of losing his life by the assaults of violent, ignorant, and semi-heathen mobs, as at Wednesbury, Walsall, Colne, Shoreham, and Devizes. Sometimes he was denounced by bishops as an enthusiast, a fanatic, and a sower of dissent. Often—far too often—he was preached against and held up to scorn by the parochial clergy, as a heretic, a mischief-maker, and a meddling troubler of Israel. But none of these things moved the good man. Calmly, resolutely, and undauntedly he held on his course, and in scores of cases lived down all opposition. His letters in reply to the attacks made upon him are always dignified and sensible, and do equal honour to his heart and head.

I have now probably told the reader enough to give him a general idea of John Wesley's life and history. I dare not go further. Indeed, the last fifty years of his life were so entirely of one complexion, that I know not where I should stop if I went further. When I have said that they were years of constant travelling, preaching, organizing, conferring, writing, arguing, reasoning, counselling, and warring against sin, the world, and the devil, I have just said all that I dare enter upon.

He died at length in 1791, in the eighty-eighth year of his life and the sixty-fifth of his ministry, full of honour and respect, and in the "perfect peace" of the gospel. He had always enjoyed wonderful health, and never hardly knew what it was to feel weariness or pain till he was eighty-two. The weary wheels of life at length stood still, and he died of no disease but sheer old age.

The manner of his dying was in beautiful harmony with his life. He preached within a very few days of his death, and the texts of his two last sermons were curiously characteristic of the man. The last but one was at Chelsea, on February the 18th, on the words, "The king's business requireth haste" (1 Sam. xxi. 8). The last of all was at Leatherhead, on Wednesday the 23rd, on the words, "Seek ye the Lord while he may be found" (Isa. lv. 6). After this he gradually sunk, and died on Tuesday the 29th. He retained his senses to the end, and showed clearly where his heart and thoughts were to the very last.

The day but one before he died he slept much and spoke little. Once he said in a low but distinct manner, "There is no way into the holiest but by the blood of Jesus." He afterwards inquired what the words were from which he had preached a little before at Hampstead. Being told they were these, "Ye know the grace of our Lord Jesus Christ, that though he was rich, yet for your sakes he became poor, that ye through his poverty might be rich" (2 Cor. viii. 8); he replied, "That is the foundation, the only foundation; there is no other."

The day before he died, he said suddenly, "I will get up." While they were preparing his clothes, he broke out in a manner which, considering his weakness, astonished all present, in singing,—

> " I'll praise my Maker while I've breath,
> And when my voice is lost in death,
> Praise shall employ my noblest powers;
> My days of praise shall ne'er be past,
> While life, and thought, and being last,
> Or immortality endures."

Not long after, a person coming in, he tried to speak, but could not. Finding they could not understand him, he paused a little, and then with all his remaining strength cried out, " The best of all is, God is with us;" and soon after, lifting up his dying voice in token of victory, and raising his feeble arm with a holy triumph, he again repeated the heart-reviving words, " The best of all is, God is with us." The night following he often attempted to repeat the hymn before mentioned, but could only utter the opening words, " I'll praise; I'll praise." About ten o'clock next morning he was heard to articulate the word " Farewell," and then without a groan fell asleep in Christ and rested from his labours. Truly this was a glorious sunset! "Let me die the death of the righteous, and let my last end be like his."

Wesley was once married. At the age of forty-eight he married a widow lady of the name of Vizelle, of a suitable age, and of some independent property, which she took care to have settled upon herself. The union was a most unhappy one. Whatever good qualities Mrs. Wesley may have had, they were buried and swallowed up in the fiercest and most absurd passion of jealousy. One of his biographers remarks, "Had he searched the whole kingdom, he could hardly have found a woman more unsuitable to him in all important respects." After making her husband as uncomfortable as possible for twenty years, by opening his letters, putting his papers in the hands of his enemies in the vain hope of blasting his character, and even sometimes laying violent hands on him, Mrs. Wesley at length left her home, leaving word that she never intended to return Wesley simply states the fact in his journal, saying that he knew not the cause, and briefly adding, "I did not forsake her, I did not dismiss her, I will not recall her."

Like Whitefield, John Wesley left no children. But he left behind him a large and influential communion, which he not only saw spring up, but lived to see it attain a vigorous and healthy maturity. The number of Methodist preachers at the time of his death amounted in the British dominions to 313, and in the United States of America to 198. The number of Methodist members in the British dominions was 76,968, and in the United States 57,621. Facts like these need no comment; they speak for themselves. Few labourers for Christ have ever been so successful as Wesley, and to none certainly was it ever given to see so much with his own eyes.

In taking a general view of this great spiritual hero of the last century, it may be useful to point out some salient points of his character which demand particular attention. When

God puts special honour on any of his servants, it is well to analyze their gifts, and to observe carefully what they were. What, then, were the peculiar qualifications which marked John Wesley?

The first thing which I ask the reader to notice is his extra-ordinary *singleness of eye and tenacity of purpose.* Once embarked on his evangelistic voyage, he pressed forward, and never flinched for a day. "One thing I do," seemed to be his motto and constraining motive. To preach the gospel, to labour to do good, to endeavour to save souls,—these seemed to become his only objects, and the ruling passion of his life. In pursuit of them he compassed sea and land, putting aside all considera-tions of ease and rest, and forgetting all earthly feelings. Few men but himself could have gone to Epworth, stood upon their father's tombstone, and preached to an open-air congregation, "The kingdom of God is not meat and drink, but righteous-ness, and peace, and joy in the Holy Ghost." Few but himself could have seen fellow-labourers, one after another, carried to their graves, till he stood almost alone in his generation, and yet preached on, as he did, with unabated spirit, as if the ranks around him were still full. But his marvellous singleness of eye carried him through all. "Beware of the man of one book," was the advice of an old philosopher to his pupils. The man of "one thing" is the man who in the long run does great things, and shakes the world.

The second thing I ask the reader to notice is his extra-ordinary *diligence, self-denial, and economy of time.* It puts one almost out of breath to read the good man's Journals, and to mark the quantity of work that he crowded into one year. He was to all appearance always working, and never at rest. "Leisure and I," he said, "have taken leave of one another. I propose to be busy as long as I live, if my health is so long indulged to me." This resolution was made in the prime of life ; and never was resolution more punctually observed.

" Lord, let me not live to be useless," was the prayer which he uttered after seeing one, whom he once knew as an active and useful man, reduced by age to be a picture of human nature in disgrace, feeble in body and mind, slow of speech and under-standing.   Even the time which he spent in travelling was not lost. " History, poetry, and philosophy," said he, " I commonly read on horseback, having other employment at other times." When you met him in the street of a crowded city, he attracted notice not only by his bands and cassock, and his long silvery hair, but by his pace and manner ; both indicating that all his minutes were numbered, and that not one was to be lost. " But though I am always in haste," he said, " I am never in a hurry, because I never undertake any more work than I can go through with perfect calmness of spirit."   Here, again, is one secret of great usefulness.   We must abhor idleness ; we must redeem time.   No man knows how much can be done in twelve hours until he tries.   It is precisely those who do most work who find that they can do most.

The last thing which I ask the reader to notice is his marvel-lous *versatility of mind and capacity for a variety of things.*   No one perhaps can fully realize this who does not read the large biographies which record all his doings, or study his wonderful Journals.   Things the most opposite and unlike — things the most petty and trifling — things the most thoroughly secular — things most thoroughly spiritual, — all are alike mastered by his omnivorous mind.   He finds time for all, and gives directions about all.   One day we find him condensing old divinity, and publishing fifty volumes of theology, called the " Christian Library ;"—another day we find him writing a complete com-mentary on the whole Bible ;—another day we find him com-posing hymns, which live to this day in the praises of many a congregation ;—another day we find him drawing up minute directions for his preachers, forbidding them to shout and scream and preach too long, insisting on their reading regularly

lest their sermons became threadbare, requiring them not to
drink spirits, and charging them to get up early in the morning;—another day we find him calmly reviewing the current
literature of the day, and criticizing all the new books with cool
and shrewd remarks, as if he had nothing else to do. Like
Napoleon, nothing seems too small or too great for his mind to
attend to ; like Calvin, he writes as if he had nothing to do
but write, preaches as if he had nothing to do but preach, and
administers as if he had nothing to do but administer. A versatility like this is one mighty secret of power, and is a striking
characteristic of most men who leave their mark on the world.
To be a steam-engine and a penknife, a telescope and a micro-
scope, at the same time, is probably one of the highest attainments of the human mind.

I should think my sketch of Wesley incomplete if I did not
notice the objection continually made against him—that he was
an Arminian in doctrine. I fully admit the seriousness of the
objection. I do not pretend either to explain the charge away,
or to defend his objectionable opinions. Personally, I feel
unable to account for any well-instructed Christian holding
such doctrines as perfection and the defectibility of grace, or
denying such as election and the imputed righteousness of
Christ.

But, after all, we must beware that we do not condemn
men too strongly for not seeing all things in our point of view,
or excommunicate and anathematize them because they do not
pronounce our shibboleth. It is written in God's Word, " Why
dost thou judge thy brother ? or why dost thou set at nought
thy brother ?" We must think and let think. We must learn
to distinguish between things that are of the *essence* of the
gospel and things which are of the *perfection* of gospel. We
may think that a man preaches an imperfect gospel who denies
election, considers justification to be nothing more than forgiveness, and tells believers in one sermon that they may attain

perfection in this life, and in another sermon that they may entirely fall away from grace. But if the same man strongly and boldly exposes and denounces sin, clearly and fully lifts up Christ, distinctly and openly invites men to believe and repent, shall we dare to say that the man does not preach the gospel at all? Shall we dare to say that he will do no good? I, for one, cannot say so, at any rate. If I am asked whether I prefer Whitefield's gospel or Wesley's, I answer at once that I prefer Whitefield's : I am a Calvinist, and not an Arminian. But if I am asked to go further, and to say that Wesley preached no gospel at all, and did no real good, I answer at once that I cannot do so. That Wesley would have done better if he could have thrown off his Arminianism, I have not the least doubt ; but that he preached the gospel, honoured Christ, and did extensive good, I no more doubt than I doubt my own existence.

Let those who depreciate Wesley as an Arminian, read his own words in the funeral sermon which he preached on the occasion of Whitefield's death. He says of his great fellow-labourer and brother : —

" His fundamental point was to give God all the glory of whatever is good in man. In the business of salvation he set Christ as high and man as low as possible. With this point he and his friends at Oxford — the original Methodists so-called — set out. Their grand principle was, there is no power by nature, and no merit in man. They insisted, ' all grace to speak, think, or act right, is in and from the Spirit of Christ ; and all merit is not in man, how high soever in grace, but merely in the blood of Christ.' So he and they taught. There is no power in man, till it is given him from above, to do one good work, to speak one good word, or to form one good desire. For it is not enough to say all men are sick of sin : no, we are all *dead* in trespasses and sins.

" And we are all helpless, both with regard to the power and the guilt of sin. For who can bring a clean thing out of an unclean? None less than the Almighty. Who can raise those .that are dead, spiritually dead, in sin? None but he who raised us from the dust of the earth. But on what consideration will he do this? Not for works of righteousness that we have done. The dead cannot praise thee, O Lord, nor can they do anything for which they should be raised to life. Whatever, therefore, God does, he does it merely for the sake of his well-beloved Son. 'He was wounded for our transgressions, he was bruised for our iniquities. He himself bore all our sins in his own body on the tree. He was delivered for our offences, and rose again for our justification.' Here, then, is the sole meritorious cause of every blessing we can or do enjoy, and, in particular, of our pardon and acceptance with God, of our full and free justification. But by what means do we become interested in what Christ has done and suffered? 'Not by works, lest any man should boast, but by faith alone.' 'We conclude,' says the apostle, 'that a man is justified by faith without the deeds of the law.' And 'to as many as receive Christ he gives power to become sons of God; even to them which believe in his name, who are born not of the will of man but of God.'

"Except a man be thus born again he cannot enter into the kingdom of God. But all who are thus born of the Spirit have the kingdom of God within them. Christ sets up his kingdom in their hearts—righteousness, peace, and joy in the Holy Ghost. That mind is in them which was in Christ Jesus, enabling them to walk as Christ walked. His indwelling Spirit makes them holy in mind, and holy in all manner of conversation. But still, seeing all this is a free gift through the blood and righteousness of Christ, there is eternally the same reason to remember—he that glorieth, let him glory in the Lord.

"You are not ignorant that these are the fundamental doctrines which Mr. Whitefield everywhere insisted on; and may they not be summed up, as it were, in two words—'the new birth, and justification by faith?' These let us insist upon with all boldness, and at all times, in all places, in public and in private. Let us keep close to these good old unfashionable doctrines, how many soever contradict and blaspheme."

Such were the words of the Arminian, John Wesley. I make no comment on them. I only say, before any one despises this great man because he was an Arminian, let him take care that he really knows what Wesley's opinions were. Above all, let him take care that he thoroughly understands what kind of doctrines he used to preach in England a hundred years ago.

CHAPTER II.

ENGLAND a hundred years ago received such deep impressions from John Wesley, that I should not feel I did him justice if I did not give my readers a few select specimens of his writings. Before we turn away from the father of Methodism, let us try to get some distinct idea of his style of thought and his mode of expressing himself. Let us see how his mind worked.

The man who could leave his mark so indelibly on his fellow-countrymen as John Wesley did, we must all feel could have been no ordinary man. The man who could keep his hold on assemblies till he was between eighty and ninety years old, and produce effects second only to those produced by Whitefield, must evidently have possessed peculiar gifts. Two or three extracts from his sermons and other writings will probably be thought interesting and instructive by most Christian readers.

The materials for forming a judgment in this matter are happily abundant, and easily accessible. A volume of fifty-seven sermons lies before me at this moment, prepared for publication by Wesley's own hands, and first published in 1771. It is a volume that deserves far more attention than it generally receives in the present day. The doctrine of some of the discourses, I must honestly confess, is sometimes very defective. Nevertheless, the volume contains many noble passages; and there are not a few pages in it which, for clearness, terseness, pointedness, vigour, and pure Saxon phraseology, are perfect models of good style.

Wesley's preface to his volume of sermons is of itself very remarkable. I will begin by giving a few extracts from it. He says,—

"I design plain truth for plain people. Therefore, of set purpose, I abstain from all nice and philosophical speculations; from all perplexed and intricate reasonings; and, as far as possible, from even the show of learning, unless in sometimes citing the original Scriptures. I labour to avoid all words which are not easy to be understood—all which are not used in common life; and in particular those technical terms that so frequently occur in Bodies of divinity—those modes of speaking which men of reading are intimately acquainted with, but which to common people are an unknown tongue. Yet I am not assured that I do not sometimes slide into them unawares; it is so extremely natural to imagine that a word which is familiar to ourselves is so to all the world.

"Nay, my design is, in some sense, to forget all that ever I have read in my life. I mean to speak in the general, as if I had never read one author, ancient or modern, always excepting the inspired. I am persuaded that, on the one hand, this may be a means of enabling me more clearly to express the sentiments of my heart, while I simply follow the chain of my own thoughts without entangling myself with those of other men; and that, on the other, I shall come with fewer weights upon my mind, with less of prejudice and prepossession, either to search for myself or to deliver to others the naked truth of the gospel.

"To candid, reasonable men I am not afraid to lay open what have been the inmost thoughts of my heart. I have thought, 'I am a creature of a day, passing through life as an arrow through the air. I am a spirit come from God, and returning to God, just hovering over the great gulf, till a few moments hence I am no more seen! I drop into an unchangeable eternity! I want to know one thing,—the way to heaven—how to land safe on that happy shore. God himself has condescended to teach the way; for this very end he came from heaven. He hath written it down in a book. Oh, give me that book! At any price give me the book of God! I have it: here is knowledge enough for me. Let me be a man of one book. Here, then, I am free from the busy ways of men. I sit down alone: only God is here. In his presence I open, I read his book; for this end—to find the way to heaven. Is there a doubt concerning the meaning of what I read?—does anything appear dark and intricate?—I lift up my heart to the Father of lights: Lord, is it not thy word, "If any man lack wisdom, let him ask of God:" thou givest liberally, and upbraidest not. Thou hast said, if any be willing to do thy will he shall know. I am willing to do; let me know thy will. I then search after and consider parallel passages of Scripture, comparing spiritual things with spiritual. I meditate thereon with all the earnestness and attention of which my mind is capable. If any doubt still remains, I consult those who are experienced in the ways of God; and then the writings whereby, being dead, they yet speak. And what I thus learn that I teach.'

"But some may say, I have mistaken the way myself, although I have undertaken to teach it to others. It is probable that many will think this, and it is very possible that I have. But I trust, whereinsoever I have mistaken, my mind is open to conviction. I sincerely desire to be better informed. I say to God and man, 'What I know not teach thou me.'

"Are you persuaded you see more clearly than me? It is not unlikely that you may. Then treat me as you would desire to be treated yourself upon a change of circumstances. Point me out a better way than I have yet known. Show me it is so by plain proof of Scripture. And if I linger in the path I have been accustomed to tread, and therefore I am unwilling to leave it, labour with me a little; take me by the hand and lead me as I am able to bear. But be not discouraged if I entreat you not to beat me down in order to quicken my pace: I can go but feebly and slowly at best: *then* I should not be able to go at all. May I not request you, further, not to give me hard names, in order to bring me into the right way. Suppose I was ever so much in the wrong, I doubt this would not set me right. Rather it would make me run so much the further from you, and so get more and more out of the way.

"Nay! perhaps if you are angry, so shall I be too; and then there will be small hopes of finding the truth. If once anger arises, its smoke will so dim the eyes of my soul that I shall be able to see nothing clearly. For God's sake, if it be possible to avoid it, let us not provoke one another to wrath. Let us not kindle in each other this fire of hell; much less blow it up into a flame. If we could discern truth by that dreadful light, would it not be loss rather than gain? For how far is love, even with many wrong opinions, to be preferred before truth itself without love! We may die without the knowledge of many truths, and yet be carried into Abraham's bosom. But if we die without love, what will knowledge avail? Just as much as it avails the devil and his angels!"

The next specimen of John Wesley's mind shall be an extract from a sermon preached by him at St. Mary's, Oxford, before the University, on June 18, 1738, from the words, "By grace ye are saved through faith" (Ephes. ii. 8). It concludes with the following passages :—

"At this time more especially will we speak, that *by grace ye are saved through faith*, because never was the maintaining this doctrine more seasonable than it is at this day. Nothing but this can effectually prevent the increase of the Romish delusion among us. It is endless to attack one by one all the errors of that Church. But salvation by faith strikes at the root, and all fall at once when this is established. It was this doctrine. which our Church justly calls the strong rock and foundation of the Christian religion, that first drove Popery out of these kingdoms, and it is this alone can keep it out. Nothing but this can give a check to that immorality which hath overspread the land as a flood. Can you empty the great deep drop by drop? Then you may reform us by dissuasion from particular vices. But let the righteousness which is of God by faith be brought in, and so shall its proud waves be stayed. Nothing but this can stop the mouths of those who glory in their shame, and openly 'deny the Lord that bought them.' They can talk as sublimely of the law as he that hath it written by God in his heart. To hear them speak on this head might incline one to think they were not far from the kingdom of God. But take them out of the law into the gospel; begin with the righteousness of faith, with *Christ the end of the law to every one that believeth;* and those who but now appeared almost if not altogether Christians, stand confessed the sons of perdition, as far from life and salvation (God be merciful unto them) as the depth of hell from the height of heaven.

" For this cause the adversary so rages whenever salvation by faith is declared to the world. For this reason did he stir up earth and hell to destroy those who preached it. And for the same reason, knowing that faith alone could overturn the foundation of his kingdom, did he call forth all his forces, and employ all his arts of lies and calumny, to affright that champion of the Lord of hosts, Martin Luther, from reviving it. Nor can we wonder thereat; for as that man of God observes, How would it enrage a proud, strong man, armed, to be stopped and set at nought by a little child coming against him with a reed in his hand? Especially when he knew that little child would surely overthrow him and tread him under foot. Even so, Lord Jesus! thus hath thy strength been even made perfect in weakness! Go forth then, thou little child that believest in Him, and his right hand shall teach thee terrible things. Though thou art helpless and weak as an infant of days, the strong man shall not be able to stand before thee. Thou shalt prevail over him, and subdue him, and overthrow him, and trample him under thy feet. Thou shalt march on with the great Captain of thy salvation, conquering and to conquer, until all thine enemies are destroyed, and death is swallowed up in victory."

The next specimen that I will give of John Wesley's preaching is the conclusion of his sermon on justification by faith. It ends with the following striking paragraph. The text is Romans iv. 5 :—

"Thou ungodly one who hearest or readest these words, thou vile, helpless, miserable sinner, I charge thee before God, the judge of all, go straight unto Jesus with all thy ungodliness. Take heed thou destroy not thine own soul by pleading thy righteousness more or less. Go as altogether ungodly, guilty, lost, destroyed, deserving and dropping into hell; and thus shalt thou find favour in his sight, and know that he justifieth the ungodly. As such thou shalt be brought unto the blood of sprinkling, as an undone, helpless, damned sinner. Thus look unto Jesus! There is the Lamb of God, who taketh away thy sins! Plead thou no works, no righteousness of thine own! no humility, contrition, sincerity. In no wise. That were, in very deed, to deny the Lord that bought thee. No! Plead thou singly the blood of the covenant, the ransom paid for thy proud, stubborn, sinful soul. Who art thou that now seest and feelest both thine inward and outward ungodliness? Thou art the man! I want thee for my Lord. I challenge thee for a child of God by faith. The Lord hath need of thee. Thou who feelest thou art just fit for hell art just fit to advance his glory, the glory of free grace, justifying the ungodly and him that worketh not. Oh, come quickly! Believe in the Lord Jesus; and thou, even thou, art reconciled to God."

The last example of John Wesley's preaching that I will bring before the reader, is a portion of a sermon preached by him at St. Mary's, Oxford, before the University, in 1744. The text is Acts iv. 31, and the title of the sermon is "Scriptural Christianity." After asking the question, "Where does Scriptural Christianity exist?" he proceeds to address his hearers in the following manner.—These hearers, we must remember, were the University of Oxford, Heads of Houses, Professors, Fellows, Tutors, and other residents :—

"I beseech you, brethren, by the mercies of God, if ye do account me a madman or a fool, yet as a fool bear with me. It is utterly needful that some one should use great plainness of speech towards you. It is more especially needful at this time; for who knoweth but it may be the last. Who knoweth how soon the righteous Judge may say: 'I will no more be entreated for this people. Though Noah, Daniel, and Job were in this land, they should but deliver their own souls.' And who will use this plainness if I do not? Therefore I, even I, will speak. And I adjure you, by the living God, that ye steel not your hearts against receiving a blessing at my hands. Do not say in your hearts, '*non persuadebis etiamsi persuaseris;*' or, in other words, 'Lord, thou shalt not send by whom thou wilt send. Let me rather perish in my blood than be saved by this man.'

"Brethren, I am persuaded better things of you, though I thus speak. Let me ask you then, in tender love, and in the spirit of meekness, is this city of Oxford a Christian city? Is Christianity, Scriptural Christianity, found here? Are we, as a community of men, so *filled with the Holy Ghost* as to enjoy in our hearts, and show forth in our lives, the genuine fruits of the Spirit? Are all the magistrates, all heads and governors of colleges and halls, and their respective societies (not to speak of inhabitants of the town), of one heart and one soul? Is the love of God shed abroad in our hearts? Are our tempers the same that were in Him? Are our lives agreeable thereto? Are we holy, as He who hath called us is holy, in all manner of conversation?

"In the fear, and in the presence of the great God before whom both you and I shall shortly appear, I pray you that are in authority over us (whom I reverence for your office' sake), to consider not after the manner of dissemblers with God, Are you filled with the Holy Ghost? Are you lively portraitures of him whom ye are appointed to represent among men? *I have said, ye are gods*, ye magistrates and rulers; ye are by office so nearly allied to the God of heaven. In your several stations and degrees ye are to show forth to us the Lord our Governor. Are all the thoughts of your hearts, all your tempers and desires, suitable to your high calling? Are all your words like unto those which come out of the mouth of God? Is there in all your actions dignity and love, a greatness which words cannot express, which can flow only from a heart full of God, and yet consistent with the character of man that is a worm, and the son of man that is a worm?

"Ye venerable men, who are more especially called to form the tender minds of youth, to dispel therein the shades of ignorance and error, and train them up to be heirs unto salvation, are you filled with the Holy Ghost, and with those fruits of the Spirit which your important office so indispensably requires? Is your heart whole with God, and full of love and zeal to set up his kingdom on earth? Do you continually remind those under your care that the one rational end of all our studies is to know, love, and serve the only true God and Jesus Christ whom he hath sent? Do you inculcate upon them day by day that love alone never faileth, and that without love all learning is but splendid ignorance, pompous folly, vexation of spirit? Has all

you teach an actual tendency to the love of God, and of all
mankind for his sake ? Have you an eye to this end, in whatever you prescribe, touching the kind, manner, and measure of
their studies, desiring and labouring that wherever the lot of
these young soldiers of Christ is cast, they may be so many
burning and shining lights, adorning the gospel of Christ in all
things ? And, permit me to ask, do you put forth all your
strength in the vast work you have undertaken ? Do you
labour herein with all your might, exerting every faculty of
your souls, using every talent which God hath lent you, and that
to the uttermost of your power ?

"Let it not be said that I speak here as if all under your care
were intended to be clergymen. Not so ; I only speak as if
they were all intended to be Christians. But what example is
set them by us who enjoy the beneficence of our forefathers,
by fellows, students, scholars, more especially those who are of
some rank and eminence ? Do ye, brethren, abound in the
fruits of the Spirit, in lowliness of mind, in self-denial and
mortification, in tenderness and composure of spirit, in patience,
meekness, sobriety, temperance, and in unwearied, restless en-
deavours to do good unto all men, to relieve their outward
wants and to bring their souls to the true knowledge and love
of God ? Is this the general character of Fellows of colleges ?
I fear it is not. Rather, have not pride and haughtiness of
spirit, impatience and peevishness, sloth and indolency, glut-
tony and sensuality, and even a proverbial uselessness, been
objected to us, perhaps not always by our enemies nor wholly
without ground ? Oh ! that God would roll away this reproach
from us, that the very memory of it might perish for ever !

"Many of us are men immediately consecrated to God, called
to minister in holy things. Are we, then, patterns to the rest,
in word, in conversation, in charity, in spirit, in faith, in purity ?
Is there written on our foreheads and on our hearts, Holiness
to the Lord ? From what motive did we enter upon the office ?

Was it indeed with a single eye to serve God, trusting that we were inwardly moved by the Holy Ghost to take upon us this ministration for the promotion of his glory, and the edifying of his people? And have we clearly determined, by God's grace, to give ourselves wholly to this office? Do we forsake and set aside, as much as in us lies, all worldly cares and studies? Do we apply ourselves wholly to this one thing, and draw all our cares and studies this way? Are we apt to teach? Are we taught of God, that we may be able to teach others also? Do we know God? Do we know Jesus Christ? Hath God revealed his Son in us? And hath he made us able ministers of the new covenant? Where, then, are the seals of our apostleship? Who that were dead in trespasses and sins, have been quickened by our word? Have we a burning zeal to save souls from death, so that for their sakes we often forget even to eat our bread? Do we speak plainly, by manifestation of the truth commending ourselves to every man's conscience? Are we dead to the world, and the things of the world, laying up all our treasure in heaven? Do we lord it over God's heritage, or are we the least, the servants of all? When we bear the reproach of Christ does it sit heavy on us, or do we rejoice therein? When we are smitten on the one cheek, do we resent it? Are we impatient of affronts? or do we turn the other cheek also, not resisting evil, but overcoming evil with good? Have we a bitter zeal, inciting us to strive sharply and passionately with them that are out of the way? or, is our zeal the flame of love, so as to direct all our words with sweetness, lowliness, and meekness of wisdom?

"Once more, what shall we say concerning the youth of this place?—Have you either the form or the power of Christian godliness? Are you humble, teachable, advisable; or stubborn, self-willed, heady, and high-minded? Are you obedient to your superiors as to parents, or do you despise those to whom ye owe the tenderest reverence? Are you diligent in your every business, pursuing your studies with all your strength? Do you redeem the time, crowding as much work into every day as it can contain? Rather are ye not conscious to yourselves that you waste away day after day, either in reading what has no tendency to Christianity, or in gambling, or in—you know not what? Are you better managers of your fortune than of your time? Do you, out of principle, take care to owe no man anything? Do you remember the Sabbath day to keep it holy, to spend it in the more immediate worship of God! When you are in his house, do you consider God is there? do you behave as seeing him that is invisible? Do you know how to possess your bodies in sanctification and honour? Are not drunkenness and uncleanness found among you? Yea, are there not a multitude of you who glory in their shame? Do not many of you take the name of God in vain, perhaps habitually, without either remorse or fear? Yea, are there not a multitude among you that are forsworn? I fear a swiftly-increasing multitude? Be not surprised, brethren. Before God and this congregation I own myself to have been of this number, solemnly swearing to observe all those customs which I then knew nothing of, and those statutes which I did not so much as read over, either then or for some years after. What is perjury if this is not? But if it be, oh, what a weight of sin, yea, sin of no common dye, lieth upon us! And doth not the Most High regard it?

" May it not be one of the consequences of this that so many of you are a generation of triflers, triflers with God, with one another, and with your own souls? For how few of you spend, from one week to another, a single hour in private prayer? How few of you have any thought of God in the general tenor of your conversation? Who of you is in any degree acquainted with the work of his Spirit, his supernatural work in the souls of men? Can you hear, unless now and then in a church, any talk of the Holy Spirit? Would you not take it for granted, if one began such a conversation, that it was either hypocrisy or enthusiasm? In the name of the Lord God Almighty, I ask what religion are you of? Even the talk of Christianity, ye cannot, will not bear. Oh, my brethren, what a Christian city is this! It is time for thee, Lord, to lay to thine hand.

"For, indeed, what probability—what possibility rather, speaking after the manner of men—is there that Christianity, Scriptural Christianity, should be again the religion of this place, and that all orders of men among us should speak and live as men filled with the Holy Spirit? By whom should this Christianity be restored? By those of you that are in authority? Are you convinced, then, that this is Scriptural Christianity? Are you desirous it should be restored? Do you count your fortune, liberty, life, not dear unto yourselves so you may be instrumental in restoring of it? But suppose you have the desire, who hath any power proportioned to effect? Perhaps some of you have made a few vain attempts, but with how small success! Shall Christianity, then, be restored by young, unknown, inconsiderable men? I know not whether ye yourselves would suffer it. Would not some of you cry out, 'Young man, in so doing thou reproachest us!' But there is no danger of your being put to the proof; so hath iniquity overspread us like a flood. Whom then shall God send? The famine, the pestilence (God's last messengers to a guilty land), or the sword? the armies of Romish aliens to reform us into our first love? Nay, rather let us fall into thy hand, O Lord; and let us not fall into the hand of man.

"Lord, save, or we perish! Take us out of the mire, that we sink not! Oh, help us against these enemies, for vain is the help of man. Unto thee all things are possible. According to the greatness of thy power, preserve thou those that are appointed to die, and preserve us in the manner that seemeth to thee good; not as we will, but as thou wilt."

The reader will probably agree with me that this is a remarkable sermon, and one of a class that is not frequently heard in University pulpits. What was thought of it in 1744 by the Vice-chancellor, the Heads of Houses, and the Fellows and Tutors of Colleges, we have little means of knowing. In his journal, Wesley only remarks : " I preached this day for the last time, I suppose, at St. Mary's. Be it so. I am now clear of the blood of these men. I have fully delivered my own soul. The beadle came to me afterwards, and told me, 'that the Vice-chancellor had sent him for my notes.' I sent them without delay, not without admiring the wise providence of God. Perhaps few men of note would have given a sermon of mine the reading, if I had put it in their hands. But by this reason it came to be read, probably more than once, by every man of eminence in the University." Many, perhaps, will agree with me that, if Oxford had heard more of such plain preaching during the last one hundred and twenty years, it would have been well for the Church of England.

Turning away from Wesley's preaching, I will now give a specimen of his mind of a very different description. I will give the twelve rules which he laid down for the guidance of his helpers in evangelistic work in the Methodist communion. They serve to illustrate, I think, in a very striking manner, the great shrewdness and good sense of the man, and are also good examples of his terse, pithy style of composition. He says to his helpers :—

" 1. Be diligent. Never be unemployed for a moment; never be triflingly employed. Never while away time ; neither spend any more time at any place than is strictly necessary.

" 2. Be serious. Let your motto be, Holiness to the Lord. Avoid all lightness, jesting, and foolish talking.

" 3. Converse sparingly and cautiously with women, particularly with young women in private.

" 4. Take no step towards marriage without first acquainting me with your design.

"5. Believe evil of no one ; unless you see it done, take heed how you credit it. Put the best construction on everything : you know the judge is always supposed to be on the prisoner's side..

"6. Speak evil of no one ; else your words especially would eat as doth a canker. Keep your thoughts within your own breast till you come to the person concerned.

"7. Tell every one what you think wrong in him, and that plainly, and as soon as may be, else it will fester in your heart. Make all haste to cast the fire out of your bosom.

"8. Do not *affect* the gentleman. You have no more to do with this character than with that of a dancing-master. A preacher of the gospel is the servant of all.

"9. Be ashamed of nothing but sin ; not of fetching wood (if time permit), or of drawing water ; not of cleaning your own shoes, or your neighbour's.

"10. Be punctual. Do everything exactly at the time ; and, in general, do not mend our rules, but keep them ; not for wrath, but for conscience' sake.

"11. You have nothing to do but to save souls. Therefore spend and be spent in this work. And go always not to those who want you, but to those who want you most.

"12. Act in all things, not according to your own will, but as a son in the gospel. As such, it is your part to employ your time in the manner which we direct, partly in preaching and visiting the flock from house to house ; partly in reading, meditation, and prayer. Above all, if you labour with us in the Lord's vineyard, it is needful that you should do that part of the work which we advise, at those times and places which we judge most for his glory."

Comment on these rules is needless. They speak for themselves. Though originally drawn up with a special view to the wants of the Methodist helpers, they contain wisdom for all bodies of Christians. Happy would it be for all the churches of Christ, if all the ministers of the gospel would carry out the spirit of these rules, and remember their wise suggestions far more than they do.

Let us next take an illustration of the manner in which he used to advise his preachers individually. To one who was in danger of becoming a noisy, clamorous preacher, he writes :—

"Scream no more at peril of your soul. God now warns you by me, whom he has set over you. Speak as earnestly as you can, but do not scream. Speak with all your heart, but with a moderate voice. It was said of our Lord, 'He shall not *cry.*' The word means properly, he shall not *scream.* Herein be a follower of me, as I am of Christ. I often speak loud, often vehemently ; but I never scream ; I never strain myself ; I dare not ; I know it would be a sin against God and my own soul."

To one who neglected the duty of private reading and regular study, he wrote as follows :—

"Hence your talent in preaching does not increase ; it is just the same as it was seven years ago. It is lively, but not deep ; there is little variety ; there is no compass of thought. Reading only can supply this, with daily meditation and daily prayer. You wrong yourself greatly by omitting this ; you never can be a deep preacher without it, any more than a thorough Christian. Oh begin ! Fix some part of every day for private exercises. You may acquire the taste which you have not ; what is tedious at first will afterwards be pleasant. Whether you like it or not, read and pray daily. It is for your life ! There is no other way ; else you will be a trifler all your days, and a pretty superficial preacher. Do justice to your own soul ; give it time and means to grow : do not starve yourself any longer."

The last specimen of John Wesley's mind that I will give, is an extract from a letter which he wrote to the Bishop of Lincoln, by way of public protest, on account of the disgraceful persecution which some intolerant magistrates carried on against the Lincolnshire Methodists. It is an interesting letter, not only on account of the holy boldness of its style, but also on account of the age of the writer. He says:—

"My Lord, I am a dying man, having already one foot in the grave. Humanly speaking, I cannot long creep upon the earth, being now nearer ninety than eighty years of age. But I cannot die in peace before I have discharged this office of Christian love to your Lordship. I write without ceremony, as neither hoping nor fearing anything from your Lordship or from any man living. And I ask, in the name and in the presence of Him, to whom both you and I are shortly to give an account, why do you trouble those that are quiet in the land, those that fear God and work righteousness? Does your Lordship know what the Methodists are—that many thousands of them are zealous members of the Church of England, and strongly attached, not only to His Majesty, but to his present ministry? Why should your Lordship, setting religion out of the question, throw away such a body of respectable friends? Is it for their religious sentiments? Alas, my Lord, is this a time to persecute any man for conscience' sake? I beseech you, my Lord, do as you would be done to. You are a man of sense; you are a man of learning; nay, I verily believe (what is of infinitely more value), you are a man of piety. Then think, and let think. I pray God to bless you with the choicest of his blessings."

With this letter I conclude my illustrations of John Wesley's mind and its working. It would be easy to add to the extracts I have given from the large stock of materials which are still within reach of all who choose to look for them. But there is such a thing as overloading a subject, and injuring it by over-quotation. I believe I have said enough to supply my readers with the means of forming a judgment of John Wesley's mental calibre.

Has any one been accustomed to regard the father of

Methodism as a mere fanatic, as a man of moderate abilities and superficial education, as a successful popular preacher and leader of an ignorant sect, but nothing more? I ask such an one to examine carefully the specimens I have given of Wesley's mind, and to reconsider his opinion. Whether men like Methodist doctrine or not, I think they must honestly concede that the old Fellow of Lincoln was a scholar and a sensible man. The world, which always sneers at evangelical religion, may please itself by saying that the men who shook England a hundred years ago were weak-minded, hot-headed enthusiasts, and unlearned and ignorant men. The Jews said the same of the apostles in early days. But the world cannot get over facts. The founder of Methodism was a man of no mean reputation in Oxford, and his writings show him to have been a well-read, logical-minded, and intelligent man. Let the children of this world deny this if they can.

Finally, has any one been accustomed to regard Wesley with dislike on account of his Arminian opinions? Is any one in the habit of turning away from his name with prejudice, and re-fusing to believe that such an imperfect preacher of the gospel could do any good? I ask such an one to remould his opinion, to take a more kindly view of the old soldier of the cross, and to give him the honour he deserves.

What though John Wesley did not use all the weapons of truth which our great Captain has provided? What though he often said things which you and I feel we could not say, and left unsaid things which we feel ought to be said? Still, not-withstanding this, he was a bold fighter on Christ's side, a fear-less warrior against sin, the world, and the devil, and an unflinching adherent of the Lord Jesus Christ in a very dark day. He honoured the Bible. He cried down sin. He made much of Christ's blood. He exalted holiness. He taught the absolute need of repentance, faith, and conversion. Surely these things ought not to be forgotten. Surely there is a deep lesson in those words of our Master, "Forbid him not : for there is no man which shall do a miracle in my name, that can lightly speak evil of me. For he that is not against us is on our part" (Mark ix. 39, 40).

Then let us thank God for what John Wesley *was*, and not keep poring over his deficiencies, and only talking of what he *was not*. Whether we like it or not, John Wesley was a mighty instrument in God's hand for good ; and, next to George White-field, was the first and foremost evangelist of England a hundred years ago.

V.

William Grimshaw of Haworth, and his Ministry.

CHAPTER I.

Born at Brindle, 1708—Educated at Christ's College, Cambridge—Ordained, 1731—Curate of Rochdale and Todmorden—Death of his Wife—Minister of Haworth, 1742—Description of Haworth—Style of his Ministry—His Manner of Life, Diligence, Charity, Love of Peace, Humility—His Ministerial Success.

THE third spiritual hero of the last century whom I wish to introduce to my readers, is one who is very little known. The man I mean is William Grimshaw, Perpetual Curate of Haworth, in Yorkshire.

Thousands, I can well believe, are familiar with the history of Whitefield and Wesley, who have not so much as heard of Grimshaw's name. Yet he was a mighty man of God, of whom the Church and the world were not worthy. If greatness is to be measured by usefulness to souls, I believe there were not in England a hundred years ago three greater men than William Grimshaw.

The reasons why this good man is so little known are soon explained.

For one thing, Grimshaw never withdrew from his position as a beneficed clergyman of the Church of England. He lived and died incumbent of a Yorkshire parochial district. He founded no new sect, and drew up no new articles of faith. He found as much liberty as he wanted within the pale of a beneficed clergyman's position, and with that liberty he was content. Such a man, in the very nature of things, will rarely emerge from comparative obscurity. No zealous partisan will chronicle his actions and movements. No persecuted followers will publish accounts of his life and opinions. The man who remains in the ranks, or behind the intrenchments, will never be so conspicuous as he who carries on a guerilla warfare single-handed, or stands forth outside on the plain.*

For another thing, Grimshaw never went to London, or opened his mouth so much as once in a London pulpit. He moved in a purely provincial orbit, in days when railways, telegraphs, and penny postage were not even dreamed of. Within that orbit, no doubt, he was a star of the first magnitude; but beyond it he was never heard or seen. We need not wonder that he was little known in his day and generation. The minister who never preaches in London, and writes nothing, must not be surprised if the world knows nothing of him. Like some of the judges of Israel, he may be great in his own district, but some of the tribes will scarcely be acquainted with his name.

After all, the being famous is a thing that depends greatly on position and opportunity. It is not enough to possess gifts and powers: there must also be the means of exhibiting them. For want of opportunity some of the greatest men perhaps are buried in obscurity. There may be great physicians who could never find a practice, great lawyers who could never get a brief, and great soldiers who never had a chance of distinguishing themselves. The main reason why the Church has done so little honour to Grimshaw's name may be, that it had so little opportunity of knowing him.

William Grimshaw was born at Brindle, in Lancashire, on the

---

* It ought to be remembered that neither Wesley nor Whitefield ever held a living in the Church of England. It is, therefore, not correct to speak of them as men who *seceded* from the Church. They resigned no living or official position, simply because they had none to resign. They were practically excluded from the pulpits of the Establishment, because the clergy as a body refused to admit them. But they never formally separated themselves from the communion in which they had been ordained.

3rd of September 1708. Brindle is an agricultural parish, containing at present about thirteen hundred people, and lies not far from the three manufacturing towns of Preston, Chorley, and Blackburn. Nothing whatever is known of the rank and position of his parents. Who his mother was, whether he had any brothers and sisters, what was his father's occupation and employment, are all points which are now veiled in complete obscurity. Beyond the fact that one of the churchwardens of Brindle in 1728 was a certain William Grimshaw, nothing has ever been ascertained.*

About Grimshaw's early life and education I can tell my readers almost nothing. That he went to the Grammar Schools of Blackburn and Hesketh, was admitted to Christ's College, Cambridge, at the age of eighteen, and in due course of time took his degree as Bachelor of Arts, are the only facts that I can collect about the first twenty-one years of his life. But his character as a boy and young man, and his conduct at school and college, are matters about which I cannot supply the slightest information, because none exists. There are, however, no grounds for supposing that he spent his time at all better than other young men of his day, or that he evinced any concern about religion.

In the year 1731 Grimshaw was ordained deacon, and entered holy orders as curate of Rochdale. He seems to have taken on him this solemn office without any spiritual feeling, and in utter ignorance of the duties of a minister of Christ's gospel. Like too many young clergymen, he appears to have been ordained without knowing anything aright either about his own soul, or about the way to do good to the souls of others. In fact, in after-life he deeply lamented that he sought ordination from the lowest and most unworthy of motives—the desire to

---

* I think it right to say, that almost the only accessible source of information about Grimshaw is a biography of him lately published by Mr. Spence Hardy. It is an interesting volume, and well worth reading, though the author's predilections in favour of Methodism are rather too manifest.

be in a respectable profession, and, if possible, to get a good living.

Grimshaw's stay at Rochdale, for some reason which we cannot now explain, was a very short one. In September 1731, the very year that he was ordained, he became curate of Todmorden, and left Rochdale entirely. Todmorden lies in a romantic valley between Rochdale and Leeds, well known to all who travel by the Lancashire and Yorkshire Railway. Before the steam-engine was invented, it must have been a singularly beautiful place. Ecclesiastically, it is a chapelry in the patronage of the Vicar of Rochdale, and stands partly in the great parish of Rochdale and partly in the equally large parish of Halifax. Here Grimshaw continued for no less than eleven years.

The eleven years during which Grimshaw resided at Todmorden were, beyond doubt, the turning-point in his spiritual history. It is much to be regretted that we possess nothing but the most scanty information about this period of his life. Enough, however, exists to throw some light on the way through which he was led to become the man of God that he was in after-days.

It appears then, according to Middleton, one of his biographers, that about the year 1734, three years after he came to Todmorden, Grimshaw began for the first time to feel deep concern about his own soul, and the souls of his parishioners. A change came over his life and outward behaviour. He laid aside the diversions in which he had hitherto spent the greater part of his time—such as hunting, fishing, card-playing, revelling, and merry-making—and began to visit his people, and press on them the importance of religion, like one who really believed it. At the same time he commenced the practice of praying in secret four times a-day, a practice which there is reason to believe he never left off.

There is nothing to show that his views of Christianity at

this period were any but the most dark and obscure. Of the
distinctive doctrines of the gospel, of salvation by grace, justification by faith, free pardon through Christ's blood, and the
converting power of the Holy Ghost, he probably knew nothing
at all.   He had none but books of a very legal character, most
of them given by Dr. Dunster, Vicar of Rochdale, when he was
his curate.   He had no friend to deal with him, as Peter did
with Cornelius, or Aquila and Priscilla did with Apollos, and
" show him the way of God more perfectly."   But he was
honest in seeking light, and light came, though not immediately.
He prayed much, like Saul in the house of Judas at Damascus,
and after many days his prayer was heard.   He used such
means as he had, and in so using means God met him and
helped him.   He had a sincere desire to do God's will, and the
promise of the Lord Jesus was verified, " He shall know of the
doctrine whether it be of God" (John vii. 17).

The struggle between light and darkness in Grimshaw's mind
appears to have continued several years.   Long as this delay
may seem to us, we must not forget that he was entirely without
help from man, and had to work out every spiritual problem
unassisted and alone.   But though the work within him went
on slowly, it went on solidly and surely.   The illness and death
of his first wife, leaving him a desolate widower with two children, after four years of married life, appears to have been a
powerful means of drawing him nearer to God.   The perusal
of two most valuable Puritan books, "Brooks' Precious Remedies
against Satan's Devices," and " Owen on Justification," seems
to have been extremely helpful and establishing to his soul.
And the final result was, that after several years of severe conflict, Grimshaw no longer " walked in darkness, but had the
full light of life" (John viii. 12).   The scales completely fell
from his eyes.   He saw and knew the whole truth, and the
truth made him free.   He left Todmorden a far wiser and hap-
pier man than he entered it.   Hard as the schooling was, he

there learned lessons which he never forgot to his life's end. Few men, perhaps, have ever so thoroughly verified the truth of Luther's saying, " Prayer and temptation, the Bible and meditation, make a true minister of the gospel."

Grimshaw's testimony to the power of the Scriptures at this crisis in his spiritual history, is very striking and instructive. Like many others, he found the Bible almost a new book to his mind. Up to this time he had known it only in the letter, but now he became acquainted with it in its spiritual power. He afterwards told a friend that "if God had drawn up his Bible to heaven, and sent him down another, it could not have been newer to him." So true is it that when man becomes a new creature "old things pass away and all things become new."

Grimshaw's people at Todmorden soon found that a change had come over their minister's mind. In the middle of his spiritual conflict, and before he had found peace, it is related that a poor woman came to him in great distress of soul, and asked him what she must do. He could only say, " I cannot tell what to say to you, Susan, for I am in the same state myself; but to despair of the mercy of God would be worse than all." Another woman, named Mary Scholefield, of Calf Lees, had sought his advice in the beginning of his ministry, and got the following answer: " Put away these gloomy thoughts. Go into merry company. Divert yourself; and all will be well at last." At a later period he went to her house and said, " O Mary, what a blind leader of the blind was I, when I came to take off thy burden by exhorting thee to live in pleasure, and to follow the vain amusements of the world!" Incidents like these, we may be sure, would soon be known throughout Todmorden. True conversion, like the presence of Christ, is a thing that cannot be hid.

It would indeed be interesting if we had any authentic records of Grimshaw's history during these momentous eleven

years at Todmorden.   But God has thought fit to withhold
them from us.   It is certainly very curious that without the
least concert with the other great evangelists who were his
contemporaries, he should have arrived at the same doctrinal
conclusions and taken up the same line of action.   But it is
an established fact, and well ascertained, that all the time he
was at Todmorden he was an entire stranger to Whitefield and
Wesley, and never read a line of their writings.   It is no less
curious to observe how God was pleased to wean him from the
love of worldly things, by taking away his beloved wife, whose
loss he seems to have felt most keenly.   But the well-instructed
Christian will see in all this part of his history the hand of
perfect wisdom.   The tools that the great Architect intends to
use much, are often kept long in the fire, to temper them and
fit them for work.   The discipline that Grimshaw went through
at Todmorden was doubtless very severe.   But the lessons he
learned under it could probably have been learned in no other
school.

In the month of May 1742, Grimshaw was appointed
minister of Haworth in Yorkshire, and remained there twenty-
one years, until his death.   How and by what interest he got
the appointment, we do not know.   At the present time,
the patronage is in the hands of the Vicar of Bradford and
certain trustees.   It is not unlikely that his first wife's family
had something to do with it.*   Haworth is a chapelry in the
parish of Bradford, and about four miles from the town of
Keighley.   It stands in a cold, desolate, bleak moorland
country, on the hills which divide Yorkshire from Lancashire,
and, running down from the Lake district to the peak of
Derbyshire, form the "backbone" of England.   None but
those who have travelled from Manchester to Leeds by the
Lancashire and Yorkshire Railway, or from Manchester to

* Haworth is best known at present as the birth-place and residence of the unhappy
Charlotte Brontë, whose father was incumbent of the place.

Huddersfield by the London and North-Western, or from Manchester to Sheffield by the Great Northern line, can have any adequate idea of the rugged, weather-beaten, mountainous character of this district. Its valleys are beautiful, highly cultivated, and teeming with life and manufacturing activity. But the upper parts of the country are often as wild, and steep, and uncultivated, and unapproachable, as a Highland moor. At the top of one of the roughest parts of the mountain district lies the village of Haworth, the principal scene of Grimshaw's ministerial labour.

Haworth a hundred years ago was perhaps as rough and uncivilized a place as a minister could go to. Even Doomsday-Book specially describes it as "desolate and waste." It is a long narrow village, built of brown stone, approached by a steep ascent from Keighley or Hebden bridge. The street is so steep that one can understand it must have been only recently that wheeled carriages went there. Indeed, there is a legend that when the first carriage came to Haworth the villagers brought out hay to feed it, under the idea that it was an animal! Such was the parish in which Grimshaw set up the standard of the cross. A less promising field can hardly be imagined.

Grimshaw began his work at Haworth after a manner very different from his beginning at Todmorden. He commenced preaching to his wild and rough parishioners the gospel of Christ in the plainest and most familiar manner, and followed up his preaching by house to house visitation. His preaching was not confined to the walls of the church. Wherever he could get people together, whether in a room, a barn, a field, a quarry, or by the roadside, he was ready to preach. His visiting was not a mere going from family to family to gossip about temporal matters, sickness, and children. Wherever he went he took his Master with him, and spoke plainly to people about their souls. In this kind of work his whole life was spent at

Haworth. Preaching publicly and privately repentance to-ward God, and faith toward our Lord Jesus Christ, after the manner of St. Paul, was his one employment throughout the whole twenty-one years of his ministry. He himself describes his mode of action in the following letter :—

" The method which I, the least and most unworthy of my Lord's ministers, take in my parish, is this : I preach the gospel —glad tidings of salvation to penitent sinners through faith in Christ's blood only—twice every Sunday the year round, save when I expound the Church Catechism and thirty-nine articles, or read the Homilies, which in substance I think my duty to do in some part of the year annually, on the Lord's day morn-ings. I have found this practice, I bless God, of inexpressible benefit to my congregation, which consists, especially in the summer season, of perhaps ten or twelve hundred souls, or, as some think, many more. We have also prayer, and a chapter expounded every Lord's Day evening. I visit my parish in twelve several places monthly, convening six, eight, or ten families in each place, allowing any people of the neighbouring parishes that please to attend the exhortation. This I call my monthly visitation. I am now entering into the fifth year of it, and wonderfully has the Lord blessed it. The only thing more are our funeral expositions and exhortations, and visiting our societies in one or other of the three last days of the month. This I purpose, through the grace of God, to make my con-stant business in my parish so long as I live."

In carrying on this kind of work, Grimshaw gladly availed himself of every help that he could obtain from like-minded men. He became acquainted with John Nelson, the famous Yorkshire stone-mason, one of the most remarkable lay-preachers whom Wesley sent forth, and frequently received him at Haworth. He welcomed those few clergymen who were of one heart with himself, and seized every opportunity of getting them to preach to his people. Whitefield, the two

Wesleys, Romaine, and Venn, were among those whom he was only too glad to place in his pulpit. On such occasions it was no uncommon thing to leave the church and preach in the churchyard, in order to meet the convenience of the crowds who came together. When the Lord's Supper was administered at such seasons, it was sometimes necessary for the first congregation of communicants to retire from the church and give way to others, until all had partaken of the ordinance. In one instance, when Whitefield was present, the numbers who came to the Lord's Table were so great that no less than thirty-five bottles of wine were used !

The effect produced by this new and fervent style of ministration, as might well be expected, was very great indeed. An interest about religion was aroused throughout the whole district round Haworth, and multitudes began to think who had never thought before. Grimshaw himself says, in a letter to Dr. Gillies, author of the "Historical Collections:" "Souls were affected by the word, brought to see their lost estate by nature, and to experience peace through faith in the blood of Jesus. My church began to be crowded, insomuch that many were obliged to stand out of doors. Here, as in many places, it was amazing to see and hear what weeping, roaring, and agony, many people were seized with, at the apprehension of their sinful state and wrath of God. After a season I joined people, such as were truly seeking, or had found the Lord, in society, for meetings and exercises. These meetings are held once a week, about two hours, and are called classes, consisting of about ten or twelve members each. We have much of the Lord's presence among them, and greatly in consequence must such meetings conduce to Christian edification."

The style of preaching which Grimshaw adopted was peculiarly well suited to the rough and uneducated population with which he had to do. He was eminently a plain preacher. His first aim undoubtedly was to preach the whole truth as it is in

Jesus ; his second was to preach so as to be understood. To accomplish this end he was willing to make many sacrifices, to crucify his natural taste as an educated clergyman who had been at Cambridge, and to be thought a fool by intellectual men. But he cared nothing so long as he could succeed in reaching the hearts and consciences of his hearers. John Newton, who knew him well, has left some remarks on this characteristic of Grimshaw's preaching which are well worth reading. He says : " The desire of usefulness to persons of the weakest capacity, or most destitute of the advantages of education, influenced his phraseology in preaching. Though his abilities as a speaker, and his fund of general knowledge, rendered him very competent to stand before great men, yet, as his stated hearers were chiefly of the poorer and more unlettered classes, he condescended to accommodate himself, in the most familiar manner, to their ideas, and to their modes of expression. Like the apostles, he disdained that elegance and excellence of speech which is admired by those who seek entertainment perhaps not less than instruction from the pulpit. He rather chose to deliver his sentiments in what he used to term ' market language.' And though the warmth of his heart and the rapidity of his imagination might sometimes lead him to clothe his thoughts in words which even a candid critic could not justify, yet the general effect of his plain manner was striking and impressive, suited to make the dullest understand, and to fix for a time the attention of the most careless. Frequently a sentence which a delicate hearer might judge quaint or vulgar, conveyed an important truth to the ear, and fixed it on the memory for years after the rest of the sermon and the general subject were forgotten. Judicious hearers could easily excuse some escapes of this kind, and allow that, though he had a singular felicity in bringing down the great truths of the gospel to a level with the meanest capacity, he did not degrade them. The solemnity of his manner, the energy with which he spoke, the spirit of love which beamed in his eyes and breathed through his addresses, were convincing proofs that he did not trifle with his people. I may give my judgment on this point, something in his own way, by quoting a plain and homely proverb which says, 'That is the best cat which catches the most mice.' His improprieties, if he was justly chargeable with any, are very easily avoided; but few ministers have had equal success. But if his language was more especially suited to the taste of his unpolished rustic hearers, his subject-matter was calculated to affect the hearts of all, whether high or low, rich or poor, learned or ignorant; and they who refused to believe were often compelled to tremble."

The manner in which he conducted public worship at Haworth seems to have been as remarkable as his preaching. There was a life, and fire, and reality, and earnestness about it, which made it seem a totally different thing from what it was in other churches. The Prayer-Book seemed like a new book; and the reading-desk was almost as arresting to the congregation as the pulpit. Middleton, in his life of him, says: "In performance of divine service, and especially at the communion, he was at times like a man with his feet on earth and his soul in heaven. In prayer, before sermon, he would indeed 'take hold (as he used to say) of the very horns of the altar,' which, he added, 'he could not, he would not, let go till God had given the blessing.' And his fervency often was such, and attended with such heartfelt and melting expressions, that scarcely a dry eye was to be seen in his numerous congregation."

The life which Grimshaw lived appears, by the testimony of all his contemporaries, to have been as remarkable as his preaching. In the highest sense he seems to have adorned the doctrine of the gospel, and to have made it beautiful in the eyes of all around him. He was not like some of whom the bitter remark has been made, that when they are in the pulpit it is a pity they ever get out of it, and when out of it, a pity that they should ever get in. The same Christ that he preached in the pulpit was the Christ that he endeavoured to follow in his daily life.

He was a man of rare diligence and self-denial. None ever worked harder than he did in his calling, and few worked so hard. He seldom preached less than twenty, and often nearly thirty times in a week. In doing this he would constantly travel scores of miles, content with the humblest fare and the roughest accommodation.

He was a man of rare charity and brotherly love. He loved all who loved Christ, by whatever name they might be called, and he was kind to every one in temporal as well as spiritual things. "In fact," says Middleton, "his charity knew no bound but his circumstances. As his grace and faithfulness rendered him useful to all, so his benevolent liberality particularly endeared him to the poor. He frequently used to say, 'If I shall die to-day I have not a penny to leave behind me.' And yet he did not quit the world in debt, for he had prudence as well as grace."

He was pre-eminently a peacemaker. "The animosities and differences of men," says Middleton, "afforded his affectionate spirit nothing but pain. No labour was too great or too long if their reconciliation might be his reward. When he has met with cases of uncommon perseverance or obduracy, he has been known to fall on his knees before them, beseeching them, for Christ's sake, to love one another, and offering to let them tread on his neck if they would only be at peace among themselves."

He was, above all, a man of rare humility. Few gifted men, perhaps, ever thought so meanly of themselves, or were so truly ready in honour to prefer others. "What have we to boast of?" he said. "What have we that we have not received? Freely by grace we are saved. When I die I shall then have my greatest grief and my greatest joy,—my greatest grief that I have done so little for Jesus, and my greatest joy that Jesus has done so much for me. My last words shall be, *Here goes an unprofitable servant !"*

That such a man as Grimshaw should soon obtain immense influence in Haworth is nothing more than we might expect. Preaching as he did and living as he did, we can well understand that he produced a mighty impression on his wild parishioners. Sin was checked, Sabbath-breaking became unfashionable, immorality was greatly restrained. Like John the Baptist in the wilderness, he shook the little corner of Yorkshire where he was placed, and stirred men's minds to the very bottom. Hundreds learned to fear hell who did not really love heaven. Scores were restrained from sin though they were not converted to God.

But this was not all. There can be no doubt that Grimshaw was the means of true conversion to many souls. Year after year the Holy Ghost applied his sermons to the hearts and consciences of not a few of his hearers, and added to the true Church of Christ such as should be saved. In one single year, after burying eighteen persons, he said that " he had great reason to believe that sixteen of them were entered into the kingdom of God."

" Not long before his death," says one of his biographers, " he stood with the Rev. John Newton upon a hill near Haworth surveying the romantic prospect. He then said that at the time he first came into that part of the country he might have gone half a day's journey on horseback toward the east, west, north, and south, without meeting one truly serious person, or even hearing of one. But now, through the blessing of God upon his labours, he could tell of several hundreds of persons who attended his ministry, and were devout communicants with him at the Lord's Table ; and of nearly all the last-named he could say that he was as well acquainted with their several temptations, trials, and mercies, both personal and domestic, as if he had lived in their families."

The extra-parochial labours which Grimshaw undertook, and the persecutions which they entailed upon him, his early death, and some account of his few literary remains, are subjects of so much interest that I must defer them to another chapter.

CHAPTER II.

Extra-Parochial Labour in Yorkshire, Lancashire, and Cheshire—The Nature of this Labour Explained and Defended—Persecution at Colne—The Archbishop of York's Visit to Haworth—His Love to the Articles and Homilies—His Last Illness, Dying Sayings, Death, and Funeral.

THE religious condition of England a hundred years ago was so deplorably bad, that a man like Grimshaw was not likely to confine his labours to his own parish. Led by the force of circumstances, he soon began to preach outside his parochial boundaries, and finally " did the work of an evangelist" throughout the whole region within fifty miles of Haworth.

The circumstances which led Grimshaw into this course of action are soon explained. Hundreds of his regular hearers at Haworth were not his parishioners, and came together from distant places. Once taught of God to know the value of the gospel, they went out of their own parishes to get the spiritual food which they could not find at home. It was only natural that these people should feel for their families and neighbours, and desire that they might hear what had done good to themselves. They asked Grimshaw to come and preach at their houses, and represented to him the ignorance and spiritual destitution of all around their own homes. They entreated him to come and tell their friends and relatives the same things he was every week telling his congregation at Haworth. They told him that souls were perishing for lack of knowledge, unshepherded, uncared for, and untaught, and promised him a hearty welcome if he would " come over" his parish boundaries and "help" them. Appeals like these, we can well believe, were not made in vain. In a short time these extra-parochial labours became a regular and systematic business. The voice of the incumbent of Haworth was soon heard in many other places beside his parish-church, and for many years he was known throughout Yorkshire, Lancashire, Cheshire, and North Derbyshire, as the apostle and preacher of the district.

It would be interesting to name all the places which Grimshaw was in the habit of visiting as an evangelist, but it is impossible to do so. No accurate record remains of the extent of his labours, and he left no journal behind him. It is known, however, that in Yorkshire he used to preach at Leeds, Halifax, Bradford, Manningham, Todmorden, Birstal, Keighley, Otley, Bingley, Bramley, Heptonstall, Luddenden, and Osmotherley. In Lancashire, he used to visit Manchester, Bolton, Rochdale, Colne, Padiham, Holme, Bacop, and Rossendale. In Cheshire, we find him at Stockport, Tarvin, and Rostherne ; and in Derbyshire at Mellor. These places are probably not a tenth part of those he visited, but they are places specially mentioned by his biographers.

In all these places the people who valued such preaching as Grimshaw's were banded together in societies, and generally under the direction of one man. The incumbent of a large parish like Haworth, of course, could only leave his own work for a short time, and visit distant preaching-stations at long intervals. Between his visits, the societies were necessarily left very much to themselves and their local leaders. Conference with these leaders, receiving reports from them of the spiritual condition of the societies, and arranging with them for breaking up new ground as well as keeping old ground in cultivation, made no small part of Grimshaw's extra-parochial work. To these leaders of societies was left the provision of rooms, or barns, or convenient fields for preaching, and the collection of money to defray expenses. Thus, when the incumbent of

Haworth, or some like-minded friend, paid his periodical visit, he had nothing to do but to preach.

The managers or leaders of these societies, scattered about Yorkshire, Lancashire, and Cheshire, were seldom above the middle class, and frequently no more than intelligent small farmers. There is no evidence that Grimshaw's ministry ever had much effect upon the upper ranks, or indeed was ever brought to bear upon them. But none but an ignorant man will ever think the worse of it on that account. To get hold of the lower middle and lower classes of society, and enlist them in the service of Christ, is at this day one of the greatest problems the Churches have to solve. If Grimshaw succeeded in doing this, it is enough to prove that he was no common man. A church is never in so healthy a state as it is when "the common people hear gladly."

Let the following extract from Hardy's "Life of Grimshaw" supply an instance of the sort of people that Grimshaw got hold of in his itinerant labours outside his own parish :—" At Booth Bank, in the parish of Rostherne, Cheshire, Grimshaw's services used to be held in the house of John and Alice Cross. Alice was a woman of great spirit and intrepidity, and a heroine in Christ's service. Her husband was a quiet sober man, but for some time after her conversion he remained in his old ways. When going out to worship, with her straw hat in one hand and the door-latch in the other, she would say to him, 'John Cross, wilt thou go to heaven with me ? If thou wilt not, I am determined not to go to hell with thee !' John yielded at last ; a pulpit was fixed in the largest room of their house at Rostherne, and the messengers of God were made welcome to their fare and farm. When beggars came to the door she told them of the riches that are in Christ Jesus, and, kneeling by their side, commended them to the grace of God, and then sent them away, grateful for her charity, and impressed by her earnestness in seeking their souls' good. Nor were the more honourable of the land beyond the reach of her reproofs. On one occasion she stopped the Cheshire hunt, when passing her house, and addressed the horsemen, especially Lord Stamford and Sir Harry Main-waring, who listened to her warning and rode on. When the expected preacher did not come, though the pulpit was not occupied, the congregation did not go empty away. Alice Cross herself, in her simple and earnest way, dealt out the bread of life." Such were the kind of households that Grimshaw used to make centres of operation in his extra-parochial evangelism. Such were the kind of people who valued his labours, welcomed his visits, and proved the value of his preaching, in the district within fifty miles of Haworth.

No doubt these extra-parochial labours of Grimshaw will appear wrong to many in the present day. Many are such excessive lovers of parochial order that they feel scandalized at the idea of an incumbent preaching in other men's parishes. Such people would do well to remember the condition of England in Grimshaw's times. There were scores and hundreds of parishes all over the north of England in which there was no resident clergyman ; and the services of the Church, even when performed, were cold, brief, and utterly unprofitable. To tell us that Grimshaw ought to have left the inhabitants of these parishes to perish in ignorance rather than commit a breach of parochial order, is simply ridiculous. Men might as well tell us that we must not knock at a person's door and awaken him, when his house is on fire, because we have not the honour of his acquaintance ! The parochial system of the Church of England was designed for the good of men's souls. It was never intended to ruin souls by cutting them off from the sound of the gospel.

The thing that is really wonderful, in the history of Grimshaw's extra-parochial labours, is the non-interference of ecclesiastical authorities. How the incumbent of Haworth can have gone on for fifteen or twenty years preaching all over

Lancashire, Yorkshire, and Cheshire, without being stopped by bishops and archdeacons, is very hard to understand! Let us charitably hope that many felt in their secret hearts that some such evangelism as his was absolutely needed. The enormous size of such parishes as Bradford and Halifax in Yorkshire—as Whalley, Rochdale, and Prestwich, in Lancashire—as Stockport, Astbury, and Prestbury, in Cheshire, made it utterly impossible for the clergymen of the mother-churches to provide means of grace for their parishioners. We may well believe, that to arrest such labours as Grimshaw's in these unwieldy parishes would have been so unwise, that even bishops and archdeacons of the last century shrank from attempting it. Be the cause what it may, it is a most curious fact that Grimshaw was never entirely stopped in his extra-parochial ministry. The hand of the Lord was with him, and he carried on his itinerant work, as well as his regular services at Haworth, up to his death.

But though Grimshaw was never actually stopped, we must not suppose that he escaped persecution. The prince of this world will never willingly part with any of his subjects. He will stir up opposition against any one who tries to pull down his kingdom. The incumbent of Haworth was often obliged to face abuse and personal violence of a kind that we can hardly imagine in the present day. "Mad Grimshaw" was the name given to him by many throughout the district in which he laboured. None opposed him more than some of the clergy. With the true dog-in-the-manger spirit, they neither did good themselves nor liked any one else to do it for them.

The most violent of Grimshaw's opponents was the Rev. George White, perpetual curate of Colne and Marsden, in Lancashire. This worthy commenced his attack by publishing a sermon against the Methodists, preached at his two churches in August 1748. In this sermon he charged Grimshaw and all his fellow-labourers with being "authors of confusion; open destroyers of the public peace ; flying in the face of the very Church they craftily pretend to follow ; occasioning many bold insurrections, which threaten our spiritual government ; schismatical rebels against the best of Churches ; authors of a further breach in our unhappy divisions ; contemners of the great command, 'Six days shalt thou labour ;' defiers of all laws, civil and ecclesiastical ; professed disrespecters of learning and education ; causing a visible ruin of trade and manufactures ; and, in short, promoters of a shameful progress of enthusiasm and confusion not to be paralleled in any other Christian dominion."

Not content with preaching this stuff and nonsense, White proceeded to stir up a mob to stop the preaching of Grimshaw and his companions by force and violence. He actually issued a proclamation, in order to collect a mob, in the following words : " Notice is hereby given, that if any men be mindful to enlist into His Majesty's service, under the command of the Rev. George White, commander-in-chief, and John Banister, lieutenant-general of His Majesty's forces, for the defence of the Church of England, and the support of the manufactures in and about Colne, both which are now in danger, let them now repair to the cross, when each man shall have a pint of ale for advance, and other proper encouragements. "

The consequence of this outrageous proclamation was just what might have been expected. " Lewd fellows of the baser sort" are always ready to make a riot against religion, as they were in the days of St. Paul. When Grimshaw and John Wesley went to Colne to preach, on the 24th of August 1748, they were attacked by an overwhelming mob of drunken people armed with clubs, and dragged before White like thieves and malefactors. After a vain endeavour to extort a promise from them that they would desist from coming to preach at Colne, they were allowed to leave the house. As soon as they got outside, " the mob closed in upon them, and tossed them about with great violence, throwing Grimshaw down, and covering both of them with mire, there being no one to come to their rescue. The people who had assembled to hear the word of God were treated with even greater cruelty. They had to run for their lives, amidst showers of dirt and stones, and no regard was paid to either sex or age. Some were trampled in the mire; others dragged by the hair; and many were unmercifully beaten with clubs. One was forced to leap from a rock, ten or twelve feet high, into the river, to prevent being thrown in headlong. When he crawled out, wet and bruised, they swore they would throw him in again, and were with difficulty prevented from executing their threat. White, well-pleased, was watching his mad followers all this time without a word to stay them."*

None of these things moved the lion-hearted incumbent of Haworth. Not long afterwards he went to Colne again, and was again shamefully treated—pelted with mud and dirt, and dragged violently along the road. In the following year, 1749, he published a long reply to White's sermon, extending to eighty-six pages, in which he powerfully and triumphantly refuted White's charges.†

Persecution of this rough kind was not the only hard measure that Grimshaw had to undergo in consequence of his extra-parochial evangelism. He was more than once called to account for his conduct by the Archbishop of York, and seems to have escaped suspension or deprivation in a most marvellous manner.

On one occasion "a charge was preferred against him for having preached in a licensed meeting-house at Leeds. Had proof been forthcoming to substantiate the charge, he would have been dismissed from his cure for irregularity. Though no

---

* See Hardy's " Life of Grimshaw," p. 82.

† White must have been a very extreme specimen of the careless, worthless clergyman of the last century. He was educated at Douay College for the Romish priesthood, and after his recantation was recommended for preferment to the vicar of Whalley, by Archbishop Potter. He frequently abandoned his parish for weeks together; and, on one occasion, is said to have read the funeral-service more than twenty times in a single night over the dead bodies that had been buried in his absence! He died at Langroyd in 1751; and it is pleasant to record, that he is said to have sent for Grimshaw on his death-bed, and expressed his sorrow for the part he took in the riotous proceedings above described.

act of delinquency was proved, he was obliged to promise the archbishop that he would not preach in any place that had been *licensed* for the worship of dissenters; while he repeated his determination to continue preaching abroad so long as there were souls for whom no one seemed to care. On another occasion, when accused of preaching out of his own parish, he was asked by the archbishop, ' How many communicants had you when you first came to Haworth ?' He answered, ' Twelve, my lord.' ' How many have you now ?' was the next question. The reply was, ' In the winter, from three to four hundred ; and in the summer, near twelve hundred.' On hearing this the archbishop expressed his approbation, and said, ' We cannot find fault with Mr. Grimshaw when he is instrumental in bringing so many persons to the Lord's Table.' "*

On another occasion, "when complaint was made to the archbishop of his ramblings and intrusions into other men's folds, the archbishop announced his intention to hold a confirmation-service in Mr. Grimshaw's church, and to have an interview with him on the occasion. On the day appointed they met in Haworth vestry, and while the clergy and laity were assembling in great numbers, the following conversation took place : ' I have heard,' said the archbishop, ' many extraordinary reports respecting your conduct, Mr. Grimshaw. It has been stated to me that you not only preach in private houses in your parish, but also travel up and down, and preach where you have a mind, without consulting your diocesan or the clergy into whose parishes you obtrude your labours ; and that your discourses are very loose ; that, in fact, you can and do preach about anything. That I may be able to judge for myself, both of your doctrine and manner of stating it, I give you notice that I shall expect you to preach before me and the clergy present in two hours hence, and from the text which I am about to name.' After repeating the text, the archbishop added : ' Sir,

* Hardy's " Life of Grimshaw," p. 232.

you may now retire, and make what preparation you can while I confirm the young people.' — 'My lord,' said Grimshaw, looking out of the vestry-door into the church, 'see what multitudes of people are here ! Why should the order of the service be reversed, and the congregation kept out of the sermon for two hours ?* Send a clergyman to read prayers, and I will begin immediately.' After prayers Mr. Grimshaw ascended the pulpit, and began an extempore prayer for the archbishop, the people, and the young persons about to be confirmed, and wrestled with God for his assistance and blessing, until the congregation, the clergy, and the archbishop himself, were moved to tears. After the service was over, the clergy gathered round the archbishop to ascertain what proceedings he intended to adopt in order to restrain the preacher from such rash and extemporaneous expositions of God's Word. To their surprise the archbishop, taking Mr. Grimshaw by the hand, said with a tremulous voice, 'I would to God that all the clergy in my diocese were like this good man !' Mr. Grimshaw afterwards observed to a party of friends who came to take tea with him that evening, 'I did expect to be turned out of my parish on this occasion ; but if I had been I would have joined my friend John Wesley, taken my saddle-bags and gone to one of his poorest circuits.'"†

It is impossible to turn from this part of Grimshaw's history without feelings of righteous indignation. There is something revolting in the idea of a holy and zealous minister of the Church of England being persecuted for overstepping the bounds of ecclesiastical etiquette, while hundreds of clergymen were let alone and undisturbed whose lives and doctrine were beneath contempt. All over England country livings were often filled by hunting, shooting, gambling, drinking, card-playing, swear-

* It is evident that the confirmation described in this story must have been held on a Sunday.

† From Strachan's " Life of Rev. G. Lowe," a Methodist minister.

ing, ignorant clergymen, who cared neither for law nor gospel, and utterly neglected their parishes. When they did preach, they either preached to empty benches, or else "the hungry sheep looked up and were not fed." And yet these men lived under their own vines and fig-trees enjoying great quietness, untouched by bishops, eating the fat of the land, and calling themselves the true supporters of the Church! But the moment a man rose up like Grimshaw, who gloried in the Articles, Liturgy, and Homilies, and preached the Gospel, he was treated like a felon and malefactor, and his name cast out as evil! Truly God's patience with the Church of England a hundred years ago was something marvellous. Marvellous that he did not remove our candlestick altogether! Marvellous that he granted her such a revival, and raised up so many burning and shining lights amongst her ministers!

To talk of Grimshaw being no Churchman and being an enemy to the Church of England, is preposterous and absurd. If attachment to the standards and formularies of his own communion is a mark of Churchmanship, he was a Churchman in the truest sense. No doubt he loved all who loved Jesus Christ in sincerity. No doubt he made nothing of parochial boundaries when souls were perishing, and other clergymen neglected their duties. But to the day of his death he was a steady adherent of the Church in which he had been ordained, used her services devoutly and regularly, and did more for her real interests than any clergyman in the north of England. One of his biographers specially mentions "that he greatly admired the Homilies, and regarded their disuse, and neglect of the Thirty-nine Articles, as the chief occasion of all the mischief to the Church, believing it probable that if they had been constantly read Methodism would never have appeared." He said once, that an old clergyman of his acquaintance, being asked by his curate if he might read the Homilies in the pulpit, answered "No! for if you should do so, the whole congregation would turn Methodists." On another occasion he wrote to Charles Wesley the following remarkable words: "I see nothing so materially amiss in the liturgy, or the Church constitution, as to disturb my conscience or justify my separation. No: where shall I go to mend myself? I believe the Church of England to be the soundest, purest, and most apostolical national Christian Church in the world. Therefore I can in good conscience (as I am determined, God willing, to do) live and die in her." Yet this is the man who, some dare to tell us, was no Churchman!

Grimshaw's holy and useful career was brought to an end on the 7th of April 1763. He died in his own house at Haworth of a putrid fever, in the fifty-fifth year of his age and the twenty-first of his ministry at Haworth. The fever of which he died had been raging in his parish from the beginning of the year, and had proved fatal to many of the inhabitants. "On its first breaking out," says Hardy, "he had a presentiment that it would prove fatal to some member of his family, and had exhorted all to be ready." When visiting a parishioner he caught the prevailing epidemic, and at once predicted that he would not recover.

To the physician who attended him "he expressed in strong terms the humiliating feelings he had on a retrospect of his whole life, and how disproportionate, defective, and defiled his best services had been, compared with the obligation under which he felt himself, and the importance of the cause in which he had been engaged; and that he hoped, if the Lord should prolong his days and raise him up, to be much more active and diligent."

To his friend and brother in the gospel, the Rev. Mr. Ingham, he said: "My last enemy is come! The signs of death are upon me. But I am not afraid. No! no! Blessed be God, my hope is sure, and I am in his hands." Afterwards, when Mr. Ingham prayed for the lengthening of his life, that he might yet be useful to Christ's cause, he said, " Alas ! what have my wretched services been ? I have now need to cry, at the end of my unprofitable course, God be merciful to me a sinner !" At another time, laying his hand on his heart, he said, " I am quite exhausted ; but I shall soon be at home—for ever with the Lord—a poor miserable sinner redeemed by his blood."

His valued fellow-labourer, the Rev. Henry Venn, then vicar of Huddersfield, came over to see him from Huddersfield, and asked him how he felt. To him he replied, " Never had I such a visit from God since I first knew him. I am as happy as I can be on earth, and as sure of glory as if I were in it." After this, finding that his disease was peculiarly infectious and dangerous, he requested his friends to visit him as little as possible. But his peace and hope are reported to have continued unshaken to the end. As he lived so he died, rejoicing in Christ Jesus, and putting no confidence in the flesh."

He was buried, by his own desire, by the side of his first wife in the chancel of Luddenden Church, in the valley of the Calder, not far from Haworth. Like Joseph, " he gave commandment concerning his bones." He had drawn up full and particular directions about his funeral long before he was taken ill, and these directions were carefully followed. The number of attendants was to be twenty, " religious or relative friends, or both." He would have only a plain, poor man's burial suit, and a plain, poor man's coffin of elm boards, with the words on the cover, " To me to live is Christ, and to die is gain." All the way to the church suitable verses were to be sung, in various selected metres and tunes, out of the 23rd, 39th, and 91st Psalms, and also suitable hymns. One of the attendants, at least, was to be a Methodist preacher, and he was to preach a funeral sermon from the text on his coffin (Phil. i. 21). The Methodist preacher selected for the occasion was his old friend and fellow-labourer, Henry Venn.* The church at Luddenden was too small to contain the immense congregation which assembled, and the preacher had to take his position in the grave-yard. "Tradition reports," says Hardy, "that Venn's voice rose like the swell of a full-toned bell as he told forth the virtues of his departed friend, and exhorted the people to follow him as he had followed Christ." Never, indeed, had any man a more honourable burial. Like Stephen, "devout men carried him to his grave, and made great lamentation over him." He had, as Venn well remarks, "what is more ennobling than all the pomp of solemn dirges, or of a royal funeral. He was followed to the tomb by a great multitude, who beheld his corpse with affectionate sighs and many tears, and who cannot still hear his much-loved name without weeping for the guide of their souls."

Grimshaw was twice married, and twice left a widower. His first wife was Sarah, daughter of John Lockwood of Ewood Hall. She had been twice married before, first to William Sutcliffe of Scaitcliffe Hall, and secondly to John Ramsden, both of whom died without children. He was evidently greatly attached to his first wife, and her death, on the 1st of November 1739, made a deep impression on him. His second wife was Elizabeth, daughter of Henry Cockcroft of Mayroyd, near Hebden Bridge. I can find no record of the date of her death.

Grimshaw had only two children, both by his first wife, a son and a daughter. His daughter died when only twelve years old, when at school at Kingswood, near Bristol. Charles Wesley says that "she departed in the Lord." His son survived his father only three years, and died childless. During his father's lifetime he had been careless and intemperate, and the cause of great grief. When he visited him on his death-

---

* All evangelical clergymen of the Church of England used to be called "Methodists" a hundred years ago.

bed, Grimshaw told him to take care what he did, as he was not fit to die. To him also he used the remarkable words that "his body felt like a boiling vessel, but his soul was as happy as it could be made by God." John Grimshaw died at Ewood on the 17th May 1766, and by God's great mercy there was hope in his death. His father's dying words perhaps sunk into his heart, and at any rate his father's many prayers for him were heard. After his father's death, he used to ride a horse which formerly belonged to him, and one day meeting an inhabitant of Haworth, the man remarked, "I see you are riding the old parson's horse."—"Yes," was the reply; "once he carried a great saint, and now he carries a great sinner." Long before his death young Grimshaw had given clear evidence of repentance unto salvation, and found pardon and peace in Christ ; and a little time before he died, he was heard to exclaim, "What will my old father say when he sees I have got to heaven?"

CHAPTER III.

Literary Remains—Covenant and Summary of Belief—Letter to Christians in London—Anecdotes and Traditions—Influence in his Parish—Haworth Races Stopped—Mode of Discovering False Professors—Peculiarities in his Conduct of Divine Service—Testimony of Romaine, Venn, and Newton.

IN order to form a correct estimate of a great man's character, there are two sources of information to which we should always turn, if possible, in addition to the events of his life. The literary remains he leaves behind him form one of these sources; the anecdotes handed down about him by contemporaries form another. From both these sources I will endeavour to supply the reader of these pages with some further information about William Grimshaw.

The literary remains of a man like Grimshaw are necessarily few and scanty. It could hardly be otherwise. A clergyman who was constantly preaching twenty or thirty times a-week, and carrying on a system of aggressive evangelism all over Yorkshire, Lancashire, and Cheshire, was not likely to have much time for writing. In fact, his "Reply to White," already referred to, is the only formal publication that he ever put forth. He says himself in the Reply, "I have as little leisure for writing as for anything I do." There are, however, a few valuable relics of his thoughts still extant, which are useful, as indicating his turn of mind, and will probably be thought interesting by all Christian readers.

His covenant with God, given at length by Hardy, is a very striking and interesting document, though too long for the pages of a memoir like this.* The following disconnected extracts will give some idea of it :—

"Eternal and unchangeable Jehovah ! thou great Creator of heaven and earth, and adorable Lord of angels and men ! I desire with the deepest humiliation and abasement of soul to fall down at this time in thine awful presence, and earnestly pray that thou wilt penetrate my heart with a suitable sense of thine unutterable and inconceivable glories." . . .

"I know that through Jesus, the Son of thy love, thou condescendest to visit sinful mortals, and to allow their approach to thee and this covenant intercourse with thee. Nay, I know that the scheme and plan are entirely thine own, and that thou hast graciously sent to propose it unto me, as none untaught by thee could have been able to join it, or inclined to embrace it, even when actually proposed." . . .

"To thee, therefore, do I now come, invited by thy love, and trusting his righteousness alone, laying myself at thy feet with shame and confusion of face, and smiting on my breast, saying with the publican, God be merciful to me a sinner ! I acknowledge, O Lord, that I have been a great transgressor. My sins have reached unto heaven, and mine iniquities have been lifted up unto the skies. My base corruptions and lusts have numberless ways wrought to bring forth fruit unto death, and if thou wert extreme to mark what I have done amiss, I could never abide it. But thou hast graciously called me to return unto thee, though I am a prodigal son and a backsliding child. Behold, therefore, I solemnly come before thee. O my Lord, I am convinced of my sin and folly. Thou knowest, O Lord, I solemnly covenanted with thee in the year 1738. And now, once more and

---

* In giving this covenant to my readers, I would carefully abstain from saying that such covenants ought always to be made, or to be pressed on all Christians. So far from that, I think them likely to do harm to some minds. Let every one use his liberty. He that finds it good to make a covenant, let him make it. But let him not condemn his neighbour who makes none.

for ever, I most solemnly give up, devote, and resign all I am, spirit, soul, and body to thee, and to thy pleasure and commands in Christ Jesus my Saviour, this 4th of December 1752 ; sensible of my vileness and unworthiness, but yet sensible that I am thy pardoned, justified, and regenerated child in the spirit and blood of my dear and precious Saviour, Jesus Christ, by clear experience." . . .

"Glory be to thee, O my Triune God ! Permit me to repeat and renew my covenant with thee. I desire and resolve to be wholly and for ever thine. Blessed God, I most solemnly surrender myself unto thee. Hear, O heaven, and give ear, O earth ! I avouch this day the Lord to be my God, Father, Saviour, and portion for ever. I am one of his covenant children for ever. Record, O eternal Lord, in thy book of remembrance that henceforth I am thine for ever. From this day I solemnly renounce all former lords—world, flesh, and devil—in thy name. No more, directly or indirectly, will I obey them. I renounced them many years ago, and I renounce them for ever. This day I give up myself to thee, a living sacrifice, holy and acceptable unto thee ; which I know is my reasonable service. To thee I consecrate all my worldly possessions ; in thy service I desire and purpose to spend all my time, desiring thee to teach me to spend every moment of it to thy glory and the setting forth of thy praise, in every station and relation of life I am now or may hereafter be in. And I earnestly pray that whatever influence thou mayest in any wise give me over others, thou wouldest give me strength and courage to exert it to the utmost to thy glory, resolving not only myself to do it, but that all others, so far as I can rationally and properly influence them, shall serve the Lord. In that cause would I, O Lord, steadfastly persevere to my last breath, steadfastly praying that every day of my life may supply the defects and correct the irregularities of the former ; and that by divine grace I may be enabled not only in that happy way to hold on, but to grow daily more active in it. Nor do I only consecrate all I have to thy service, but I also most humbly resign and submit to thy holy and sovereign will all that I have. I leave, O Lord, to thy management and direction all I possess and all I wish, and set every enjoyment and interest before thee to be disposed of as thou pleasest. Continue or remove what thou hast given me, bestow or refuse what I imagine I want, as thou seest good ; and though I dare not say I will never repine, yet I hope I may say I will labour not only to submit but to acquiesce ; not only to bear thy heaviest afflictions on me, but to consent to them and praise thee for them ; contentedly resolving, in all thy appointments, my will into thine ; esteeming myself as nothing, and thee, O God, as the great Eternal All, whose word shall determine, and whose power shall order all things in the world." . . .

"Dispose my affairs, O God, in a manner which may be wholly subservient to thy glory and my own true happiness ; and when I have done, borne, and endured thy will upon earth, call me home at what time and in what manner thou pleasest. Only grant that in my dying moments, and the near approach of eternity, I may remember this my engagement to thee, and may employ my latest breath in thy service ; and do thou, when thou seest me in the agonies of death, remember this covenant too, though I should be incapable of recollecting it. Look down upon me, O Lord, thy languishing, dying child ; place thine everlasting arms underneath my head ; put strength and confidence into my departing spirit, and receive it to the embrace of thine everlasting love." . . .

"And when I am thus numbered with the dead and all the interests of mortality are over with me for ever, if this solemn memorial should fall into the hands of any surviving friends or relations, may it be the means of mak‑ ing serious impressions on their minds, and may they read it not only as my language, but as their own, and learn to fear the Lord my God, and with me to put their trust under the shadow of his wings for time and for eternity." . . .

"I solemnly subscribe this dedication of myself to the ever-blessed Triune God, in the presence of angels and all invisible spectators, this fourth day of December 1752.   WILLIAM GRIMSHAW."

The next document from which I will supply some extracts, is a Creed or Summary of Belief which Grimshaw sent to Romaine in December 1762, only four months before his death. It is to be found at length in Middleton's Biographia Evangelica. This creed is a regular systematic statement of Grimshaw's religious views, drawn out into twenty-six heads, and is of course far too long to be inserted in this place. A few paragraphs are all that I can give the reader. They prove, at any rate, that, however much Grimshaw may have agreed with Wesley on many points, he certainly was not an Arminian.*

"XXII.—I believe it is by the Spirit we are enabled, not to eradicate (as some affirm), for that is absurd, but to subjugate the old man; to suppress, not extirpate, the exorbitancies of our fleshly appetites ; to resist and over‑ come the world and the devil, and to grow in grace gradually, not suddenly, unto the perfect and eternal day. This is all I acknowledge or know to be Christian perfection or sanctification.

"XXIII.—I believe that all true believers will be daily tempted by the flesh, as well as by the world and the devil, even to their lives' end ; and they will feel an inclination, more or less, to comply, yea and do comply

---

* It is worthy of remark, that in one of his letters, on another occasion, Grimshaw uses the following language : "My perfection is to see my own imperfection ; my comfort, to feel that I have the world, flesh, and devil to overthrow through the Spirit and merits of my dear Saviour ; and my desire and hope is to love God with all my heart, mind, soul, and strength, to the last gasp of life. This is my perfection. I know no other, expecting to lay down my life and my sword together."

therewith. So that the best believer, if he knows what he says, and says the truth, is but a sinner at the best.

"XXIV.—I believe that their minds are incessantly subject to a thousand impertinent, unprofitable thoughts, even amidst their reading, meditation, and prayers; that all their religious exercises are deficient; that all their graces, how eminent soever, are imperfect; that God sees iniquity in all their holy things; and though it be granted that they love God with all their hearts, yet they must continually pray with the psalmist, 'Enter not into judgment with thy servant.'

"XXV.—But I believe that Jesus is a full as well as a free Saviour, the same yesterday, to-day, and for ever. He alone is not only the believer's wisdom and righteousness, but his sanctification and redemption; and in him is a fountain ever open for sin and uncleanness unto the last breath of his life. This is my daily, necessary privilege, my relief, and my comfort.

"XXVI.—I believe, lastly, that God is faithful and unchangeable; that all his promises are yea and amen; that he never, never will, as the apostle says, leave me; will never, never, never forsake me; but that I, and all that believe, love, and fear him, shall receive the end of our faith—the salvation of our souls.

"Here is the sum and substance of my creed. It is at least what I presume to call my form of sound words. In it I can truly say I have no respect to men or books, ancient or modern, but to the Holy Scriptures, reason, and experience. According to this creed hitherto I have, and I hope hereafter to proceed in all my preaching, debasing man and exalting my dear Lord in all his offices."

The last specimen that I will give of Grimshaw's remains is a letter addressed by him to certain Christians in London. It is dated January 9, 1760, and is to be found in Hardy's Life.

"Grace, mercy, and peace be to you from God our Father and from our Lord Jesus. It is well with some sorts of people that you have had, or now have to do with. It is well with those of you in Christ who are gone to God; it is well with those of you in Christ who are not gone to God; it is well with those of you who earnestly long to be in Christ, that they may go to God; it is well for those who neither desire to be in Christ nor to go to God; and it is only bad with such who, being out of Christ, are gone to the devil. Them it is best to let alone, and say no more about them.

"It is well with those of you who, being in Christ, are gone to God. You, ministers and members of Christ, have no more doubt or pain about them. They are now and for ever out of the reach of the world, flesh, and devil. They are gone where the wicked cease from troubling, and where the weary are at rest. They are sweetly reposing in Abraham's bosom. They dwell in His presence who hath redeemed them, where there is fulness of joy and pleasure for evermore. They are waiting the joyful morning of the resurrection, when their vile bodies shall be made like unto his glorious body, shall be re-united to the soul, shall receive the joyful sentence, and inherit the kingdom prepared for them from the foundation of the world.

"It is well also with those of you who are in Christ though not gone to God. You live next door to them. Heaven is begun with you too. The kingdom of God is within you; you feel it. This is a kingdom of righteousness, and peace, and joy in the Holy Ghost. It is begun in grace, and shall terminate in glory. Yea, it is Christ within you the hope of glory. Christ the rock, the foundation laid in your hearts, hope in the middle, and glory at the top. Christ, hope, glory! Christ, hope, glory! You are washed in the blood of the Lamb; justified, sanctified, and shall shortly be glorified. Yea, your lives are already hid with Christ in God. You have your conversation already in heaven. Already you sit in heavenly places in Christ Jesus. What heavenly sentences are these! What can come nearer Paradise? Bless the Lord, O ye happy souls, and let all that is within you bless his holy name. Sing unto the Lord as long as you live, and praise your God while you have your being. And how long will that be? Through the endless ages of a glorious eternity!

"It is well with all those of you who truly desire to be in Christ, that you may go to God. Surely he owns you. Your desires are from him; you shall enjoy his favour. By-and-by you shall have peace with him through our Lord Jesus Christ. Go forth by the footsteps of the flock, and feed by the Shepherd's tents. Be constant in every means of grace. He will be found of them that diligently seek him. Blessed are they that mourn, for they shall be comforted. Though your sins be never so many, never so monstrous, all shall be forgiven. He will have mercy upon you, and will abundantly pardon. For where sin hath abounded, grace doth much more abound. He who hath begun this good work in you will accomplish it to your eternal good and his eternal glory. Therefore doubt not, fear not; a broken and a contrite heart God will not despise. The deeper is your sorrow, the nearer is your joy. Your extremity is God's opportunity. It is usually darkest just before daybreak. You shall shortly find pardon, peace, and plenteous redemption, and at last rejoice in the common and glorious salvation of his saints.

"And lastly, it is well for you who neither truly desire to be in Christ, nor to go to God. For it is well for you that you are not in hell. It is well your day of grace is not utterly past. Behold, now is your accepted time; behold, now is your day of salvation! Oh that you may employ the remainder of it in working out your salvation with fear and trembling. Now is faith to be had—saving faith. Now you may be washed from all sins in the Redeemer's blood, justified, sanctified, and prepared for heaven. Take, I beseech you, the time, while the time is. You have now the means of grace to use, the ordinances of God to enjoy, his Word to read and hear, his ministers to instruct you, and his members to converse with. You know not what a day may bring forth. You may die suddenly. As death leaves you judgment will find you. And if you should die as you are—out of Christ, void of true faith, unregenerate, unsanctified—fire and brimstone, storm and tempest, God will rain upon you, as your eternal, intolerable portion to drink.

"Suffer me, therefore, thus far, one and all of you. God's glory and your everlasting salvation is all I aim at. What I look for in return from you is, I confess, much more than I deserve—your prayers."

It would be easy to supply many more extracts than these. But I forbear. I make no apology, however, for the length of those I have already given. The reader will probably agree with me that they are in themselves full of interesting matter. But this is not all. They possess an additional value as supplying a most graphic picture of Grimshaw's mode of expressing himself, and of the topics on which his mind was constantly dwelling. In fact, they furnish a pretty correct idea of what the good man's preaching must have been. He evidently wrote as he thought and spoke. His remains are just the overflowings of a heart full of Scripture, full of Christ, full of deep thoughts on the sinfulness of sin, the value of the soul, the need of repentance and faith, the happiness of holy living, the importance of a world to come. Let a man analyze Grimshaw's remains carefully and thoughtfully, and I suspect he will have a very fair conception of the style in which Grimshaw used to preach.

The anecdotes and traditions that have been handed down about the good Incumbent of Haworth are very many and very curious. All of them, perhaps, are not true. Some, perhaps, are greatly exaggerated. Many, however, after making every fair deduction, are undoubtedly credible and genuine. I will mention some of them.

The influence he gradually obtained in his own parish was very great. Even those who were not converted looked up to him and feared him. John Newton says: "One Sunday, as a man was passing through Haworth on horseback, his horse lost a shoe. He applied to a blacksmith to put it on. To his surprise, the man told him he could not shoe a horse on the

Lord's day without the minister's leave. They went together to Mr. Grimshaw, and the man satisfying him that he was really in haste, going for a doctor, Mr. Grimshaw permitted the blacksmith to shoe the horse, which otherwise he would not have done for double pay."

"It was his frequent custom," adds Newton, "to leave the church at Haworth while the psalm before sermon was singing, to see if any were absent from worship and idling their time in the churchyard, the street, or the ale-houses ; and many of those whom he so found he would drive into church before him.* A friend of mine, passing a public-house in Haworth on a Lord's day morning, saw several persons making their escape out of it, some jumping out of the lower windows, and some over a low wall. He was at first alarmed, fearing the house was on fire ; but upon inquiring what was the cause of the commotion, he was only told that they saw the parson coming. They were more afraid of the parson than of a justice of the peace. His reproof was so authoritative, and yet so mild and friendly, that the stoutest sinner could not stand before him.

"He endeavoured likewise to suppress the common custom of walking in the fields on the Lord's day in summer, instead of coming to God's house. He not only bore his testimony against it from the pulpit, but went into the fields in person to detect and reprove the delinquents. There was a spot at some distance from the village, where many young people used to assemble on Sundays in spite of all his warnings. At last he disguised himself one evening, that he might not be known till he was near enough to discover who they were. He then threw off his disguise, and charged them not to move. He took down all their names with his pencil, and ordered them to attend on

---

* According to Hardy, there is a tradition in Haworth that Grimshaw sometimes used a stick or horse-whip on these occasions, and that he occasionally gave out the 119th Psalm to be sung during his absence from church, in order that he might have the longer time for prosecuting his search after the disorderly. These stories, however, are probably apocryphal.

him on a day and hour which he appointed. They all waited on him accordingly, as punctually as if they had been served with a warrant. When they came, he led them into a private room, when, after forming them into a circle and commanding them to kneel down, he kneeled down in the midst of them, and prayed for them with much earnestness for a considerable time. After rising from his knees, he gave them a close and affecting lecture. He never had occasion to repeat this friendly discipline. He entirely broke the objectionable custom."

One of the most remarkable and well-authenticated anecdotes about Grimshaw is in connection with Haworth races. These races were an annual festival got up by the innkeepers, and a great occasion of drunkenness, riot, profligacy, and confusion. For some time Grimshaw attempted in vain to stop these races. "At last," says John Newton, "unable to prevail with men, he addressed himself to God. For some time before the races he made it a subject of fervent prayer that the Lord would be pleased to interfere, and to stop these evil proceedings in his own way. When the race-time came, the people assembled as usual, but they were soon dispersed. Before the races could begin, dark clouds covered the sky, and such excessively heavy rain fell, that the people could not remain on the ground, and it continued to rain incessantly during the three days appointed for the races. This event was much spoken of at Haworth. It became a sort of proverbial saying among the people that old Grimshaw put a stop to the races by his prayers. And it proved an effectual stop. There were no more races at Haworth."

"He was particularly watchful," says Newton, "over those of his flock who made an open profession of religion, to see if they adorned the doctrine of God our Saviour in all things, and maintained a consistent character; and he was very severe in his censures if he found any of his communicants guilty of wrong practices. When he suspected hypocrisy, he sometimes took such strange methods to detect it, as perhaps few men but himself would have thought of. He had a suspicion of the sincerity of some of his hearers, who made great pretence to religion. In order to find out one of them, he disguised himself as a poor man, and applied to him for relief and a lodging; and, behold! this person who wished to be thought very good and charitable, treated him with some abuse.—He then went to another house, to a woman who was almost blind. He touched her gently with his stick, and went on doing it until she, supposing it was done by some children in the neighbourhood, began not only to threaten but to swear at them. Thus he was confirmed in his apprehensions."

" At a cottage prayer-meeting," says Hardy, " some of Grimshaw's people had to endure much annoyance and persecution, and for a long time no one could discover who the delinquents were. At last the incumbent came to their assistance and solved the mystery. He put on an old woman's cap, and peeped stealthily from behind the door, and then appeared to grow rather bolder, while he quietly made the observation he wished. He found there was a set of rude boys who only came to make sport and annoy others. They soon began to make fun of the old woman (as she seemed to be), and defied her with mocks and menaces. In this way they were all found out and brought to justice, and then the persecution ceased."

He carried his humility and simplicity of living to such an extent that he thought anything good enough for himself, if he could only show a Christian brother kindness and hospitality. A godly friend who once came to stay a night with him, was horrified on looking out of his bedroom window in the morning, to see Grimshaw with his own hands cleaning his guest's boots! Nor was this all. On coming down stairs he discovered that Grimshaw had actually given up his own bedroom for his accommodation, and had spent the night in a hay-loft!

His ways in his own parish, as he went about doing the work of a pastor, were very peculiar. Hardy says, " When he met with any one in the lanes he would enter into familiar conversation with them, and generally asked if they were accustomed to pray. When they answered in the affirmative, and he doubted their sincerity, he bade them kneel down and show him how they performed this duty. There were sometimes scenes by the road-side, in consequence, that a stranger could not look at without a smile ; but to the persons concerned these inquiries were, in some instances, the means of awakening concern about their souls. The tradition of the district is, that ' *he would rive them* from horseback to make them pray.' But he was as ready to do an act of courtesy as to administer reproof. Once on his way to Colne, he overtook an old woman, and asked her where she was going. She replied, ' To hear Grimshaw.' He pitied her many infirmities ; but she said her heart was already there, and she would make the body follow. Struck by her earnestness, he actually took her up behind him on the pillion of his own horse, and thus enabled her to reach the place without further toil."

Hardy adds, " Grimshaw was not unmindful of himself, whilst watchful over the souls of others. Once he had a very fine cow, in which he took so much pride, that the thought of her followed him into the service of the Church, and hindered his communion with God. He determined that she should no longer ruffle his mind, and so announced her for sale. When a farmer came to look at her, he asked, as usual, whether she had any fault. To this Grimshaw made this quaint reply, ' Her fault in my eyes will be no fault to you ; she follows me into my pulpit.'"

The things that he did inside his church, both in the reading-desk and the pulpit, may certainly seem to us very eccentric and strange in the present day.* Undoubtedly, they are not

---

* Hardy, in his biography, gives an interesting description of Haworth Parish Church, which according to him, is very little altered since Grimshaw's death. Among other things,

examples for imitation ; and unless a man is " a Grimshaw," he has no right to attempt them.   Before condemning them too strongly, however, men should call to mind the times and the population with which he had to do.   We are, in fact, dealing with a man who lived a hundred years ago.

He was very particular in enforcing order and devout be-haviour among the worshippers in his church at Haworth. Carelessness and inattention were instantly observed and openly rebuked ; and he would not proceed with the service until he saw every person present in the attitude of devotion.   Some of his hearers certainly deserved great attention and encouragement. Not a few came ten or twelve miles every Sunday to attend his ministry.   One John Madden of Bacup often walked to Ha-worth on the Sabbath, and returned the same evening, a distance, out and home, of nearly forty miles.*

In giving out the hymns to be sung in church, he sometimes took singular liberties.   A valued friend of mine was told by an old man in Haworth that he remembered his grandfather speaking of Grimshaw, and telling the following story :—His grandfather was in Haworth Church, when Grimshaw gave out the well-known hymn of Dr. Watts, beginning,—

> "Come, ye that love the Lord,
>   And let your joys be known ;
> Join in a song with sweet accord,
>   And so surround the throne."

He said, that when Grimshaw had read the first verse, he looked at the people, and cried out, " Now, unconverted sinners here present, can you sing that ?"

His sermons were seldom short when he occupied his own pulpit at Haworth.   Indeed, he sometimes preached for two

---

he says : " Appropriate inscriptions, in various parts of the church, remind the worship-pers of their duty.   Under the sounding board of the pulpit, in gilt letters, there is the sentence, ' I determined not to know anything save Jesus Christ and him crucified.'   His favourite text, ' To me to live is Christ,' appears on the pulpit, on the brass chandelier, and on a tablet with the names of the church officers.   On the baptismal font is the sentence ' I indeed baptize with water, but he shall baptize with the Holy Ghost.' "

* *Methodist Magazine* for 1811, p. 521.

hours! For this he once made an apology to John Newton: "If I were in some places," he said, "I might not think it needful to speak so much. But many of my hearers, who are wicked and careless, are likewise very ignorant and slow of apprehension. If they do not understand me, I cannot hope to do them good; and when I think of the uncertainty of life, that, perhaps, it may be the last opportunity, and that it is not impossible I may never see them again till the great day, I know not how to be explicit enough. I try to set the subject in a variety of lights. I express the same thoughts in different words, and can scarcely tell how to leave off, lest I should have omitted something, for want of which my preaching and their hearing should be vain."

His prayers after sermon must have been sometimes very remarkable. John Pawson, a well-known Methodist preacher, said, in 1803, that he heard him, fifty years before, preach a most comforting discourse on the words, "O fear the Lord, ye his saints, for there is no want to them that fear him" (Ps. xxxiv. 9), in which he spoke very strongly about God's faithfulness to his promises, and said, "Before the Lord will suffer his promise to fail, he will lay aside his divinity and un-God himself." He then offered the following prayer: "Lord, dismiss us with thy blessing. Take all these poor people under thy care, and bring them in safety to their own houses, and give them their supper when they get home. But let them not eat a morsel till they have said a grace. Then let them eat and be satisfied, and return thanks to thee when they have done. Then let them kneel down and say their prayers before they go to bed. Let them do this for once at any rate, and then thou wilt preserve them till the morning."

Though Grimshaw's ministry was almost entirely among the poor and lower middle classes, he was quite able to take his position and speak wisely and shrewdly in any company. On one occasion he was invited to meet a nobleman who had imbibed infidel principles, and had resisted the efforts of two eminent clergymen to convince him of his error. He wished at once to draw Grimshaw into a discussion, but Grimshaw firmly and decidedly declined. "My lord," he said, "I do not refuse to argue because I have nothing to say, or because I fear for my cause. I refuse because argument will do you no good. If you really needed any information, I would gladly assist you. But the fault is not in your head, but in your heart, which can only be reached by a divine power. I shall pray for you, but I will not dispute with you." The nobleman afterwards said that he was more impressed by the honesty and firmness of those simple words than by all the arguments he had heard.

"To a lady," says Hardy, "with whom Grimshaw was conversing, he once gave a striking reproof. She was expressing her admiration of a certain minister who had more talents than grace. 'Madam,' said Grimshaw, 'I am glad you never saw the devil. He has greater talents than all the ministers in the world. I fear, if you saw him, you would fall in love with him, as you have so high a regard for talents without sanctity. Pray, do not be led away with the sound of talents.'"

Anecdotes like these tell a tale that ought not to be overlooked. The subject of them must surely have been no ordinary man. When sayings and doings are so carefully treasured up and handed down from generation to generation, the character round which they cluster was one of no common mould. I repeat the opinion that I expressed at the beginning of this biography. There were not three greater spiritual heroes in England one hundred years ago than William Grimshaw.

I will now conclude this paper with three short extracts from men of approved characters in the last century, which serve to show the high estimation in which Grimshaw was held by his contemporaries.

Romaine said publicly in a sermon preached at St. Dunstan's in the West, shortly after Grimshaw's death,—

" Mr. Grimshaw was one of the most laborious and indefatigable ministers of Christ that I ever knew. For the good of souls he rejected all hopes of affluent fortune, and for the love of Christ cheerfully undertook difficulties, dangers, and tribulations. He preached Christ and Christ alone ; and God gave him very numerous seals to his ministry. Himself hath told me that not fewer than 1200 were in communion with him, most of whom, in the judgment of charity, he could not but believe to be one with Christ. When some of his friends, in tenderness to his health, would wish him to spare himself, he would answer, —' Let me labour now : I shall have rest enough by-and-by. I cannot do enough for Christ, who has done so much for me.' He was the most humble walker with God I ever met with ; inasmuch that he could never bear to hear any commendations of his usefulness, or anything which belonged to him. His last words were, ' Here goes an unprofitable servant !'"

Henry Venn, who preached his funeral sermon, said, among other things,—" It is hard to determine whether we have more cause to lament his removal from our world, or to rejoice that God was pleased to enrich him with divine knowledge in so large a measure, to make him so long an eminent instrument in his hand of converting sinners, and to enable him to persevere with an unblemished character till he finished his course with joy. Few have ever expressed so great ardency of affection to the service of Christ as your late much-loved pastor.

" Never was there any sordid child of this world more engrossed by the love of money, and more laborious in heaping it up, than your late pastor was in teaching and preaching the kingdom of God, and the things concerning the Lord Jesus Christ."

John Newton says,—" I knew Mr. Grimshaw, and had repeated conversations with him for four or five years. I number it among the many great mercies of my life, that I was favoured with his notice, edified (I hope) by his instruction and example,

VI.

William Romaine and his Ministry.

CHAPTER I.

Born at Hartlepool in 1714—Educated at Houghton le-Spring and Christ Church, Oxford—Character for Learning at Oxford—Ordained 1736—Curate of Lewtrenchard and Banstead—Lectures at St. Botolph's 1748, and St. Dunstan's 1749—Troubles at St. Dunstan's—Morning Preacher at St. George's, Hanover Square, 1750—Loses his Preachership 1755—Gresham Professor of Astronomy—Morning Preacher at St. Olave, Southwark, and St. Bartholomew the Great—Preaches before the University of Oxford—Gives great Offence.

THE true Church of Christ is curiously like a well-appointed army.

The soldiers of an army all owe allegiance to one common sovereign, and are engaged in one common cause. They are commanded by one general, and fight against one common foe. And yet there are marked varieties and diversities among them. Cavalry, infantry, and artillery have each their own peculiar mode of fighting. Each arm in its own way is useful. It is the well-balanced combination of all three which gives to the whole army efficiency and power.

It is just the same with the true Church of Christ. Its members all love the same Saviour, and are led by the same Spirit; all wage the same warfare against sin and the devil, and all believe the same gospel. But the work of one soldier of Christ is not the work of another. Each is appointed by the

Great Captain to fill his own peculiar position, and each is specially useful in his own department.

Thoughts such as these come across my mind, when I turn from Whitefield, Wesley, and Grimshaw, to the fourth spiritual hero of the last century—William Romaine. In doctrine and practical piety, the four good men were, in the main, of one mind. In their mode of working, they were curiously unlike one another. Whitefield and Wesley were spiritual cavalry, who scoured the country, and were found everywhere. Grimshaw was an infantry soldier, who had his head-quarters at Haworth, and never went far from home. Romaine, in the meantime, was a commander of heavy artillery, who held a citadel in the heart of a metropolis, and seldom stirred beyond his walls. Yet all these four men were mighty instruments in God's hand for good ; and not one of them could have been spared. Each did good service in his own line ; and not the least useful, I hope to show, was the Rector of Blackfriars, William Romaine. In what are called *popular* gifts, no doubt, he was not equal to his three great contemporaries. But none of the three, probably, was so well fitted as he was to fill the position which he occupied in London.

William Romaine was born at Hartlepool, in the county of Durham, on the 25th of September 1714. His father was one of the French Protestants who took refuge in England after the revocation of the edict of Nantes. He settled at Hartlepool as a corn merchant, and appears to have prospered in business. At any rate, he brought up a family of two sons and three daughters, and left behind a high character as a kind and estimable man when he died, 1757, at the ripe age of eighty-five.

There is every reason to believe that Romaine's parents were decidedly religious people, and that from his earliest years he saw true Christianity both taught and exemplified in his own home. The value of this rare privilege can hardly be overrated. The seeds of a long life of service and usefulness were certainly sown by the Holy Ghost in this Hartlepool home. Romaine never forgot this. In a letter written to a friend when he was seventy years old, he uses the following expressions: " Mr. Whitefield used often to put me in mind how singularly favoured I was. He had none of his family converted ; while my father, mother, and three sisters were like those blessed people of whom it is written, ' Jesus loved Martha and her sister, and Lazarus.' And as they loved him again, so do we."

At the age of ten, Romaine was sent to a well-known grammar school at Houghton-le-Spring, in the county of Durham, founded by the famous Bernard Gilpin at the time of the Protestant Reformation. At this school he remained seven years. From thence, in the year 1731, he was sent to Oxford ; and after first entering Hertford College, was finally removed to Christ Church. For the next six years he appears to have resided principally at Oxford, until he took his degree as Master of Arts in October 1737.

Of Romaine's manner of life at Oxford we know nothing, except the fact that he was a hard reader, and had a high reputation as a man of ability. Of his friends, companions, and associates, we have no record. This at first sight seems somewhat remarkable, when we remember that it was precisely at this period that " Methodism," so-called, took its rise at the University. In fact, it was just the time when John Wesley, Charles Wesley, Whitefield, Ingham, and Hervey, were beginning to work for Christ in Oxford, and had formed a kind of religious society. There is not, however, the slightest trace of any communication between them and Romaine. The most natural supposition is, that he was wholly absorbed in literary pursuits, and allowed himself no time for other work. To this we may add the fact, that the natural bent of his character would probably incline him to keep by himself and stand alone.

The high character which he attained in the university, as a learned man, is clearly shown by an anecdote related of him by his curate and successor, Mr. Goode, after his death. He says in his funeral sermon: "Dress was never a foible of Mr. Romaine's. His mind was superior to such borrowed ornaments. Immersed in the noble pursuit of literature, before his consecration to a still more exalted purpose, he paid but little attention to outward decoration. Being observed at Oxford, on one occasion, to walk by rather negligently attired, a visitor inquired of a friend, Master of one of the colleges: 'Who is that slovenly person with his stockings down?' The master replied: 'That slovenly person, as you call him, is one of the greatest geniuses of the age, and is likely to be one of the greatest men in the kingdom.'"

Commendation like this was, of course, somewhat exaggerated and extravagant. But at any rate, there can be no doubt that Romaine left Oxford a thorough scholar and a well-read man. His worst enemies in after-life could never lay to his charge that he was "unlearned and ignorant." They might dislike his doctrinal views, but they could never deny that in any matter of Hebrew, Greek, or Latin criticism, his opinion was entitled to respect. Well would it be for the Churches, if in this respect there were more evangelical ministers who walked in the steps of Romaine. Grace and soundness in the faith, diligence and personal piety, are undoubtedly the principal things. But book-learning ought not to be despised. An ignorant and ill-read ministry, in days of intellectual activity, must sooner or later fall into contempt.

Romaine was ordained deacon at Hereford in 1736, by Bishop Egerton; and priest in 1738, by the Bishop of Winchester, the notorious Dr. Hoadley. The history of the first eleven years of his ministerial life is involved in much uncertainty. I am unable to tell the reader who gave him a title for orders, or why he was ordained at Hereford. I can only find out that his first engagement was the curacy of Lewtrenchard, near Okehampton, in Devonshire. He went there on a visit to an Oxford friend, whose father lived at Lidford, and upon the express condition that his friend should find him work. He only remained here about six months. From Lewtrenchard he removed into the diocese of Winchester, and was curate of Banstead, near Epsom, for anything we can see, for an unbroken period of ten years. Much of his after-course in life probably hinged on this curacy. It was here that he became acquainted with Sir Daniel Lambert, an alderman of London, who lived in the parish, and was lord-mayor in 1741. He thought so highly of Romaine that he appointed him his chaplain during the year of his mayoralty—a circumstance which brought him into notice as a preacher, both at St. Paul's Cathedral and in many other London pulpits.

It is highly probable that the ten years which Romaine spent at Banstead were years of deep study and literary pursuits. It was at this time that he published two volumes in reply to Warburton's " Divine Legation of Moses," in which he ably controverted the main positions of that mischievous book. He also prepared for the press a new edition of the Hebrew Concordance and Lexicon of Marius de Calasio, in four large volumes—a work which required very close attention, and which employed him no less than seven years. The small size of his cure at Banstead no doubt left him abundant time for study; and this time was well spent. The extremely firm and unwavering position which he assumed on points of doctrine in after-life, may be traced in all probability to the quiet ten years which he spent in his Surrey curacy. Foundation-stones are often laid in a young minister's mind during his residence in such a position, which nothing in after-life can ever shake or displace.

One thing, at all events, is very certain, whatever else is uncertain, about Romaine's ministerial beginnings. There never seems to have been a period, from the time of his ordination, when he did not preach clear, distinct, and unmistakable evangelical doctrines. The truths of the glorious gospel appear to have been applied to his heart by the Holy Spirit from the days of his childhood at Hartlepool. From the very first he was a well-instructed divine, and, unlike many clergymen, had nothing to unlearn after he was ordained.

The proof of this may be seen in the sermon which he preached in St. Paul's Cathedral, as chaplain to the Lord Mayor, on September 2, 1741. At this time, it will be remembered, he was only twenty-seven years old. The title of this sermon is, "No Justification by the Law of Nature," and the text is Romans ii. 14, 15. Cadogan, his biographer, justly remarks on this sermon : "Although we do not discover in this discourse the same fertile experience, use, and application of the truth as are to be found in his later writings, yet we discover the same truth itself by which he was then made free from the errors of the day, and in the enjoyment of which he lived and died. . . . . The truth is, he was a believer possessed of that unfeigned faith which dwelt in his father and mother before him, and we are persuaded that it was in him also."

The second marked period in Romaine's ministerial life extends from 1748 to 1766. Within this space of eighteen years he met with some of his greatest trials, and filled many different posts in the Lord's vineyard, but always in London. I may add, that at no time in his life, perhaps, was he more useful and more popular. He was in the full vigour of body and mind, and enjoyed a reputation as a bold and uncompromising preacher of evangelical doctrine throughout the metropolis, which few other living men equalled, and fewer still surpassed.

The first post that Romaine regularly occupied in London was that of lecturer at St. Botolph's, Billingsgate. The circumstances which led to his appointment were so singular that I think it well to mention them. They supply an admirable

These sermons gave great offence, and he was never allowed to enter the University pulpit again after delivering them. They are to be found among his published works at the present day, and furnish a melancholy proof of the spiritual darkness in which Oxford was sunk a hundred years ago! The governing body of an University which could exclude a man from its pulpit for preaching such doctrine as these sermons contain, must indeed have been in a miserably benighted state of mind. Romaine's dedication of them to Dr. Randolph, President of Corpus Christi, and Vice-chancellor of the University, is well worth reading. He says, " When I delivered these discourses I had no design to make them public; but I have been since compelled to it. I understand they gave great offence, especially to you, and I am in consequence thereof refused the university pulpit. In justice, not to myself, for I desire to be out of the question, but to the great doctrine here treated of, namely, the righteousness of the Lord Jesus Christ, as the only ground of our acceptance and justification before God the Father, I have sent to the press what was delivered from the pulpit. I leave the friends of our Church to judge, whether there be anything herein advanced contrary to the Scriptures and to the doctrines of the Reformation. If not, I am safe. If there be, you are bound to make it appear. You have a good pen, and have great leisure; make use of them; and I hope and pray you may make use of them for your good and mine." Comment on the whole affair is needless. The treatment which Romaine received at Oxford was as little creditable to the University as that which he received in the west end of London was to the parishioners of St. George's, Hanover Square.

It was about this period of his life that Romaine became intimate with the well-known Lady Huntingdon, who made him one of her domestic chaplains. In this capacity he used to preach frequently at her house, both in London and near Ashby-de-la-Zouch, and at the various chapels, or preaching-

esteemed, that his various letters on the subject were collected into a pamphlet and reprinted by his friends in the City in 1753.

From the date of Romaine's removal from St. George's, Hanover Square, until his appointment to the Rectory of St. Anne's, Blackfriars, we find him occupying several different positions, and never long in any one. The only post which he never vacated was the Lectureship of St. Dunstan's, Fleet Street. In the beginning of 1756 he became curate and morning-preacher at St. Olave's, Southwark. He continued in this office until the year 1759, residing most of the time in Walnut Tree Walk, Lambeth. After leaving St. Olave's, he was morning-preacher for two years at St. Bartholomew the Great, near West Smithfield. From thence he removed to Westminster Chapel, but only preached there six months. The abrupt termination of his engagement there was occasioned by a fresh piece of persecution. The Dean and Chapter of Westminster withdrew their patronage and protection from the chapel, and refused him their nomination for a licence to preach there. From this time he had no stated employment in the Church, except the Lectureship of St. Dunstan's, until he was chosen Rector of St. Anne's, Blackfriars, in 1766.

We must not, however, suppose for a moment that Romaine was an idle man during the years when he had no settled employment in the morning of Sundays. He appears to have been constantly preaching charity sermons in London churches; for which purpose, from his great popularity, his services were eagerly sought after. He also preached very frequently at the chapel of the Lock Hospital, upon the first institution of that charity.

At this period of his life he was several times called upon to preach before the University of Oxford. This, however, came to an end after he had preached two sermons, entitled, "The Lord our Righteousness," on March 20, 1757, in St. Mary's.

parochial annals of the diocese of London. An eminent and godly clergyman was removed from his post because he attracted too many hearers! And yet, at this very time, scores of clergymen in London churches were no doubt preaching every week to empty benches or to congregations of half-a-dozen people, without any one interfering with them!

It is consolatory to think that there was one parishioner at least in St. George's, Hanover Square, who made a noble protest against the treatment which Romaine received. This was the old Earl of Northampton. He rebuked those who complained that the parish-church was crowded, by reminding them that they bore the greater crowd of a ball-room, an assembly, or a play-house, without the least complaint. "If," said he, "the power to attract be imputed as a matter of admiration to Garrick, why should it be urged as a crime against Romaine? Shall excellence be considered exceptionable only in divine things?"—Another member of the congregation who is said to have adhered steadfastly to Romaine's cause at this juncture, was Mr. John Sanderson, afterwards state-coachman to George III. This worthy man lived to the great age of eighty-nine, and died in 1799, after long adorning the doctrine he professed by an exemplary and godly life.

During the five years that Romaine was preaching at St. George's, he occupied for a short time the situation of Professor of Astronomy at Gresham College. There is little record extant of what he did in this office, and it is doubtful whether he was very successful in it. In all probability he was a much better theologian than an astronomer, and was better fitted for lecturing about Christ and heaven than about the sun, moon, and stars. But whatever credit he lost as a professor of astronomy, he retrieved a hundred-fold by his conduct about the Bill for removing Jewish disabilities. This he thought it his duty to oppose vehemently, to the great gratification of many citizens of London. In fact, his arguments were so highly

to a Careless World ;" and the other, " The Duty of Watchfulness Enforced." Delivered at the time they were, we cannot doubt that they are specimens of the kind of sermons which Romaine usually preached at that period of his ministry. I think it impossible to read them without feeling deep regret that the Church of England in the west end of London has not had more of such preaching.

Romaine's ministry, as assistant morning-preacher at St. George's, Hanover Square, began in April 1750 and ended in September 1755. During that time he preached occasionally at Bow Church, in exchange with Dr. Newton, afterwards Bishop of Bristol ; and also at Curzon Chapel, then called St. George's, Mayfair, in exchange with the Rector. The circumstances under which he left St. George's are so remarkable that they deserve special notice.

It appears that the office which he filled as assistant morning-preacher was not a regularly endowed and independent appointment, but one entirely dependent on the Rector, and kept up at his own option, discretion, and expense. The Rector of St. George's, who first invited Romaine to take the office, and then at the end of five years removed him from it, was Dr. Andrew Trebeck. His appointment was owing to his high character and reputation, and not to personal friendship ; his removal was caused by the popularity and plainness of his ministry. The real truth was, that his preaching attracted such crowds to the old parish-church, that the regular seat-holders took offence, and complained that they were put to inconvenience. Strong pressure was brought to bear upon the Rector ; and he, " willing to please " the parishioners, gave Romaine notice to terminate his engagement. This notice he received quietly, saying, that " he was willing to relinquish the office, hoping that his doctrine had been Christian, and owning the inconvenience which had attended the parishioners." A more discreditable affair than this probably never disfigured the

Christianity prevailed widely among the upper and middle classes of society. Bishop Butler had complained not long before, that "many persons seemed to take it for granted that Christianity was fictitious, and that nothing remained but to set it up as a principal object of mirth and ridicule." That such principles naturally produced the utmost profligacy, recklessness, and immorality of practice, no Bible reader will be surprised to hear. In fact, the utter ungodliness of the age was so thorough that few living in the present day can have the slightest conception of it. Against this ungodliness Romaine boldly lifted up a standard, and blew the trumpet of the gospel with no uncertain sound. He was in the highest sense a man for the times, and he was exactly in the right place. Those who would like to see how boldly and powerfully he delivered his Master's message, would do well to read two sermons which he delivered at St. George's, one of them entitled, "A Method for Preventing the Frequency of Robberies and Murders;" and the other, "A Discourse on the Self-Existence of Jesus Christ."

Just about the time that he was removed from the pulpit of St. George's, the inhabitants of London were dreadfully frightened by two severe shocks of an earthquake. Happening simultaneously with the awful earthquake which in a moment overthrew Lisbon and destroyed forty thousand persons, this event caused great alarm. Thousands of persons fled to Hyde Park and spent the night there. Hundreds crowded to the places of worship where so-called Methodist doctrines were preached, and anxiously sought consolation. Even Sherlock, Bishop of London, thought it necessary to publish a Letter to his Diocese on the subject, in which he exhorted the clergy "to awaken the people, to call them from their lethargy, and make them see their own danger." Here again Romaine was just the man for the occasion. He preached and printed two sermons, which even now will amply repay perusal. One of them is called, "An Alarm

tion were waiting outside St. Dunstan's. Observing the crowd, he asked the cause of it, and being told that it was Romaine's congregation, he interfered with the rector and churchwardens on their behalf, expressed great respect for the lecturer, and obtained for him and his hearers that the service should begin at six, that the doors should be opened in proper time, and that lights should be provided in the winter season. From this time forth Romaine continued in the quiet exercise of his ministry at St. Dunstan's, without disturbance, and to the edification of many, to the end of his life. In fact, he held this lectureship for no less than forty-six years, though it was only worth eighteen pounds a-year!

In the year 1750, Romaine was appointed assistant morning-preacher at St. George's, Hanover Square, and held the office for five years. Of all the many pulpits which he occupied during his long ministry, this was by far the most important. Standing, as the church does, in an extremely prominent position in the west end of London, and well known as the mother-church of the most fashionable quarter of the metropolis, it opened up to him a great and effectual door of usefulness. Romaine, in many respects, was just the man for the post. His undeniable powers as a preacher attracted attention. His well-known scholarship commanded respect even from those who did not agree with him. And best of all, his bold, uncompromising declarations of the real gospel of Christ, and plain denunciations of fashionable sins, were precisely the message which the Bible leads us to expect God will bless. It is not, perhaps, too much to say, that from the day St. George's, Hanover Square, was built, to this very day, it has never had its pulpit so well filled on Sunday mornings as it was for five years by Romaine.

The circumstances of the times in which he preached at St. George's made his testimony peculiarly valuable and important. A cold heartless scepticism about all the leading truths of

called him to a city-lectureship, and so detained him in London, where he was kept to the end of his existence as a witness for Jesus Christ, with abilities as truly suited to this meridian as those of the Apostle Paul to the meridian of Ephesus, Corinth, or Rome."

In the year 1749, he was chosen lecturer of St. Dunstan's in the West—an appointment which brought down on him one of the fiercest storms of persecution which he had to face in the course of his ministry. The Rector of St. Dunstan's, for some reason, disputed his right to the pulpit, and occupied it himself during the time of prayers, in order to exclude him from it. Romaine, in the meantime, appeared constantly in his place to assert his claim to the lectureship, and his readiness to perform the duties of the office. The affair was at length carried into the Court of King's Bench, and after hearing the cause argued, Lord Mansfield decided that Romaine was legally entitled to the lectureship, and that seven o'clock in the evening was a convenient time to preach the lecture.

Even then, however, the troubles of the lectureship were not over. Cadogan says that even after Lord Mansfield's decision, the churchwardens refused to open the doors of the church till seven o'clock, and to light it when there was occasion. The result was, that Romaine frequently read prayers and preached by the light of a single candle, which he held in his own hand. Besides this, as the church doors were kept shut until the precise moment fixed for preaching the lecture, the congregation was usually assembled in Fleet Street waiting for admission. The consequence was a great concourse of people, collected in a principal thoroughfare of the metropolis, and though not noisy or disorderly, occasioning much inconvenience to those who passed that way. This state of things actually continued for some time. Happily for all parties, Dr. Terrick, Bishop of London, who had once held the lectureship himself, happened to pass through Fleet Street one evening when the congrega-

illustration of the manner in which God works by his providence in finding a right position for his people. It seems, then, to have been Romaine's intention, after finishing his edition of Calasio's Lexicon, to return to his native county, and to seek employment near his home. In fact, he had actually packed up his trunks, and sent them on board ship with this view. But as he was going to the water-side, in order to secure his own passage, he was met by a gentleman, an entire stranger to him, who stopped and asked him if his name was Romaine. The gentleman had formerly known his father, and was led to make the inquiry by observing a strong resemblance to him in the clergyman whom he met. After some conversation about his family, this gentleman, who was a man of some influence in the city, told him that the lectureship of St. Botolph's, Billingsgate, was then vacant, and that if he liked to become a candidate for the post, he would gladly exert his influence in his behalf. Romaine, seeing in this unexpected providence the finger of God, at once consented, provided he was not obliged to canvass the voters in person, a custom which he always thought inconsistent with the office of a clergyman. The result was, that in the autumn of 1748 he was chosen lecturer of St. Botolph's, and commenced his long career as a London clergyman.

It is deeply instructive to observe in a case like this, how God chooses the habitation of his people, and places them where he knows it is best for them to be. Cadogan, Romaine's excellent biographer, remarks on this part of his history: " A settlement in the metropolis was the thing of all others which he last thought of, and to which he was the least inclined. From the bent of his genius to the study of nature, of minerals, fossils, and plants, and the wonders of God in creation, a country life, so favourable to these pursuits, would have been chosen by him. But God chose otherwise for him; and by a circumstance trivial and accidental to appearance, but in reality a turn of providence such as decides the condition of most men,

houses which she built at Brighton, Bath, and elsewhere. To her friendship, indeed, he was finally indebted for his appointment to the Rectory of St. Anne's, Blackfriars, in the fifty-second year of his age. The circumstances, however, of his appointment to this post, the history of his twenty-nine years' ministry in it, and some account of his writings, letters, and character, are matters which I shall reserve for another chapter.

CHAPTER II.

Rector of St. Anne's, Blackfriars, 1764—Difficulties in the way of his Appointment—Letter to Lady Huntingdon—Usefulness at Blackfriars—Peculiarities of Address and Temperament—Last Illness and Dying Saying—Death 1795—Public Funeral—Literary Remains.

The biographer of William Romaine can hardly fail to observe that his life naturally divides itself into three portions. The first extends from his birth to the commencement of his London ministry in 1746. The second ranges from 1746 to his final settlement at St. Anne's, Blackfriars, in 1764. The third comprises his ministry at Blackfriars, up to the time of his death in 1795. It is this third and last portion of his history which I propose to deal with in this chapter.

Romaine's appointment to the rectory of St. Anne's, Blackfriars, took place at a very critical period in his ministerial life. He was now about fifty years old. After preaching as a lecturer in London for eighteen years, he was still without a stated position as the incumbent of a parish. Every door seemed shut against him. Opposition and persecution followed him wherever he went. It seemed, in short, a question whether he had not better give up London altogether, and turn his steps elsewhere. Lord Dartmouth offered him a living in the country. Whitefield urged him to accept a large church at Philadelphia, in America. Hot-headed friends pressed him to let them build him a chapel. It seemed far from improbable that he might fulfil the predictions of his enemies, and end by leaving the Church of England and becoming a regular dissenter.

But Romaine had a very deep sense of the value of the Church of England. He loved her Articles and Prayer-Book with no common love. Whatever her defects in administration, and however ill she treated her best children, he believed that the occupant of her pulpits had peculiar advantages ; and he steadfastly refused to leave her. He was catholic, and kind, and liberal to those who were not churchmen, and lived in habits of friendly communion with many of them. To this even John Wesley, Arminian as he was, bears strong testimony. In a letter to Lady Huntingdon, in 1763, he says, " Mr. Romaine has shown a truly sympathizing spirit, and acted like a brother." But nothing could induce him to give up his own position and become a Nonconformist. At this juncture he was greatly strengthened in his determination by the advice of that excellent clergyman, Walker of Truro. He resolved to stick by the Church in which he had been ordained, and to wait patiently for some door to be opened. His patience was at length rewarded. By a singular train of providences, he became rector of an important parish in the City, and there spent the last twenty-nine years of his life in the undisturbed exercise of his ministry.

The circumstances under which Romaine was appointed to his new sphere of duty were somewhat remarkable. The patronage of the united parish of St. Andrew by the Wardrobe with St. Anne's, Blackfriars, is vested in the Lord-Chancellor and the parishioners alternately. The immediate predecessor of Romaine was Mr. Henley, nephew of the then Lord-Chancellor Henley. He only held the living about six years, and died of putrid fever, caught in visiting a parishioner. Upon his death the appointment fell to the turn of the parishioners ; and at once some friends of Romaine, without his knowledge and consent, resolved to nominate him as a candidate for the vacant living. It was soon found that at least two-thirds of the parishioners were in his favour; and though he refused to canvass for votes himself, his interest was warmly supported by Lady Huntingdon, Mr. Thornton, and Mr. Madan.

There were two other candidates beside Romaine, and in accordance with the custom on such occasions, he was called on to preach a probationary sermon before the parishioners. This sermon, preached on September 30, 1764, from 2 Cor. iv. 5, is to be found among his printed works, and is creditable both to his heart and head. One part of it, in which he assigned his reason for not canvassing the electors in person, deserves particular notice. He says,—

" Some have insinuated that it was from pride that I would not go about the parish, from house to house, canvassing for votes; but truly it was from another motive,—I could not see how this could promote the glory of God. How can it be for the honour of Jesus that his ministers, who have renounced fame, riches, and ease, should be most anxious and earnest in the pursuit of those very things which they have renounced? Surely this would be getting into a worldly spirit, as much as the spirit of parliamenteering. And as this method of canvassing cannot be for Jesus' sake, so neither is it for our honour; it is far beneath our function: nor is it for your profit. What good is it to your souls—what compliment to your understanding—what advantage to you, in any shape, to be directed and applied to by every person with whom you have any connection, or on whom you have any dependence? Is not this depriving you of the freedom of your choice? Determined by these motives, when my friends, of their own accord, put me up as a candidate, to whom I have to this hour made no application, directly or indirectly, I left you to yourselves. If you choose me, I desire to be your servant for Jesus' sake; and if you do not, the will of the Lord be done."

It deserves notice that this sermon did the preacher's cause no harm, but rather operated in his favour. It was well received by the parishioners, and was published at their request.

Notwithstanding the strong support Romaine received, his appointment was not finally secured without great difficulty and opposition. A hotly contested election, a poll, a scrutiny and an appeal to the Court of Chancery, interposed between the first movement of his friends and the final accomplishment of their wishes. At length, after eighteen months' delay, all obstacles were overcome, a decree was given in his favour by Lord Henley, and he was instituted and inducted rector of St. Anne's, Blackfriars, in February 1766. No one, perhaps, throughout this anxious period of suspense, worked more heartily in his behalf than Lady Huntingdon. She saw clearly the immense importance of such a champion of Christ's gospel being settled in a prominent position in London; and she left no stone unturned to secure his success. Help, too, was raised up in some quarters of a most unexpected kind. A publican in the parish is said to have been one of his most active supporters and canvassers; and at first no one could understand the reason. But after all was over, on Romaine's calling on him to thank him, the worthy publican replied, " Indeed, sir, I am more indebted to you than you to me; for you have made my wife, who was one of the worst, the best woman in the world."

Romaine entered on his new sphere with a very deep sense of his own insufficiency. He who intended him to be a wise master-builder, taught him to lay a sound foundation of self-abasement and humility. His own letters on the occasion of his election give a very graphic picture of his feelings.

In one he says : " My friends are rejoicing all around me, and wishing me a joy that I cannot take. It is my Master's will, and I submit. He knows best what is for his own glory and his people's good ; and I am certain he makes no mistakes on either of these points. But my head hangs down upon the occasion, through the awful apprehension which I ever had of the care of souls. I am frightened to think of watching over two or three thousands, when it is work enough to watch over one. The plague of my own heart almost wearies me to death; what can I do with so vast a number?"

In a letter to Lady Huntingdon, of the same date, he says: " Now, when I was setting up my rest, and had begun to say unto my soul, Soul, take thine ease, I am called into a public station, and to the sharpest engagement, just as I had got into winter quarters. I can see nothing before me, so long as breath is in my body, but war; and that with unreasonable men, a divided parish, an angry clergy, and a wicked world, all to be resisted and overcome. Besides all these, a sworn enemy, subtle and cruel, with whom I can make no peace—no, not a moment's time, night and day—with all his children and his host, is aiming at my destruction. When I take counsel of the flesh I begin to faint; but when I go to the sanctuary, I see my good cause, and my almighty Master and true Friend, and then he makes my courage revive. Although I am no way fit for the work, yet he called me to it, and on him I depend for strength to do it, and for success to crown it. I utterly despair of doing anything as of myself, and therefore the more I have to do, the more I shall be forced to live by faith on Him. In this view I hope to get a great income by my *living*. I shall want Jesus more, and shall get closer to him."

Whatever anticipations of trouble Romaine may have formed in his mind, he met with comparatively little at Blackfriars. In fact, his twenty-nine years' ministry there, compared to his earlier days, was a season of quietness. Enemies and opponents no doubt he had, like every faithful clergyman who preaches the gospel. But they could do little to disturb him. The result was that the latter years of his life, though not less useful than the former, were certainly less eventful. Like the river that at first dashes brawling down the mountain-side, but glides silently along when it reaches the plains and becomes navigable, so Romaine's ministry from the time of his settlement at Blackfriars, though it made less noise, was probably more beneficial to the Church of Christ. He necessarily became less of an itinerant and missionary preacher. The claims of his own parish and pulpit obliged him to stay much at home, and absorbed much of his time and attention. But his usefulness, whatever some hasty judges might think, was not only not diminished, but was probably much increased.

The plain truth is, that as rector of a London parish, Romaine became a rallying point for all in London who loved evangelical truth in the Church of England. Man after man, and family after family, gathered round his pulpit, until his congregation became the nucleus of a vast amount of good in the metropolis. His constant, unflinching declaration of Christ's whole truth insensibly produced a powerful impression on men's minds, and made them understand what a true clergyman of the Church of England ought to be. His undeniable learning made him an adversary that few cared to cope with, and gave a weight to his assertions which they did not always possess when they came from the lips of half-educated men. His position gave him peculiar advantages. Almost within sight both of St. Paul's and Westminster Abbey, he held a post from which he was always ready to go forth and do battle, either with tongue or pen. If error arose rampant, he was on the spot prepared to attack it. If truth was assaulted, he was equally prepared to sally forth and defend it. In short, the good that he did, as rector of Blackfriars, though less showy, was probably more solid and permanent than the good that he did all the rest of his life.

To attempt to chronicle all the events of his life during his twenty-nine years at Blackfriars would be of little use, even if we possessed materials for doing it. From the very beginning of his incumbency, he took great pains to have the services of his church conducted with strict reverence and good order. Like many other clergymen, he never rested till he had put the fabric of his church in good repair, had built a good parsonage, and made the parochial schools thoroughly efficient. These things once accomplished, he gave himself entirely to the direct work of his office. He was never idle, and seldom passed a silent Sabbath. Preaching, visiting, writing for the press, or corresponding with the many who asked his advice, occupied nearly all his time to his life's end.

He was not perhaps what would be called now-a-days a "genial" man. He was "naturally close and reserved," says Cadogan, "irritable to a certain degree, short and quick in his replies, and frequently mistaken as being rude and morose where he meant nothing of the kind. Had he paid more attention than he did to the various distresses of soul and body which were brought before him, he would have had no time left for reading, meditation, and prayer, and, in short, for what every man must attend to in private who would be useful in public. It was not uncommon for him to tell those who came to him with cases of conscience and questions of spiritual concern, that he said all he had to say in the pulpit. Thus people might be hurt for the moment by such a dismissal, but they had only to attend his preaching, and they soon found that their difficulties had impressed him as well as themselves; that they had been submitted to God, and that they had been the subject of his serious and affectionate consideration."

These observations of Cadogan's deserve special attention. Romaine, unhappily, is not the only minister whose reputation has suffered from gross misrepresentation and misconstruction. Few men, unfortunately, are so liable to be unfairly judged as ministers who fill prominent posts, and are eminent for gifts and graces. Even Christians are too ready to set them down as haughty, proud, cold, distant, reserved, and unsocial, without any just ground for so doing. The immense demands continually made on their time and strength, the many private difficulties they frequently have to contend with, the absolute necessity they are under of much daily reading, meditation, and communion with God—all these things are too often entirely forgotten. Many indeed are the wounds of feeling which ministers have to endure from the unkind remarks of unreasonable friends. The cup which Romaine had to drink is a cup which many clergymen have to drink in the present day.

The few anecdotes preserved about Romaine are all somewhat characteristic of the man as Cadogan describes him. They all give the idea of one who was short and abrupt to an extreme in his communications; so much so, in fact, that we can quite understand captious people being offended by him. And yet the anecdotes always tend to prove that he was a man of no common graces, gifts, and good sense.

He was one evening invited to a friend's house, and, after tea, the lady of the house asked him to play at cards, to which he made no objection. The cards were brought out, and when all were ready to begin playing, Romaine said, " Let us ask the blessing of God." "Ask the blessing of God!" said the lady in great surprise; " I never heard of such a thing before a game of cards." Romaine then inquired, " Ought we to engage in anything on which we cannot ask God's blessing?" This reproof put an end to the card-playing.

On another occasion he was addressed by a lady, who expressed the great pleasure she had enjoyed under his preaching, and added that she could comply with his requirements, with the exception of one thing. "And what is that?" asked Romaine. " Cards, sir," was the reply. " You think you could not be happy without them?" " No, sir, I know I could not." " Then, madam," said he, " cards are your god, and they must save you." It is recorded that this pointed remark led to serious reflections, and finally to the abandonment of card-playing.

When the unhappy Dr. Dodd was sentenced to death for forgery, Romaine, among others, felt a deep and melancholy interest about him. There was once a time when he and Dodd had been on terms of intimacy, from their common zeal for the prosecution of Hebrew learning. When, however, poor Dodd began to love the world better than Christ, the intimacy gradually ceased, and he actually told Romaine that he hoped he would not acknowledge him if they met in public! Before his execution, Romaine visited him in Newgate at his particular request, and many were anxious to know what he thought of the prisoner's spiritual state. But the only answer that could be extracted from him was this: "I hope he may be a real penitent; but there is a great difference between saying, 'God be merciful to me a sinner,' and really feeling it."

Short and abrupt as the rector of Blackfriars evidently was in his demeanour, he was very sensible of his own deficiencies of temper, and very willing to confess himself in the wrong. On one occasion a dissenting minister who often attended his lectures, called on him to complain of some severe reflections which he thought Romaine had made upon Dissenters. Having made his complaint, Romaine replied, "I do not want to have anything to say to you, sir."—"If you will hear me," added the other, "I will tell you my name and profession. I am a Protestant dissenting minister."—"Sir," said Romaine, "I neither wish to know your name nor your profession." Upon this the unfortunate Nonconformist bowed and took his leave. Not long after Romaine, to the great surprise of his hearer and reprover, returned the visit, and after the usual salutation, began: "Well, Mr. T., I am not come to renounce my principles, I have not changed my sentiments, I will not give up my preference for the Church of England; but I am come as a Christian to make some apology. I think my behaviour to you sir, the other day, was not becoming, nor such as it should have been." They then shook hands, and parted good friends.

Romaine's last illness found him still doing his Father's business, and happy in his work. He lived to the great age of eighty-one, and enjoyed the full use of his faculties to the very last. During the last ten years of his life he seems to have become greatly mellowed and softened, and to have been a beautiful example of that lovely sight, a godly old man, "a hoary head found in the way of righteousness." He went gradually down the valley toward the river, with all the golden richness of a setting sun in summer. There appeared to be little but heaven in his sermons or in his life ; and, like dying Baxter, he spoke of his future home with great familiarity, like one who had already seen it.

It was well remarked by some of his friends, in these last days of his ministry, that he was a true diamond, naturally rough and pointed, but the more he was broken by years the more he appeared to shine. There was often a light upon his countenance—and particularly when he preached—which looked like the dawn, or a faint appearance of glory. If any one asked him how he did, his general answer was, "As well as I can be out of heaven." He made this reply, shortly before his death, to a friend of a different communion, and then added, "There is but one central point, in which we must all meet—Jesus Christ and him crucified." This was the object which he always kept in sight—the wonderful God-man, whom, according to his own words, "He had taken for body and for soul, for time and for eternity, his present and everlasting all."

Romaine's simple and regular habits of life, no doubt, had much to say to his length of days and vigorous old age. There are ministers, unquestionably, who seem independent of regular food and hours, and whose iron constitutions appear to stand any strain. But their number is small. Of Romaine, Cadogan says, " His hour of breakfast was six in the morning ; of dinner, half-past one in the afternoon; and of supper, seven in the evening. His family were assembled to prayer at nine o'clock in the morning, and at the same hour at night. His Hebrew Psalter was his constant companion at breakfast, and he often said how much his first repast was sanctified by the Word of God and prayer. From ten o'clock to one he was generally employed in visiting the sick and friends. He retired to his study after dinner, and sometimes walked again after supper in summer. After evening service in his family, he retired again to his study, and to his bed at ten. From this mode of living he never deviated, except when he was a guest in the house of friends; and then he breakfasted at seven, dined at two, and supped at eight. His adherence to rules, in this respect, was never more marked than in a circumstance which happened during the last years of his life. He was invited by an eminent dignitary of the Church to dine with him at five o'clock. He felt respect for the inviter, and wished to show it. Instead, therefore, of sending a written apology, he waited upon him himself, thanked him for the invitation, and excused himself by pleading his long habits of early hours, his great age, and his often infirmities."

Romaine's death-bed was a beautiful illustration of the truth of John Wesley's saying, " Our people die well! The world may find fault with our opinions, but the world cannot deny that our people die well." This was eminently the case with Romaine. His fatal illness attacked him on Saturday, the 6th of June 1795, and put an end to his life on the 26th of July. The last sermon which he preached was on the preceding Thursday evening at St. Dunstan's. It was an exposition of the eighteenth chapter of St. John's Gospel; and he remarked to his curate that he must get on as fast as he could, lest he should not get through the Gospel before the lectures closed for the summer. His concluding sermon at Blackfriars was on the preceding Tuesday morning, from the thirteenth verse of

the 103rd Psalm—" Like as a father pitieth his children, so the
Lord pitieth them that fear him." These dates are worthy of
special notice. This fine old servant of Christ, at the age of
eighty-one, was evidently preaching at least three days in every
week !

From the moment he was seized with his illness, he considered it to be his last ; and though he had occasional
symptoms of recovery during the seven weeks that his illness
continued, he never entered the pulpit again. He spoke of
himself as a dying man, but always as one that had peace
in believing. On the morning of his seizure he came down to
breakfast as usual, in the house at Balham Hill, where he was
staying, and presided in family devotion. It was observed that
he prayed most earnestly to God that " he would fit them for,
and support them in their trials that day, which might be many."
He returned the same day to his own house in London, and
conversed most profitably and comfortably in the way, on the
approach of death and near prospect of eternity. He said,
" How animating is the view which I have now of death, and
the hope laid up for me in heaven, full of glory and immortality !" On arriving at home his last illness struck him.

He continued at his own house in London under medical
advice for three weeks, and used all the means which his physician thought fit to prescribe. But he said, " You are taking
much pains to prop up this feeble body ; I thank you for it ;
it will not do now." His Hebrew Psalter lay close by him,
and out of it he frequently read a verse or two, not being able
to attend to more. From the nature of his illness he could
speak but little ; and being once asked if he would see some of
his friends, he replied, " He needed no better company than he
enjoyed."

" On the 26th of June," says his biographer, Cadogan, " he
left town, and went to a friend's house at Tottenham for a
fortnight, where he was so much better that he was able to

walk about the garden. Upon his return to town, he told his curate that he had laid long in the arms of death, and if recovering, it was very slowly. ' But,' said he, ' this is but a poor dying life at best ; however, I am in His hands who will do the best for me ; I am sure of that. I have lived to experience all I have spoken and all I have written, and I bless God for it.'—To another friend he said, ' I have the peace of God in my conscience, and the love of God in my heart ; and that, you know, is sound experience. I knew before that the doctrines I preached were truths, but now I experience them to be blessings.'—Thanking another friend for a visit, he told him ' that he had come to see a saved sinner.'—This he often affirmed should be his dying breath ; he desired to die with the language of the publican in his mouth—' God be merciful to me a sinner !' "

He continued in London for a few days in this blessed frame of mind, and then returned on the 13th of July to the house of his friend, Mr. Whitridge, at Balham Hill, where he had been the day that he was first taken ill. From this date his strength rapidly decayed, but his faith and patience never failed him. He was often saying, " How good is God ! What comforts does he give me ! What a prospect do I see before me of glory and immortality ! He is my God in life, in death, and throughout eternity." On the 23rd of July, as he sat at breakfast, he said, " It is now nearly sixty years since God opened my mouth to publish the everlasting sufficiency and eternal glory of the salvation in Christ Jesus ; and it has now pleased him to shut my mouth, that my heart might feel and experience what my mouth has so often spoken."

On the 24th of July, after being helped down-stairs for the last time, he said, " Oh, how good is God ! With what a night has he favoured me !" requesting at the same time that prayer without ceasing might be made for him, that his faith and patience might not fail. He spoke with great kindness and affection of his wife; and, thanking her for all her care of him, said, " Come, my love, that I may bless you : the Lord be with you a covenant God for ever to save and bless you !"—Mrs. Whitridge, in whose house he was dying, on seeing and hearing him bless his wife, said, " Have you not a blessing for me, sir ?" " Yes," he replied ; " I pray God to bless you." And so he said to every one that came to him.

On Saturday the 25th of July he was not able to get down stairs, but lay upon a couch all day, in great weakness of body, but strong in faith, giving glory to God, and the power of Christ resting on him. Towards the close of the day some thought they heard him say, " Though I walk through the valley of the shadow of death I will fear no evil, for thou art with me."— About an hour before his death, Mr. Whitridge, his host and friend, said, " I hope, my dear sir, you now find the salvation of Jesus Christ precious, dear, and valuable to you." His answer was, " He is a precious Saviour to me now." These were the last words he spoke to man. To the Lord he was heard to say, " Holy ! holy ! holy ! blessed Jesus ! to thee be endless praise !" About midnight, as the Sabbath began, he breathed his last, and entered that eternal rest which remains for the people of God. Well saith the Scriptures, " Mark the perfect man, and behold the upright : for the end of that man is peace" (Ps. xxxvii. 37).

Romaine's friends and relations had fully intended to give him a private funeral. But this proved impossible. The many hearers of a minister who had preached the gospel in London for forty-five years could not be prevented showing their respect and affection by following him to the grave. Scores looked up to him as their spiritual father. Hundreds venerated his character and consistency, even though they did not fully embrace the gospel he had preached. The consequence was that his funeral, in spite of all wishes and intentions, was a peculiarly public one. Fifty coaches followed the hearse from Clapham

Common, besides many persons on foot. By the time the procession reached the obelisk in St. George's Fields, the multitude collected was very great indeed; but silence, solemnity, and decorum prevailed. At the foot of Blackfriars' Bridge the city marshals were waiting with their men in black silk scarfs and hatbands, and rode before the hearse to the entrance of the church. They had been ordered out by the lord mayor, as his token of respect for the memory of a man whose character had stood so high in the city of London. Thus went to his long home on August 3rd, 1795, amidst every outward mark of respect and affection, the venerable rector of Blackfriars. At the end of his long forty-five years' ministry no one lifted up his tongue against him. The winds and waves of persecution had at length ceased. He had fairly lived down all opposition, and he died honoured and lamented. So true is that word of Scripture, "When a man's ways please the Lord, he maketh even his enemies to be at peace with him" (Prov. xvi. 7).

Romaine was once married, though rather later in life than many ministers. His wife was a Miss Price, and, as we have already seen, she survived him. He had children, of whom one son died at Trincomalee in 1782, to his great sorrow. Another son was with him in his last illness, of whom he spoke with great affection, expressing his hope of him as a son in the faith, as well as a son in the flesh. Of his other children I can find no account.

Most of Romaine's literary works are so well known that I need not trouble my readers with any account of them. His largest work, "The Life, Walk, and Triumph of Faith," has been often reprinted, and holds a respectable position among English evangelical classics. His "Twelve Sermons on the Law and the Gospel" have also been more than once republished, and in my judgment deservedly so. I regard it as the best and most valuable work he ever sent to the press. His expository sermons on the 107th Psalm and on Solomon's Song

are not so well known as they ought to be. The latter especially throws more light on a most difficult book of Scripture
than many works of much higher pretensions. His single sermons are of course very little known. But no one who wants
to get a just idea of the kind of preacher Romaine was, should
omit to read them. For simplicity, pith, point, and forcible-
ness,—for short, true, vigorous sentences,—they will bear a
favourable comparison with almost any evangelical sermons of
the last century.

Many of his letters in his published correspondence are very
valuable. Like John Newton, he wrote in days when the
modern machinery of societies, committee meetings, Exeter Hall
gatherings, &c., was totally unknown, and when a man had
more leisure to write long letters than he has now. Those who
like reading Newton's " Cardiphonia" and " Omicron," would
find Romaine's correspondence well worth perusing. Christ
and the Bible are the two golden threads which seem to run
through all his letters.

Perhaps, after all, one of the most useful publications that
Romaine ever sent forth is one that is hardly known at all. I
may be wrong, but my firm belief is, that my estimate of its
usefulness will be found correct at the last day. The publication I refer to is called " An Earnest Invitation to the Friends of
the Established Church to join with several of their brethren,
clergy and laity, in London, in setting apart an hour of every
week for Prayer and Supplication during the present troublesome times." There is strong reason to believe that this little
publication was made eminently useful when it first appeared,
and has led to an amazing succession of supplications, intercessions, and prayers down to the present day. It was beyond
all doubt a move in the right direction. It sent men to Him
who alone has all hearts in his hands, and alone can revive his
Church in dead times. Who can tell but that much of the
Spirit's work in the last sixty years will be found at last to have

been the answer to Romaine's prayers? One fact, at any rate, deserves to be specially remembered. When Romaine first sent forth this Invitation in 1757, he only knew about a dozen clergymen in all England who were willing to unite with him, and join his scheme of prayer. But when he died, in 1795, he reckoned that the number of like-minded men in the Establishment had swelled to at least three hundred. That fact alone speaks for itself.

I leave the fourth spiritual hero of the eighteenth century here, and ask my readers to give his name the honour that it deserves. He had not all the popular gifts of some of his contemporaries. He had not the genial attractive characteristics of many in his day. But take him for all in all, he was a great man, and a mighty instrument in God's hand for good. He stood in a most prominent position in London for forty-five years, testifying the gospel of the grace of God, and never flinching for a day. He stood alone, with almost no backers, supporters, or fellow-labourers. He stood in the same place, constantly preaching to the same hearers, and not able, like Whitefield, Wesley, Grimshaw, and other itinerant brethren, to preach old sermons. He stood there witnessing to truths which were most unpopular, and brought down on him opposition, persecution, and scorn. He stood in a most public post, continually watched, observed, and noticed by unfriendly eyes, ready to detect faults in a moment if he committed them. Yet, during all these forty-five years, he maintained a blameless character, firmly upheld his first principles to the last, and died at length, like a good soldier at his post, full of days and honour. The man of whom these things can be said must have been no common man. It is place and position that specially prove what we are. In England one hundred years ago there were not four spiritual champions greater and more honourable than William Romaine.

VII.

Daniel Rowlands and his Ministry.

CHAPTER I.

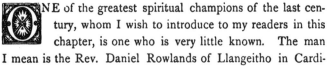NE of the greatest spiritual champions of the last century, whom I wish to introduce to my readers in this chapter, is one who is very little known. The man I mean is the Rev. Daniel Rowlands of Llangeitho in Cardiganshire. Thousands of my countrymen, I suspect, have some little acquaintance with Whitefield, Wesley, and Romaine, who never even heard the name of the great apostle of Wales.

That such should be the case need not surprise us. Rowlands was a Welsh clergyman, and seldom preached in the English language. He resided in a very remote part of the Principality, and hardly ever came to London. His ministry was almost entirely among the middle and lower classes in about five counties in Wales. These circumstances alone are enough to account for the fact that so few people know anything about him. Whatever the causes may be, there are not many Englishmen who understand Welsh, or can even pronounce the names of the parishes where Rowlands used to preach. In the face of these circumstances, we have no right to be surprised if his reputation has been confined to the land of his nativity.

In addition to all this, we must remember that no biographical account of Rowlands was ever drawn up by his contemporaries. Materials for such an account were got together by one of his sons, and forwarded to Lady Huntingdon. Her death, unfortunately, immediately afterwards, prevented these materials being used, and what became of them after her death has never been ascertained. The only memoirs of Rowlands are two lives, written by clergymen who are still living. They are both excellent and useful in their way, but of course they labour under the disadvantage of having been drawn up long after the mighty subject of them had passed away.* These two volumes, and some very valuable information which I have succeeded in obtaining from a kind correspondent in Wales, are the only mines of matter to which I have had access in drawing up this memoir.

Enough, however, and more than enough, is extant, to prove that Daniel Rowlands, in the highest sense, was one of the spiritual giants of the last century. It is a fact that Lady Huntingdon, no mean judge of clergymen, had the highest opinion of Rowlands. Few people had better opportunities of forming a judgment of preachers than she had, and she thought Rowlands was second only to Whitefield. It is a fact that no British preacher of the last century kept together in one district such enormous congregations of souls for fifty years as Rowlands did. It is a fact, above all, that no man a hundred years ago seems to have preached with such unmistakable power of the Holy Ghost accompanying him as Rowlands. These are great isolated facts that cannot be disputed. Like the few

---

* The memoirs of Rowlands to which I refer are two small volumes by the Rev. John Owen, Rector of Thrussington, and the Rev. E. Morgan, Vicar of Syston, both in the county of Leicester. The private information which I have received has been supplied by a relative of the great Welsh apostle, though not in lineal descent, the Rev. William Rowlands of Fishguard, South Wales. Some few facts, it may be interesting to my readers to know, come from an old man of eighty-five, who, when a boy, heard Rowlands preach.

scattered bones of extinct mammoths and mastodons, they speak volumes to all who have an ear to hear. They tell us that, in considering and examining Daniel Rowlands, we are dealing with no common man.

Daniel Rowlands was born in the year 1713, at Pant-y-beudy in the parish of Llancwnlle, near Llangeitho, Cardiganshire. He was the second son of the Rev. Daniel Rowlands, rector of Llangeitho, by Jennet, his wife. When a child of three years old, he had a narrow escape of death, like John Wesley. A large stone fell down the chimney on the very spot where he had been sitting two minutes before, which, had he not providentially moved from his place, must have killed him. Nothing else is known of the first twenty years of his life, except the fact that he received his education at Hereford Grammar School, and that he lost his father when he was eighteen years old. It appears, from a tablet in Llangeitho Church, that when Rowlands was born, his father was fifty-four and his mother forty-five years old. His father's removal could not therefore have been a premature event, as he must have attained the ripe age of seventy-two.

From some cause or other, of which we can give no account, Rowlands appears to have gone to no University. His father's death may possibly have made a difference in the circumstances of the family. At any rate, the next fact we hear about him after his father's death, is his ordination in London at the early age of twenty, in the year 1733. He was ordained by letters dimissory from the Bishop of St. David's, and it is recorded, as a curious proof both of his poverty and his earnestness of character, that he went to London on foot.

The title on which Rowlands was ordained was that of curate to his elder brother John, who had succeeded his father, and held the three adjacent livings of Llangeitho, Llancwnlle, and Llandewibrefi. He seems to have entered on his ministerial duties like thousands in his day—without the slightest adequate sense of his responsibilities, and utterly ignorant of the gospel of Christ. According to Owen he was a good classical scholar, and had made rapid progress at Hereford School in all secular learning. But in the neighbourhood where he was born and began his ministry, he is reported never to have given any proof of fitness to be a minister. He was only known as a man remarkable for natural vivacity, of middle size, of a firm make, of quick and nimble action, very adroit and successful in all games and athletic amusements, and as ready as any one, after doing duty in church on Sunday morning, to spend the rest of God's day in sports and revels, if not in drunkenness. Such was the character of the great apostle of Wales for some time after his ordination! He was never likely, afterwards, to forget St. Paul's words to the Corinthians, "Such were some of you" (1 Cor. vi. 11), or to doubt the possibility of any one's conversion.

The precise time and manner of Rowlands' conversion are points involved in much obscurity. According to Morgan, the first thing that awakened him out of his spiritual slumber, was the discovery that, however well he tried to preach, he could not prevent one of his congregations being completely thinned by a dissenting minister named Pugh. It is said that this made him alter his sermons, and adopt a more awakening and alarming style of address. According to Owen, he was first brought to himself by hearing a well-known excellent clergyman, named Griffith Jones, preach at Llandewibrefi. On this occasion his appearance, as he stood in the crowd before the pulpit, is said to have been so full of vanity, conceit, and levity, that Mr. Jones stopped in his sermon and offered a special prayer for him, that God would touch his heart, and make him an instrument for turning souls from darkness to light. This prayer is said to have had an immense effect on Rowlands, and he is reported to have been a different man from that day. I do not attempt to reconcile the two accounts. I can quite believe that both are true. When the Holy Ghost takes in hand the conversion of a soul, he often causes a variety of circumstances to concur and co-operate in producing it. This, I am sure, would be the testimony of all experienced believers. Owen got hold of one set of facts, and Morgan of another. Both happened probably about the same time, and both probably are true.

One thing, at any rate, is very certain. From about the year 1738, when Rowlands was twenty-five, a complete change came over his life and ministry. He began to preach like a man in earnest, and to speak and act like one who had found out that sin, and death, and judgment, and heaven, and hell, were great realities. Gifted beyond most men with bodily and mental qualifications for the work of the pulpit, he began to consecrate himself wholly to it, and threw himself, body, and soul, and mind, into his sermons. The consequence, as might be ex pected, was an enormous amount of popularity. The churches where he preached were crowded to suffocation. The effect of his ministry, in the way of awakening and arousing sinners, was something tremendous. "The impression," says Morgan, "on the hearts of most people, was that of awe and distress, and as if they saw the end of the world drawing near, and hell ready to swallow them up. His fame soon spread throughout the country, and people came from all parts to hear him. Not only the churches were filled, but also the churchyards. It is said that, under deep conviction, numbers of the people lay down on the ground in the churchyard of Llancwnlle, and it was not easy for a person to pass by without stumbling against some of them."

At this very time, however curious it may seem, it is clear that Rowlands did not preach the full gospel. His testimony was unmistakably truth, but still it was not the whole truth. He painted the spirituality and condemning power of the law in such vivid colours that his hearers trembled before him, and cried out for mercy. But he did not yet lift up Christ crucified in all his fulness, as a refuge, a physician, a redeemer, and a friend ; and hence, though many were wounded, they were not healed. How long he continued preaching in this strain it is, at this distance of time, extremely difficult to say. So far as I can make out by comparing dates, it went on for about four years. The work that he did for God in this period, I have no doubt, was exceedingly useful, as a preparation for the message of later days. I, for one, believe that there are places, and times, and seasons, and congregations, in which powerful preaching of *the law* is of the greatest value. I strongly suspect that many evangelical congregations in the present day would be immensely benefited by a broad, powerful exhibition of God's law. But that there was too much law in Rowlands' preaching for four years after his conversion, both for his own comfort and the good of his hearers, is very evident from the fragmentary accounts that remain of his ministry.

The means by which the mind of Rowlands was gradually led into the full light of the gospel have not been fully explained by his biographers. Perhaps the simplest explanation will be found in our Lord Jesus Christ's words, "If any man will do his will, he shall know of the doctrine" (John vii 17) Rowlands was evidently a man who honestly lived up to his light, and followed on to know the Lord. His Master took care that he did not long walk in darkness, but showed him "the light of life." One principal instrument of guiding him into the whole truth was that same Mr. Pugh who, at an earlier period, had thinned his congregation ! He took great interest in Rowlands at this critical era in his spiritual history, and gave him much excellent advice. " Preach the gospel, dear sir," he would say ; " preach the gospel to the people, and apply the balm of Gilead, the blood of Christ, to their spiritual wounds, and show the necessity of faith in the crucified Saviour." Happy indeed are young ministers who have an Aquila or

Priscilla near them, and when they get good advice are willing to listen to it ! The friendship of the eminent layman, Howell Harris, with whom Rowlands became acquainted about this time, was no doubt a great additional help to his soul. In one way or another, the great apostle of Wales was gradually led into the full noontide light of Christ's truth; and about the year 1742, in the thirtieth year of his age, became established as the preacher of a singularly full, free, clear, and well-balanced gospel.

The effect of Rowlands' ministry from this time forward to his life's end was something so vast and prodigious, that it almost takes away one's breath to hear of it. We see unhappily so very little of spiritual influences in the present day, the operations of the Holy Ghost appear confined within such narrow limits and to reach so few persons, that the harvests reaped at Llangeitho a hundred years ago sound almost incredible. But the evidence of the results of his preaching is so abundant and incontestable, that there is no room left for doubt. One universal testimony is borne to the fact that Rowlands was made a blessing to hundreds of souls. People used to flock to hear him preach from every part of the Principality, and to think nothing of travelling fifty or sixty miles for the purpose. On sacrament Sundays it was no uncommon thing for him to have 1500, or 2000, or even 2500 communicants! The people on these occasions would go together in companies, like the Jews going up to the temple feast in Jerusalem, and would return home afterwards singing hymns and psalms on their journey, caring nothing for fatigue.

It is useless to attempt accounting for these effects of the great Welsh preacher's ministry, as many do, by calling them religious excitement. Such people would do well to remember that the influence which Rowlands had over his hearers was an influence which never waned for at least forty-eight years. It had its ebbs and flows, no doubt, and rose on several occasions to the spring-tide of revivals; but at no time did his ministry appear to be without immense and unparalleled results. According to Charles of Bala, and many other unexceptionable witnesses, it seemed just as attractive and effective when he was seventy years old as it was when he was fifty. When we recollect, moreover, the singular fact that on Sundays, at least, Rowlands was very seldom absent from Llangeitho, and that for forty-eight years he was constantly preaching on the same spot, and not, like Whitefield and Wesley, incessantly addressing fresh congregations, we must surely allow that few preachers have had such extraordinary spiritual success since the days of the apostles.

Of course it would be absurd to say that there was no excitement, unsound profession, hypocrisy, and false fire among the thousands who crowded to hear Rowlands. There was much, no doubt, as there always will be, when large masses of people are gathered together. Nothing, perhaps, is so infectious as a kind of sham, sensational Christianity, and particularly among unlearned and ignorant men. The Welsh, too, are notoriously an excitable people. No one, however, was more fully alive to these dangers than the great preacher himself, and no one could warn his hearers more incessantly that the Christianity which was not practical was unprofitable and vain. But, after all, the effects of Rowlands' ministry were too plain and palpable to be mistaken. There is clear and overwhelming evidence that the lives of many of his hearers were vastly improved after hearing him preach, and that sin was checked and distinct knowledge of Christianity increased to an immense extent throughout the Principality.

It will surprise no Christian to hear that, from an early period, Rowlands found it impossible to confine his labours to his own parish. The state of the country was so deplorable as to religion and morality, and the applications he received for help were so many, that he felt he had no choice in the matter.

The circumstances under which he first began preaching out of his own neighbourhood are so interesting, as described by Owen, that I shall give his words without abbreviation :—

"There was a farmer's wife in Ystradffin, in the county of Carmarthen, who had a sister living near Llangeitho. This woman came at times to see her sister, and on one of these occasions she heard some strange things about the clergyman of the parish—that is, Rowlands. The common saying was, that he was not right in his mind. However, she went to hear him, and not in vain ; but she said nothing then to her sister or to anybody else about the sermon, and she returned home to her family. The following Sunday she came again to her sister's home at Llangeitho. 'What is the matter?' said her sister, in great surprise. 'Are your husband and your children well?' She feared, from seeing her again so soon and so un-expectedly, that something unpleasant had happened. 'Oh, yes,' was the reply, 'nothing of that kind is amiss.' Again she asked her, 'What, then, is the matter?' To this she replied, 'I don't well know what is the matter. Something that your *cracked* clergyman said last Sunday has brought me here to-day. It stuck in my mind all the week, and never left me night nor day.' She went again to hear, and continued to come every Sunday, though her road was rough and mountainous, and her home more than twenty miles from Llangeitho.

"After continuing to hear Rowlands about half a year, she felt a strong desire to ask him to come and preach at Ystradffin. She made up her mind to try ; and, after service one Sunday, she went to Rowlands, and accosted him in the following man-ner:—'Sir, if what you say to us is true, there are many in my neighbourhood in a most dangerous condition, going fast to eternal misery. For the sake of their souls, come over, sir, to preach to them.' The woman's request took Rowlands by surprise ; but without a moment's hesitation he said, in his usual quick way, 'Yes, I will come, if you can get the clergyman's permission.' This satisfied the woman, and she returned home as much pleased as if she had found some rich treasure. She took the first opportunity of asking her clergyman's permission, and easily succeeded. Next Sunday she went joyfully to Llangeitho, and informed Rowlands of her success. According to his promise he went over and preached at Ystradffin, and his very first sermon there was wonderfully blessed. Not less than thirty persons, it is said, were converted that day! Many of them afterwards came regularly to hear him at Llangeitho."

From this time forth, Rowlands never hesitated to preach outside his own parish, wherever a door of usefulness was opened. When he could, he preached in churches. When churches were closed to him, he would preach in a room, a barn, or the open air. At no period, however, of his ministerial life does he appear to have been so much of an itinerant as some of his contemporaries. He rightly judged that hearers of the gospel required to be built up as well as awakened, and for this work he was peculiarly well qualified. Whatever, therefore, he did on week days, the Sunday generally found him at Llangeitho.

The circumstances under which he first began the practice of field-preaching were no less remarkable than those under which he was called to preach at Ystradffin. It appears that after his own conversion he felt great anxiety about the spiritual condition of his old companions in sin and folly. Most of them were thoughtless headstrong young men, who thoroughly disliked his searching sermons, and refused at last to come to church at all. "Their custom," says Owen, "was to go on Sunday to a suitable place on one of the hills above Llangeitho, and there amuse themselves with sports and games." Rowlands tried all means to stop this sinful profanation of the Lord's day, but for some time utterly failed. At last he determined to go there himself on a Sunday. As these rebels against God would not come to him in church, he resolved to go to them on their own ground. He went therefore, and suddenly breaking into the ring as a cock-fight was going on, addressed them powerfully and boldly about the sinfulness of their conduct. The effect was so great that not a tongue was raised to answer or oppose him, and from that day the Sabbath assembly in that place was completely given up. For the rest of his life Rowlands never hesitated, when occasion required, to preach in the open air.

The extra-parochial work that Rowlands did by his itinerant preaching was carefully followed up and not allowed to fall to the ground. No one understood better than he did, that souls require almost as much attention after they are awakened as they do before, and that in spiritual husbandry there is need of watering as well as planting. Aided, therefore, by a few zealous fellow-labourers, both lay and clerical, he established a regular system of Societies, on John Wesley's plan, over the greater part of Wales, through which he managed to keep up a constant communication with all who valued the gospel that he preached, and to keep them well together. These societies were all connected with one great Association, which met four times a-year, and of which he was generally the moderator. The amount of his influence at these Association-meetings may be measured by the fact that above one hundred ministers in the Principality regarded him as their spiritual father! From the very first this Association seems to have been a most wisely organized and useful institution, and to it may be traced the existence of the Calvinistic Methodist body in Wales at this very day.

The mighty instrument whom God employed in doing all the good works I have been describing, was not permitted to do them without many trials. For wise and good ends, no doubt —to keep him humble in the midst of his immense success and to prevent his being exalted overmuch—he was called upon to drink many bitter cups. Like his divine Master, he was "a man of sorrows and acquainted with grief." The greatest of these trials, no doubt, was his ejection from the Church of England in 1763, after serving her faithfully for next to nothing as an ordained clergyman for thirty years. The manner in which this disgraceful transaction was accomplished was so remarkable, that it deserves to be fully described.

Rowlands, it must be remembered, was never an incumbent. From the time of his ordination in 1733, he was simply curate of Llangeitho, under his elder brother John, until the time of his death in 1760. What kind of a clergyman his elder brother was is not very clear. He was drowned at Aberystwith, and we only know that for twenty-seven years he seems to have left everything at Llangeitho in Daniel's hands, and to have let him do just what he liked. Upon the death of John Rowlands, the Bishop of St. David's, who was patron of Llangeitho, was asked to give the living to his brother Daniel, upon the very reasonable ground that he had been serving the parish as curate no less than twenty-seven years ! The bishop unhappily refused to comply with this request, alleging as his excuse that he had received many complaints about his irregularities. He took the very singular step of giving the living to John, the son of Daniel Rowlands, a young man twenty-seven years old. The result of this very odd proceeding was, that Daniel Rowlands became curate to his own son, as he had been curate to his own brother, and continued his labours at Llangeitho for three years more uninterruptedly.*

The reasons why the Bishop of St. David's refused to give Rowlands the living of Llangeitho may be easily divined. So long as he was only a curate, he knew that he could easily silence him. Once instituted and inducted as incumbent, he would have occupied a position from which he could not have

---

* For a clue to all this intricacy, I am entirely indebted to the Rev. W. Rowlands of Fishguard. Unless the facts I have detailed are carefully remembered, it is impossible to understand how Daniel Rowlands was so easily turned out of his position. The truth is, that he was only a curate

been removed without much difficulty. Influenced, probably, by some such considerations, the bishop permitted Rowlands to continue preaching at Llangeitho as curate to his son, warning him at the same time that the Welsh clergy were constantly complaining of his irregularities, and that he could not long look over them. These "irregularities," be it remembered, were neither drunkenness, breach of the seventh commandment, hunting, shooting, nor gambling ! The whole substance of his offence was preaching out of his own parish wherever he could get hearers ! To the bishop's threats Rowlands replied, "that he had nothing in view but the glory of God in the salvation of sinners, and that as his labours had been so much blessed he could not desist."

At length, in the year 1763, the fatal step was taken. The bishop sent Rowlands a mandate, revoking his license, and was actually foolish enough to have it served on a Sunday ! The niece of an eye-witness describes what happened in the following words : " My uncle was at Llangeitho church that very morning. A stranger came forward and served Mr. Rowlands with a notice from the bishop, at the very time when he was stepping into the pulpit. Mr. Rowlands read it, and told the people that the letter which he had just received was from the bishop, revoking his license. Mr. Rowlands then said, 'We must obey the higher powers. Let me beg you will go out quietly, and then we shall conclude the service of the morning by the church gate.' And so they walked out, weeping and crying. My uncle thought there was not a dry eye in the church at the moment. Mr. Rowlands accordingly preached outside the church with extraordinary effect."

A more unhappy, ill-timed, blundering exercise of episcopal power than this, it is literally impossible to conceive! Here was a man of singular gifts and graces, who had no objection to anything in the Articles or Prayer-book, cast out of the Church of England for no other fault than excess of zeal.

And this ejection took place at a time when scores of Welsh clergymen were shamefully neglecting their duties, and too often were drunkards, gamblers, and sportsmen, if not worse! That the bishop afterwards bitterly repented of what he did, is very poor consolation indeed. It was too late. The deed was done. Rowlands was shut out of the Church of England, and an immense number of his people all over Wales followed him. A breach was made in the walls of the Established Church which will probably never be healed. As long as the world stands, the Church of England in Wales will never get over the injury done to it by the preposterous and stupid revocation of Daniel Rowlands' license.

There is every reason to believe that Rowlands felt his expulsion most keenly. However, it made no difference whatever in his line of action. His friends and followers soon built him a large and commodious chapel in the parish of Llangeitho, and migrated there in a body. He did not even leave Llangeitho rectory; for his son, being rector, allowed him to reside there as long as he lived. In fact, the Church of England lost every-thing by ejecting him, and gained nothing at all. The great Welsh preacher was never silenced practically for a single day, and the Church of England only reaped a harvest of odium and dislike in Wales, which is bearing fruit to this very hour.

From the time of his ejection to his death, the course of Rowlands' life seems to have been comparatively undisturbed. No longer persecuted and snubbed by ecclesiastical superiors, he held on his way for twenty-seven years in great quietness, undiminished popularity, and immense usefulness, and died at length in Llangeitho rectory on October the 16th, 1790, at the ripe old age of seventy-seven.

" He was unwell during the last year of his life," says Morgan, " but able to go on with his ministry at Llangeitho, though he scarcely went anywhere else. It was his particular wish that he might go direct from his work to his everlasting rest, and not be kept long on a death-bed. His heavenly Father was pleased to grant his desire, and when his departure was drawing nigh, he had some pleasing idea of his approaching end."

One of his children has supplied the following interesting account of his last days:—"My father made the following observations in his sermons two Sundays before his departure. He said, 'I am almost leaving, and am on the point of being taken from you. I am not tired of work, but in it. I have some presentiment that my heavenly Father will soon release me from my labours, and bring me to my everlasting rest. But I hope that he will continue his gracious presence with you after I am gone.' He told us, conversing on his departure after worship the last Sunday, that he should like to die in a quiet, serene manner, and hoped that he should not be disturbed by our sighs and crying. He added, 'I have no more to state, by way of acceptance with God, than I have always stated : I die as a poor sinner, depending fully and entirely on the merits of a crucified Saviour for my acceptance with God.' In his last hours he often used the expression, in Latin, which Wesley used on his death-bed, 'God is with us ;' and finally departed in great peace."

Rowlands was buried at Llangeitho, at the east end of the church. His enemies could shut him out of the pulpit, but not out of the churchyard. An old inhabitant of the parish, now eighty-five years of age, says: "I well remember his tomb, and many times have I read the inscription, his name, and age, with that of his wife's, Eleanor, who died a year and two months after her husband. The stone was laid on a three feet wall, but it is now worn out by the hand of time."

Rowlands was once married. It is believed that his wife was the daughter of Mr. Davies of Glynwchaf, near Llangeitho. He had seven children who survived him, and two who died in infancy. What became of all his family, and whether there are any lineal descendants of his, I have been unable to ascertain with accuracy.

The engraving of him which faces the title-page of the lives drawn up by Morgan and Owen, gives one the idea of Rowlands being a grave and solemn-looking man. It is probably taken from the picture of him which Lady Huntingdon sent an artist to take at the very end of his life. The worthy old saint did not at all like having his portrait taken. "Why do you object, sir?" said the artist at last. "Why?" replied the old man, with great emphasis; "I am only a bit of clay like thyself." And then he exclaimed, "Alas! alas! alas! taking the picture of a poor old sinner! alas! alas!"—"His countenance," says Morgan, "altered and fell at once, and this is the reason why the picture appears so heavy and cast down."

I have other things yet to tell about Rowlands. His preaching and the many characteristic anecdotes about him deserve special notice. But I must reserve these points for another chapter.

———

CHAPTER II.

Analysis of his Preaching—Much of Christ—Richness of Thought—Felicity of Language —Large Measure of Practical and Experimental Teaching—Manner, Delivery, and Voice—Christmas Evans' Description of his Preaching—Testimony of Mr. Jones of Creaton—Specimens of Rowlands' Sermons—Inner Life and Private Character— Humility, Prayerfulness, Diligence, Self-Denial, Courage, Fervour—Rowland Hill's Anecdote.

IN taking a general survey of the ministry of Daniel Rowlands of Llangeitho, the principal thing that strikes one is the extraordinary power of his *preaching*. There was evidently something very uncommon about his sermons. On this point we have the clear and distinct testimony of a great cloud of witnesses. In a day when God raised up several preachers of very great power, Rowlands was considered by competent judges to be equalled by only one man, and to be excelled by none.

Whitefield was thought to equal him ; but even Whitefield was not thought to surpass him. This is undoubtedly high praise. Some account of the good man's sermons will probably prove interesting to most of my readers. What were their peculiar characteristics ? What were they like ?

I must begin by frankly confessing that the subject is surrounded by difficulties. The materials out of which we have to form our judgment are exceedingly small. Eight sermons, translated out of Welsh into English in the year 1774, are the only literary record which exists of the great Welsh apostle's fifty years' ministry. Besides these sermons, and a few fragments of occasional addresses, we have hardly any means of testing the singularly high estimate which his contemporaries formed of his preaching powers. When I add to this, that the eight sermons extant appear to be poorly translated, the reader will have some idea of the difficulties I have to contend with.

Let me remark, however, once for all, that when the generation which heard a great preacher has passed away, it is often hard to find out the secret of his popularity. No well-read person can be ignorant that Luther and Knox in the sixteenth century, Stephen Marshall in the Commonwealth times, and George Whitefield in the eighteenth century, were the most popular and famous preachers of their respective eras. Yet no one, perhaps, can read their sermons, as we now possess them, without a secret feeling that they do not answer to their reputation. In short, it is useless to deny that there is some hidden secret about pulpit power which baffles all attempts at definition. The man who attempts to depreciate the preaching of Rowlands on the ground that the only remains of him now extant seem poor, will find that he occupies an untenable position. He might as well attempt to depreciate the great champions of the German and Scottish Reformations.

After all, we must remember that no man has a right to pass unfavourable criticisms on the remains of great popular preachers, unless he has first thoroughly considered what kind of thing a popular sermon must of necessity be. The vast majority of sermon-hearers do not want fine words, close reasoning, deep philosophy, metaphysical abstractions, nice distinctions, elaborate composition, profound learning. They delight in plain language, simple ideas, forcible illustrations, direct appeals to heart and conscience, short sentences, fervent, loving earnestness of manner. He who possesses such qualifications will seldom preach to empty benches. He who possesses them in a high degree will always be a popular preacher. Tried by this standard, the popularity of Luther and Knox is easily explained. Rowlands appears to have been a man of this stamp. An intelligent judge of popular preaching can hardly fail to see in his remains, through all the many disadvantages under which we read them, some of the secrets of his marvellous success.

Having cleared my way by these preliminary remarks, I will proceed at once to show my readers some of the leading characteristics of the great Welsh evangelist's preaching. I give them as the result of a close analysis of his literary remains. Weak and poor as they undoubtedly look in the garb of a translation, I venture to think that the following points stand out clearly in Rowlands' sermons, and give us a tolerable idea of what his preaching generally was.

The first thing that I notice in the remains of Rowlands is the *constant presence of Christ* in all his addresses. The Lord Jesus stands out prominently in almost every page. That his doctrine was always eminently "evangelical" is a point on which I need not waste words. The men about whom I am writing were all men of that stamp. But of all the spiritual champions of last century, none appear to me to have brought Christ forward more prominently than Rowlands. The blood, the sacrifice, the righteousness, the kindness, the patience, the saving grace, the example, the greatness of the Lord Jesus, are subjects which appear to run through every sermon, and to crop out at every turn. It seems as if the preacher could never say enough about his Master, and was never weary of commending him to his hearers. His divinity and his humanity, his office and his character, his death and his life, are pressed on our attention in every possible connection. Yet it all seems to come in naturally, and without effort, as if it were the regular outflowing of the preacher's mind, and the language of a heart speaking from its abundance. Here, I suspect, was precisely one of the great secrets of Rowlands' power. A ministry full of the Lord Jesus is exactly the sort of ministry that I should expect God to bless. Christ-honouring sermons are just the sermons that the Holy Spirit seals with success.

The second thing that I notice in the remains of Rowlands is a singular *richness of thought* and matter. Tradition records that he was a diligent student all his life, and spent a great deal of time in the preparation of his sermons. I can quite believe this. Even in the miserable relics which we possess, I fancy I detect strong internal evidence that he was deeply read in Puritan divinity. I suspect that he was very familiar with the writings of such men as Gurnall, Watson, Brooks, Clarkson, and their contemporaries, and was constantly storing his mind with fresh thoughts from their pages. Those who imagine that the great Welsh preacher was nothing but an empty declaimer of trite commonplaces, bald platitudes, and hackneyed phrases, with a lively manner and a loud voice, are utterly and entirely mistaken. They will find, even in the tattered rags of his translated sermons, abundant proof that Rowlands was a man who read much and thought much, and gave his hearers plenty to carry away. Even in the thin little volume of eight sermons which I have, I find frequent quotations from Chrysostom, Augustine, Ambrose, Bernard, and Theophylact. I find frequent reference to things recorded by Greek and Latin classical writers. I mark such names as Homer, Socrates, Plato, Æschines,

Aristotle, Pythagoras, Carneades. Alexander the Great, Julius Cæsar, Nero, the Augean stable, Thersites, and Xantippe, make their appearance here and there. That Rowlands was indebted to his friends the Puritans for most of these materials, I make no question at all. But wherever he may have got his learning, there is no doubt that he possessed it, and knew how to make use of it in his sermons. In this respect I think he excelled all his contemporaries. Not one of them shows so much reading in his sermons as the curate of Llangeitho. Here again, I venture to suggest, was one great secret of Rowlands' success. The man who takes much pains with his sermons, and never brings out what has "cost him nothing," is just the man I expect God will bless. We want well-beaten oil for the service of the sanctuary.

The third thing that I notice in the remains of Rowlands is the curious *felicity of the language* in which he expressed his ideas. Of course this is a point on which I must speak diffidently, knowing literally nothing of the Welsh tongue, and entirely dependent on translation. But it is impossible to mistake certain peculiarities in style which stand forth prominently in everything which comes from the great Welsh apostle's mind. He abounds in short, terse, pithy, epigrammatic, proverbial sentences, of that kind which arrests the attention and sticks in the memory of hearers. He has a singularly happy mode of quoting Scriptures in confirming and enforcing the statement he makes. Above all, he is rich in images and illustrations, drawn from everything almost in the world, but always put in such a way that the simplest mind can understand them. Much of the peculiar interest of his preaching, I suspect, may be traced to this talent of putting things in the most vivid and pictorial way. He made his hearers feel that they actually saw the things of which he was speaking. No intelligent reader of the Bible, I suppose, needs to be reminded that in all this Rowlands walked in the footsteps of his divine Master. The sermons of Him who " spake as never man spake," were not elaborate rhetorical arguments. Parables founded on subjects familiar to the humblest intellect, terse, broad, sententious statements, were the staple of our Lord Jesus Christ's preaching. Much of the marvellous success of Rowlands, perhaps, may be traced up to his wise imitation of the best of patterns, the great Head of the Church.

The fourth and last thing which I notice in the remains of Rowlands, is the large measure of *practical and experimental teaching* which enters into all his sermons. Anxious as he undoubtedly was to convert sinners and arouse the careless, he never seems to forget the importance of guiding the Church of God and building up believers. Warnings, counsels, encouragements, consolations suited to professing Christians, are continually appearing in all his discourses. The peculiar character of his ministerial position may partly account for this. He was always preaching in the same place, and to many of the same hearers, on Sundays. He was not nearly so much an itinerant as many of his contemporaries. He could not, like Whitefield, and Wesley, and Berridge, preach the same sermon over and over again, and yet feel that probably none of his hearers had heard it before. Set for the defence of the gospel at Llangeitho every Sunday, and seeing every week the same faces looking up to him, he probably found it absolutely necessary to " bring forth new things as well as old," and to be often exhorting many of his hearers not to stand still in first principles, but to " go on unto perfection." But be the cause what it may, there is abundant evidence in the sermons of Rowlands that he never forgot the believers among his people, and generally contrived to say a good many things for their special benefit. Here again, I venture to think, we have one more clue to his extraordinary usefulness. He " rightly divided the word of truth," and gave to every man his portion. Most preachers of the gospel, I suspect, fail greatly in this matter. They either neglect the unconverted or the true Christians in their congregations. They either spend their strength in perpetually teaching elementary truths, or else they dwell exclusively on the privileges and duties of God's children. From this one-sided style of preaching Rowlands seems to have been singularly free. Even in the midst of the plainest addresses to the ungodly, he never loses the opportunity of making a general appeal to the godly. In a word, his ministry of God's truth was thoroughly well-balanced and well-proportioned ; and this is just the ministry which we may expect the Holy Ghost will bless.

The manner and delivery of this great man, when he was in the act of preaching, require some special notice. Every sensible Christian knows well that voice and delivery have a great deal to say to the effectiveness of a speaker, and above all of one who speaks in the pulpit. A sermon faultless both in doctrine and composition will often sound dull and tiresome, when tamely read by a clergyman with a heavy monotonous manner. A sermon of little intrinsic merit, and containing perhaps not half-a-dozen ideas, will often pass muster as brilliant and eloquent, when delivered by a lively speaker with a good voice. For want of good delivery some men make gold look like copper, while others, by the sheer force of a good delivery, make a few halfpence pass for gold. Truths divine seem really " mended" by the tongue of some, while they are marred and damaged by others. There is deep wisdom and knowledge of human nature in the answer given by an ancient to one who asked what were the first qualifications of an orator : " The first qualification," he said, " is action ; and the second is action ; and the third is action." The meaning of course was, that it was almost impossible to overrate the importance of manner and delivery.

The voice of Rowlands, according to tradition, was remarkably powerful. We may easily believe this, when we recollect that he used frequently to preach to thousands in the open air, and to make himself heard by all without difficulty. But we must not suppose that power was the only attribute of his vocal organ, and that he was nothing better than one who screamed, shouted, and bawled louder than other ministers. There is universal testimony from all good judges who heard him, that his voice was singularly moving, affecting, and tender, and possessed a strange power of drawing forth the sympathies of his hearers. In this respect he seems to have resembled Baxter and Whitefield. Like Whitefield, too, his feelings never interfered with the exercise of his voice; and even when his affections moved him to tears in preaching, he was able to continue speaking with uninterrupted clearness. It is a striking feature of the moving character of his voice, that a remarkable revival of religion began at Llangeitho while Rowlands was reading the Litany of the Church of England. The singularly touching and melting manner in which he repeated the words, " By thine agony and bloody sweat, good Lord, deliver us," so much affected the whole congregation, that almost all began to weep loudly, and an awakening of spiritual life commenced which extended throughout the neighbourhood.

Of the manner, demeanour, and action of Rowlands in the delivery of his sermons, mention is made by all who write of him. All describe them as being something so striking and remarkable, that no one could have an idea of them but an eye-witness. He seems to have combined in a most extraordinary degree solemnity and liveliness, dignity and familiarity, depth and fervour. His singular plainness and directness made even the poorest feel at home when he preached; and yet he never degenerated into levity or buffoonery. His images and similes brought things home to his hearers with such graphic power that they could not help sometimes smiling. But he never made his Master's business ridiculous by pulpit joking. If he did say things that made people smile occasionally, he far more often said things that made them weep.

The following sketch by the famous Welsh preacher, Christmas Evans, will probably give as good an idea as we can now obtain of Rowlands in the pulpit. It deserves the more attention, because it is the sketch of a Welshman, an eye-witness, a keen observer, a genuine admirer of his hero, and one who was himself in after-days a very extraordinary man :—

"Rowlands' mode of preaching was peculiar to himself— inimitable. Methinks I see him now entering in his black gown through a little door from the outside to the pulpit, and making his appearance suddenly before the immense congregation. His countenance was in every sense adorned with majesty, and it bespoke the man of strong sense, eloquence, and authority. His forehead was high and prominent; his eye was quick, sharp, and penetrating; he had an aquiline or Roman nose, proportionable comely lips, projecting chin, and a sonorous, commanding, and well-toned voice.

"When he made his appearance in the pulpit, he frequently gave out, with a clear and audible voice, Psalm xxvii. 4 to be sung. Only one verse was sung before sermon, in those days notable for divine influences; but the whole congregation joined in singing it with great fervour. Then Rowlands would stand up, and read his text distinctly in the hearing of all. The whole congregation were all ears and most attentive, as if they were on the point of hearing some evangelic and heavenly oracle, and the eyes of all the people were at the same time most intensely fixed upon him. He had at the beginning of his discourse some stirring, striking idea, like a small box of ointment which he opened before the great one of his sermon, and it filled all the house with its heavenly perfume, as the odour of Mary's alabaster box of ointment at Bethany; and the congregation being delightfully enlivened with the sweet odour, were prepared to look for more of it from one box after the other throughout the sermon.

"I will borrow another similitude in order to give some idea of his most energetic eloquence. It shall be taken from the trade of a blacksmith. The smith first puts the iron into the fire, and then blows the bellows softly, making some inquiries respecting the work to be done, while his eye all the time is fixed steadily on the process of heating the iron in the fire. But as soon as he perceives it to be in a proper and pliable state, he carries it to the anvil, and brings the weighty hammer and sledge down on the metal, and in the midst of stunning noise and fiery sparks emitted from the glaring metal, he fashions and moulds it at his will.

" Thus Rowlands, having glanced at his notes as a matter of form, would go on with his discourse in a calm and deliberate manner, speaking with a free and audible voice ; but he would gradually become warmed with his subject, and at length his voice became so elevated and authoritative, that it resounded through the whole chapel. The effect on the people was wonderful ; you could see nothing but smiles and tears running down the face of all. The first flame of heavenly devotion under the first division having subsided, he would again look on his scrap of notes, and begin the second time to melt and make the minds of the people supple, until he formed them again into the same heavenly temper. And thus he would do six or seven times in the same sermon.

" Rowlands' voice, countenance, and appearance used to change exceedingly in the pulpit, and he seemed to be greatly excited ; but there was nothing low or disagreeable in him—all was becoming, dignified, and excellent. There was such a vehement, invincible flame in his ministry, as effectually drove away the careless, worldly, dead spirit ; and the people so awakened drew nigh, as it were, to the bright cloud—to Christ, to Moses, and Elias—eternity and its amazing realities rushing into their minds.

" There was very little, if any, inference or application at the end of Rowlands' sermon, for he had been applying and enforcing the glorious truths of the gospel throughout the whole of his discourse. He would conclude with a very few striking and forcible remarks, which were most overwhelming and invincible; and then he would make a very sweet, short prayer, and utter the benediction. Then he would make haste out of the pulpit through the little door. His exit was as sudden as his entrance. Rowlands was a star of the greatest magnitude that appeared the last century in the Principality; and perhaps there has not been his like in Wales since the days of the apostles."

It seems almost needless to add other testimony to this graphic sketch, though it might easily be added. The late Mr. Jones of Creaton, who was no mean judge, and heard the greatest preachers in England and Wales, used to declare that "he never heard but one Rowlands." The very first time he heard him, he was so struck with his manner of delivery, as well as his sermon, that it led him to a serious train of thought, which ultimately ended in his conversion.—Charles of Bala, himself a very eminent minister, said that there was a peculiar "dignity and grandeur" in Rowlands' ministry, "as well as profound thoughts, strength and melodiousness of voice, and clearness and animation in exhibiting the deep things of God."—A Birmingham minister, who came accidentally to a place in Wales where Rowlands was preaching to an immense congregation in the open air, says: "I never witnessed such a scene before. The striking appearance of the preacher, and his zeal, animation, and fervour were beyond description. Rowlands' countenance was most expressive; it glowed almost like an angel's."

After saying so much about the gifts and power of this great preacher, it is perhaps hardly fair to offer any specimens of his sermons. To say nothing of the fact that we only possess them in the form of translations, it must never be forgotten that true pulpit eloquence can rarely be expressed on paper. Wise men know well that sermons which are excellent to listen to, are just the sermons which do not "read" well. However, as I have hitherto generally given my readers some illustrations of the style of my last century heroes, they will perhaps be disappointed if I do not give them a few passages from Rowlands'.

My first specimen shall be taken from his sermon on the words, "All things work together for good to them that love God" (Rom. viii. 28).

"Observe what he says. Make thou no exception, when he makes none. *All!* remember he excepts nothing. Be thou confirmed in thy faith; give glory to God, and resolve, with Job, 'Though he slay me, yet will I trust in him.' The Almighty may seem for a season to be your enemy, in order that he may become your eternal friend. Oh! believers, after all your tribulation and anguish, you must conclude with David, 'It is good for me that I have been afflicted, that I might learn thy statutes.' Under all your disquietudes you must exclaim, 'O the depth of the riches both of the wisdom and knowledge of God! how unsearchable are his judgments, and his ways past finding out!' His glory is seen when he works by means; it is more seen when he works without means; it is seen, above all, when he works contrary to means. It was a great work to open the eyes of the blind; it was a greater still to do it by applying clay and spittle, things more likely, some think, to take away sight than to restore. He sent a horror of great darkness on Abraham, when he was preparing to give him the best light. He touched the hollow of Jacob's thigh, and lamed him, when he was going to bless him. He smote Paul with blindness, when he was intending to open the eyes of his mind. He refused the request of the woman of Canaan for a while, but afterwards she obtained her desire. See, therefore, that *all* the paths of the Lord are mercy, and that *all* things work together for good to them that love him.

"Even affliction is very useful and profitable to the godly. The prodigal son had no thought of returning to his father's house till he had been humbled by adversity. Hagar was haughty under Abraham's roof, and despised her mistress; but in the wilderness she was meek and lowly. Jonah sleeps on board ship, but in the whale's belly he watches and prays. Manasseh lived as a libertine at Jerusalem, and committed the most enormous crimes; but when he was bound in chains in the prison at Babylon his heart was turned to seek the Lord his God. Bodily pain and disease have been instrumental in rousing many to seek Christ, when those who were in high health have given themselves no concern about him. The ground which is not rent and torn with the plough bears nothing but thistles and thorns. The vines will run wild, in process of time, if they be not pruned and trimmed. So would our wild hearts be overrun with filthy, poisonous weeds, if the true Vine-dresser did not often check their growth by crosses and sanctified troubles. 'It is good for a man that he bear the yoke in his youth.' Our Saviour says, 'Every branch that beareth fruit, my Father purgeth, that it may bring forth more fruit.' There can be no gold or silver finely wrought without being first purified with fire, and no elegant houses built with stones till the hammers have squared and smoothed them. So we can neither become vessels of honour in the house of our Father till we are melted in the furnace of affliction, nor lively stones in the walls of new Jerusalem till the hand of the Lord has beaten off our proud excrescences and tumours with his own hammers.

"He does not say that all things *will*, but *do*, work together for good. The work is on the wheel, and every movement of the wheel is for your benefit. Not only the angels who encamp around you, or the saints who continually pray for you, but even your enemies, the old dragon and his angels, are engaged in this matter. It is true, this is not their design. No! They think they are carrying on their own work of destroying you, as it is said of the Assyrian whom the Lord sent to punish a hypocritical nation, 'Howbeit, he meaneth not so;'

yet it was God's work that he was carrying on, though he did not intend to do so. All the events that take place in the world carry on the same work—the glory of the Father and the salvation of his children. Every illness and infirmity that may seize you, every loss you may meet with, every reproach you may endure, every shame that may colour your faces, every sorrow in your hearts, every agony and pain in your flesh, every aching in your bones, are for your good. Every change in your condition—your fine weather and your rough weather, your sunny weather and your cloudy weather, your ebbing and your flowing, your liberty and your imprisonment, all turn out for good. Oh, Christians, see what a harvest of blessings ripens from this text! The Lord is at work; all creation is at work; men and angels, friends and foes, all are busy, working together for good. Oh, dear Lord Jesus, what hast thou seen in us that thou shouldst order things so wondrously for us, and make *all things*—all things to work together for our good?"

My second specimen shall be taken from his sermon on Rev. iii. 20 :—

"Oh, how barren and unfruitful is the soul of man, until the word descends like rain upon it, and it is watered with the dew of heaven! But when a few drops have entered and made it supple, what a rich harvest of graces do they produce! Is the heart so full of malice that the most suppliant knee can expect no pardon? Is it as hard to be pacified and calmed as the roaring sea when agitated by a furious tempest? Is it a covetous heart; so covetous that no scene of distress can soften it into sympathy, and no object of wretchedness extort a penny from its gripe? Is it a wanton and adulterous heart, which may as soon be satisfied as the sea can be filled with gold? Be it so. But when the word shall 'drop on it as the rain, and distil as the dew,' behold, in an instant the flint is turned into flesh, the tumultuous sea is hushed into a calm, and the mountains of Gilboa are clothed with herbs and flowers, where before

not a green blade was to be seen! See the mighty change!
It converts Zaccheus, the hard-hearted publican and rapacious
tax-gatherer, into a restorer of what he had unjustly gotten, and
a merciful reliever of the needy. It tames the furious perse-
cuting Saul, and makes him gentle as a lamb. It clothes Ahab
with sackcloth and ashes. It reduces Felix to such anguish of
mind that he trembles like an aspen leaf. It disposes Peter to
leave his nets, and makes him to catch thousands of souls at
one draught in the net of the gospel. Behold, the world is converted to the faith, not by the magicians of Egypt, but by the
outcasts of Judæa!"

The last specimen that I will give is from his sermon on
Heb. i. 9:—

"Christ took our nature upon him that he might sympathize
with us. Almost every creature is tender toward its own kind,
however ferocious to others. The bear will not be deprived of
her whelps without resistance: she will tear the spoiler to
pieces if she can. But how great must be the jealousy of the
Lord Jesus for his people! He will not lose any of them. He
has taken them as members of himself, and as such watches
over them with fondest care. How much will a man do for
one of his members before he suffers it to be cut off? Think
not, O man, that thou wouldst do more for thy members than
the Son of God. To think so would be blasphemy, for the
pre-eminence in all things belongs to him. Yea, he is acquainted
with all thy temptations, because he was in all things tempted
as thou art. Art thou tempted to deny God? So was he.
Art thou tempted to kill thyself? So was he. Art thou
tempted by the vanities of the world? So was he. Art thou
tempted to idolatry? So was he; yea, even to worship the
devil. He was tempted from the manger to the cross. He
was a man of sorrows and acquainted with grief. The Head in
heaven is sympathizing with the feet that are pinched and pressed
on earth, and says, 'Saul, Saul, why persecutest thou me?'"

I should find no difficulty in adding to these extracts, if the space at my command did not forbid me. Feeble and unsatisfactory, as they undoubtedly are, in the form of a translation, they will perhaps give my readers some idea of what Rowlands was in the pulpit, so far as concerns the working of his mind. Of his manner and delivery, of course, they cannot give the least idea. It would be easy to fill pages with short, epigrammatic, proverbial sayings culled from his sermons, of which there is a rich abundance in many passages. But enough, perhaps, has been brought forward to give a general impression of the preaching that did such wonders at Llangeitho. Those who want to know more of it should try to get hold of the little volume of translated sermons from which my extracts have been made. Faintly and inadequately as it represents the great Welsh preacher, it is still a volume worth having, and one that ought to be better known than it is. Scores of books are reprinted in the present day which are not half so valuable as Rowlands' eight sermons.

The inner life and private character of the great Welsh preacher would form a deeply interesting subject, no doubt, if we knew more about them. But the utter absence of all materials except a few scattered anecdotes leaves us very much in the dark. Unless the memoirs of great men are written by relatives, neighbours, or contemporaries, it stands to reason that we shall know little of anything but their public conduct and doings. This applies eminently to Daniel Rowlands. He had no Boswell near him to chronicle the details of his long and laborious life, and to present him to us as he appeared at home. The consequence is, that a vast quantity of interesting matter, which the Church of Christ would like to know, lies buried with him in his grave.

One thing, at any rate, is very certain. His private life was as holy, blameless, and consistent, as the life of a Christian can be. Some fifteen years ago, the *Quarterly Review* contained an article insinuating that he was addicted to drunkenness, which called forth an indignant and complete refutation from many competent witnesses in South Wales, and specially from the neighbourhood of Llangeitho. That such charges should be made against good men need never surprise us. Slander and lying are the devil's favourite weapons, when he wants to injure the mightiest assailants of his kingdom. Satan is pre-eminently "a liar." Bunyan, Whitefield, and Wesley had to drink of the same bitter cup as Rowlands. But that the charge against Rowlands was a mere groundless, malicious falsehood, was abundantly proved by Mr. Griffith, the vicar of Aberdare, in a reply to the article of the *Quarterly Review*, printed at Cardiff. We need not be reminded, if we read our Bibles, who it was of whom the wicked Jews said, "Behold a man gluttonous, and a winebibber, a friend of publicans and sinners" (Matt. xi. 19). If the children of this world cannot prevent the gospel being preached, they try to blacken the character of the preacher. What saith the Scripture? "The disciple is not above his master, nor the servant above his lord. It is enough for the disciple that he be as his master, and the servant as his lord. If they have called the Master of the house Beelzebub, how much more shall they call them of his household?" (Matt. x. 24, 25).

The only light that we can throw on the character and private habits of Rowlands is derived from the few anecdotes which still survive about him. I shall, therefore, conclude my account of him by presenting them to my readers without note or comment.

One leading feature in Rowlands' character was his *humility*. Like every eminent servant of God of whom much is known, he had a deep and abiding sense of his own sinfulness, weakness, and corruption, and his constant need of God's grace. On seeing a vast concourse of people coming to hear him, he would frequently exclaim: "Oh, may the Lord have mercy on me, and help me, a poor worm, sinful dust and ashes !"—When a backslider was pointed out to him, who had once been one of his followers, he said: "It is to be feared indeed that he is one of *my* disciples; for had he been one of *my Lord's* disciples, he would not have been in such a state of sin and rebellion." He often used to say, during his latter days, that there were four lessons which he had laboured to learn throughout the whole course of his religious life, and yet that he was but a dull scholar even in his old age. These lessons were the following —(1.) To repent without despairing; (2.) To believe without being presumptuous; (3.) To rejoice without falling into levity; (4.) To be angry without sinning. He used also often to say, that a self-righteous legal spirit in man was like his shirt, a garment which he puts on first, and puts off last.

A habit of *praying much* was another leading characteristic of Rowlands. It is said that he used often to go to the top of Aeron Hills, and there pour out his heart before God in the most tender and earnest manner for the salvation of the numerous inhabitants of the country which lay around him. "He lived," says Morgan, "in the spirit of prayer, and hence his extraordinary success. On one occasion having engaged to preach at a certain church which stood on an eminence, he had to cross a valley in sight of the people, who were waiting for him in the churchyard. They saw him descend into the bottom of the valley, but then lost sight of him for some time. At last, as he did not come up by the time they expected, and service-time had arrived, some of them went down the hill in search of him. They discovered him, at length, on his knees in a retired spot a little out of the road. He got up when he saw them, and went with them, expressing sorrow for the delay; but he added, 'I had a delightful opportunity below.' The sermon which followed was most extraordinary in power and effect."

Diligence was another distinguishing feature in the character of Rowlands. He was continually improving his mind, by reading, meditation, and study. He used to be up and reading as early as four o'clock in the morning; and he took immense pains in the preparation of his sermons. Morgan says, "Every part of God's Word, at length, became quite familiar to him. He could tell chapter and verse of any text or passage of Scripture that was mentioned to him. Indeed the word of God dwelt richly in him. He had, moreover, a most retentive memory, and when preaching, could repeat the texts referred to, off-hand, most easily and appropriately."

Self-denial was another leading feature of Rowlands' character. He was all his life a very poor man ; but he was always a contented one, and lived in the simplest way. Twice he refused the offer of good livings—one in North Wales, and the other in South Wales—and preferred to remain a dependent curate with his flock at Llangeitho. The offer in one case came from the excellent John Thornton. When he heard that Rowlands had refused it, and ascertained his reasons, he wrote to his son, saying, "I had a high opinion of your father before, but now I have a still higher opinion of him, though he declines my offer. The reasons he assigns are highly creditable to him. It is not a usual thing with me to allow other people to go to my pocket; but tell your father that he is fully welcome to do so whenever he pleases." The residence of the great Welsh evangelist throughout life was nothing but a small cottage possessing no great accommodation. His journeys, when he went about preaching, were made on horseback, until at last a small carriage was left him as a legacy in his old age. He was content, when journeying in his Master's service, with very poor fare and very indifferent lodgings. He says himself, "We used to travel over hills and mountains, on our little nags, without anything to eat but the bread and cheese we carried in our pockets, and without anything to drink but water from the springs. If we had a little buttermilk in some cottages we thought it a great thing. But now men must have tea, and some, too, must have brandy!" Never did man seem so thoroughly to realize the primitive and apostolic rule of life— "Having food and raiment, let us be therewith content."

Courage was another prominent feature in Rowlands' character. He was often fiercely persecuted when he went about preaching, and even his life was sometimes in danger. Once, when he was preaching at Aberystwith, a man swore in a dreadful manner that he would shoot him immediately. He aimed his gun, and pulled the trigger, but it would not go off.—On another occasion his enemies actually placed gunpowder under the place where he was about to stand when preaching, and laid a train to a distant point, so that at a given time they might apply a match, and blow up the preacher and congregation. However, before the time arrived, a good man providentially discovered the whole plot, and brought it to nothing.—On other occasions riotous mobs were assembled, stones were thrown, drums beaten, and every effort made to prevent the sermon being heard. None of these things ever seems to have deterred Rowlands for a moment. As long as he had strength to work he went on with his Master's business, unmoved by opposition and persecution. Like Colonel Gardiner, he "feared God, and beside him he feared nothing." He had given himself to the work of preaching the gospel, and from this work he allowed neither clergy nor laity, bishops nor gentry, rich nor poor, to keep him back.

Fervent and deep feeling was the last characteristic which I mark in Rowlands. He never did anything by halves. Whether preaching or praying, whether in church or in the open air, he seems to have done all he did with heart and soul, and mind and strength. "He possessed as much animal spirits," says one witness, "as were sufficient for half-a-dozen men." This energy seems to have had an inspiring effect about it, and to have swept everything before it like a fire. One who went to hear him every month from Carnar-vonshire, gives a striking account of his singular fervour when Rowlands was preaching on John iii. 16. He says, " He dwelt with such overwhelming, extraordinary thoughts on the love of God, and the vastness of his gift to man, that I was swallowed up in amazement. I did not know that my feet were on the ground ; yea, I had no idea where I was, whether on earth or in heaven. But presently he cried out with a most powerful voice, ' Praised be God for keeping the Jews in ignorance respecting the *greatness* of the Person in their hands! Had they known who he was, they would never have presumed to touch him, much less to drive nails through his blessed hands and feet, and to put a crown of thorns on his holy head. For had they known, they would not have cruci-fied the Lord of glory.' "

I will wind up this account of Rowlands by mentioning a little incident which the famous Rowland Hill often spoke of in his latter days. He was attending a meeting of Metho-dist ministers in Wales in one of his visits, when a man, nearly a hundred years old, got up from a corner of the room and addressed the meeting in the following words:— " Brethren, let me tell you this: I have heard Daniel Row-lands preach, and I heard him once say, Except your con-sciences be cleansed by the blood of Christ, you must all perish in the eternal fires." Rowlands, at that time, had been dead more than a quarter of a century. Yet, even at that interval, " though dead he spoke." It is a faithful saying, and worthy of all remembrance, that the ministry which exalts Christ crucified most, is the ministry which produces most last-ing effects. Never, perhaps, did any preacher exalt Christ more than Rowlands did, and never did preacher leave behind him such deep and abiding marks in the isolated corner of the world where he laboured a hundred years ago.

VIII.

John Berridge and his Ministry.

CHAPTER I.

 HUNDRED years ago there were spiritual giants in the Eastern Counties of England, as well as in Lancashire and Wales. The sixth leader of the great revival of last century whom I wish to introduce to my readers, was a man as remarkable in his way as either Grimshaw or Rowlands. Like them, he lived in an obscure and out-of-the-way village. But, like them, he shook the earth around him, and was one of those who "turn the world upside down." The man I mean is John Berridge, Vicar of Everton, in the county of Bedfordshire.

Of all the English evangelists of the eighteenth century, this good man was undeniably the most quaint and eccentric. Without controversy he was a very odd person, a comet rather than a planet, a man who must be put in a class by himself, a minister who said and did things which nobody else could say or do. But the eccentricities of the Vicar of Everton are probably better known than his graces. With all his peculiarities, he was a man of rare gifts, and deeply taught by the Holy Ghost. Above all, he was a mighty instrument for good in the orbit in which he moved. Few preachers, perhaps, a hundred years ago, were more honoured by God and more useful to souls than the eccentric John Berridge.

My account of this good man is compiled from very scanty materials. A single volume, of no great size, containing his literary remains, and a short biography by his curate, Mr. Whittingham, is the only source of information about him that I can find. In this, however, there is nothing that should surprise us. He was never married, and lived entirely alone. He resided in an isolated rural parish, far away from London, in days when there were no railways, and even turnpike roads were not good. He was settled at a distance from his own family, in a county where, apparently, he had no relatives or connections. He wrote very little, and was chiefly known by his preaching. Add to these facts the mighty one, that Berridge belonged to "a sect everywhere spoken against," and we need not wonder that the records remaining of him are very few. But there is a memorial of him that will never perish. The last day will show that his Master kept "a book of remembrance," and that "his record was on high."

John Berridge was born at Kingston, in the county of Nottinghamshire, on March 1, 1716, within a very few years of Whitefield, Wesley, Grimshaw, Romaine, and Rowlands. The village in which he was born may be seen any day from Kegworth Station by those who travel to the north along the Midland Railway. His father was a wealthy farmer and grazier at Kingston, who married a Miss Sarah Hathwaite, in the year 1714. John Berridge was his eldest son. He had three other sons, about whom I can find out nothing, except that his brother Thomas lived and died at Chatteris, in the Isle of Ely, and survived the subject of this memoir.*

---

* A well-informed correspondent expresses some doubt as to Thomas Berridge having died at Chatteris. He says there is reason to think that he lived and died at Draycott in Derbyshire. He also says that in 1841 a direct lineal descendant of one of John Berridge's brothers was living at Sutton-Bonnington, in Nottinghamshire.

The first fourteen years of Berridge's life were chiefly spent with an aunt at Nottingham, with whom he was a particular favourite. Here also he received the groundwork of his education, but at what school, and under what teacher, I have been unable to ascertain. It is evident that even when a boy he was remarkable for seriousness and steadiness; so much so, as to excite the attention of all who knew him. There is not, however, the slightest proof that he knew anything at this time of scriptural religion; nor was it likely, I fear, in those days, that he would hear anything about it in Nottingham. No doubt, in after-life he had abundant reason to be thankful for his early morality. Steadiness and correctness of life, of course, are not conversion, and save no man's soul. But still they are not to be despised. The scars left by youthful sins, even after forgiveness and complete reconciliation with God, are never wholly effaced, and the recollection of them often causes bitter sorrow.

Berridge himself ascribes his first serious impressions to a singular circumstance :—"One day, as he was returning from school, a boy, who lived near his aunt, invited him into his house, and asked if he might read to him out of the Bible. He consented. This, however, being repeated several times, he began to feel a secret aversion, and would gladly have declined if he had dared. But having obtained the reputation of being *pious*, he was afraid to risk it by refusal. One day, however, as he was returning from a fair, where he had been spending a holiday, he hesitated to pass the door of his neighbour, lest he should be invited as before. The boy, however, was waiting for him, and not only invited him to come in and read the Bible, but also asked if they should pray together. It was then that Berridge began to perceive he was not right before God, or else he would not have felt the aversion that he did to the boy's invitations. And such, he says, was the effect of that day's interview, that not long afterwards he himself began a similar practice with his companions."

Facts such as these are always interesting to those who study God's ways of dealing with souls. It is clear that he often "moves on the face" of hearts by his Spirit long before he introduces light, order, and life. We must never despise the "day of small things." The impressions and convictions of children, especially, ought never to be rudely treated or over-looked. They have often a green spot in their characters which ought to be carefully cultivated by good advice, kind encourage-ment, and prayer. Berridge, unfortunately, seems to have had no one near him at this critical period to guide and direct him. Who can tell but the counsel of some Aquila or Priscilla, if they had found him at Nottingham, might have saved him from many years of darkness, and from many agonizing exercises of mind?

At the age of fourteen Berridge left school, and returned to his home at Kingston, with the intention of taking up his father's business. This plan, however, soon fell to the ground. For some time his father used to take him about to markets and fairs, in order that he might become familiar with the price of cattle, sheep, and pigs, and learn his business by observa-tion and experience. The next step, of course, was to ask him to give his judgment of the value of animals which his father wished to purchase—a matter in which necessarily lies the whole secret of a grazier's success. Here, however, poor John was so invariably wrong in his estimates, that old Mr. Berridge began to despair of ever making him fit to be a grazier; and used often to say, "John, I find you cannot form any idea of the price of cattle, and I shall have to send you to college to be a light to the Gentiles."

How long this state of suspense about Berridge's future life continued, we have no means of ascertaining. In all proba-bility it went on for two or three years, and was a cause of much family trouble. An old Nottinghamshire grazier was not likely to let his eldest son forsake oxen and sheep, and go to college, without a hard struggle to prevent him.   But the son's distaste for his father's calling was deep and insuperable.   His religious impressions, moreover, were kept up and deepened by conversation with a tailor in Kingston, with whom he became so intimate that his friends threatened to bind him to articles of apprenticeship under him.   At last old Mr. Berridge, seeing that his son had no apparent inclination for anything but reading and religion, had the good sense to give up his cherished plans, and to consent to his going to Cambridge.   And thus John Berridge was finally entered at Clare Hall on October 28, 1734, in the nineteenth year of his age.

God's ways are certainly not like man's ways.   Curious as it may appear, for fourteen or fifteen years after entering Clare Hall, John Berridge seems to have gone backward rather than forward in spiritual things.   He took his degree as B.A. in 1738, and as M.A. in 1742; and about the same time was elected Fellow of his College, and resided there, doing comparatively nothing, till 1749.   He was a hard-reading man, and made such progress in every branch of literature that he obtained a high reputation in the University as a thorough scholar.   A clergyman who knew him well for fifty years, said that he was as familiar with Greek and Latin as he was with his mother tongue. He says himself that he sometimes, at this period of his life, read fifteen hours a-day.   But his very cleverness became a snare to him.   His natural love of humour and social disposition entailed on him many temptations.   His acquaintance was courted by people of high rank and position ; and men like the elder Pitt, afterwards Lord Chatham, were among his intimate associates and friends.   All this, no doubt, was very pleasant to flesh and blood, but very bad for his soul.   In short, he had to learn, by bitter experience, that wit and brilliant powers of conversation, like beauty, musical skill, and a fine voice, are very perilous possessions.   They seem to help people forward in this world, but they are in reality most dangerous to their possessors.

Whittingham, his biographer, says of him at this time :—
" ' Hudibras ' was so familiar to him, that he was at no loss in
using any part of it on any occasion. While he was at college,
if it was known he would be present at any public dinner, the
table was sure to be crowded with company, who were delighted
with the singularity of his conversation and his witty sayings.
But as ' evil communications corrupt good manners,' so Berridge speedily caught the spirit of his company, and drank in
the Socinian scheme of religion to such a degree that he lost
all his serious impressions, and discontinued private prayer for
the space of ten years, a few intervals excepted ! In these intervals he would weep bitterly, reflecting on his sad state of
mind compared with what it was when he first came to the
University ; and he would often say to a fellow-student, afterwards an eminent clergyman, ' Oh that it were with me as in
years past !' "

This part of Berridge's history is indeed a melancholy picture.
It is the more so when we remember that it was during this
period of his life that he must have taken holy orders as a Fellow of Clare Hall, and professed that he was " inwardly moved
by the Holy Ghost" to take upon him the office of a minister !
He was probably ordained by the Bishop of Ely. How utterly
unfit he was for the ministerial office, we may see at a glance
from the account given of him by Whittingham. Yet it is a
sorrowful fact, I fear, that the case of Berridge has only been
that of thousands. No earthly condition appears to be so
deadening to a man's soul as the position of a resident Fellow
of a college, and the society of a Common room at Oxford or
Cambridge. If Berridge fell for a season before the influences
brought to bear upon his soul at Clare Hall, we must in justice
remember that he was exposed to extraordinary temptations.
How hardly shall resident Fellows of colleges enter the kingdom
of God ! It was a miracle of grace that he was not cast away for
ever, and did not sink beneath the waters, never to rise again.

In the year 1749 it pleased God to awaken his conscience once more, and to revive within him his old religious impressions. In that year, after eleven years of apparent idleness, he began to feel a desire to do something as a clergyman, and accepted the curacy of Stapleford, near Cambridge. At this period, it will be remembered, he was thirty-three years old, and thus had lost no less than ten valuable years of time.

Berridge entered on his duties as curate of Stapleford with great zeal, and a sincere desire to do good, and served his church regularly from college for no less than six years. He took great pains with his parishioners, and pressed upon them very earnestly the importance of sanctification, but without producing the slightest effect on their lives. His preaching, even at this time, was striking, plain, and attractive. His life was moral, upright, and correct. His diligence as a pastor was undeniable. Yet his ministry, throughout these six years, was entirely without fruit, to his own great annoyance and mortification. The fact was, that up to this time he was utterly ignorant of the gospel. He did not really know what message he had to deliver to his hearers. He knew nothing aright of Christ crucified, of justification by faith in his blood, of salvation by grace, of the complete present forgiveness of all who believe, and of the absolute necessity of coming to Christ as our Saviour, as the very first step towards heaven. At present these blessed truths were hidden from the Fellow of Clare College, and he could tell his people nothing about them. No wonder that he did no good! If he wounded, he could not heal. If he pulled down, he could not build up. If he showed his flock that they were wrong, he had no idea what could set them right. In short, his Christianity was like a solar system without the sun, and of course did no good to his congregation. There can be no doubt that he learned lessons as curate of Stapleford which he remembered to the last day of his life. He learned the thorough uselessness of a ministry, however zealous, in which

Christ has not his rightful office, and faith has not its rightful place. But we may well believe that the clever and accomplished Fellow of Clare learned his lesson with much humiliation and with many bitter tears.

In the year 1755 Berridge was presented by his college to the vicarage of Everton, in Bedfordshire. He took up his residence at once on his living, and never moved again till he was called away to a better world, after holding his cure for no less than thirty-eight years. It was at this place that his eyes were opened to the whole truth as it is in Jesus, and the whole tone of his ministry was changed. It was here that he first found out the enormous mistakes of which he had been guilty as a teacher of others, and began to preach in a scriptural manner the real gospel of Christ. The circumstances under which this change took place are so well described by his biographer Whittingham, that I think it best to give the account in his own words.

" At Everton," he says, " Mr. Berridge at first pressed sanctification and regeneration on his hearers as strenuously as he had at Stapleford, but with as little success. Nor was it to be wondered at, as his preaching rather tended to make them trust in themselves as righteous, than to depend on Christ for the remission of sins. Having continued for two years in this unsuccessful mode of preaching, and his desire to do good continually increasing, he began to be discouraged. A doubt arose in his mind whether he was right himself, and preached as he ought to do. This suggestion he rejected for some time with disdain, supposing the advantages of education, which he had improved to a high degree, could not have left him ignorant of the best mode of instructing his people. This happened about Christmas 1757. But not being able to repel these secret misgivings, his mind was brought into a state of embarrassment and distress to which hitherto he had been a stranger. However, this had the happy effect of making him cry mightily to

God for direction. The constant language of his heart was this—'Lord, if I am right, keep me so; if I am not right, make me so, and lead me to the knowledge of the truth as it is in Jesus.'—After the incessant repetition of this child-like prayer, it is no wonder that God should lend a gracious ear, and return him an answer, which he did almost two days after. As he sat one morning musing on a text of Scripture, the following words seemed to dart into his mind like a voice from heaven—'Cease from thine own works; only believe.' At once the scales seemed to fall from his eyes, and he perceived the application. He saw the rock on which he had been splitting for many years, by endeavouring to blend the Law and the Gospel, and to unite Christ's righteousness with his own. Immediately he began to think on the words 'faith' and 'believe,' and looking into his Concordance, found them very frequently used. This surprised him so much, that he instantly resolved to preach Jesus Christ and salvation by faith. He therefore composed several sermons of this description, and addressed his hearers in a manner very unusual, and far more pointed than before.

"God very soon began to bless this new style of ministry. After he had preached in this strain two or three Sabbaths, and was wondering whether he was yet right, as he had perceived no better effect from them than from his former discourses, one of his parishioners came to inquire for him. Being introduced, he said, 'Well, Sarah, what is the matter?'—'Matter!' she replied; 'why, I don't know what is the matter. Those new sermons! I find we are all to be lost now. I can neither eat, drink, nor sleep. I don't know what is to become of me.' The same week came two or three more on a like errand. It is easy to conceive what relief these visits must have afforded his mind in a state of anxiety and suspense. So confirmed was he thereby in the persuasion that his late impressions were from God, that he determined in future to know nothing but Jesus Christ and him crucified. He was deeply humbled that he should have spent so many years of his life to no better purpose than to confirm his hearers in their ignorance. He therefore immediately burned all his old sermons, and shed tears of joy over their destruction. This circumstance aroused the neighbourhood. His church soon became crowded with hearers, and God gave testimony to the word of his grace in the frequent conviction and conversion of sinners."

In describing this period of his life, Berridge says himself, in a letter to a friend: "I preached up sanctification by the works of the law very earnestly for six years in Stapleford, and never brought one soul to Christ. I did the same at Everton for two years, without any success at all. But as soon as I preached Jesus Christ, and faith in his blood, then believers were added to the Church continually; then people flocked from all parts to hear the glorious sound of the gospel; some coming six miles, others eight, and others ten. And what is the reason why my ministry was not blessed, when I preached up salvation partly by faith and partly by works? It is because this doctrine is not of God, and because he will prosper no ministers but such as preach salvation in his own appointed way; namely, by faith in Jesus Christ."

I pity the man who can read such an account as this without interest. If ever there was a case in which we can see clearly the hand of the Holy Spirit, it was this case of John Berridge. Here is a clergyman in the prime of bodily and mental vigour, suddenly changed from being a preacher of morality into a preacher of Christ's gospel. He is not a mere boy, but a man of forty-two years of age, well read, of acknowledged literary attainments, and the very reverse of a fool. He is not persuaded and influenced by any living person, and seems to have no earthly friend or adviser. Yet all of a sudden he begins to preach the very same doctrine as Whitefield, Wesley, Grimshaw, Romaine, and Rowlands, and with the same effects. One account alone can be given of the whole affair. It was the finger of God. Flesh and blood did not reveal the truth to Berridge, but our Father who is in heaven. Well would it be for the churches if there were more cases like his!

Once enlightened by the Holy Ghost and brought into the liberty of God's children, John Berridge made rapid advances both in preaching and practice. He was not a man to do anything by halves, whether converted or unconverted; and as soon as he was converted he threw himself with constitutional energy into his Master's service, with all his might, and soul, and strength. The learned Fellow of Clare soon ceased to preach written sermons, having discovered, by a providential accident, that he possessed the happy gift of preaching without book. His next step was to commence preaching outside his own parish, all over the district in which he lived, like a missionary. This he began on June 22, 1758. One of the first-fruits of this itinerant aggression was a clergyman named Hicks, rector of Wrestlingworth, near Everton, who afterwards became a very useful man, and a faithful labourer in Christ's vineyard. His third and crowning step was to commence preaching out of doors. This he began doing on May 14, 1759, and describes it himself in a letter quoted by Whittingham :— " On Monday week, Mr. Hicks accompanied me to Meldred. On the way we called at a farm-house. After dinner, I went into the yard, and seeing nearly a hundred and fifty people, I called for a table, and preached for the first time in the open air. We then went to Meldred, where I preached in a field to about four thousand people. In the morning, at five, Mr. Hicks preached in the same field to about a thousand. Here the presence of the Lord was wonderfully among us; and I trust, beside many that were slightly wounded, nearly thirty received heart-felt conviction."

Berridge had now climbed to the top of the tree as an evangelist. He preached the pure gospel; he preached extempore; he preached anywhere and everywhere where he could get hearers; he preached, like his Master, in the open air, if need required. We cannot therefore wonder that he was soon publicly known as a fellow-labourer with Whitefield, Wesley, Grimshaw, and Romaine, and, as a popular preacher, little inferior to any of these great men. His life from this time forth, with little intermission, for more than thirty years, was spent in preaching the gospel. To this work he gave himself wholly. In season and out of season, out of doors or in doors, in churches or in barns, in streets or in fields, in his parish or out of his parish, the old Fellow of Clare College was constantly telling the story of the Cross, and exhorting sinners to repent, believe, and be saved. He became acquainted with Lady Huntingdon, John Thornton, John Wesley, Fletcher, John Newton, and other eminent Christians of his day, and kept up friendly intercourse with them. He went to London sometimes in the winter, and preached occasionally in the well-known Tabernacle in Tottenham Court Road. But, as a general rule, he seldom went far from his own district, and rarely went into society. He found enough, and more than enough, to do in meeting the spiritual wants of congregations within that district, and seldom went to regions beyond.

The extent of his labours was prodigious. He used to preach in every part of Bedfordshire, Cambridgeshire, and Huntingdonshire, and in many parts of Hertfordshire, Essex, and Suffolk.* He would often preach twelve times, and ride a hundred miles in a week. Nor was he content with preaching. He watched carefully over those who were aroused by his sermons, and provided lay evangelists to look after them when he left them. Some of these evangelists appear to have been nothing but humble labouring men, for whose maintenance he had to provide out of his own pocket. But expenses like these

---

* It is a singular fact that I can find no record of Berridge ever having visited Nottinghamshire, or preached in his own county. I can only suppose that his relatives did not sympathize with him, and gave him no encouragement to come among them.

he cheerfully defrayed out of his own purse as long as he had a shilling to spare, counting it an honour to spend his income in furthering Christ's gospel. When he had nothing of his own to give, he would ask help of the well-known John Thornton, the London merchant; and to the honour of that good man he never seems to have asked in vain.

The spiritual effects that were produced by his preaching were immense. In fact, a singular blessing appears to have attended his ministry from the very moment that he began to preach the gospel. When we find that he was the means of awakening no less than four thousand persons in one single year, we may have some little idea of the good that he did in his district by his thirty years' preaching. In calculations like these, allowance must always be made for a vast amount of exaggeration, and for an equally vast amount of excitement and false profession. Still, after every reasonable deduction has been made, there is no just ground for doubting that Berridge was the means of doing good to thousands of souls. Wherever he went he produced some impression. Some were reclaimed from sin, some were awakened and convinced, and some were thoroughly converted to God. If this is not doing good, there is no such thing as doing good in the world. Spiritual work done in rural parishes is, perhaps, less "seen of men" than any work within the province of the Christian ministry. The work that Berridge did among farmers and labourers had few to proclaim and chronicle it. But I strongly suspect the last day will prove that he was a man who seldom preached in vain. How few there are of whom this can be said!

It is undeniable that at certain periods of Berridge's ministry very curious physical effects were produced on those who were aroused by his preaching. Some of his hearers cried out aloud hysterically, some were thrown into strong convulsions, and some fell into a kind of trance or catalepsy, which lasted a long time. These physical effects were carefully noticed by John

Wesley and others who witnessed them, and certainly tended to bring discredit on the gospel, and to prejudice worldly people. But it is only fair to Berridge to say, that he never encouraged these demonstrations, and certainly did not regard them as a necessary mark of conversion. That such phenomena will sometimes appear in cases of strong religious excitement—that they are peculiarly catching and infectious, especially among young women—that even the most scientific medical men are greatly puzzled to explain them,—all these are facts which have been thoroughly established within the last twenty years during the Irish revival. To attempt to depreciate Berridge's usefulness because of these things, is simply ridiculous. Whatever the faults of the vicar of Everton were, he certainly does not seem to have favoured fanaticism. That he was perplexed by the physical demonstrations I have described, and at first attached more value to them than they deserved, is the utmost that can be said against him on the subject. But, after all, the same may be said of many calm and sober-minded witnesses who saw the Ulster revival in 1858. In short, the whole subject, like demoniacal possession, is a very deep and mysterious one, and there we must be content to leave it. But a minister ought certainly not to be put down as a fanatic because people go into convulsions under his preaching

It is needless to tell any Christian that Berridge was fiercely persecuted by the world throughout the whole period of his ministry. No name was too bad to be given to him. No means were left untried by his enemies to stop him in his useful career. Foremost, of course, among his persecutors were the unconverted clergy of Bedfordshire, Huntingdonshire, and Cambridgeshire, who, like the dog in the manger, would neither do good themselves nor let any one else do it for them. But, singularly enough, no weapon forged against the vicar of Everton seemed to prosper. Like Grimshaw at Haworth, there was an invisible wall of protection around him, which his bitterest foes could not pull down.   Irregular as his proceedings undoubtedly were, offensive as they necessarily must have been to the idle, worldly clergymen who lived near him, they appeared unable to lay hold upon him and shut his mouth, from one end of his ministry to the other.   From some extraordinary cause which we cannot now explain, the itinerant evangelist of Everton was never stopped by his persecutors for a single day!   So true is the Word of God: "When a man's ways please the Lord, he maketh even his enemies to be at peace with him."

One special interposition of God in order to protect Berridge from his enemies was so remarkable that it deserves particular notice.   It derives a peculiar interest from the fact that the record of it has been handed down in the good man's own words.   He says :—

"Soon after I began to preach the gospel of Christ at Everton, the church was filled from the villages around us, and the neighbouring clergy felt themselves hurt at their churches being deserted.   A person of my own parish, too, was much offended. He did not like to see so many strangers, and be so incommoded.   Between them both, it was resolved, if possible, to turn me out of my living.   For this purpose, they complained of me to the bishop of the diocese, that I had preached out of my parish.   I was soon after sent for by the bishop; I did not much like my errand, but I went.   When I arrived, the bishop accosted me in a very abrupt manner: 'Well, Berridge, they tell me you go about preaching out of your own parish.   Did I institute you to the livings of A——y, or E——n, or P——n?' —'No, my lord,' said I; 'neither do I claim any of these livings.   The clergymen enjoy them undisturbed by me.'— 'Well, but you go and preach there, which you have no right to do!'—'It is true, my lord, I was one day at E——n, and there were a few poor people assembled together, and I admonished them to repent of their sins, and to believe in the Lord Jesus Christ for the salvation of their souls; and I remember seeing five or six clergymen that day, my lord, all out of their own parishes upon E——n bowling-green.'—' Poh!' said his lordship ; ' I tell you, you have no right to preach out of your own parish ; and if you do not desist from it, you will very likely be sent to Huntingdon gaol.'—' As to that, my lord,' said I, ' I have no greater liking to Huntingdon gaol than other people ; but I had rather go thither with a good conscience, than live at my liberty without one.'—Here his lordship looked very hard at me, and very gravely assured me ' that I was beside myself, and that in a few months' time I should either be better or worse.'—' Then,' said I, ' my lord, you may make yourself quite happy in this business ; for if I should be better, you suppose I should desist from this practice of my own accord ; and if worse, you need not send me to Huntingdon gaol, as I shall be provided with an accommodation in Bedlam.'—His lordship now changed his mode of attack. Instead of threatening, he began to entreat. ' Berridge,' said he, ' you know I have long been your friend, and I wish to be so still. I am continually teazed with the complaints of the clergymen around you. Only assure me that you will keep to your own parish ; you may do as you please there. I have but little time to live ; do not bring down my gray hairs with sorrow to the grave.'—At this instant two gentlemen were announced, who desired to speak with his lordship. ' Berridge,' said he, ' go to your inn, and come again at such an hour, and dine with me.'—I went, and, on entering a private room, fell immediately upon my knees. I could bear threatening, but knew not how to withstand entreaty, especially the entreaty of a respectable old man.

" At the appointed time I returned. At dinner I was treated with great respect. The two gentlemen also dined with us. I found they had been informed who I was, as they sometimes cast their eyes towards me, in some such manner as one would glance at a monster. After dinner his lordship took me into the garden. ' Well, Berridge,' said he, ' have you considered of my request ?'—' I have, my lord,' said I, ' and have been upon my knees concerning it.'—' Well, and will you promise me that you will preach no more out of your own parish ?'—' It would afford me great pleasure,' said I, ' to comply with your lordship's request, if I could do it with a good conscience. I am satisfied the Lord has blessed my labours of this kind, and I dare not desist.'—' A good conscience !' said his lordship ; ' do you not know that it is contrary to the canons of the Church ?'—' There is one canon, my lord,' I replied, ' which says, " Go preach the gospel to every creature." '—' But why should you wish to inter-fere with the charge of other men ? One man cannot preach the gospel to all the world '—' If they would preach the gospel themselves,' said I, ' there would be no need for my preaching it to their people ; but, as they do not, I cannot desist.'—His lordship then parted with me in some displeasure. I returned home not knowing what would befall me, but thankful to God that I had preserved a conscience void of offence.

" I took no measures for my own preservation ; but Divine Providence worked for me in a way I never expected. When I was at Clare Hall I was particularly acquainted with a certain Fellow of that college, and we were both on terms of intimacy with Mr. Pitt, the late Lord Chatham, who was at that time also at the university. This Fellow of Clare Hall, when I began to preach the gospel, became my enemy, and did me some injury. At length, however, when he heard that I was likely to come into trouble, and to be turned out of my living at Everton, his heart relented. He began to think within himself, ' We shall ruin this poor fellow among us.' This was just about the time that I was sent for by the bishop. Of his own accord he writes a letter to Mr. Pitt, saying nothing about my Methodism, but to this effect :— Our old friend Berridge has got a living in Bedfordshire, and I am told there is one of his neighbours who gives him a great deal of trouble, has accused him to the bishop, and, it is said, will turn him out of his living. I wish you would contrive to stop his proceedings.' Mr. Pitt was then a young man, and, not desiring to apply himself to the bishop, spoke to a certain nobleman about it to whom the bishop was indebted for his promotion. This nobleman made it his business, within a few days, to see the bishop, who was then in London. ' My lord,' he said, ' I am informed you have a very honest fellow named Berridge in your diocese, and that he has been ill-treated by a litigious neighbour. I hear he has accused him to your lordship, and wishes to turn him out of his living. You would oblige me, my lord, if you would take no notice of this person, and not suffer the honest man to be interrupted.'—The bishop was astonished, and could not imagine in what manner things could thus have got round. It would not do, however, to object; he was obliged to bow compliance, and so I continued ever after uninterrupted in my sphere of action."

Great as Berridge's labours were, they do not appear to have materially affected his bodily health. He seems to have possessed one of those iron constitutions, which nothing but old age can quite break down. He lived to be seventy-seven; and though in his latter years a feeble old man, and very solitary, without wife, sister, or brother, to minister to him, he was mercifully kept in great peace to the last. Henry Owen's account of a visit to him in 1792, the year before he died, is very touching and interesting. He says, " I lately visited my dear brother Berridge. His sight is very dim, his ears can scarcely hear, and his faculties are fast decaying, so that, if he continues any time, he may outlive the use of them. But in this ruin of his earthly tabernacle it is surprising to see the joy in his countenance, and the lively hope with which he looks for the day of his dissolution. In his prayer with me and my children, we were much affected by his commending himself to the Lord, as quite *alone*, not able to read or hear, or do anything. But he said, ' Lord, if I have thy presence and love, *that* sufficeth.' "

Berridge died at Everton vicarage on January 22nd, 1793.

For some little time the infirmities natural to his years had prevented him doing much public work. But he was most mercifully spared any long season of pain and disease, and died after only a few days' illness, the weary wheels of life not so much broken by sickness as worn out and standing still. His frame of mind during his last days was very comfortable. He spoke but little, but what he did say was in terms of gratitude for the rich support he experienced in the prospect of eternity. He felt the stability of the rock on which he had been long resting his hopes of heaven; and while speaking of the excellency and preciousness of the Saviour, he said in an emphatic manner, "What should I do now if I had no better foundation to rest upon than what Dr. Priestley the Socinian points out?"

He was buried in Everton churchyard on the following Sunday, amidst an immense concourse of people assembled from all parts of the country.

Six clergymen, "devout men, carried him to his grave, and made great lamentation over him." A funeral sermon was then preached by the well-known Charles Simeon, from 2 Tim. iv. 7, 8, a text admirably well suited to the occasion. Old Henry Venn of Yelling, his son John Venn, and Charles Simeon, were among the few neighbours with whom the good old Vicar of Everton felt entire sympathy; and his letters give frequent evidence of the value he set on them, and the pleasure he took in their society.

Berridge's tomb is placed on the north-east side of Everton churchyard, where formerly those only were buried who had come to some dishonourable end. But before he died he frequently said that his remains should be laid in that part of the churchyard, which, he said with characteristic pleasantry, might be "a means of consecrating it." His epitaph, composed by himself, is so remarkable in its way, that I think it needless to make any excuse for giving it entire. It is inscribed on the south side of his tomb, and at the time of his death required

size that we cannot understand how they are used. There are beasts, like the Mandril baboon, marked with such brilliant blue and red colours that we are fairly at a loss to explain their object. Yet they are all the work of an all-wise Creator. Our Father made them all. Not one of them could have been made better. Each and all, we need not doubt, is perfectly adapted for the place in creation which it was intended to fill.

Thoughts such as these come across my mind when I survey the character of John Berridge, Vicar of Everton. Never, probably, did the grace of God dwell in a vessel of such singularly tempered clay. There was a strange vein of quaintness in his mental constitution, which seemed to crop out and bubble up on every occasion. He was continually saying odd things, and employing odd illustrations to convey his meaning. I do not for a moment think that he was an intentional " joker of jokes," or really wished to set people laughing ; but his mind was so peculiarly compounded that he could not help putting things in a ludicrous way. It was in vain that his friends warned him of his besetting sin, and entreated him to lay it aside. The poor old evangelist acknowledged his infirmity, and pleaded that he was born with a fool's cap on, and that a fool's cap was not so easily put off as a night-cap. Hard as he strove to keep down his enemy, it was never completely subdued. " Odd things," he said, " break from me as abruptly as croaking from a raven." The habit of quaintness was bone of his bones and flesh of his flesh. It stuck to him as closely as his skin, and never left him until he was laid in the grave. Quaintly he thought and quaintly he spoke, quaintly he preached and quaintly he wrote, quaint he lived and quaint he died. In this respect I fully concede he was a beacon to be avoided, and not an example to be followed.

While, however, I admit that Berridge was painfully quaint and odd, I do not at all admit the justice of Southey's remark, that he was " buffoon as well as fanatic." This judgment is unwarrantably severe. The twenty-six Outlines of Sermons, which his biographer has published, contain abundant proof that the Vicar of Everton never deliberately prepared buffoonery for the pulpit. On the contrary, with one or two trifling exceptions, there is a "conspicuous absence" of anything that could create a smile. The reader of these Outlines will find them very simple, very full of Scripture, very spiritual, and very evangelical. He will find in them, no doubt, nothing very deep or profound, nothing very striking or original; though he will always find man painted in his true colours and put in his right place, and Christ magnified, glorified, and exalted in every page. But if he expects to find anything ludicrous, jocose, or absurd, any quaint anecdotes, or ridiculous illustrations, he will be utterly and entirely disappointed. I should like those who decry poor Berridge as a mere pulpit jester, to read over, with attention, the hundred pages in which Whittingham has recorded the remains of the good man's preaching. If they do not alter their opinion very materially, I shall be much surprised. They will probably agree with me that if the composer of such Outlines of Sermons was a "buffoon and a fanatic," it would do no harm to the Church of England if she had a few more such "buffoons and fanatics" among her clergy.

In justice to Berridge, I give it as my own deliberate opinion, that whatever quaintness there was in his sermons, was strictly confined to the extemporaneous part of them, or to the illustrations which struck him on the spur of the moment. At any rate, there is little or no trace of it in his written Outlines. A man like the old Fellow of Clare Hall, of great natural genius, and a keen sense of the ludicrous, with his mind full of Aristophanes and Hudibras, might surely be lightly judged if he sometimes said odd things in his sermons. The excitement of seeing a great multitude hanging on his lips was doubtless great. The anxiety to say what would arrest and arouse was, doubtless, overwhelming. What wonder if he sometimes broke away from the outlines of his sermons, and said things in the heat of his zeal which in calmer moments he might condemn? One thing, at any rate, is very clear from the remains of his preaching, and that is, that he was a methodical preacher. If he did occasionally break over the fence, and let fall odd sayings, he managed to get back into the road, and was sooner or later marching along in good order.

After all, I venture to think that men are often far too squeamish in their judgment of preachers. Great allowance ought always to be made for those who, like Berridge, are constantly preaching in rural districts to uneducated congregations. None but those who have preached for many years in such districts can have the least idea of the preacher's difficulties. There is a gulf between his mind and the minds of his hearers of which few have the smallest conception. How to get at their understandings, how to make them comprehend what we are saying, is the grand problem that has to be solved. Their standard of taste is not that of Oxford or Cambridge. Things that sound coarse and vulgar and unrefined to a trained mind and a well educated ear, do not sound so to them. Their first and foremost want is to understand what the preacher is talking about; and he that can make poor farmers and labourers understand what he says is a preacher deserving of the highest praise. They care nothing for fine abstract ideas and rhetorical figures. They only care to hear what they can *carry away.* Now this, I suspect, was precisely the thing that Berridge never forgot. His grand aim was to make his hearers understand, and to attain that aim he sacrificed everything. If he made them smile, he also made them weep. If he excited them, he did not let them go to sleep. If he broke the rules of taste, and made men laugh, he also succeeded in breaking hard hearts, and making them repent. All honour be to him for his boldness! Better a thousand times for men to smile and be converted, than to look stiff, and grave, and sleepy in their pews, and remain dead in trespasses and sins. I do not defend Berridge's escapades and transgressions of good taste. I do not recommend him as a model to young preachers. I only say that those who run him down and depreciate him because of his quaintness, would do well to remember that he did what many do not—he awakened and converted souls. Thousands of correct, and smooth, and prim, and proper clergymen are creeping through this world, who never broke a canon of taste in the pulpit, never told an anecdote, never used a vulgar illustration, and never raised a smile. They have their reward! Their educated friends and relations admire them, and the world praises them. But they never prick a conscience, never frighten a sinner, never build up a saint, never pull down a single stone of the devil's kingdom—never save a soul. Give me the man who, like Berridge, may commit many mistakes, and offend many scrupulous ears, but yet reaches hearts, and helps to fill heaven.

Those who wish to form a correct idea of the singularly quaint workings of Berridge's mind, must turn from the Outlines of his Sermons to his other literary remains. These remains consist of a collection of hymns called "Zion's Songs," a prose work entitled "The Christian World Unmasked," and a selection of private letters to friends. The hymns I shall leave alone. The Vicar of Everton was no more a poet than Cicero or Julius Cæsar; and although the doctrine of his hymns is very sound, poetry of them is very poor, while the ideas they occasionally present are painfully ludicrous. The "Christian World Unmasked" is a dialogue between two imaginary characters about the way of salvation, and contains much that is pointed and clear; but it is written throughout in such a very unrefined style, that it is not likely to be extensively useful. The letters to private friends are excellent, and are worth all the rest of Whittingham's volume put together. From these and the "Christian World" I will now select a few specimens of

Berridge's quaintness. I have spoken a good deal about it, and it is only just and fair to let the reader see what it was like.

Let us hear how Berridge speaks of human nature: "Nature lost her legs in Paradise, and has not found them since; nor has she any will to come to Jesus. The way is steep and narrow, full of self-denials, crowded up with stumbling-blocks: she cannot like it; and when she does come, it is with huge complaining. Moses is obliged to flog her tightly, and make her heart ache, before she casts a weeping look on Jesus. Once she doated on this Jewish lawgiver, was fairly wedded to him, and sought to please him by her works—and he seemed a kindly husband; but now, he grows so grim a tyrant, there is no bearing of him. When she takes a wrong step, his mouth is always full of cursing, and his resentment so implacable, no weeping will appease him, nor promise of amendment." *

Let us hear Berridge about the "Whole Duty of Man:" "The 'Whole Duty of Man' was sent abroad with a good intent, but has failed of its purpose, as all such teaching ever will. Morality has not thriven since its publication; and never can thrive, unless founded wholly upon grace. The heathen, for want of this foundation, could do nothing. They spoke some noble truths, but spoke to men with withered hearts and loathing appetites. They were like way-posts, which show a road, but cannot help a cripple forward; and yet many of them preached higher morals than are often taught by their modern friends. In their way they were skilful fishermen, but fished without the gospel-bait, and could catch no fry. And after they had toiled long in vain, we take up their angle-rods, and dream of more success, though not possessed of half their skill. God has shown how little human wit and strength can do to compass reformation. Reason has explored the moral path,

* "Christian World," p. 292, Whittingham's Edition.

planted it with roses, and fenced it round with motives; but all in vain.*

Let us hear him again: "Men are rightly treated in the reading-desk, and called by their proper name of *miserable sinners.* But in the pulpit they are complimented on the dignity of their earthly, sensual, devilish natures, are flattered with a princely will and power to save themselves, and ornamented with a lusty seam of merit. Justification by faith, the jewel of the Gospel covenant, the groundwork of the Reformation, the glory of the British Church, is now derided as a poor old beggarly element, which may suit a negro or a convict, but will not save a lofty scribe nor a lewd gentleman. And the covenant of grace, though executed legally by Jesus, purchased by his life and death, written and sealed with his blood, is deemed of no value, till ratified by Moses. Paul declares no other foundation can we lay beside that which is laid, Christ Jesus. But men are growing wise above that which is written, and will have two foundations for their hopes. These are, fancied merit, added to the meritorious life and death of Christ. If an angel should visit our earth, and proclaim such a kind of gospel as is often hawked from the press and pulpit, though he preached morality with most seraphic power, and till his wings dropped off, he would never turn one soul to God, nor produce a single grain of true morality, arising from the love of God, and aiming only at his glory." †

Let us hear him again: "Once I went to Jesus as a coxcomb, and gave myself fine airs, fancying, if He were something, so was I; if He had merit, so had I. I used him as a healthy man will use a walking-staff—lean an ounce upon it, and vapour with it in the air. But now He is my whole crutch; no foot can stir a step without him. He is my all, as he ought to be if he will become my Saviour, and bids me cast all my care on him. My heart can have no rest unless it leans upon

* "Christian World," p. 335.   † "Christian World," p. 341.

him wholly; and then it feels his peace. But I am apt to leave my resting-place; and when I ramble from it, my breast will quickly brew up mischief. Some evil temper now begins to boil, or some care would fain perplex me, or some idle wants to please me, or some deadness or lightness creeps upon my spirit, and communion with my Saviour is withdrawn. When these thorns stick in my flesh, I do not try, as heretofore, to pick them out with my own needle; but I carry all my complaints to Jesus, casting every care on him. His office is to save, and mine to look to him for help. If evil tempers arise, I go to him as some demoniac. If deadness creeps upon me, I go as a paralytic. If dissipation comes, I go as a lunatic. If darkness clouds my face, I go as a Bartimeus. And when I pray, I always go as a leper, crying, as Isaiah did, Unclean, unclean." *

Let us hear what he says in a letter to John Newton, dated October 18, 1771 : " The foulest stain and highest absurdity in our nature is pride. And yet this base hedgehog so rolls himself up in his bristly coat, we can seldom get a sight of his claws. It is the root of unbelief. Men cannot submit to the righteousness of Christ, and pride cleaves to them like a pitched shirt to the skin, or like leprosy to the wall. No sharp culture of ploughing and harrowing will clear the ground of it. The foul weed will be sure to spring up again with the next kindly rain. This diabolical sin has brought more scourges on my back than anything else ; and it is of so insinuating a nature, that I know not how to part with it. I hate it, and love it ; I quarrel with it, and embrace it ; I dread it, and yet suffer it to lie in my bosom. It pleads a right, through the fall, to be a tenant for life; and has such a wonderful appetite, that it can feed kindly both on grace and garbage—will be as warm and snug in a cloister as a palace, and be as much delighted with a fine prayer as a foul oath."

Let us hear what he says in a letter to Samuel Wilkes, dated August 16, 1774: "Sitting closely on the beach is very sweet after a stormy voyage; but I fancy you will find it more difficult to walk closely with Jesus in a calm than a storm, in easy circumstances than in straits. A Christian never falls asleep in the fire or in the water, but grows drowsy in the sunshine. We love to nestle, but cannot make a nest in a hard bed. God has given you good abilities. This, of course, will make you respected by men of business, and tempt you at times to admire yourself, and thus bring a smart rod upon your back. Sharp genius, like a sharp knife, often makes a wrong gash, and cuts a finger instead of food. We scarcely know how to turn our backs on admiration, though it comes from the vain world; yet a kick from the world does believers less harm than a kiss. I apprehend a main part of your trial will lie here. When you are tempted to think gaudily of yourself, and spread your feathers like a peacock, remember that fine parts in themselves are like the fine wings of a butterfly, which garnish out the moth and grub beneath. Remember, too, that a fiend has sharper parts than the sharpest of us, and that one grain of godly grace is of more worth than a hundred thousand headsful of Attic wit, or of philosophic, theologic, or commercial science."

Let us hear what he writes to Lady Huntingdon about the marriage of ministers, on March 23, 1770: "Before I parted with honest G., I cautioned him much against petticoat snares. He has burnt his wings already. Sure he will not imitate a foolish gnat, and hover again about the candle? If he should fall into a sleeping-lap, like Samson, he will soon need a flannel night-cap, and a rusty chain to fix him down, like a chained Bible to the reading-desk. No trap so mischievous to the field-preacher as wedlock; and it is laid for him at every hedge corner. Matrimony has quite maimed poor Charles [Wesley], and might have spoiled John [Wesley] and George [Whitefield], if a wise Master had not graciously sent them a brace of ferrets. Dear George has now got his liberty again ; and he will escape well if he is not caught by another tenter-hook.   Eight or nine years ago, having been grievously tormented with house-keeping, I truly had thought of looking out for a Jezebel myself. But it seemed highly needful to ask advice of the Lord. So, kneeling down on my knees before a table, with a Bible between my hands, I besought the Lord to give me a direction."   I may add that Jeremiah xvi. 2 settled the question, to Berridge's satisfaction, in the negative.

In another letter he says : "A man may be constitutionally meek as the lamb, constitutionally kind as the spaniel, constitutionally cheerful as the lark, and constitutionally modest as the owl ; but these things are not sanctification.   No sweet, humble, heavenly tempers, no sanctifying graces, are found but from the cross."

In another letter he says : "A Smithfield fire would unite the sheep of Christ, and frighten the goats away ; but when the world ceases to persecute the flocks, they begin to fight each other.   Indeed, the worst part of the sheep is in his head, which is not half so good as a calf's head ; and with this they are ever butting at each other."

In another letter he says: "I told my brother Mr. Henry Venn he need not fear being hanged for sheep-stealing, while he only whistles the sheep into a better pasture, and meddles neither with the flock nor fleece.   And I am sure he cannot sink much lower in credit; for he has lost his character right honestly by preaching law and gospel without mincing.   The scoffing world makes no other distinction between him and me, than between Satan and Beelzebub.   We have both got tufted horns and cloven feet; only I am thought the more impudent devil of the two."

I leave the subject of John Berridge's quaintness here.   It would be easy to multiply quotations like those I have given;

but I have probably said enough to give my readers some idea of the strange workings of the good Vicar of Everton's mind. I do not pretend to defend his odd sayings. I fully admit that they were calculated to interfere with his usefulness. But, once for all, I must request my readers not to judge them too severely, and, above all, to beware of setting down the eccentric author of them as a ranting fool. Berridge, we may depend on it, was nothing of the kind. Quaint as his sayings were, a Christian reader will seldom fail to discern in them a deep vein of common sense, shrewdness, and sagacity. Odd and unrefined as his illustrations often were, they were just the kind of thing that arrests and keeps up the attention of rural hearers. Let us grant that he erred in an excess of *quaintness*, but let us not forget that hundreds of preachers err in an excess of correct *dulness*, and never do good to a single soul.

I should be sorry to leave on my reader's mind the impression that quaintness was the leading characteristic of the good Vicar of Everton. There were other prominent features in his character which were quite as remarkable as his quaintness, but which his detractors have found it convenient to forget. There were many grand and fine points about this old evangelist, which deserve to be had in remembrance, and which all who love pure and undefiled religion will know how to appreciate. I will briefly mention a few of them, and then draw my account of him to a conclusion.

Berridge was a man of *deep humility*. That queen of all the graces, which adorned Whitefield and Grimshaw so remarkably, was a prominent feature in his character. No man could be more sensible of his infirmities than he was, and no one could speak of himself more disparagingly than he did. He says, in 1773: "Ten years ago, I hoped to be something long before this time, and seemed in a promising way; but a nearer view of the spiritual wickedness in my heart, and of the spiritual demands of God's laws, has forced me daily to cry, 'O wretched man that I am! God be merciful to me a sinner!' I am now sinking from a poor something into a vile nothing; and wish to be nothing, that Christ may be all. I am creeping down the ladder from self-complacence to self-abhorrence; and the more I abhor myself, the more I must hate sin, which is the cause of that abhorrence."—"As the heart is more washed, we grow more sensible of its remaining defilement; just as we are more displeased with a single spot on a new coat, than with a hundred stains on an old one. The more wicked men grow, the less ashamed they are of themselves; and the more holy men grow, the more they learn to abhor themselves."

For another thing, Berridge was a man who *gloried in our Lord Jesus Christ*, and in all his preaching, speaking, and writing, delighted to make much of Him. He says, in one of his letters: "Once I was sensible of my lameness, but did not know that Christ was to be my whole strength as well as righteousness. I saw His blood could purge away the guilt of sin; but I thought I had some natural might against the power of sin. Accordingly, I laboured to cut away my own corruptions, and pray away my own will, but laboured in the fire. At length, God has shown me that John Berridge cannot drive the devil out of himself; but Jesus Christ, blessed be his name, must say to the Legion, 'Come out.' I see that faith alone can purify the heart as well as purify the conscience, and that Christ is worthy to be my all in everything, in wisdom, righteousness, sanctification, and redemption."

For another thing, Berridge was a man of *singular kindness and self-denial.* No man perhaps ever carried on Christ's work with more thoroughly disinterested views. Whether at home or abroad he was always giving, and never receiving, and went through all his immense labours gratuitously. Houses and barns were rented for preaching, lay-preachers maintained in all directions, and his own travelling expenses defrayed by himself. Whenever he preached in a cottage, he invariably left half-a-crown for the use of it; and, during his itinerancy, he actually spent £500 in this way alone. Cases of distress and suffering always met with munificent help from him. His whole income, both private and professional, was annually spent in doing good, and even his family plate was sold to buy clothes for his itinerant preachers. As to his own habits at home, they were simple in the extreme. To one who came to supply his pulpit (the Hon. and Rev. W. Shirley), when absent from home, he wrote the following quaint intimation: "You must eat what is set before you, and be thankful. I get hot victuals but *once a week* for myself, namely, on Saturday; but, because you are an Honourable man, I have ordered two hot joints to be got each week for you. Use what I have just as your own. I make no feasts, but save all I can, to give all I can. I have never yet been worth a groat at the year's end, nor desire it." As to his fare abroad, when itinerating in the eastern counties, he says in another letter: "I fear my weekly circuit would not suit a London or Bath divine. Long rides, and miry roads, in sharp weather! Cold houses to sit in, with very moderate fuel, and three or four children roaring or rocking about you! Coarse food, and meagre liquor! Lumpy beds to lie on and too short for the feet, with stiff blankets like boards for a covering! Rise at five in the morning to preach; at seven, breakfast on poor tea; at eight, mount a horse with boots never cleaned, and then ride home praising God for all mercies!"

For another thing, Berridge was a man of uncommon *shrewdness, good sense, and sagacity*. Never was there a more complete mistake than to suppose that he, any more than Romaine, was a mere ranting, weak-headed fanatic. A careful perusal of his remains will show them to be replete with deep, thoughtful, and far-sighted remarks. His criticism of Cowper's Poems, his letters about Lady Huntingdon's College at Trevecca, his well-balanced statements of some of the most disputed points in the Calvinistic controversy, and his sensible treatment of enthusiasts under his ministry, are excellent evidences of this feature in his character. I know few wiser and more comprehensive letters of advice to a young minister about a sermon than one (not dated) which Whittingham has inserted at the end of his collection. Among other things, he says: "When you open your commission, begin with laying open the innumerable corruptions of the hearts of your audience. Moses will lend you a knife, which may be often whetted at his grindstone. Lay open the universal sinfulness of men's natures, the darkness of the mind, the frowardness of the will, the fretfulness of the temper, and the earthliness and sensuality of the affections. Speak of the evil of sin in its nature, its rebellion against God as our Sovereign, ingratitude to God as our Lawgiver, and contempt both of his authority and love. Declare the evil of sin in its effects, bringing all our sicknesses, pains, and snares—all the evils we feel, and all the evils we fear."—" Lay open the spirituality of the law and its extent, reaching to every thought, word, and action, and declaring every transgression, whether by omission or commission, deserving of death. Declare man's utter helplessness to change his nature, or make his peace."—"When your hearers are deeply affected with these things, which is often seen by the hanging down of their heads, then preach Christ. Lay open the Saviour's almighty power to soften the hard heart and give it repentance, to bring pardon to the broken heart, a spirit of prayer to the prayerless heart, holiness to the filthy heart, and faith to the unbelieving heart. Let them know that all the treasures of grace are lodged in Jesus Christ for the use of the poor needy sinner, and that he is full of love as well as of power; turns no beggar from his gate, but receives all comers kindly; loves to bless them, and bestows all his blessings free. Here you must wave the gospel flag, and magnify the Saviour supremely. Speak it with a full mouth, that his blood can wash away the foulest sins, and his grace subdue the stoutest corruptions. Entreat the people to seek his grace, to seek it directly, to seek it diligently, to seek it constantly; and acquaint them that all who thus seek shall assuredly find the salvation of God."

For another thing, Berridge was a man of *extraordinary courage and boldness.* He was one of those who could say with David: "I will speak of thy testimonies before kings, and not be ashamed." In doing his Master's business, and delivering his Master's message, he was never stopped for a moment by fear of personal danger or regard for the opinion of the world. Neither bishops, squires, nor parsons had any terrors for him. At an early period of his evangelical ministry he took his line, and from that line he never swerved. The occasion of his first resolving never to be afraid is strikingly described in the following anecdote, which I take from the " Churchman's Monthly Penny Magazine " for 1852 :—

" In one of the villages in which he was known as a preacher of the new doctrines, which were then beginning to excite a great sensation in different spots in England, he was exposed, when passing through it, to the hootings and revilings of the mob to an extent which frequently chafed his excitable spirit. This village was composed nearly exclusively of a long, straggling street, and, as is to be seen in many similar hamlets in England and else-where, was surrounded on one side by a narrow lane, which, jutting off at one end, joined it again, by a much wider circuit than that made by the street, at the other. On one day in which Berridge was about to pass through this village, his spirit quailed within him, in anticipation of the rough reception he would certainly meet with from the bigoted inhabitants. He felt as if he could not encounter it, and accordingly turned into the narrow lane of which we have spoken just at the moment when a pig-driver of his acquaintance entered the street with his noisy charge. It was their hap, each pursuing his own course, to meet again at the farther end of the village, when the pig-driver, who not only knew Berridge, but knew his principles, and knew the truth, looked up in his face with a most peculiar expression, and said : ' *So you are ashamed on't.*'

" The saying went to his heart. ' Yes,' he said, ' I have been ashamed *on't;* I resolve, in the strength of God, to be ashamed of it no more, but henceforth to press after it, firm unto the end.' A resolution which, under-taken by a resolute mind in the fear of God, was, perhaps, never more faithfully carried out in the future progress of a long and devoted life."

Last, but not least, Berridge was a man of deep *acquaintance with Christian experience, and tender sympathy* with the people of God. Those who fancy that he was a rough, vulgar, ranting out-door preacher, always full of jests and jokes and high spirits, and always dwelling on elementary truths, know very little of the good man's character. Let them read the following letters carefully, and mark how the itinerant evangelist of Everton could write to his friends. The first of the three was written to a friend on the occasion of his wife's death, and will be found in Whittingham's volume. The other two have come to me from private hands, and have never been printed before:—

EVERTON, *March* 26, 1771.

"DEAR BROTHER,—Mr. W—— informs me of the loss of your dear wife. You once knew she was mortal; but she has now put off mortality, and is become immortal. Can this grieve you? Oh, that I was where she now is!—

'Safe landed on that peaceful shore,
Where pilgrims meet to part no more.'

She was once a mourning sinner in the wilderness, but she is now a glorified saint in Zion; the Lord is become her everlasting light—the days of her mourning are ended. Does this trouble you?—She was once afflicted with bodily pains and weakness, encompassed with cares, and harassed with a crowd of anxious, needless fears; but she has now arrived at her Father's house, and Jesus has wiped away all tears from her eyes, and freed her in a moment from all pains, cares, fears, and wants. And shall this affect you?— You have not lost your wife; she has only left you for a few moments—left an earthly husband to visit a heavenly Father—and expects your arrival there soon, to join the hallelujah for redeeming love. Are you still weeping?—Fie upon you, brother!—weeping because your wife can weep no more! weeping because she is happy, because she is joined to that assembly where all are kings and priests! weeping because she is daily feasted with heavenly manna, and hourly drinking new wine in her Father's kingdom! weeping because she is now where you would be, and long to be eternally! weeping because she is singing, and singing sweet anthems to her God and your God!—O shameful weeping! Jesus has fetched your bride triumphantly home to his kingdom, to draw your soul more ardently thither, he has broken up a cistern to bring you nearer, and keep you closer to the fountain; has caused a moment's separation, to divorce your affections from the creature; and has torn a wedding-string from your heart, to set it a-bleeding more freely, and panting more vehemently for Jesus. Hereafter you will see how gracious the Lord has been, in calling a beloved wife home, in order to betroth the husband more effectually to himself. Re member that the house of mourning becomes and befriends a sinner; that sorrow is a safe companion for a pilgrim, who walks much astray until his heart is well broken. May all your tears flow in a heavenly channel, and every sigh waft your soul to Jesus! May the God of all consolation comfort you through life, and in death afford you a triumphant entrance into his kingdom! So prays your friend and brother in the gospel of Christ,

"J. BERRIDGE."

"EVERTON, *Sept.* 14, 1773.

"DEAR SIR,—I received your kind letter, and thank you for it. You want nothing but an opened eye to see the glory of Christ's redemption; and he must give it, and will bestow it, when it is most for his glory and your advantage. Had you Daniel's holiness, Paul's zeal, John's love, Magdalen's repentance (and I wish you had them all), yet altogether they would give you no *title* to a pardon. You must at last receive it as a *ruined* sinner, even as the Cross-thief received it.

"No graces or services of your own can give you a right to pardon; you must come to Jesus for it, weary and heavy-laden; and if you are afflicted for sin, and desirous of being delivered from its guilt and power, no past iniquities in your life, nor present corruptions of your heart, will be a bar to pardoning mercy. If we are truly seeking salvation by Jesus, we shall be disposed, as we are really bound, to seek after holiness.

"But remember, though holiness is the *walk* to heaven, Christ is the *way* to God; and when you seek for pardon, you must go wholly out of your walk, be it good or bad, and look only to Him who is the way. You must look to him as a miserable sinner, justly condemned by his law, a proper brand for hell, and look to be plucked from the fire by rich and sovereign grace. You have just as much worthiness for a pardon as the Cross-thief had, which is none at all; and in your best estate you will never have any more. A pardon was freely given to him upon asking for it freely, and given instantly because no room was left for delays; and a pardon is as ready for you as for him, when you can ask for it as he did, with self-loathing and condemnation; but the proper *seasons* of bestowing the pardon are kept in Jesus' own hand. He makes his mercy manifest to the heart when it will most glorify his grace and benefit the sinner. Only continue asking for mercy; and seek it only through the blood of the cross, without any eye to your own worthiness, and that blood in due time will be sprinkled on your conscience, and you shall cry, Abba, Father.

"Present my kindest love to my dear brother Mr. Romaine. The Lord continue his life and usefulness. Kind respects and Christian salutation to Mrs. Olney. Grace and peace be with both, and with your affectionate and obliged servant. J. BERRIDGE."

"EVERTON, *Nov.* 7, 1786.

"DEAR SIR,—I received your kind letter, along with your present. I thank you for the present, as being a token of your respect, and attended, I find, with your daily prayers for me, which I value more than human presents. The Lord bless you, and lift up the light of his countenance upon you, and give you a sweet enjoyment of his peace.

"I have hitherto found that Christian people who live in the dark, fearing and doubting, yet waiting on God, have usually a very happy death. They are kept humble, hungering and praying, and the Lord clears up their evidences at length in a last sickness, if not before, and they go off with hallelujahs.

"From what I know of you, and from the account you give of yourself, I have no doubt of the safety of your state : yet rest not here, but seek further. Two things should be carefully attended to by all upright people—one is the evidence of the Word, the other is the evidence or witness of the Spirit. The Word says: 'All that believe are justified from all things' (Acts xiii. 39). I ask, then, do you not place your whole dependence on Jesus Christ for salvation? Do you not heartily accept of Jesus Christ in all his offices, and are you not daily seeking to him to teach you and rule you, as well as to pardon you? Then you are certainly a believer, and as such are justified in God's sight from all your sins, according to the plain declaration of God's Word. Let this encourage you to seek with confidence for the evidence of the Spirit, to proclaim that justification to your heart. The evidence of the Word is given to hold up the heart in a season of doubts and fears, and the evidence of the Spirit comes to scatter those fears. Remember also that salvation does not depend on the *strength* of faith, but the *reality* of it. In the gospels, Jesus often rebukes weak faith, but never rejects it. Weak faith brings but little comfort, yet is as much entitled to salvation as strong.

"I have had much of my nervous fever this summer ; never once stirred out of my parish, and never further in it than to my church ! Through mercy I am somewhat better ; and when alone, with a Bible before me, am composed and comfortable, yet scarce able to bear visits, so weak are my spirits. . . . Give my love to Mr. G——, and tell him from first to last he has been the friend of my heart. I send my kind respects to your partner. Grace and peace be with you both, and with your affectionate servant,

"JOHN BERRIDGE."

I close my account of the good old Vicar of Everton with one remark. The man who could write such letters as these is not one who ought to be lightly esteemed. John Berridge is a minister who has never been rightly valued on account of his one besetting infirmity. The one "dead fly in his ointment" has made the Church ignore his many gifts and graces. Yet he was a man of whom the world was not worthy. Good judges of men, such as John Thornton, Lady Huntingdon, Wesley, Venn, Fletcher, John Newton, Rowland Hill, Charles

Simeon, Jones of Creaton, were all agreed about him, and all held him in honour. Let us reform our judgment of the good man, and cast our prejudices aside. Whatever some may please to say, we may rest assured that there were few greater, better, holier, and more useful ministers a hundred years ago than old John Berridge.

IX.

Henry Venn and his Ministry.

CHAPTER I.

THE seventh spiritual hero of the last century to whom I wish to direct the attention of my readers, is one better known than several of his contemporaries. The man I mean is Henry Venn, for some time Vicar of Huddersfield, in Yorkshire, and afterwards Vicar of Yelling, in Huntingdonshire. He is the only English minister of the eighteenth century whom I consider worthy to be ranked with the six whose memoirs I have already put together — viz., Whitefield, Wesley, Grimshaw, Romaine, Rowlands, and Berridge. These seven men appear to me, in some respects, to stand alone in the religious history of England a hundred years ago. Beside them, no doubt, there were many others of eminent grace and gifts. But none attained to the degree of the first seven.

One reason why Henry Venn is better known than many of his day, is the excellence of the only biography of him. Few men certainly have been so fortunate in their biographers as the evangelical Vicar of Huddersfield. In the whole range of Christian memoirs, I know few volumes so truly valuable as the single volume of "Henry Venn's Life and Letters." I never take it down from my shelves without thinking of the words which our great poet puts in the mouth of Queen Katherine :—

> " After my death I wish no other herald,
> No other speaker of my living actions,
> To keep mine honour from corruption,
> But such an honest chronicler as——."
>
> *Henry VIII.*, Act iv. sc. 2.

In fact, almost the only fault I find with the book is one which is most rare in a biography—it is too short !

Another reason why Henry Venn's name is so well known to English evangelical Christians, is the happy circumstance that he left behind him children who followed him " even as he followed Christ." His son, and his son's sons, have all been thoroughly like-minded with him. For more than a century there has never been wanting a minister of his name within the pale of the Church of England, to preach the same doctrine which he preached in the pulpit of Huddersfield. The name of "Venn" has consequently never ceased to be before the public. When Whitefield and Wesley and Berridge were laid in their graves, they left no sons "to keep their name in remembrance," however numerous their spiritual children may have been. But the family-name of Venn has been so much in men's mouths for three generations, that there are few English Christians who are not acquainted with it.

While, however, I fully admit that Henry Venn's name is well known in this country, I cannot help thinking that there is much confusion in men's minds as to the period of his ministry, and the time when he died. Some, I know, are in the habit of speaking of him as a contemporary of Scott, and Cecil, and Simeon. Even a writer like Sir James Stephen, in an article contributed to the *Edinburgh Review*, speaks of him as the

" last of four evangelical fathers," of whom Scott, Newton, and Milner were the first three! All these ideas about Venn are totally inaccurate. The authors of them, I suspect, confound Henry Venn with his son John Venn of Clapham. Henry Venn belonged to an earlier generation, and was well known and popular long before Newton, or Scott, or Cecil, or Simeon, or Milner, were ever heard of. To class him with these good men is an entire mistake. His true place is with Whitefield, and Wesley, and Grimshaw, and Rowlands, and Romaine, and Berridge. These were the men by whose side he laboured. These were the men with whom he must be ranked. To clear up Henry Venn's true history, and to convey some correct information about the main facts of his life and ministry, is the object that I set before me in the present memoir. Once for all, I wish it to be understood that the men I undertake to write about in this work are men of the last century. The men of the present century are men that I purposely leave alone.

Henry Venn was born at Barnes, in Surrey, on the 2nd of March 1724—within twenty-one years of the birth of John Wesley. He was the descendant of a long line of clergymen, reaching downwards in unbroken succession from the time of the Reformation. William Venn died vicar of Otterton, Devonshire, in 1621. Richard Venn, his son, succeeded him at Otterton; and after suffering greatly for his steadfast adherence to the Church of England in the Commonwealth times, died quietly in possession of his living. After him, his son, Dennis Venn, died vicar of Holberton, in Devonshire, in 1691. And finally his son, Richard Venn, rector of St. Antholin's, in the City of London, was the father of the subject of this memoir. These facts are full of interest. At the present day the name of Venn has appeared for seven generations in the clergy list of the Church of England!

Henry Venn's father is said to have been " an exemplary and learned minister, very zealous for the interests of the Church of

England, and remarkable for great liberality towards the poor, and especially towards distressed clergymen." Little is known about him, except the fact that he was the son of a very strong minded mother, who said that "Richard should not go to school till he had learned to say ' No.'" He was once brought into much public notice, and incurred obloquy, on account of the opposition which he made, in conjunction with Bishop Gibson, to the appointment of Dr. Rundle to the Bishopric of Gloucester. The grounds of his objection were certain expressions which he had heard Dr. Rundle use, of a deistical tendency ; and the result of his opposition was, that Dr. Rundle was actually kept out of the see of Gloucester, and was obliged to content himself with the Irish bishopric of Derry.* When we remember what times they were when these things happened, and what kind of a man Dr. Rundle's patron, Sir Robert Walpole, was, it is impossible not to admire the courage and conscientiousness which Richard Venn displayed in the affair. He died at the early age of forty-eight, when his son Henry was only fifteen years old.

The facts recorded about Henry Venn, as a boy, are few, but interesting. They are enough to show that from his earliest childhood he was a "thorough" and decided character, and one who never did anything by halves. In fact, Dr. Gloucester Ridley was so struck with his energy of character when young, that he said, "This boy will go up Holborn, and either stop at Ely Place (then the London palace of the Bishop of Ely), or go on to Tyburn !" (the place where criminals were hanged.) The following three anecdotes will show what kind of a boy he was. I give them in his son's own words :—

"While he was yet a child, Sir Robert Walpole attempted to introduce more extensively the system of Excise. A violent

* It is only fair and just to the character of one long dead to say, that living descendants or connections of Dr. Rundle deny the correctness of the statement here made about his opinions. I can only say that my authority is Mr. Venn's biography.

opposition was excited, and the popular feeling ran strongly against the measure. Young Henry Venn caught the alarm, and could not sleep in his bed lest the Excise Bill should pass; and on the day when it was to be submitted to Parliament, his boyish zeal made him leave his father's house early, and wander through the streets, crying 'No Excise!' till the evening, when he returned home exhausted with fatigue, and with his voice totally lost by his patriotic exertions."

"A gentleman, who was reported to be an Arian, called one day upon his father. Young Henry Venn, then a mere child, came into the room, and with a grave countenance earnestly surveyed him. The gentleman, observing the notice which the child took of him, began to show him some civil attentions, but found all his friendly overtures sternly rejected. At length, upon his earnestly soliciting him to come to him, the boy indignantly replied, 'I will not come near you; for you are an Arian.'"

"As he adopted with all his heart the opinions which he imbibed, he early entertained a most vehement dislike of all Dissenters. It happened that a Dissenting minister's son, two or three years older than himself, lived in the same street in London with his father; and young Henry Venn, in his zeal for the Church, made no scruple to attack and fight the unfortunate Nonconformist whenever he met him. It was a curious circumstance, that, many years after, he became acquainted with this very individual, who was then a Dissenting minister. He frankly confessed that young Venn had been the terror of his youthful days, and acknowledged that he never dared leave his father's door till he had carefully looked on every side to see that this young champion of the Church was not in the street."

Henry Venn's education began at the age of twelve, in a school at Mortlake, near Barnes. From this school he was removed to one kept by a Mr. Croft, at Fulham, but only stayed there a few months. He left at his own request under very singular circumstances. He complained to his mother, as very few boys ever do, " that his master was too indulgent, and the discipline was not sufficiently strict." From Fulham he went to a school at Bristol, kept by Mr. Catcott, author of a work on the Deluge, and an excellent scholar, though a severe master. From thence he removed to a school kept by Dr. Pitman at Markgate Street, in Hertfordshire, and there finished his early education.

In June 1742, at the age of seventeen, Henry Venn entered St. John's College, Cambridge. He only continued a member of that house three months, as he removed to Jesus College in September, on obtaining a scholarship there, and remained on the books of Jesus for seven years. In the year 1745, he took the degree of B.A. In 1747, he was appointed by Dr. Battie, who had been a ward of his father's, to one of the university scholarships which he had just founded ; and in June the same year he was ordained deacon by Bishop Gibson, without a title, from the respect which the bishop bore to his father's memory. In 1749, he became M.A., and was elected Fellow of Queen's College. This was the last of the many steps and changes in his educational career. At this date his ministerial life begins; and although he held his fellowship until his marriage, in 1757, from this time he had little more close connection with Cambridge.

Henry Venn's ministerial life began in 1749, when he was twenty-five years old.* He first served the curacy of Barton, near Cambridge, and afterwards officiated for various friends, at Wadenhoe in Northamptonshire, and Little Hedingham in Essex, and other places of which I cannot find out the names. In 1750 he ceased to reside at Cambridge, and became curate of Mr. Langley, rector of St. Matthew, Friday Street, London, and West Horsley, near Guildford. Venn's duty was to serve

---

* By a comparison of dates it would appear that Henry Venn became a Fellow, was ordained, and took a curacy near Cambridge in the very same year that the famous John Berridge became curate of Stapleford, near Cambridge. But I can find no proof that they were friends at this time.

the church in London during part of the summer, and to reside the remainder of the year at Horsley. In this position he remained continuously for four years, until he became curate of Clapham in 1754.

I can find no evidence that Venn had any distinct theological views for some little time after he was ordained. In fact, he appears, like too many, to have taken on him the holy office of a minister without any adequate conception of its duties and responsibilities. It is clear that he was moral and conscientious, and had a high idea of the deportment suited to the clerical life. But it is equally clear that he knew nothing whatever of evangelical religion; and in aftertime he regarded his college days as " days of vanity and ignorance."

One thing, however, is very plain in Venn's early history—he was scrupulously honest and conscientious in acting up faithfully to anything which he was convinced was right. Indeed, he used often to say " that he owed the salvation of his soul to the resolute self-denial which he exercised, in following the dictates of conscience in a point which seemed itself of only small importance."

" The case," says his son, " was this : He was extremely fond of cricket, and was reckoned one of the best players in the university. In the week before he was ordained he played in a match between Surrey and All England, which excited great interest, and was attended by a very numerous body of spectators. When the game terminated in favour of the side on which he was playing, he threw down his bat, saying, ' Whoever wants a bat which has done me good service may take that, as I have no further occasion for it.' His friends inquiring the reason, he replied, ' Because I am to be ordained on Sunday; and I will never have it said of me, " Well struck, parson." ' To this resolution, notwithstanding the remonstrances of friends, he strictly adhered; and, though his health suffered by a sudden transition from a course of most violent exercise to a life of comparative inactivity, he never could be persuaded to play any more. From being faithful in a little, more grace was imparted to him."

" His first considerable religious impressions," adds his son, " arose from an expression in the form of prayer, which he had been accustomed to use daily, but, like most persons, without paying much attention to it—' That I may live to the glory of thy name.' The thought powerfully struck his mind, ' What is it to live to the glory of God? Do I live as I pray? What course of life ought I to pursue to glorify God?' After much reflection, he came to the conclusion that to live to God's glory required that he should live a life of piety and religion in a degree in which he had not yet lived ; and that he ought to be more strict in prayer, more diligent in reading the Scriptures and pious books, and more generally holy in his conduct. And, seeing the reasonableness of such a course of life, he showed his honesty and uprightness by immediately and steadily pursuing it. He set apart stated seasons for meditation and prayer, and kept a strict account of the manner in which he spent his time and regulated his conduct. I have heard him say that, at this period, he used to walk almost every evening in the cloisters of Trinity College while the great bell of St. Mary's was tolling at nine o'clock, and amidst the solemn tones of the bells, and in the stillness and darkness of the night, he would indulge in impressive reflections on death and judgment, heaven and hell."*

" In this frame of mind," his son continues, " Law's ' Serious Call to a Devout and Holy Life' was particularly useful to him. He read it repeatedly, with peculiar interest, and immediately began, with great sincerity, to frame his life according to the Christian model there delineated. He kept a diary of the state

---

* The close resemblance between Henry Venn's experience at Cambridge, and George Whitefield's at Oxford, cannot fail to strike any one who reads attentively the biographies of the two men

of his mind—a practice from which he derived great benefit, though not in the way he expected, for it chiefly made him better acquainted with his own deficiencies. He also allotted the hours of the day, as far as was consistent with the duties of his station, to particular acts of meditation and devotion. He kept frequent fasts; and was accustomed often to take solitary walks, in which his soul was engaged in prayer and communion with God. I have heard him mention, that in these retired walks in the meadow behind Jesus College he had such a view of the goodness, mercy, and glory of God, as elevated his soul above the world, and made him aspire toward God as his supreme good."

Such was the religious condition of Henry Venn's mind when he first began the active work of the Christian ministry. Earnest, zealous, moral, conscientious, and scrupulously determined to do his duty, he put his hand to the plough and went forward. At Barton he distributed religious tracts and conversed with the poor in such an affectionate manner, that some remembered him after an interval of thirty years. At Horsley he instructed many of the poor on the week-days at his own home. His family prayers were attended by thirty or forty poor neighbours, and the number of communicants increased from twelve to sixty. In fact, the neighbouring clergy began to regard him as an enthusiast and a Methodist. But his zeal, unhappily, was so far entirely without knowledge. He knew nothing whatever of the real gospel of Christ, and, of course, could tell his hearers nothing about it. The consequence was, that for nearly four years of his ministerial life his labours were in vain.

Henry Venn's four years at Horsley, however, were by no means thrown away. If he did little good to others, he certainly learned lessons there of lasting benefit to his soul. The solitude and seclusion of his position gave him abundant time for reading, meditation, and prayer, and in the honest use of such means as he had, God was graciously pleased to show him more light, and to lead him onward towards the full knowledge of the gospel. Little by little he began to find out that "Law's" divinity was very defective, and that his favourite author did not give sufficient honour to Christ. Little by little he began to discover that he was, in reality, trying to "work out a righteousness" of his own, while, in truth, he had nothing to boast of; and that, with all his straining after perfection, he was nothing better than a poor weak sinner. Little by little he began to see that true Christianity was a scheme providing for man's wants as a ruined, fallen, and corrupt creature; and that the root of all vital religion is faith in the blood and righteousness and mediation and mercy of a Divine Saviour—Christ the Lord. The scales began to fall from his eyes. The tone of his preaching began sensibly to alter. And though, when he left Horsley for Clapham he had not even yet attained full light, it is perfectly evident that he went out of the parish in a totally different state of mind from that with which he entered. It was true that even now he "saw men as trees, walking;" but it is no less true that he could have said, "I was blind, and now I see."

I pity the man who can read the story of Henry Venn's religious experience without deep interest. The steps by which God leads his children on from one degree of light to another are all full of instruction. Seldom does He seem to bring his people into the full enjoyment of spiritual knowledge all at once. We must not, therefore, "despise the day of small things." We should rather respect those who fight their way out of darkness and grope after truth. What has been won by hard fighting is often that which wears the longest. Theological principles taken up second-hand have often no root, and endure but for a little season. Striking and curious is the similarity in the experience of Whitefield, Berridge, and Venn. They all had to fight hard for spiritual light; and having found it, they held it fast, and never let it go.

The five years during which Henry Venn was curate of Clapham completely settled his theological creed, and formed a turning-point in his religious history. His work there was very heavy, as he held two lectureships in London, beside his curacy. His regular duty on Sunday consisted of a full service at Clapham in the morning ; a sermon in the afternoon at St. Alban's, Wood Street ; and another in the evening at Swithin's, London Stone. On Tuesday morning, he preached again at Swithin's ; on Wednesday morning, at seven o'clock, at his father's old church, St. Antholin's ; and on Thursday evening at Clapham. To preach six sermons every week was undoubtedly a heavy demand on a curate of only four years' standing ! Yet it is not unlikely that the very necessity for exertion which his position entailed on him was the means of calling forth latent power. Men never know how much they can do, until they are put under the screw, and obliged to exert themselves. At any rate Venn was compelled to learn how to preach from notes, from sheer inability to write six sermons a-week, and thus attained a facility in extemporaneous speaking which he afterwards found most useful.

In a spiritual point of view, Venn's character was greatly influenced, during his five years' residence at Clapham, by three circumstances. The first of these was a severe illness of eight months' duration, which laid him aside from work in 1756, and gave him time for reflection and self-examination. The second was his marriage, in 1757, to the daughter of Dr. Bishop, minister of the Tower Church, Ipswich ; a lady who, from her piety and good sense, seems to have been admirably qualified to be a clergyman's wife. The third, and probably the most important circumstance of his position, was the friendship that he formed with several eminent Christians, who were of great use to his soul. At Horsley he seems to have had no help from any one, and whatever he learned there he did not learn from man. At Clapham, on the contrary, he at once became intimate with the well-known layman John Thornton and Dr. Haweis, and afterwards with George Whitefield and Lady Huntingdon.

To Lady Huntingdon, Henry Venn seems to have been under peculiar obligations for advice and counsel. The following extract from a letter which she addressed to him about the defects in his first preaching at Clapham, is an interesting example of her faithfulness, and throws much light on the precise state of her correspondent's mind at this period. She says: " O my friend, we can make no atonement to a violated law ; we have no inward holiness of our own ; the Lord Jesus Christ is 'the Lord our righteousness.' Cling not to such beggarly elements, such filthy rags, mere cobwebs of Pharisaical pride ; but look to him who hath wrought out a perfect righteousness for his people. You find it a hard task to come naked and miserable to Christ ; to come divested of every recommendation but that of abject wretchedness and misery, and receive from the outstretched hand of our Immanuel the riches of redeeming grace. But if you come at all you must come thus ; and, like the dying thief, the cry of your heart must be, ' Lord, remember me.' There must be no conditions ; Christ and Christ alone must be the only mediator between God and sinful men ; no miserable performance can be placed between the sinner and the Saviour. And now, my dear friend, no longer let false doctrine disgrace your pulpit. Preach Christ crucified as the only foundation of the sinner's hope. Preach him as the Author and Finisher as well as the sole Object of faith, that faith which is the gift of God. Exhort Christless sinners to fly to the City of Refuge ; to look to Him who is exalted as Prince and Saviour, to give repentance and the remission of sins. Go on, then, and may your bow abide in strength. Be bold, be firm, be decided. Let Christ be the Alpha and Omega of all you advance in your addresses to your fellow-men. Leave the consequences to your Divine Master

May his gracious benediction rest upon your labours! and may you be blessed to the conversion of very many, who shall be your joy and crown of rejoicing in the great day when the Lord shall appear."—The date of this faithful letter is not given. I am inclined, however, to conjecture that it was written between the time of Venn's illness in 1756 and his marriage in 1757. At any rate, it is a remarkable fact, recorded by his son, that he used to observe that after 1756 he was no longer able to preach the sermons which he had previously composed. Lady Huntingdon's faithful letter was probably not written in vain.

Whatever defects there may have been in Venn's doctrinal views during the first few years of his Clapham ministry, they appear to have completely vanished after his restoration to health in 1757. He was soon recognized as a worthy fellow-labourer with that noble little company of evangelists which, under the leading of Whitefield and Wesley, was beginning to shake the land; and from his gifts as a preacher took no mean position among them. Whitefield seems especially to have delighted in him. In a letter written some time in 1757, he says to Lady Huntingdon: "The worthy Venn is valiant for the truth, a son of thunder. He labours abundantly, and his ministry has been owned of the Lord to the conversion of sinners. Thanks be to God for such an instrument to strengthen our hands! I know the intelligence will rejoice your ladyship. Your exertions in bringing him to a clearer knowledge of the everlasting gospel have indeed been blessed. He owes your ladyship much, under God, and I believe his whole soul is gratitude to the Divine Author of mercies, and to you the honoured instrument in leading him to the fountain of truth." Testimony like this is unexceptionable. George Whitefield was one of the last men on earth to be satisfied with any preaching which was not the full gospel. We cannot for a moment doubt that during the last two years of Venn's curacy at Clapham, he at length walked in the full light of Christ's truth, and "declared all the counsel of God."

In the year 1759, Henry Venn was appointed vicar of Huddersfield, in Yorkshire, by Sir John Ramsden, at the solicitation of Lord Dartmouth. He accepted the appointment from the purest of all motives, a desire to do good to souls. The town itself presented no great attractions. In point of income he was positively a loser by the move from Clapham. But he felt deeply that the offer opened "a great and effectual door" of usefulness, and he did not dare to turn away from it. He seems also to have had a strong impression that he had not been successful at Clapham, and that this was an indication that he ought not to refuse a change. His wife was averse to his moving; and her opinion no doubt placed him in much perplexity. But the result showed beyond doubt that he decided rightly. In leaving Clapham for Yorkshire, he was in God's way.

Henry Venn became vicar of Huddersfield at the age of thirty-five, and continued there only twelve years. He went there a poor man, without rank or influence, and with nothing but God's truth on his side. He found the place a huge, dark, ignorant, immoral, irreligious, manufacturing town. He left it shaken to the centre by the lever of the gospel, and leavened with the influence of many faithful servants of Jesus Christ, whom he had been the means of turning from darkness to light. Few modern ministers appear to have had so powerful an influence on a town population as Henry Venn had on Huddersfield. The nearest approach to it seems to have been the work of Robert M'Cheyne at Dundee.

The story of Henry Venn's life from the time of his settlement at Huddersfield is a subject which I must reserve for another chapter. I do not feel that I could possibly do justice to it now. How he lived, and worked, and preached, and prospered in his great manufacturing parish—how he turned the world upside down throughout the district around, and became a centre of light and life to hundreds—how his health finally gave way under the abundance of his labours, and obliged him to leave Huddersfield—how he spent the last twenty years of his life in the comparative retirement of a little rural parish in Huntingdonshire,—all these are matters which I cannot enter into now. I hope to tell my readers something about them in another chapter.

CHAPTER II.

Mode of Working at Huddersfield—Effect of his Ministry—Fruits found in 1824—Extra-parochial Labours—Friendly relation with Whitefield—Health Fails—Wife Dies—Leaves Huddersfield for Yelling, 1771—Description of Yelling—Second Marriage—Description of Life at Yelling—Dies, 1797.

HENRY VENN was Vicar of Huddersfield from 1759 to 1771. These twelve years, we need not doubt, were the period of his greatest public usefulness. In the full vigour of his bodily and mental faculties, with his mind thoroughly made up about all the leading doctrines of the gospel, with his heart thoroughly set on his Master's business, he entered his new sphere with peculiar power and acceptance, and soon " made full proof of his ministry." His time there was certainly short, if measured by years alone, in consequence of his failing health; but it measured by action and usefulness, like Edward the Sixth's reign, it was very long indeed.

For more than one reason a peculiar interest attaches to Venn's ministry at Huddersfield. For one thing, he was the only one of the seven spiritual heroes of the last century who ever became incumbent of a large town population. Wesley and Whitefield were itinerant evangelists, whose parish was the world. Romaine was the rector of a little confined district in the City. Rowlands lived and died among Welsh mountains, Grimshaw on Yorkshire moors, and Berridge on Bedfordshire plains. Venn was the only man among the seven who could number his lawful parishioners by thousands.—For another thing, he was the first evangelical clergyman in the Church of England who proved that the manufacturing masses of our fellow-countrymen can be thoroughly reached by the gospel. He proved to a demonstration that the working-classes in our great northern towns are to be got at just like other men, if they are approached in the proper way. He proved that the preaching of the cross suits the wants of all Adam's children, and that it can "turn the world upside down" among looms and coal-mines, just as thoroughly as it can in watering-places, country parishes, or metropolitan chapels-of-ease. We all know this now. Nobody would dream of denying it. But we must remember it was not so well known a hundred years ago. Let honour be given where honour is due. The first clergyman in England who fairly proved the power of evangelical aggression on a manufacturing parish, was Henry Venn.

A clergyman's work in a large town district in the last century was very unlike what it is in these times. A vast quantity of religious machinery, with which every one is familiar now, in those days did not exist. City missions, Scripture readers' societies, Pastoral aid societies, Bible women, mothers' meetings, were utterly unknown. Even schools for the children of the poor were few, and comparatively defective, and utterly out of proportion to the wants of the population. In short, the evangelical minister of a great town a hundred years ago was almost entirely shut up to the use of one weapon. The good old apostolical plan of incessant preaching, both " publicly and from house to house," was nearly the only machine that he could use. He was forced to be pre-eminently a man of one thing, and a soldier with one weapon, a perpetual preacher ot God's Word. Whether in the long run the minister of last century did not do more good with his one weapon than many do in modern times with an immense train of parochial machinery, is a question which admits of much doubt. My own private opinion is, that we have too much lost sight of apostolical simplicity in our ministerial work. We want more men of " one thing " and " one book," men who make everything secondary to preaching the Word. It is hard to have many irons in the fire at once, and to keep them all hot. It is quite possible to make an idol of parochial machinery, and for the sake of it to slight the pulpit.

These things ought to be carefully remembered in forming an estimate of Venn's ministry at Huddersfield. Let us never forget that he went to his great Yorkshire parish, like David against Goliath, with nothing but his sling and stones, and an unwavering faith in the power of God. He went there with no sympathizing London committee to correspond with him, encourage him, and assist him with funds. He went there with no long-tried plans and approved modes of evangelical aggression in his pocket. He went there with nothing but his Bible, and his Master at his side. Bearing these things in mind, I think the following extracts from his admirable biography ought to possess a peculiar interest in our eyes.

His son, John Venn, says : " As soon as he began to preach at Huddersfield, the church became crowded to such an extent that many were not able to procure admission. Numbers became deeply impressed with concern about their immortal souls; persons flocked from the distant hamlets, inquiring what they must do to be saved. He found them in general utterly ignorant of their state by nature, and of the redemption that is in Christ Jesus. His bowels yearned over his flock, and he was never satisfied with his labours among them, though they were continued to a degree ruinous to his health. On the Sunday he would often address the congregation from the desk, briefly explaining the psalms and the lessons. He would frequently begin the service with a solemn and most impressive address, exhorting the worshippers to consider themselves as in the presence of the great God of heaven, whose eye was in a particular manner upon them, while they drew nigh to him in his own house. His whole soul was engaged in preaching; and as at this time he only used short notes in the pulpit, ample room was left to indulge the feelings of compassion, tenderness, and love, with which his heart overflowed towards his people. In the week he statedly visited the different hamlets in his extensive parish; and collecting some of the inhabitants at a private house, he addressed them with a kindness and earnestness which moved every heart." A letter written in 1762 to Lady Huntingdon, informs us that in that year, beside his stated work on the Lord's day, the Vicar of Huddersfield generally preached eight or ten sermons in the week in distant parts of the parish, when many came to hear who would not come to church. It also mentions that his outdoor preaching was found especially useful.

His grandson, Henry Venn, has gathered some additional facts about his Huddersfield ministry, which are well worth recording. He tells us that "Mr. Venn made a great point of the due observance of the Sabbath, both in the town and parish. He induced several of the most respectable and influential inhabitants to perambulate the town, and by persuasion, rather than by legal intimidation, to repress the open violation of the day. By such means a great and evident reformation was accomplished."

"He endeavoured to preserve the utmost reverence and devotion in public worship, constantly pressing this matter upon his people. He read the service with peculiar solemnity and effect. The *Te Deum*, especially, was recited with a triumphant air and tone, which often produced a perceptible sensation throughout the whole congregation. He succeeded in inducing the people to join in the responses and singing. Twice in the course of his ministry at Huddersfield he preached a course of sermons in explanation of the Liturgy. On one occasion, as he went up to church, he found a considerable number of persons in the churchyard, waiting for the commencement of the service. He stopped to address them, saying, he hoped they were preparing their hearts for the service of God, and that he had himself much to do to preserve his heart in a right frame. He concluded by waving his hand for them to go into the church before him, and waited till they had all entered."

"He took great pains in catechizing the younger members of his congregation, chiefly those who were above fourteen years of age. The number was often very considerable ; and he wrote out for their use a very copious Explanation of the Church Catechism, in the way of questions and answers." *

The immediate effects produced by Henry Venn's preaching appear to have been singularly deep, powerful, and permanent. Both his son and grandson have supplied some striking illustrations of them.

His son says : " A club, chiefly composed of Socinians, in a neighbouring market-town, having heard much censure and ridicule bestowed upon the preaching of Henry Venn, sent two of their ablest members to hear this strange preacher, detect his absurdities, and furnish matter of merriment for the next meeting. They accordingly went to Huddersfield Church ; but were greatly struck, on entering, by seeing the multitude that was assembled together, and by observing the devotion of their behaviour, and their anxiety to attend the worship of God. When Mr. Venn ascended the reading-desk, he addressed his flock, as usual, with a solemnity and dignity which showed him to be deeply interested in the work in which he was engaged. The subsequent earnestness of his preaching, and the solemn appeals he made to conscience, deeply impressed the visitors,

* I cannot make out whether this Explanation of the Church Catechism was ever published. It certainly does not appear in a complete manuscript catalogue of Mr. Venn's writings which, by the kindness of one of his descendants, is now lying before me. If it was ever published, it seems a pity that it has fallen out of sight, and is not better known. Something, perhaps, would be known of it in the town of Huddersfield at this day. Can any reader throw light on the point ?

so that one of them observed, as they left the church, ' Surely God is in this place ! There is no matter for laughter here !' This gentleman immediately called on Mr. Venn, told him who he was, and the purpose for which he had come, and earnestly begged his forgiveness and his prayers. He requested Mr. Venn to visit him without delay, and left the Socinian congregation ; and from that time to the hour of his death became one of Mr. Venn's most faithful and affectionate friends." *

"Another gentleman, highly respectable for his character, talents, and piety, the late William Hey, Esq., of Leeds, used frequently to go to Huddersfield to hear Mr. Venn preach, and he assured me that once returning home with an intimate friend, they neither of them opened their lips to each other till they came within a mile of Leeds, a distance of fifteen miles, so deeply were they impressed by the truths which they had heard, and the manner in which they had been delivered."

Henry Venn's grandson visited Huddersfield in 1824, fifty-three years after his honoured grandfather had left the place. On inquiry he found that even after the lapse of half a century, the fruits of his wonderful ministry were yet remaining on earth. The memorials he gathered together from these survivors of the old congregation are so deeply interesting that I am sure my readers will be glad to hear them, though in a somewhat abridged form.

Mr. Venn's grandson says : " Through the kind assistance of Benjamin Hudson, Esq., of Huddersfield, I saw all the old people then living in the town and neighbourhood who had received their first religious impressions under my grandfather's ministry, and still maintained a religious character. They were all in the middle or lower ranks of life ; none of a superior class had survived. What I am about to record must, therefore, be received as the genuine and unstudied testimony of persons of plain, unpolished sense.

* This gentleman was James Kershaw, Esq., of Halifax.

" Mr. William Brook of Longwood gave me the following account of the first sermon he heard at Huddersfield Church : ' I was first led to go by listening with an uncle of mine, named W. Mellor, at the door of a prayer-meeting : we thought there must be something uncommon to make people so earnest. My uncle was about nineteen, and I was about sixteen ; and we went together to the church one Thursday evening.   There was a great crowd within the church, all silent, and many weeping. The text was, " Thou art weighed in the balances, and art found wanting."   W. Mellor was deeply attentive ; and when we came out of church we did not say a word to each other till we got some way into the fields.   Then W. Mellor stopped, leaned his back against a wall, and burst into tears, saying, " I can't stand this."   His conviction of sin was from that time most powerful, and he became quite a changed character.   I was not so much affected at that time ; but I could not after that sermon be easy in sin.   I began to pray regularly ; and so, by degrees, I was brought to know myself, and to seek salvation in earnest.   The people used to go from Longwood in droves, to Huddersfield Church, three miles off.   Some of them came out of church together, whose ways home were in this direction ; and they used to stop at the Firs' End, about a mile off, and talk over, for some time, what they had heard, before they separated to go to their homes.   That place has been to me like a little heaven below !

" ' I never heard a minister like him.   He was most powerful in unfolding the terrors of the law.   When doing so, he had a stern look that would make you tremble.   Then he would turn off to the offers of grace, and begin to smile, and go on entreating till his eyes filled with tears.'

" The next person I saw was George Crow, aged eighty-two, of Lockwood, a hamlet about a mile from the town.   When I asked him whether he ever thought of old times, he answered, ' Ah, yes ! and shall do to the last.   I thought when Mr. Venn

went I should be like Rachel for the rest of my days, weeping
and refusing to be comforted. I was abidingly impressed the
first time I heard him, at an early period of his ministry. He
was such a preacher as I never heard before or since; he struck
upon the passions like no other man. Nobody could help
being affected : the most wicked and ill-conditioned men went
to hear him, and fell like slaked lime in a moment, even though
they were not converted. I could have heard him preach all
the night through.'

"I also visited Ellen Roebuck, eighty-five, living at Almond-
bury. She was very deaf and infirm, but when she understood
the object of my visit she talked with great energy. 'I well
remember his first coming to Huddersfield, and the first sermon
he preached. It was on that text, "My heart's desire and
prayer to God for Israel is that they may be saved :" and it was
as true of himself as it was of St. Paul. He took every method
for instructing the people ; he left nothing unturned. Always
at work ! it was a wonder he had not done for himself sooner.
The lads he catechized used to tell him that people said he was
teaching a new doctrine, and leading us into error ; but he
always replied, "Never mind them ; do not answer them; read
your Bibles, and press forward, dear lads ; press forward, and
you cannot miss heaven."'

"I saw also John Starkey of Cawcliff, aged eighty. As I
conversed with him, he seemed gradually to wake up, till his
countenance glistened with joy. He said, 'I esteemed Mr.
Venn too much for a man. I almost forgot that he was a
creature and an instrument. His going away went nearer to
my heart than anything. He was a wonderful preacher. When
he got warm with his subject, he looked as if he would jump
out of his pulpit. He made many weep. I have often wept
at his sermons. I could have stood to hear him till morning.
When he came up to the church, he used to go round the
churchyard and drive us all in before him.' "

I make no excuse for making the above extracts. They speak for themselves. I pity the man who can read them without interest. If after fifty years such living witnesses to the power of Henry Venn's ministry could be found, what may we suppose must have been the effect of his preaching in his day and generation? If the direct good he did was so marked and unmistakable, what a vast amount of indirect good must have been done by his presence in the district where God placed him?

We must not for a moment suppose that Henry Venn's labours in Christ's cause were entirely confined to Huddersfield during the time that he was vicar of that parish. So far from this being the case, there is abundant evidence that he occasionally did the work of an evangelist in many parts of England very distant from Yorkshire. We possess no journal of his movements, but a close examination of that interesting but oddly-arranged book, "Lady Huntingdon's Life and Times," shows plainly that the Vicar of Huddersfield preached every year in many pulpits besides his own. It could hardly be otherwise. He was on terms of intimate friendship with all the leading evangelists of his day, such as Wesley, Whitefield, Grimshaw, and Fletcher. These apostolic men not unfrequently found their way to Huddersfield vicarage, and preached for him in his pulpit. We cannot wonder that, so long as health permitted, Venn helped them in return. In fact, he seems frequently to have made excursions through various parts of England, and to have laboured in every way to preach the gospel, as an itinerant, so far as parochial engagements would allow him. We hear of him constantly in Lady Huntingdon's chapel at Oathall near Brighton, and at Bath. At one time he is at Bretby near Burton-on-Trent. At another he is at Fletcher's famous establishment at Trevecca in South Wales. Occasionally we read of his preaching at Bristol, Cheltenham, Gloucester, Worcester, and London. The half of his labours, probably, outside his own parish, is entirely unknown.

The truth must be spoken on this point. It is vain to attempt to draw any broad line of distinction between Henry Venn and his great contemporaries in the revival of the last century. No doubt he had a large town parish, and of course found it more difficult than others to be long absent from home. But in all spiritual points, in matters of doctrine and practice, and in his judgment of what the times required, he was entirely one with Whitefield and Grimshaw. He delighted in their labours. He stood by their side and helped them, whenever he had an opportunity. When Grimshaw died, it was Henry Venn who preached his funeral sermon in Luddenden Church. When Whitefield died, the man who preached the noblest funeral sermon in Lady Huntingdon's chapel at Bath was the same Henry Venn. Conduct like this, I am afraid, will not recommend my hero to some Churchmen. They will think he would have done better had he confined his labours to Huddersfield, and abstained from apparent irregularities. I content myself with saying that I cannot agree with them. I think that in keeping up intimate relations with the itinerant *evangelists* of last century, Venn did what was best and wisest in the days in which he lived. I think his unhesitating attachment to Whitefield to the very last a singularly noble trait in his character. It ought never to be forgotten that the last sermon preached by Whitefield in Yorkshire, before he sailed for America to die, was delivered in the pulpit of Huddersfield Church.

An extract from a letter written by Venn to Lady Huntingdon, about the year 1768, will give a very clear idea of the unhesitating course of action which the Vicar of Huddersfield adopted, and the boldness with which he supported Whitefield. It was written on the occasion of Whitefield preaching on a tombstone in the churchyard of Cheltenham Parish Church, after permission had been refused to preach in the church.

Venn says: "To give your ladyship any just description of what our eyes have witnessed and our hearts have felt within the last few days at Cheltenham, exceeds my feeble powers. My inmost soul is penetrated with an overwhelming sense of the power and presence of Jehovah, who has visited us with an effusion of his Spirit in a very eminent manner. There was a visible appearance of much soul-concern among the crowd that filled every part of the burial-ground. Many were overcome with fainting; others sobbed deeply; some wept silently; and a solemn concern appeared on the countenance of almost the whole assembly. But when he pressed the injunction of the text (Isa. lv. 1) on the unconverted and ungodly, his words seemed to act like a sword, and many burst out into piercing cries. At this juncture Mr. Whitefield made an awful pause of a few seconds, and wept himself. During this interval Mr. Madan and myself stood up and requested the people, as much as possible, to restrain themselves from making a noise. Oh, with what eloquence, what energy, what melting tenderness, did Mr. Whitefield beseech sinners to be reconciled to God, to come to Him for life everlasting, and to rest their weary souls on Christ the Saviour! When the sermon was ended the people seemed chained to the ground. Mr. Madan, Mr. Talbot, and myself, found ample employment in trying to comfort those who seemed broken down under a sense of guilt. We separated in different directions among the crowd, and each was quickly surrounded by an attentive audience still eager to hear all the words of this life. Of such a season it may well be said, I have heard thee in a time accepted, and in the day of salvation I have succoured thee; behold! now is the accepted time—behold! now is the day of salvation!"

In the year 1771, Henry Venn's useful Yorkshire ministry came to an end. Most reluctantly he left Huddersfield, and became the rector of Yelling, a small country living in Huntingdonshire. This happened when he was only forty-seven years old. There were many who blamed him for the step, and thought that he ought to have died at his post in Yorkshire. But really, when the circumstances of the case are fairly considered, it seems impossible to say that he was wrong. His health during the latter period of his residence at Huddersfield failed so completely, that his public usefulness was almost at an end. He had a cough and spitting of blood, beside other symptoms of approaching consumption. He was only able to preach once a fortnight; and even then the exertion rendered him incapable of rising from his couch for several days. In short, it is very evident that if he had continued at Huddersfield much longer, he would have died. Just at this crisis, his friend the Lord Chief Baron Smythe, who was one of the Commissioners of the Great Seal, offered him the Chancellor's living of Yelling. The offer appears to me to have been a providential opening, and I think Venn was quite right to accept it.

It is easy to find fault with Venn for "overworking" himself at Huddersfield, and to hold him up as a beacon and warning to young ministers who are full of zeal and abundant in labours. I venture to doubt, however, whether it is quite just and fair. It was not "overworking" alone that made his health break down. There were mental causes as well as physical. Nothing, I suspect, had so much to do with his removal from Huddersfield as the death of his wife in 1767, leaving him a widower with five young children. Up to this time, his position at Huddersfield had been one of many trials, partly from the bitter opposition of many who hated evangelical religion, partly from the straitened circumstances to which his very scanty income often reduced him. But so long as his wife lived, none of these things seemed to have moved him. Mrs. Venn was a woman of rare prudence, calmness, good sense, affection, and sympathy. She was, in fact, her husband's right hand. When she died, such a load of care and anxiety was accumulated on his head, that his health gradually gave way. People who have not been placed in similar circumstances, may probably not understand all this. Those who have had this cross to carry, can testify that there is no position in this world so trying to body and soul as that of the minister who is left a widower, with a young family and a large congregation. There are anxieties in such cases which no one knows but he who has gone through them; anxieties which can crush the strongest spirit, and wear out the strongest constitution. This, I strongly suspect, was one chief secret of Venn's removal from Huddersfield. He left it, no doubt, because he felt himself too ill to do any more work there. But the true cause probably of his breaking down was the load of care entailed on him by the death of his wife. It was just one of those secret blows from which a man's bodily health never recovers.

Venn's own private feelings, on leaving Huddersfield, are best described in a letter which he wrote at the time to Lady Huntingdon :—" No human being," he says, " can tell how keenly I feel this separation from a people I have dearly loved. But the shattered state of my health, occasioned by my unpardonable length and loudness in speaking, has reduced me to a state which incapacitates me for the charge of so large a parish. Providence has put it into the heart of the Lord Commissioner to offer this small living to me. Pray for me, my most faithful friend, that God's blessing may go with me, and render my feeble attempts to speak of his love and mercy efficacious to the conversion of souls. At Yelling, as at Huddersfield, I shall still be your ladyship's willing servant in the service of the gospel ; and when I can be of any use in furthering your plans for the salvation of souls and the glory of Christ, I am your obedient servant at command."

It is recorded that the last two or three months of Venn's residence at Huddersfield were peculiarly affecting. At an early hour the church was crowded when he preached, so that vast numbers were compelled to go away. Many came from a great distance to take leave of him, and tell him how much they owed him for benefits received under his ministry. Mothers held up their children, saying, "There is the man who has been our faithful minister and our best friend!" The whole parish was deeply moved; and when he preached his farewell sermon (Col. iii. 2) he could hardly speak for deep emotion.

The parish of Yelling, to which Henry Venn retired on leaving Huddersfield, is a little agricultural district on the south-east border of Huntingdonshire, about seven miles south of Huntingdon, five east of St. Neots, and twelve miles west of Cambridge. At this present day it has a population of about 400 souls. It would be difficult to imagine a greater contrast than the great evangelist of Yorkshire found between his new cure and his old. Vast indeed is the transition from the warm-hearted and intelligent worshippers of a northern manufacturing district to the dull, and cold, and impassive inhabitants of a purely agricultural parish in the south of England! Venn felt it deeply. He says himself in a letter to Stillingfleet, "Your letter found me under great searchings of heart, upon the point of beginning my ministry in this place. What a change from thousands to a company of one hundred! from a people generally enlightened, and many converted, to one yet sitting in darkness, and ignorant of the first principles of the gospel! from a house resounding with the voice of thanksgiving, like the noise of many waters, to one where the solitary singers please themselves with empty sounds, or gratify their vanity by the imagination of their own excellence! from a Bethel to myself, and many more, to a nominal worship of the God of Christians! A change painful indeed, yet unavoidable. With a heavy heart, therefore, did I begin yesterday to address my new hearers."

Trying, however, as the change was to Henry Venn's mind, there can be little doubt that it was exceedingly beneficial to his body. The comparative rest and entire change of his new position in all probability saved his life. Little by little his constitution rallied and recovered his tone, until he was able to get through the work of his small parish with comparative ease. In short, after going away from Huddersfield, apparently to die, he lived on no less than twenty-six years, to the great joy of his friends, the great advantage of his family, and the great benefit of the Church of Christ. How little man knows what is best for his fellow-creatures! If the Vicar of Huddersfield had remained at his post, and died in harness, his children would have lost the best training that children perhaps ever had, and the world would have lost a quantity of most valuable correspondence.

Venn's life at Yelling was singularly quiet and uneventful. His second marriage, soon after his settlement there, appears to have added much to his happiness. The lady whom he married was the widow of Mr. Smith of Kensington, and daughter of the Rev. James Ascough, Vicar of Highworth, Wilts. In her he had the comfort of finding a thorough help, and a most wise and affectionate stepmother to his children. She lived with him twenty-one years, and was buried at Yelling. The domestic arrangements and employments at his country home were truly simple and edifying. The following sketch, drawn out by himself for a Huddersfield friend, gives a pleasing impression of the way in which his life went on : " You tell me you have no idea how we go on. Take the following sketch. I am up one of the first in the house, soon after five o'clock ; and when prayer and reading the blessed Word is done my daughters make their appearance, and I teach them till Mrs. Venn comes down at half-past eight. Then family prayer begins, which is often very sweet, as my own servants are all, I believe, born of God. The children begin to sing prettily ; and our praises, I trust, are heard on high. From breakfast we are all employed till we ride out, in fine weather, two hours for health, and after dinner employed again. At six, I have always one hour for solemn meditation and walking in my house till seven. We have then sometimes twenty, and sometimes more, of the people, to whom I expound God's Word. Several appear much affected; and sometimes Jesus stands in the midst, and says, 'Peace be unto you!' Our devotions end at eight, we sup and go to rest at ten. On Sundays I am still enabled to speak six hours, at three different times, to my own great surprise. Oh the goodness of God in raising me up!"

Quiet, however, as Henry Venn's life was at Yelling, we must not suppose that he had no opportunities of being useful to souls. Far from it. He was within reach of good old John Berridge, and the two fellow-labourers often met and strengthened one another's hands. Though he seldom came before the public as he did in his Huddersfield days, he still found many ways of doing his Master's business, and proclaiming the gospel which he loved. The value of his preaching was soon discovered even in his secluded neighbourhood, and he had the comfort of seeing fruit of his ministry in Huntingdonshire as real and true, if not so abundant, as in Yorkshire. Occasionally he preached out of his own parish, though not perhaps so often as his friend and neighbour Berridge could have wished him. He delighted in the society of the good Vicar of Everton whenever he could have it. "Just such a Calvinist as Mr. Berridge is," he used to say, "I wish all ministers of Christ to be." Sometimes he preached in London, and was not ashamed to appear in the pulpit of Surrey Chapel so late as 1786. His vicinity to Cambridge gave him many opportunities of seeing members of the University who valued evangelical truth, and men like Simeon, Jowett, Robinson, and Farish, long testified their deep sense of the advantage they derived from his society and conversation. Above all, the leisure that he enjoyed at Yelling enabled him to keep up a very extensive correspondence. He lived in the good old time when letters were really well thought over and worth reading, and the letters that left Yelling parsonage are a proof to this day how wisely and well he used his pen.

On the whole, the evening of Henry Venn's life seems to have been a singularly happy one.   He had the immense comfort of seeing his four children walking in their father's footsteps, clinging firmly to the doctrines he had loved and preached, and steadily serving their father's God.   Not least, he had the joy of seeing his son John an able minister of the New Testament, and of leaving him rector of Clapham, and a man honoured by all who knew him.   Indeed, it is recorded that there were few texts so frequently on Henry Venn's lips, in his latter years, as the saying of Solomon, " A wise son maketh a glad father."

At the age of sixty-eight, he withdrew almost entirely from the public work of the ministry.   His constitution had never entirely recovered from the effect of his work at Huddersfield, and old age came prematurely upon him.   Yet even then he was never idle.   In fact, he knew not what it was to have a tedious or a vacant hour.

His last days are so beautifully described by his grandson, in his admirable biography, that I shall give the account just as he has set it down.   He tells us that " he found constant employment in reading and writing, and in the exercise of prayer and meditation.   He often declared that he never felt more fervency of devotion than whilst imploring spiritual blessings for his children and friends, and especially for the success of those who were still engaged in the ministry of the blessed gospel, from which he was himself laid aside.   For himself, his prayer was, that he might die to the glory of Christ   ' There are some moments,' he once said, ' when I am afraid of what is to come in the last agonies ; but I trust in the Lord to hold me up.   I have a great work before me, to suffer and to die to his glory.'   But the spread of his Redeemer's kingdom lay nearer to his heart than any earthly or personal concerns.   Even when the decay of strength produced occasional torpor, this subject would rouse him to a degree of fervency and joy, from which his bodily frame would afterwards suffer. I have understood that nothing so powerfully excited his spirits as the presence of young ministers whose hearts he believed to be devoted to Christ.

"About six months before his death he finally left Yelling, and settled at Clapham, near his son. His health from this time rapidly failed, and he was often on the brink of the grave. A medical friend, named Pearson, who often visited him, observed that the near prospect of death so elated his mind with joy, that it actually proved a stimulus to life. On one occasion Mr. Venn remarked some fatal appearances, and said, 'Surely these are good symptoms.' Mr. Pearson replied, 'Sir, in this state of joyous excitement you cannot die!'

"At length, on the 24th of June 1797, his happy spirit was released, and, at the age of seventy-three, Henry Venn entered into the long anticipated joy of his Lord."

I have yet more to say about this good man. His preaching, his literary remains, his correspondence, and the leading features of his character, all seem to deserve further notice. But I must reserve all to another chapter.

CHAPTER III.

His Preaching Analysed—His Literary Remains examined—Extraordinary Power as a Letter-writer—Soundness of Judgment about Doctrine—Wisdom and Good Sense about Duties—Prudent Management of his Children—Unworldliness and Cheerfulness—Catholicity and Kindliness of Spirit—Testimony of Cowper, Simeon, and Sir James Stephen.

IT is no easy matter, in the latter part of the nineteenth century, to form a correct estimate of Henry Venn's gifts and character. In fact, the materials for forming it are singularly scanty. He was peculiarly a man of one thing, absorbed in the direct work of his calling, always about his Master's business, and regardless of the verdict of posterity. He spent the greater part of his life in Yorkshire and Bedfordshire, in days when the public press was in its infancy, and there was but little communication between county and county. The only trustworthy biography of the man is a short account begun by his son, but not completed, and finished by a grandson who never saw him. As a specimen of biography, Venn's "Life" is beyond all praise; but still it is the work of a loving relative, and not of a bystander. Under these circumstances I feel unusual difficulty in handling the subject of this chapter. I cannot help thinking that the famous Vicar of Huddersfield was a man who is scarcely understood by the present generation. However, I must throw myself on the indulgence of my readers, and do the best I can.

There are two things which I propose to do in this chapter, I will first give some account of my hero, as a preacher, a writer, and a correspondent. I will then point out certain prominent features in his character, which appear to me of such rare beauty and excellence that they deserve the special notice of Christians.

As a *preacher*, I venture to think we know next to nothing of what Venn was. His sermons still extant, consisting of fourteen preached at Clapham, before he removed to Huddersfield, and eight single discourses preached on various special occasions between 1758 and 1785, most certainly fail to give us any idea of his pulpit powers. Perhaps the best of them are his funeral sermons for Grimshaw and Whitefield. In doctrine they are all, no doubt, sound, scriptural, and evangelical. But it is useless to deny that, at this day, they seem, as you read them, rather tame and commonplace. There is nothing striking, brilliant, or powerful about them. There is nothing that appears likely to lay hold of men's minds, to arrest or to keep up attention. In short, you find it hard to believe that the man who preached these sermons could ever have been considered a great preacher.

Yet it is clear as daylight that Henry Venn was a great preacher. The extraordinary effects that his sermons produced at Huddersfield—his undeniable popularity with congregations accustomed to hear such mighty orators as Whitefield—the high opinion entertained of his powers by Lady Huntingdon and other good judges—all these are facts that cannot possibly be explained away. The Vicar of Huddersfield may not have possessed the glowing eloquence of Rowlands or Whitefield. But for all that he must evidently have been a man of great pulpit powers.

The truth of the matter, I suspect, is simply this. Venn's sermons were precisely of that sort which are excellent to hear, but not excellent to read. Listened to, they are clear, satisfying, interesting, and instructive. Written down, they seem poor, and ungrammatical, and diffuse, and commonplace. Whether men will believe it or not, it is a fact that English for hearing, and English for reading, are almost two different languages, and that speeches and sermons which sound admirable when you listen to them, seem curiously flat and lifeless when you sit down to read them in cold blood. Of all the illustrations of this principle in rhetoric, I venture the conjecture that there seldom was a more remarkable one than Venn. To read his sermons over, there seems no more life or fire in them than there is in an empty stove in July. And yet the Vicar of Huddersfield, by the universal testimony of all his contemporaries, was a mighty preacher.

Let us add to all this that Venn's action and delivery, by all accounts, were singularly lively and forcible. The witness of his hearers at Huddersfield, on this point, was unanimous. His face, his voice, his hands, his eyes, his whole manner in preaching, arrested attention, and clothed all that he said with power. Who can deny the immense effect of good delivery? The ancients went so far as to call it the first, second, and third qualification of a good orator. Who can fail to see, from the traditional account, already quoted, that Venn had a peculiar gift of delivery? The sermons of a man who "looked as if he would jump out of the pulpit," may contain nothing that is original or remarkable, but they are just the sermons that often turn the world upside down. Printed sermons can show us a preacher's matter, but they cannot show us his manner as delivered. Second-rate matter, if only well delivered, will never fail to beat first-rate matter badly delivered, as long as the world stands.

After all, we must never forget that we know nothing of the nature of Venn's sermons in the days of his greatest power. They were extempore sermons, or sermons preached from notes; and that fact alone speaks volumes. Not one of these sermons, I believe, was taken down shorthand, as most of Whitefield's were, and the consequence is that we have not an idea what they were like. But every intelligent hearer of the present day knows well that a man may be a most powerful extempore preacher, who is a very dull and uninteresting writer. There are scores of men whom it is very pleasant to hear, but very wearying to read. Perhaps if we possessed good shorthand reports of some of Venn's best Huddersfield sermons, we should see at a glance the secrets of his popularity as a preacher. As matters stand, I must frankly confess it is a subject which is now wrapped in some obscurity. I have done my best to throw some conjectural light upon it, and must leave it here. I only wish to remind my readers, in passing on, that there are few things so little understood in the world as the true causes of pulpit power.

As a *writer*, Venn's reputation rests almost entirely on two works, which are pretty well known,—"The Complete Duty of Man," and "Mistakes in Religion." The first of them is a "System of doctrinal and practical Christianity," and was intended to supply something better than that mischievous and defective volume, the "Whole Duty of Man." The second of them is a collection of essays on the prophecy of Zacharias (the father of John Baptist), in which the erroneousness of many common views of religion is faithfully and scripturally exposed. Besides these, Venn published two or three smaller pamphlets, which are but little known.

The two works above-named were undoubtedly very useful in their day, and are still to be found on the shelves of most collectors of religious literature. They are sound, scriptural, and evangelical. But I strongly suspect that they stick to the shelves on which they stand, and are books which most people know better by name than by reading. The plain truth is, that every age has its own peculiar style of writing. Popular as the "Spectator," and "Tatler," and "Rambler," were in their times, it may well be doubted whether they would be much read if published now. Even the pens of Addison, Johnson, and Steele, would not command success. The same remark applies to the sound and scriptural writings of Henry Venn. They did good service in their day, when men loved a somewhat stiff and classical style, and would have turned with disdain from any other sort of English composition as unworthy of an educated person. But like the jawbone of an ass, which Samson once used so effectively, they are now laid aside. Their work is done. Like the famous long-bows which our forefathers used at Cressy and Agincourt, we still view them with respect, and are proud of the victories which they won. But we do not use them ourselves. Rifled artillery and breech-loaders have superseded them. The fashion of our weapons is changed.

After all, a close examination of Venn's two volumes will soon show an intelligent reader why they are no longer popular. The composition is of that stately and somewhat high-flown style which was thought the standard of excellence in the last century. The sentences are often very long, and somewhat involved. The words are frequently of Latin or

French origin. There is a curious absence of that rich fund of ready, happy illustration, which Whitefield and Rowlands had at their finger ends. The appeals to the imagination are few, and come in stiffly and awkwardly when they do come, like men dressed in new or borrowed clothes. In short, the style of the books is neither Saxon, nor sparkling, nor racy, nor pithy, nor anecdotal, nor pictorial. We must not wonder that they are no longer popular. Let us thank God for them. They were read in their day and generation by hundreds, who would probably have read no other evangelical literature. They may still do good to good men, and be liked by those who are really hungering for spiritual food. But we must not insist on everybody admiring them, or call people graceless and ungodly because they do not take pleasure in reading them. We must not count it a strange thing if many call them heavy, and dry, and cold.

As a *correspondent and letter-writer*, Henry Venn deserves the highest admiration. Nothing gives me such a high idea of his mental and spiritual stature, as the collection of letters which accompanies his biography. I never wonder at his reputation when I read these letters. I consider them above all praise, and commend them to the special attention of all who want to form a just estimate of the seventh great evangelist of England a hundred years ago. The true measure of the Vicar of Huddersfield and Yelling is to be found in his letters much more than his books or printed sermons.

Letter-writing, we must never forget, was a much more important business in the last century than it is at the present day. The daily newspaper was a very different affair from what it is now. Periodicals and cheap publications had a very limited circulation. The result was, that letters became most powerful instruments either for good or evil. Men of the world, like Lord Hervey, Lord Chesterfield, or Horace Walpole, were not ashamed to throw their whole minds into their correspondence.

Religious men entered so fully into doctrinal, practical, and experimental questions with their correspondents, that their letters were almost as useful as their sermons. John Newton's well-known volume of letters, called "Cardiphonia," has perhaps done as much good to Christ's cause as anything that ever came from his pen. In days like those, it is no mean praise to say that Henry Venn was second to none as a letter-writer. Compare the letters that he wrote after settling down in Huntingdonshire, with the very best that Newton published, and I venture to say boldly that no impartial judge would hesitate to pronounce that the epistolary mine at Yelling yielded quite as rich metal as that at Olney.

It is curious, indeed, to observe how free Venn's letters are, comparatively, from the faults which impair the usefulness of his books and printed sermons. There is a striking absence of that stiff and laboured mode of expression to which I have already adverted. He writes easily, naturally, and pleasantly, and makes you feel that you would like to hear again from such a correspondent. Like the letters of Mrs. Savage (Matthew Henry's sister), you cannot help regretting that the editor made so small and limited a selection from the stock he had in hand. You close the volume with the impression that you would have liked it better if it had been twice as long. For my own part, I confess to a strong suspicion that we have in Venn's published correspondence the real key of Venn's popularity as a preacher. I suspect that his extempore sermons must have closely resembled his letters. I give it, of course, as my own private conjecture, and nothing more. All I say is, that if the vicar of Huddersfield preached in his pulpit in the same clear, pithy, and direct fashion that he wrote to his friends, I do not wonder that he was a preacher of mighty power. Once more, I advise those who want to know the secret of Venn's reputation to study his letters.

It only remains for me now to point out what seem to me to

have been the prominent features in Henry Venn's character. I approach this subject with much diffidence. I have no other means of forming an opinion than a close examination of my hero's life and letters. I am very sensible that I may err in my judgment, and may say too much of some points and too little of others. But after dwelling so much on this good man's life and ministry, I cannot help inviting the attention of my readers to some characteristics which appear to me to stand out with peculiar brightness, as we look at him from a distance.

1. The first excellency that I notice in Venn's character is the *soundness of his judgment on difficult and disputable points in theology*. He lived in a day when the controversy between Calvinism and Arminianism was at its height, and when violent and exaggerated statements were continually made on both sides. In a day like this, he seems to me to have been singularly happy in observing the proportion of truth in doctrine. I can put my finger on no leading minister of last century whose views of the gospel appear to have been so truly scriptural and well balanced. Of course he was alternately claimed as an ally, or abused as an enemy, by extreme partisans on both sides. But I can find no man of that era who seems to have understood so thoroughly the relative value of every part and portion of evangelical Christianity.

Let us hear what he says about Calvinism : " As to Calvinism, you know I am moderate. Those who exalt the Lord Jesus as all their salvation, and abase man, I rejoice in. I would not have them advance further till they see more of the plan of sovereign grace, so connected with what is indisputable, that they cannot refuse their assent. Difficulties, distressing difficulties, are on every side, whether we receive that scheme or no. We must be as little children ; we must be daily exercising ourselves in humble love and prayer ; we must be looking up to our Saviour for the Holy Ghost. And after this has been our employment for many years, we shall find how much truth there is in that divine assertion, 'If any man think that he knoweth anything yet as he ought to know, that man knoweth nothing.' I used to please myself with the imagination, fifteen years ago, that by prayer for the Holy Ghost, and reading diligently the lively oracles, I should be able to understand all Scripture, and to give it all one clear and consistent meaning. That it is perfectly consistent I am very sure; but it is not so to any mortal's apprehension here. We are so proud, that we must have something to humble us; and this is one means to that end."—(15*th Feb.* 1772.)

Let us hear what he says about assurance : " I believe that the knowledge of our acceptance with God is to be constantly urged as one of the greatest motives to lead a strict life, and to abstain from all appearance of evil, seeing the Holy Ghost, whose testimony alone can satisfy the conscience, will never dwell with the slothful or lukewarm, much less with presumptuous offenders. Scripturally to state, and firmly to maintain by sound argument, the knowledge of salvation, is, I believe, a most useful way of preaching—guarding against hypocrites, who will sometimes speak great swelling words about these matters, though themselves the servants of corruption, and conscious of the lie they tell in speaking of their joy in the Lord. I judge that one great reason of the worldliness prevailing amongst orthodox Dissenters is their teachers not pressing this point; and that, amidst very much error, one great cause of Mr. Wesley's success, some years ago, was his urging Christians not to rest without joy in God from receiving the atonement."—(1775.)

Let us hear what he says about holiness : " True holiness is quite of another character than we, for a long time, in any degree conceive. It is not serving God without defect, but with deep self-abasement, with astonishment at his infinite condescension and love to sinners, to ungodly enemies, and to men who in their lost estate are exceedingly vile. It is pleasing to consider how we are all led into this point, however we may differ in others ; and were it not for the demon of controversy, and a hurry of employment which leaves no time for self-know-ledge or devout meditation on the oracles of God, I am per-suaded we should very soon be so grounded on this matter, that bystanders would no longer reproach us for our divisions." —(1776.)

Let us hear what he says about weak faith : " Weak faith seeks salvation only in Christ, and yields subjection to him, and brings the soul to his feet, though without assurance of being as yet saved by him. There is not one duty a weak believer slights. Weak faith is attended with sorrow and humili-ation ; as in his case he said with tears, ' Lord, I believe ; help thou mine unbelief.' It produces new desires and affec-tions, new principles and purposes, and a new practice, though not in such strength and vigour as is found in old established believers. Ask the weakest and most disconsolate believer, whether he would forsake and give up his hope in Christ ; and he will eagerly reply, ' Not for the whole world !' There is, therefore, no reason why weak believers should conclude against themselves ; for weak faith unites as really with Christ as strong faith, just as the least bud in the vine draws sap and life from the root no less than the strongest branch. Weak believers, therefore, have abundant cause to be thankful ; and while they reach after growth in grace, ought not to overlook what they have already received."—(1784.)

Hear, lastly, what he says about indwelling sin :—" I sympa-thize with you in your troubles from the corruption of nature. I feel myself harassed with hardness of heart and coldness of affection toward God and man, and by slightly performing secret duties, when I know so well that God is ' a rewarder (only) of those who diligently seek him.' How totally does the estimate I made of myself thirty-five years ago differ from what I know now to be my real condition ! I then confidently expected to be holy *very soon*, even as St. Paul was ; and then there would be no other difference here between me and angels than that I, by watching, fasting, and praying without ceasing, had conquered and eradicated sin, which they had never even known. *Now*, when I compare myself with the great apostle, I can scarcely perceive a diminutive feature or two of what shines so prominently in that noble saint."—(1787.)

2. The second excellency that I notice in Venn is his *singular wisdom and good sense in offering advice to others about duties* This is a rare qualification. I sometimes think it is almost easier to find a man of grace than a man of sense. How few are the people to whom we can turn for counsel on practical questions in religion, and feel a confidence that they will advise us well ! The vicar of Huddersfield appears to me to have possessed the spirit of counsel and of a sound mind in an eminent degree. His letters to Jonathan Scott, John Brasier, and Lady Mary Fitzgerald, containing directions for living a Christian life, and a solution of doubts and fears, ought to be read in their entirety to be fully appreciated. They are so thoroughly good all the way through that it is not fair to quote from them. I know nothing in the English language, of a short kind, so likely to be useful to those who are beginning a Christian life. His letter to a clergyman on the study of Hebrew and the value of translations of the Bible, is a model of sensible advice, and furnishes abundant proof that evangelical clergymen of the last century were not, as their enemies often insinuated, " unlearned and ignorant men." Last, but not least, his letters to his son and other clergymen on the ministerial office and its duties and trials, and the mistakes of young ministers, are a magazine of Christian wisdom which will amply repay examination. Indeed, there are few books which I would so strongly recommend to the attention of young clergymen as " Venn's Life and Letters." The truth is, the whole volume is full of strong Christian good sense, and it is difficult, in giving selections from it, to know

where to begin and where to stop. The following quotations must suffice.

To a friend at Huddersfield he says, in 1763 :—" The first thing I would press upon you is to beg of God more *light*. There is not a more false maxim than this, though common in almost every mouth, that ' Men know enough if they would but practice better.' God says, on the contrary, ' My people are destroyed for lack of knowledge.' And as at first men live in sin easy and well pleased, because they know not what they do ; so after they are alive and awake they do little for God, and gain little victory over sin, through the *ignorance* that is in them. They have no comfort, no establishment, no certainty that they are in the right path, even when they are going to God, because the eyes of their understanding are so little enlightened to discern the things that make for their peace. In all your prayers, therefore, call much upon God for divine teaching."

To a rich widow residing in London he says :—" In the day when the eternal state of man is determined, the greater part of those that are lost will perish, not through any gross and scandalous iniquity, but through a deadness to God and his love, an ignorance of their own sinfulness, and, in consequence of that, through reigning pride and self-sufficiency. Now, the one great source of all this miserable disorder, or that at least by which it is maintained and strengthened, is keeping much company with those whom the Scripture marks out as engaged in talk without sense—company, not with near relatives or chosen friends, not with those for whom we have any real regard, but with those who come to see us and we go to see them, only because the providence of God has brought us into one town. It is this that devours infinitely precious time, and engages us in mere trifling, when we otherwise should be drawing nigh to God and growing rich in divine knowledge and grace ; and such slaves are we naturally to the love of esteem, so eagerly desirous of having every one's good word, that we are content to go on in the circle of fashionable folly, while our hearts condemn us, and a secret voice whispers, 'This manner of spending time can never be right.' "

To the same lady he says :— " You certainly judge right not to restrain your son from balls, cards, &c., since a mother will never be judged, by a son of his age, capable of determining for him ; and perhaps, after your most strict injunctions to have done with such sinful vanities, he would be tempted even to violate your authority. The duty you are called of God to exercise now is to bear the cross borne at different times and in divers measures by all the disciples of a crucified Saviour. True, it is painful to see one's dear child a lover of pleasure more than of God—painful to see a young creature, born for communion with God and acquaintance with heavenly joys, wedded to trivial gratifications and the objects of sense alone. But such are we ! God prevented us with his goodness, and sounded an alarm in our souls, or we had been such to this hour. He expects, then, that your experience should teach you to wait for patience till mercy apprehend him also. From the whole, you see you are to learn two most important lessons from the painful situation you remain in with regard to your son. The one is, your own weakness and inability to give a single ray of light, or to excite the faintest conviction of sin, or to communicate the least particle of spiritual good, to one who is dearer to you than life. How ought this to take away every proud thought of our own sufficiency, and to keep us earnest importunate suppliants at the door of Almighty mercy and free grace ! The other lesson is, that your own conversion, and reception of the Lord Jesus Christ as your portion and righteousness, ought to be marvellous in your eyes. You have many kind thoughts and the highest esteem for me, for which I desire to retain a dear sense in my mind ; but you know I am merely a voice which said, ' Behold the Lamb of God !' "

3. The third excellency which strikes me in Venn's character is *his singular prudence and tenderness in the management of his children.* Few ministers, perhaps, have ever been more successful than he was in the education and training of his family ; few, perhaps, ever trained their sons and daughters with such unwearying pains, diligence, affection, watchfulness, and prayer. The families of pious ministers, like the sons of Samuel and David, have often brought discredit on their father's house ; or, like the children of Moses, have not been in any way remarkable. The family of Henry Venn forms a bright exception. All turned out well ; all proved Christians of no common degree ; and all gladdened their father's heart in his old age.

It would be impossible, in the narrow limits of this work, to give any adequate idea of Venn's dealing with his children. Those who feel an interest in the subject, and would like to know a most successful parent's mode of communication with his children, would do well to study the hundred pages of letters to his children which are to be found in the volume of his life and letters. Rarely indeed does a father succeed in uniting faithfulness, spirituality, and deep familiar affection so completely, in his correspondence with sons and daughters, as Henry Venn did. I can only find room for three specimens.

To his daughter Catherine he says, in 1781, writing on the due observance of the Sabbath :—" When I was of your age, I was, alas ! a mere pretender to religion. Though I constantly went to the house of God on the Sabbath, I saw not the glory of the Lord—I understood not his Word—I did not hear it when it was read—I asked for nothing—I wanted nothing for my soul,—so foolish and ignorant was I ! I was glad when the worship was over and the day was over, that my mouth might pour out foolishness, and that I might return to my sports and amusements. Oh, what a wicked stupidity of soul ! I am astonished how God could bear with me. Had he said : ' I swear thou shalt never ascend into the hill of the Lord, nor see my face, who findest it such a weariness to be at church, and art so proud and profane in spirit. No : dwell for ever with those whom you are like ; dwell with the devil and his angels, and with all who have departed this life enemies to my name and glory.' Oh ! had the Lord spoken thus to me in displeasure, I had received the due reward of my deeds. But adore him for his love to your father. In this state he opened my eyes and allured my heart, and gave me to seek him and his strength and face, and to join all his saints who keep holy his day, and to be glad to hear them say, ' Come, and let us go up to the house of the Lord.' Nay, more than this, he gave me your blessed mother for a companion, who loved exceedingly the house and day of the Lord ; and repaired to you and me her loss, by giving me another of his dear children who sanctifies each Sabbath with delight, and reverences God's house with her whole heart. Thus, instead of casting me into hell, he has made me the father of one dear saint in glory, and of four more—all of whom, I trust, fear and love the God of their father and mother, and all of whom, I have a lively hope, I shall meet in the courts above."

To his daughter Jane he writes, in 1785 :—" A great part of our warfare is to overcome our natural propensity to seek happiness in meat and drink, in dress and show ; which only nourish our disease, and keep us from communion with God as our chief good. More than thirty-seven years ago he was pleased, in his adorable mercy, to give me a demonstration that all was vanity and vexation of spirit but himself. From that hour (such is the energy of divine teaching), rising up and lying down, going out and coming in, I have felt this truth. I began and continued to seek the Lord and his strength and his face evermore. I was then led to know how the poverty and emptiness of all terrestrial good could be well supplied from the fulness of an adorable Jesus. And, oh ! how unspeakably blessed I am that I see my children impressed with the same precious and invaluable feelings, and that I hope, upon the best grounds, that we shall enjoy an eternity together in glory, where you shall know your father, not the poor, polluted, *hasty*, sinful creature he now is, but holy, without spot, wrinkle, or any such thing ; and when I shall know my dear children, not as emerging from a sea of corruption, and struggling against the law of sin in their members, and needing frequent intimations to do what is right, but when naturally and continually all within and without will be perfectly holy.   Oh ! what a meeting will that be, when all my prayers for your precious souls ever since you were born, when all my poor yet well-meant instructions and lessons from God's Word, and all your own petitions, shall be fully answered, and we shall dwell in a perfect union together !"

To his son John, on his appointment to the rectory of Clapham, he writes, in 1792 :—" Children, the old adage says, are careful comforts.   I find the truth of this now, particularly respecting you.   I was careful to see you called out to usefulness ; and now providentially a great door is found, I am in daily concern lest you should be hurt and suffer loss in your new station.   You must beware of company ; you must be much in secret and retirement.   Visiting friends, and being seldom in a solemn spirit before the throne of grace, ruin most of those who perish among professors of godliness."

The following facts, communicated to me by a connection of Henry Venn's, are in themselves so deeply interesting, and throw so much light on his mode of dealing with little children, that I make no apology for introducing them here.   It appears that one of his daughters married a widower with a family of young children.   These motherless little ones excited a strong interest in his heart, and he took one of them, only three years old, to his home at Yelling, and endeavoured to train the child for God.   My correspondent says :—

" The first thing he found out was that the poor child was

afraid of the dark. That very evening he took him by the hand, led him into his study, where the shutters were already closed, and seating him on his knee, with his arm close round him, he told the timid boy so wonderful a story out of God's Book as to make the child forget all beside. This he repeated day by day, till the evening story came to be anxiously expected. 'You will sit by my side to-day, John, and hold my hands, while you hear a new Bible story,' said the venerable man, after many a story had been told on the knee; 'and to-morrow you will like to sit by me without holding my hands, will you not?' This point once gained, a seat at a little distance was chosen, still in the dark; then one opposite; then one at the furthest end of the study; till, before winter closed, my father had entirely forgotten his fears of the dark, nor did they at any period of his life ever recur to him."

The advice given by this more than grandfather to the child, when he left Yelling for school, was often quoted; and though for a time he threw off the restraints of religion, and sought happiness in the world, the closing words of his venerable friend were never forgotten, and in after-life were repeated to his children and grandchildren scores if not hundreds of times: "Remember, little John, if anything could make heaven not heaven to me, it would be the not having you with me there."

God's blessing did follow that Christian teaching; and after a long life spent, first in actively doing, and then in suffering, his Father's will, that "Little John" rejoined his loved and honoured teacher in the skies, frequently saying, "When I get to heaven, how I shall bless God for the early lesson of dear old Henry Venn!"

4. The fourth excellency that I notice in Venn is his *singular unworldliness and cheerfulness of spirit.* He had his share of worldly trials; and these, too, of all sorts and descriptions. Sickness and severe bodily trials—the loss of his wife in the middle of his abundant labours at Huddersfield—straitened

circumstances, arising out of the extreme scantiness of his professional income,—all these things broke in upon him from time to time, and sorely tried his faith. But he seems to have been wonderfully strengthened throughout all his troubles. He preserved a cheerful frame of mind under every cross and trial, and was always able to see blue sky even in the gloomiest day.

His very portrait gives one the impression of a happy Christian. As we look at it, we can well understand the story that on more than one occasion he was asked to preach by clergymen who did not know him, under the idea that he was a jolly parson of the old school, and not a Methodist preacher! * They judged of him by his smiling face, and could not imagine that the man who had such a countenance could be the friend of Whitefield, Berridge, and Wesley. Striking, indeed, is the lesson that the incident contains. Well would it be for the Church of Christ if all preachers of the gospel were more careful to recommend their principles by their demeanour, and to show by their bearing that their Master's service is truly happy.

One single extract from his correspondence will suffice to show the vicar of Huddersfield's unworldly spirit. He heard that a lady, who knew and valued him, had made a will, leaving him a large sum of money. He at once wrote her a letter, positively declining to accept it, of which the following extract is a part: "I understand by my wife your most kind and generous intention toward me in your will. The legacy would be exceedingly acceptable; and I can assure you the person from whom it would come would greatly enhance the benefit. I love my sweet children as much as is lawful; and as I know it would give you pleasure to administer to the comfort of me and mine, I should with greater joy accept of your liberality.

"But an insurmountable bar stands in the way—the love of

* All Evangelical clergymen a hundred years ago were called " Methodists." Many people in the present day are not aware of this fact.

Him to whom we are both indebted, not for a transient benefit, for silver or gold, but, for an 'inheritance incorruptible, undefiled, and that fadeth not away, reserved in heaven for you.' His honour, his cause, is, and must be, dearer to his people than wife, children, or life itself. It is the pious resolve of his saints, 'I count all things but loss for the excellency of the knowledge of Christ Jesus my Lord.' To be, therefore, a stumbling-block in the way of any that are seeking him, to give the least countenance to any that would gladly bring his followers into contempt, would grieve me while in health, darken my mind in sickness, and load me with self-condemnation on my death-bed. After the most mature deliberation, therefore, it is our request that you will not leave us any other token of your regard than something of little value."

5. The last excellency that I note in Henry Venn is his *extraordinary catholicity and kindliness of spirit, and his readiness to love and honour his brethren.* Jealousy among ministers of Christ is, unhappily, a very common feeling. Nowhere, perhaps, will you find men so slow to recognize the gifts of others, and so quick to detect their faults, as in the ranks of preachers of religion. Of all the men of last century who attained eminent usefulness, I find none so free from jealousy as Henry Venn. He seems to delight in speaking well of his fellow-labourers, and to rejoice in their gifts and success.

It would be taking up too much room to quote all the expressions he uses about his contemporaries. Let it suffice to say that I find in his "Life" repeated kind words about the following men,—Whitefield, Wesley, Grimshaw, Romaine, Walker, Conyers, Hervey, Howell Harris, Berridge, Fletcher, Robinson, Newton, Adams, Cecil, Scott, and Abraham Booth the Baptist. That list alone is enough to show the largeness and warmth of Venn's heart. To suppose that he agreed with all these good men in all things, is simply unreasonable. But he had a quick eye to see grace, and a ready mind to acknowledge and admire it. Well would it be for the Church of Christ, if all ministers were more of his frame and spirit in this matter! Envy and jealousy are too often the greatest blots on the character of great men.

It only remains for me, now, to conclude my account of Henry Venn by quoting the language used about him by three good judges, though very different men.

Let us hear what Cowper the poet thought of him. He says, in a letter to Newton, written in 1791: "I am sorry that Mr. Venn's labours below are so near to a conclusion. I have seen few men whom I could have loved more, had opportunity been given me to know him better; so at least I have thought as often as I have seen him."

Let us hear what Charles Simeon of Cambridge thought of him. He says: "I most gladly bear my testimony that not the half, nor the hundredth part, of what might have been justly said of that blessed man of God has been spoken. If any person now living, except his children, is qualified to bear this testimony, it is I, who, from my first entrance into orders to his dying hour, had most intimate access to him, and enjoyed most of his company and conversation. How great a blessing his conversation and example have been to me will never be known till the day of judgment. I dislike the language of panegyric, and therefore forbear to expatiate on a character which, in my estimation, was above all praise. Scarcely ever did I visit him but he prayed with me, at noon-day, as well as at common seasons of family-worship. Scarcely ever did I dine with him but his ardour in returning thanks, sometimes in an appropriate hymn, sometimes in prayer, has inflamed the souls of all present. In all the twenty-four years that I knew him, I never remember him to have spoken unkindly of any one but once; and then I was struck with the humiliation he expressed for it in prayer next day."

Let us hear, lastly, what Sir James Stephen thought of Henry

Venn. In his "Essays on Ecclesiastical Biography" (amidst some things I cannot subscribe to), he concludes his account of the vicar of Huddersfield and Yelling with the following passage: "With a well-stored memory, he was an independent, if not an original, thinker. With deep and even vehement attachments, he knew how to maintain, on fit occasions, even to those he loved most, a judicial gravity, and even a judicial sternness. He acted with indefatigable energy in the throng of men, and yet in solitude could meditate with unwearied perseverance. He was at once a preacher at whose voice multitudes wept and trembled, and a companion to whose privacy the wise resorted for instruction, the wretched for comfort, and all for sympathy. In all the exigencies, and in all relations of life, the firmest reliance might always be placed on his counsel, his support, and his example. Like St. Paul, he became all things to all men, and for the same reason, that he might by any means save some."

Such was the last of the seven great spiritual heroes of the last century. I have dwelt long on his history, but I feel that he deserves it. He was not the commanding preacher that either Whitefield or Rowlands was. He did not possess the polish of Romaine, or the originality of Grimshaw or Berridge. But, take him for all in all, Henry Venn was a great man.

X.

Walker of Truro and his Ministry.

Born at Exeter, 1714—Educated at Exeter College, Oxford—Ordained, 1737—Curate of Truro, 1746—At First very ignorant of the Gospel—Mr. Conon's Influence—Effect of his Preaching—Opposition—Self-denial and Holy Life—Remarkable Effect on Soldiers —Private Unity Meetings—Died, 1761—Literary Remains—Preaching.

AN intelligent Christian needs not to be reminded that the Church of Christ has always recognized two classes of prophetical writers in the Old Testament. There are four who are called "the greater" prophets, and twelve who are called "the less." All wrote by direct and equal inspiration of God; "all spake as they were moved by the Holy Ghost;" and yet we do not hesitate to assign a higher importance to one class than to the other.

A well-informed man knows well, that in the solar system some planets exceed others in size and glory. All are bright, and beautiful, and perfect. All proclaim to the student of the heavens that the Hand which made them was divine. Yet the glory of such bodies as Jupiter and Saturn is far greater than that of Mars, or Venus, or the Moon.

Thoughts such as these come across my mind as I turn from the seven leading champions of the revival of English religion in the last century to some of their lesser contemporaries. There were not a few eminent ministers in our country who were entirely of one mind with Whitefield and his fellow-workers, and yet never attained to their greatness. They sympathized with the great leaders in all matters of doctrine.

They co-operated with them in the main, and rejoiced in their success. They cheerfully bore their share of the reproach cast on "Methodism" or evangelical religion. They shrank from no sacrifices, and spared no pains in setting forward Christ's gospel. But they did not possess the extraordinary public gifts of their seven brethren, and did not therefore leave so deep a mark on their generation. Like Silas and Timotheus in St. Paul's days, they did good work in their own positions; but not work that attracted so much public attention as that of the mighty "masters of assemblies" whom I have described in preceding chapters.

But we must beware that we do not undervalue men merely because they do not occupy prominent positions in the Church of Christ. Various and manifold are the gifts of the Holy Ghost, and he divides them to every man severally as he thinks fit. One minister is called to preach to thousands, and shake the world like a "son of thunder;" while another is called to write hymns or compose books in an obscure corner of the earth. One man has gifts of voice, and delivery, and action, and fluency, and memory, and invention, which fit him to stand up before multitudes—like Paul on Mars' Hill, or Luther at Worms, or Whitefield in Moorfields—and to carry all before him. Another is shy, and gentle, and retiring, and can only make his mind work in solitude, quiet, and silence. Yet each may be an instrument of mighty influence in God's hand. The last day, indeed, may prove that the work of him whose voice was never "heard in the street," and who dwelt among his own people, produced more permanent effect on souls than the most brilliant open-air sermons. I fear that we are all apt to exaggerate the value of public gifts, and to depreciate gifts which make no show before the world. Yet a time may come when the last shall be found first, and the first last.

Remembering these things, I wish to give some account of four men of the last century who are far less known than some of their contemporaries, and yet were eminently useful in their day and generation. The first whom I will introduce to my readers is Samuel Walker, the curate of Truro, in Cornwall.

Walker was born at Exeter in 1714, and died in 1761, at the early age of forty-seven. Partly from the circumstance that his ministerial life was entirely spent in one of the most remote corners of England, before railways were invented, and partly from his habits of mind, which made him entirely decline all public work of an aggressive and extra-parochial kind, he is a man whose name is scarcely known to many Christians. Yet he was one who, in his day, was most highly esteemed by such men as Wesley, Whitefield, Romaine, and Venn, for his eminent spirituality and soundness of judgment. Above all, he was one who cultivated his own corner of the Lord's vineyard with such singular success, that there were few places in England where such striking results could be shown from preaching the gospel as at Truro.

The facts of Walker's life of which any record remains are few, and soon told. His family resided at Exeter, and was well connected. He was lineally descended from the good Bishop Hall, who was for a time Bishop of Exeter, and whose grand-daughter married a Walker. His grandfather, Sir Thomas Walker, was member of Parliament for Exeter. John Walker, Rector of St. Mary the More, in Exeter, who wrote a well-known volume about the "Sufferings of the Ejected Clergy" under the Commonwealth, was also a relative of the subject of this chapter; in fact, the first edition of the work was published in the very year that Samuel Walker was born.

We know little of Walker's boyhood and youth, beyond the fact that he was educated at Exeter Grammar School, and was there for ten years—from the age of eight till he was eighteen. He went to Exeter College, Oxford, in 1732, and in due course of time took his degree of B.A. in that university. He seems to have made good use of his time while he was at college, and to have acquired much knowledge, which he found valuable in after-life. His biographer particularly mentions that " he cultivated logic with much success, and always considered his early devotion to that science as the foundation of the facility he afterwards attained in a clear and methodical arrangement of his ideas. When complimented by his friends, who admired the lucid and argumentative mode in which he treated every subject, he always observed that logic had been his favourite pursuit in youth, and that he recommended it to young divines." Beside being a reading man, he seems to have been thoroughly correct and moral in life ; and though utterly destitute of spiritual light or religion, he was mercifully preserved from the excesses into which many young men plunge at college, to their own subsequent bitter sorrow. We know nothing more of Walker's university life. We have no account of his companions, friends, or acquaintances. It is a curious fact, however, that it is clear, from a comparison of dates, that he must have been an undergraduate of Exeter College at the very time when the so-called Methodist movement began, and when Wesley, Whitefield, and Hervey were commencing their line of action as aggressive evangelists at Oxford. It is another curious fact that Lincoln College, of which John Wesley was a Resident Fellow, stands within fifty yards of Exeter College. Romaine also was at Christ Church at the same time. But there is not the slightest proof that Walker was acquainted with any of these good men.

Walker entered the ministry at the age of twenty-three, in the year 1737. He was first curate of Dodescomb Leigh, near Exeter, but only remained there one year. He then travelled on the Continent for two years, in the capacity of private tutor to the younger brother of Lord Rolle. On the termination of this engagement he became first curate, and immediately after vicar, of Lanlivery, near Lostwithiel, in Cornwall. He only held this living during the minority of a nephew of the patron, and finally resigned it in the year 1746. He then accepted the office of stipendiary curate of Truro, in Cornwall, and occupied that position for fifteen years, until the time of his death in 1761.

It is past all doubt that Walker was profoundly ignorant of spiritual religion at the time of his ordination. Like hundreds of clergymen, he undertook an office for which he was certainly not "inwardly moved by the Holy Ghost," and professed himself a teacher of others while he himself knew nothing of the truth as it is in Jesus. He says, in a letter dated 1756: "The week before my ordination I spent with the other candidates —as dissolute, I fear, as myself—in a very light and unbecoming manner; dining, supping, drinking, and laughing together, when, God knows, we should all have been on our knees, and warning each other to fear for our souls in the view of what we were about to put our hands to. I cannot but attribute the many careless, ungodly years I spent in pleasure after that time to this profane introduction; and, believe me, the review shocks me. While I write, I tremble in the recollection of the wounds I then gave Jesus."

In this painful and unsatisfactory state of mind Walker spent the first two years of his ministerial life. Throughout that time he was diligent and conscientious in the discharge of the outward duties of his office. He preached, visited, catechised, reproved, exhorted, and rebuked, but did no good at all. Ignorant alike of his own heart's disease and of the glorious remedy provided by Christ's gospel, he laboured entirely in vain. In fact, he said himself, in after-years, " that though he was well thought of, and, indeed, esteemed beyond most of his brethren for regularity, decency, and endeavour to keep up external attendance, and even for his public addresses, yet he felt he ought to go sorrowing to the grave, upon a review of the years so misspent."

The circumstances under which a complete change came

over Walker's heart, character, and ministerial life, were very remarkable. They supply a most instructive illustration of God's plan of leading people to Christ by ways " which they know not." Walker had come to Truro in 1746, with peculiar pleasure, on account of the notorious gaieties and festivities of the place, in which the young curate at that time took great delight. He entered the place a dancing, card-playing, party-going clergyman, and was known only in that character for the first twelve months of his ministry. It is said that at this period " his only ambition was to be courted for his gaiety and admired for his eloquence, and to become the reformer of the vicious by the power of persuasion and example." Ignorant he was not altogether, for, like every well-read man, he had historical notions of the leading doctrines of the Christian religion. But, to use his own words, " what he knew notionally, he neither felt nor sought practically." He acknowledges that, even in the midst of all his official decorum, he " was actuated by two hidden principles, as contrary to God as darkness is to light—a desire of reputation and a love of pleasure." Such were the beginnings of Walker's ministry ! Such was the unpromising material which God was pleased to take in hand, and mould and fashion into a goodly vessel of grace !

The manner of Walker's conversion is thus described by one of his biographers. " He had been at least a year in his curacy at Truro before he fell under any suspicion or uneasiness about himself or his preaching. The first impression that he was in error arose from a conversation between himself and a few of his parishioners on the subject of justifying and saving faith, to which he was judiciously led by a pious individual. This was a Mr. Conon, master of the Grammar School at Truro, who, he often said, was the first person he had ever met truly possessed of the mind of Christ, and by whose means he became sensible that all was wrong within and without." Mr. Conon was one of those rare servants of God who, like Job, are found in places where you would think no good thing could grow, and who serve to show that grace and not place makes the Christian. Intercourse between this good man and the curate of Truro gradually ripened into intimacy, and the result was the total conversion of the minister through the pious instrumentality of one of his hearers.

The change that had come over the curate of Truro was soon apparent, both in his preaching and practice. It could not be hid. He ceased to take part in the frivolous worldly amusements which at one time absorbed his attention. He frankly acknowledges that he did not take up this new line of action without a mighty inward struggle, and that it was "long before he could bring himself to any reasonable measure of indifference about the esteem of the world, and then only with heart-felt pangs of fear and disquietude." But he fought hard, and by God's grace was more than conqueror. At the same time, says his biographer, "he began to preach as he felt, declared the alteration in his views, and faithfully pointed out the evil of the empty pleasures in which the inhabitants of his parish were absorbed, and the danger of resting on the mere formalities of Sabbath worship for salvation. Repentance, faith, and the new birth became the topics of his sermons—truths which, though treated with all the power of his highly cultivated mind, brought down on him hatred as an enthusiast, derision as a madman, and vehement opposition as the destroyer of harmless joys. An infidel went even so far as to insult him in the pulpit, an affront which he bore with singular patience and dignity."

The effects of Walker's new style of preaching seem to have been very deep and extraordinary. Astonishment and surprise were the first prevailing feelings in the minds of all. To hear their curate denouncing the very practices in which he had lately indulged himself, and pressing home the very doctrines which he had neglected or despised, was enough to make men's hair stand on end! Anger and irritation were naturally excited in the hearts of hundreds who loved pleasure more than God, and were determined to cling to the world. But all alike seem to have been thoroughly aroused and impressed. His biographer says : " The earnestness of the preacher, and the striking alteration of his habits as well as of his sermons, stirred up the curiosity of the people, who, while they were enraged at the fidelity, were enchained by the eloquence and trembled at the sternness of their reprover. Even out of the pulpit they feared the presence of their minister. The Sabbath loiterers would retire at his approach, saying, ' Let us go ; here comes Walker.' His manner is said to have been commanding and solemn in the extreme, and his life so truly consistent that at length he awed into silence those who were at first most clamorous against him. At last such crowds attended his ministry, that the thoroughfares of the town seemed to be deserted during the hours of service, so that it was said you might fire a cannon down every street of Truro in church time, without a chance of killing a single human being."

No well-informed Christian will be surprised to hear that a man preaching and living as Walker did, was assailed by every kind of persecution. The great enemy of souls will never allow his kingdom to be pulled down without a struggle to preserve it. If he cannot prevent a faithful minister working, he will labour in every way to hinder and impede his work. The worldly portion of the Truro people resolved to get rid of a man who pricked their consciences and made them uncomfortable. They first tried to injure the curate of Truro with the bishop of the diocese ; but in this attempt, happily, they failed. They then endeavoured to prevail on the rector of Truro to dismiss him from his cure, a move which led to the following remarkable result. His biographer says : " Mr. Walker's enemies, being some of the wealthiest inhabitants of Truro, found the rector only too willing to listen to their complaints, and he promised that he would go to his curate and give him notice to quit his charge. He went; but like the Gaul who was sent to the Roman hero to despatch him in prison, he retired startled and abashed at his lofty tone and high bearing. On entering Walker's apartment, he was received with an elegance and dignity of manner which were natural to one who had long been the charm of society, and became so embarrassed as to be perfectly unable to advert to his errand. He at length made some remark which afforded an opportunity of speaking of the ministerial office and character, which Walker immediately embraced, and enlarged on the subject with such acuteness of reasoning and solemnity of appeal to his rector, as a fellow-labourer in the gospel, that he retreated overwhelmed with confusion, and unable to say a word about the intended dismissal. He was in consequence reproached with a breach of his promise, and went a second time to fulfil it. He again retreated without daring to allude to the object of his visit. He was pressed to go a third time by one of his principal parishioners, but replied, ' Do you go and dismiss him, if you can ; I cannot. I feel in his presence as if he were a being of superior order, and I am so abashed that I am uneasy till I can retire.' A short time after this the rector was taken ill, when he sent for Mr. Walker, entreated his prayers, acknowledged the propriety of his conduct, and promised him his hearty support if he recovered." From this time to the end of his ministry, no weapon formed against the curate of Truro seemed to prosper. He held on his way without let or hindrance, though not, of course, without much hatred, opposition, and petty persecution. But nothing that his opponents could do, or devise, was able to stop or silence him. So true is that word of Scripture : " When a man's ways please the Lord, he maketh even his enemies to be at peace with him" (Prov. xvi. 7).

There can be no doubt that Walker's position at Truro was greatly strengthened by his eminent holiness, self-denial, and consistency of life. Whatever his enemies thought of his preaching, they could not deny that he was a singularly holy man. Like Daniel, they could find no fault in him except concerning the law of his God. Two remarkable instances of his self-denial and disinterestedness deserve special mention. One is his voluntary resignation of the vicarage of Talland, to which he had been appointed about the time of his coming to Truro, with the bishop's license of non-residence. On becoming a converted man, his conscience told him that ne ought not to receive an income for which he discharged no ministerial duty. Acting on this principle, he cheerfully gave up the preferment unasked and unpersuaded, relinquished all his accustomed comforts, and went into humble lodgings of the plainest kind. The other instance is even more singular. He refused the opportunity of marrying a lady eminently suited to be his wife, who would have readily accepted his hand, on the sole ground that she had too much fortune. To a friend who seriously advised him to propose to her, he made the following remarkable reply : " I certainly never saw a woman whom I thought comparable to Miss ——, and I believe I should enjoy as much happiness in union with her as it is possible to enjoy in this world. I have reason also to think that she would not reject my suit. Still it must never be ! What would the world say of me ? Would not they imagine that the hope of obtaining such a prize influenced my profession of religion ? It is easy, they would say, to preach self-denial and heavenly-mindedness, but has not the preacher taken care to get as much of this world's good as he could possibly obtain ? It must never be ! I can never suffer any temporal happiness or advantage to be a hindrance to my usefulness." Conscientiousness like this is certainly very rare, and to many persons may seem totally incomprehensible and absurd. Whether, also, in Walker's behaviour to the lady, there was not something of morbid scrupulosity, and whether a happy marriage might not have lengthened his life and usefulness, are questions which admit of doubt. But there is no denying that not a few evangelical ministers have withered their own usefulness by marrying wealthy wives. And one thing is very certain, that Walker's character for eminent disinterestedness and unworldliness became so thoroughly established, that in this material point the breath of slander never touched him to the very end of his days.

The direct visible effects of Walker's ministry at Truro were very remarkable and extensive. Worldliness and wickedness were checked to an extraordinary extent, and even those who loved sin were ashamed to commit it so openly as they had done in time past. Not long after he began to preach the real gospel and to call men to repentance, the theatre and cockpit in the town were both forsaken, and given up to other purposes; and similar reforms extended to places in the neighbourhood through his instrumentality. The influence of his ministry, in fact, was singularly felt by many who were never converted. He said himself that he had reason to think almost all his hearers at Truro were, at one time or other, awakened more or less, "although I fear many of them have rejected the counsel of God against themselves."

Of positive spiritual results in the saving of souls by any one's ministry, a wise man will always speak cautiously. We see through a glass darkly, and are easily deceived in such matters. Yet I see every reason to believe that Walker's ministry at Truro was really the means of turning hundreds from darkness to light, and from the power of Satan unto God. It is a certain fact that in 1754, after he had preached the gospel only seven years at Truro, he recorded that no less than eight hundred persons had made particular application to him, from time to time, inquiring what they must do to be saved. Making every allowance for many of this number who doubtless drew back after their first convictions, and returned to their sins, this simple fact ought to fill our minds with astonishment. The parish of Truro, even at this day, does not contain more than ten thousand people. A hundred years ago it must have been a much smaller place. The ministry which in seven years could arrest the attention of eight hundred persons in such a parish, must have been one of singular power, and singularly blessed of God.

One of the most interesting examples of his ministerial success was the extraordinary effect that he produced on a regiment of soldiers which was quartered in Truro in 1756. As soon as they arrived, Walker set up a sermon for their special benefit on Sunday afternoon, which was called "the soldiers' sermon." After a little time the number of attendants became very large; and the mere fact that it was a voluntary service, specially intended for soldiers, no doubt helped greatly to bring hearers. The attention of the men was thoroughly arrested, and within three weeks no less than a hundred of them came to Walker's house, asking what they must do to be saved. He himself says to a correspondent: "The effects of the soldiers' sermon have been very striking. You would have seen their countenances changing, tears often bursting from their eyes, and confessions of their exceeding sinfulness and danger breaking from their mouths. I have scarcely heard such a thing as self-excusing from any of them; while the desire to be instructed, and uncommon thankfulness for any pains for them used by any of us, have been very remarkable."

His biographer says: "Mr. Walker's exertions in the regiment at first met with great opposition. The commander publicly forbade his men to go to him for private instruction, though, at last, no less than two hundred and fifty of them sought the persevering servant of Christ for that purpose. Those also whom religion had separated from the sinful habits and company of their unawakened comrades, were much derided; but grace enabled them to stand. A great alteration, however, soon took place. Punishment diminished, and order prevailed in the regiment, to a degree never before witnessed;

and at length the commander discovered the excellent cause of this salutary change. Genuine zeal had now its full triumph and rich reward. The officers waited on Mr. Walker in a body, to acknowledge the good effects of his wise and sedulous exertions, and to thank him for the reformation he had produced in their ranks."

"These interesting men left Truro after nine weeks' stay. The parting scene was indescribably affecting. They assembled the last evening in the society-room, to hear their beloved minister's farewell prayer and exhortation. 'Had you,' said Walker to a friend, 'but seen their countenances, what thankfulness, love, sorrow, and joy sat upon them! They hoped they might bring forth some fruit; they hoped to meet us again at the right hand of Jesus at the great day.' It was an hour of mingled distress and comfort; the hearts of many were so full, that they clasped the hand of the beloved instrument of their conversion, and turned away without a word. They began their morning march praising God for having brought them under the sound of the gospel; and as they slowly passed along, turned round to catch occasional glimpses of the town, as it gradually receded from their sight, exclaiming, 'God bless Truro!' They saw their spiritual leader no more upon earth, but were consoled by the hope of a triumphant meeting amongst the armies of heaven."

One grand peculiarity of Walker's ministry at Truro was the system of private meetings for mutual edification among the spiritual members of his congregation, which he succeeded in instituting. He seems to have been deeply impressed with the necessity of following up the work done in the pulpit, and with the desirableness of stirring up real Christians to be useful to one another There can be no doubt that he was right. 'Edify one another,' is an apostolic principle far too much overlooked (1 Thess. v 11) Most Christians are far too ready to leave everything to be done by their minister, and forget that a minister has only one body and one tongue, and cannot be everywhere, and do everything. Above all, most Christians forget that the mutual conference of believers is a valuable means of grace, and that in trying to water others we are likely to be watered ourselves. But the best and wisest manner of conducting these meetings for mutual edification is a subject of vast difficulty, and one on which good men differ widely. Scores of excellent ministers have attempted to do something in this direction, and have completely failed. It was precisely here that Walker seems to have been eminently gifted, and to have obtained extraordinary success.

My limited space makes it quite impossible to give a full account of all the plans and arrangements that Walker made for the conduct of these religious societies. Those who wish to know more about them will find them fully described in Sidney's "Life of Walker." One leading feature of his system deserves, however, to be specially noticed : I mean his careful classification of the members of his societies. He always formed them into two divisions, one composed entirely of men, into which no female was admitted ; the other of married men, their wives, and unmarried women, from which all single men were excluded. The wisdom and good sense of this classification will be obvious to every reflecting Christian. It is the very neglect of it, however simple it may appear, which has been the ruin of many similar private movements among religious people. The rules drawn up for the management of meetings are marked throughout by like soundness of judgment. The objects to be kept steadily in view—the admission of members, the hours to be kept, the mode of proceeding, the things to be habitually avoided by members—are all most carefully defined, and give one a most favourable idea of Walker's rare Christian good sense. I have only room to quote two rules, which are a good specimen of the tone and spirit running through all the regulations.

One rule is : " That every member of this Society do esteem himself peculiarly obliged to live in an inoffensive and orderly manner, to the glory of God and the edification of his neighbours ; that he study to advance, in himself and others, humility and meekness, faith in Christ, love to God, gospel repentance, and new obedience, in which things Christian edification consists, and not in vain janglings. And that in all his conversation and articles of faith he stick close to the plain and divine meaning of Holy Scripture, carefully avoiding all intricate niceties and refinements upon it."

The other rule, or rather explanatory definition, is : " By a disorderly carriage we mean not only the commission of gross and scandalous sins, but also what are esteemed matters of little moment in the eyes of the world, such as the light use of the words, *Lord, God, Jesus,* &c., in ordinary conversation, which we cannot but interpret as an evidence of the want of God's presence in the heart ; the buying and selling of goods which have not paid custom ; the doing needless work on the Lord's day ; the frequenting ale-houses or taverns without necessary business. And considering the consequence of vain amusements so generally practised, we do, in charity to the souls of others, as well as to avoid the danger of such things ourselves, think ourselves obliged to use particular caution about many of them, however innocent they may be in themselves, such as cards, dancings, clubs for entertainments, play-houses, sports at festivals and parish feasts, and as much as may be parish feasts themselves, lest by joining therein we are a hindrance to ourselves and others." This is sound speech that cannot be condemned. Regulations such as these need no comment. Whatever objections may be made against private societies such as Walker formed at Truro, as tending to create a church within a church, one thing at least is sure—A system which produced such a high standard of life and practice in the members of the Society, deserves serious consideration.

Walker's most useful career was brought to a termination in the year 1761. He died at the early age of forty-seven, of pulmonary consumption, accelerated, if not brought on, by his over-abundant labours in the cause of Christ at Truro. It is impossible to wonder at his breaking down at a comparatively early age, when we consider the immense amount of ministerial labour which he regularly carried on, single-handed and unassisted, for nearly fourteen years, in his large Cornish parish. He says himself, in a letter dated 1755 : " My stated business (beside the Sunday duty, prayers Wednesdays and Fridays, burials, baptisms, and attendance on the sick) is, on Mondays, Wednesdays, and Fridays, to talk with such as apply to me in private from six to ten in the evening ; Tuesday, to attend the society ; and Thursday, a lecture in church in the evening. Saturday, and as much of Friday as I can give, is bestowed in preparing the Sunday's sermons. To all this must be added what I may well call the care of the church, that is, of above a hundred people, who, on one account and another, continually need my direction. You will not wonder if my strength proves unequal to this labour, and I find myself debilitated, and under necessity of making my time shorter by lying in bed longer than formerly. In short, what I am going through seems evidently to be hastening my end, though there be no immediate danger." The plain truth is, that so far from wondering that such a man died so soon, we should rather wonder that he worked and lived so long.

He died at Blackheath, near London, after a long and suffering illness of more than a year's duration, in which he received every attention that could be bestowed on his poor earthly tabernacle from the kindness of Lord Dartmouth. He died in the full enjoyment of the peace he had so faithfully preached to others, and his death-bed was without a cloud. He had never married, and, like Berridge, had neither brother, sister, nor near relative to stand by him as he went down into the river. But he had that which is far better than earthly relatives, the strong consolation of a lively hope, and the presence of that Saviour who "sticketh closer than a brother," and who has said, "I will never leave thee nor forsake thee."

The following letter, written on his death-bed to his beloved friend Mr. Conon, only a fortnight before he died, gives a most pleasing impression of Walker's happy frame of mind in the prospect of eternity. He says :—

" My dearest, most faithful friend,—My disorder, though by no means affording the least prospect of recovery, yet seems to affect me at present more with weakness than with that violent heat which rendered me incapable of thought. I can now, blessed be God, think a little ; and with what comfort do I both receive your thoughts and communicate mine to you ! Oh, my dear friend, what do we owe to the Lord for one another ! More than I could have conceived, had not God sent me to die elsewhere. We shall have time to praise the Lord, when we meet in the other world. I stand and look upon that world with an established heart. I see the way prepared, opened, and assured unto me in Jesus Christ. For ever blessed be the name of God, that I can look upon death, that introduces that glorious scene, without any kind of fear. I find my grand duty still is submission, both as to time and circumstances. Why should I not say to you that I find nothing come so near my heart, as the fear lest my will should thwart God's will in any circumstances? Thus, I think, I am enabled to watch and pray in some poor measure. Well, my dear friend, I am but stepping a little before you. You will soon also get your release, and then we shall triumph for ever in the name, love, and power of the Lamb. Adieu ! Yours in the Lord Jesus Christ for ever. Amen."

The above touching letter was probably the last that Walker wrote. One week later, Mr. Burnet, a dear and valued friend both of Walker's and Venn's, gave the following account of him in a letter to a friend. He says: " On Saturday, the 11th July, I reached Mr. Walker's lodging at Blackheath. There I saw the dear man lying on his bed of sickness, pining away in the last stage of consumption, burnt up with raging fever, and wasted almost to a skeleton. He was perfectly sensible, and so was able to express himself much to our satisfaction. The first thing which struck me exceedingly was his patient submission under God's hand, and his thankful tender concern for all those who were near to him. So little was his mind engaged with things merely pertaining to himself, that in the smallest things concerning my own convenience and comfort he behaved as if I had been the sick person. He said he had been uneasy, at the beginning of his sickness, at the want of sensible frames of feeling, but was relieved by that Scripture, ' They that worship God must worship him in spirit,' with the noble powers of the soul ; and that he now found experimentally the worship of God's Spirit on his heart in a degree he had never before experienced. ' I am now enabled,' he said, ' to see when it was that the Lord Jesus first laid effectual hold of my heart, which I was never able to discover before. I have a perfect satisfaction in the principles I have preached, and the methods I have generally taken. I have no doubt respecting my state in Christ, or my future glory. Behold, I am going down to the gates of the grave, and holy angels wait for me. Why do you trouble yourselves, and weep? Cannot you rejoice with me? I am going to heaven. Christ died : my Lord ! Oh, had I strength to express myself, I could tell you enough to make your hearts weep for joy. God is all love to me, and my trials are very slight.' "

On Tuesday, July the 14th, Walker dictated the following words to Mr. Conon : " My dearest Friend,—With great confusion of thought, I have no doubts, great confidence, great submission, no complaining. As to actual views of the joys that are coming, I have none; but a steadfast belief of them in Christ." The same day, when one sitting by his bedside observed that his soul was ripe for heaven and eternity, he interrupted him by saying, "that the body of sin was not yet done away, but that he should continue a sinner to the last gasp, and desired that he would pray for him as such."

On Sunday, July the 19th, in the same happy and peaceful frame of mind, the holy curate of Truro fell asleep in Christ, and went home. "Let me die the death of the righteous, and let my last end be like his."

Walker's literary remains are not many, but they deserve far more attention than many writings of the period when he lived. His "Lectures on the Church Catechism," his "Nine Sermons on the Covenant of Grace," and his eleven sermons entitled "The Christian," are all excellent books, and ought to be better known and more read than they are in the present day. His sermons give me a most favourable impression of his powers as a preacher. For simplicity, directness, vivacity, and home appeals to the heart and conscience, I am disposed to assign them a very high rank among the sermons of a hundred years ago. It is my deliberate impression, that if he had been an itinerant like Whitefield, and had not confined himself to his pulpit at Truro, he would probably have been reckoned one of the best preachers of his day.

The following extract from the last sermon preached by Walker at Truro is not only interesting in itself, but is also a very fair specimen of his style of preaching. The subject was the second coming of Christ to judge the quick and the dead. He said at the conclusion: "Can I think of this day, so honourable to him whom my soul loveth, without longing and wishing for its appearing? When I consider that his people shall partake with him in the glories of that day, and hear him say those ravishing words never to be recalled, 'Come, ye blessed of my father,' can I do other than say, 'Come, Lord Jesus, come quickly?' Surely I should rejoice to see and be for ever with the Lord; to behold his beauty as the express image of his father's person; to contemplate with endless and insatiable transport the glory which the Father hath given him; to make my acknowledgment, amid the praises of heaven, among the multitude which no man can number, as saved, for ever saved, by his love and care, his power and grace. What! when the least beam of his glory let in upon my soul now turns my earth into heaven, and makes me cry out with Peter, ' It is good for us to be here,' can I wish to delay his coming? When, remaining in this vale of misery, I groan under corruptions, and am burdened with a corruptible body, can I say, ' This is better than to be fashioned in soul and body like unto the Lord?' When I find here nothing but vanity and vexation of spirit, shall I be averse to the Lord's coming to change my sorrows into joy unspeakable and full of glory? Here, beset as I am with enemies, would I not long for that blessed day when I shall see them again no more for ever? And would I not be glad to be taken from a world lying in wickedness, into that new heaven and earth wherein dwelleth righteousness? I know that my redeemer liveth. I know that he shall stand at the latter day upon the earth. I have a humble confidence that he will own me among the children. And shall I, like those who know no better joys than this world can afford them, are ignorant of a Redeemer's righteousness, and lie under the unconscious guilt of unnumbered and unpardoned sin—shall I, like them, cleave to this base life as my all for happiness, and not wait, and wish, and long for the day of my Master's glorious appearing? No! I will not abide in that low measure of faith, which only begets a hope that I may be well when the Lord comes, but knows not what it is to love the day of his appearing. My endeavour shall be to be strong in the faith, and abounding in hope through the power of the Holy Ghost, always fruitful in good works, and hasting unto the day of the Lord.

" As for you, my dear hearers, I am grieved at heart for

many, very many of you, to think how you will make your appearance before Christ's judgment-seat. You have no works to speak there for your belonging to Christ ; I can see none. I see works of various kinds that prove you do not belong to him. If a life of pleasure, idleness, indulgence, drunkenness, pride, covetousness, would recommend you to the favour of the Judge, few would be better received than numbers of you ! In the name of God, my friends, when you know this moment in your own consciences that if, as you have been and are, you should be called to judgment, you would be surely cast into hell, why will you live at such a rate? Well ! we shall all be soon before the judgment-seat of Christ. There the controversy between me, persuading you by the terrors of the Lord to repent, and you, determined to abide in your sins, will be decided. There it will appear whether your blood will be upon your own heads for your obstinate impenitences, or upon mine for not giving you warning. Christ will certainly either acquit or condemn me on this account ; and if I should be acquitted, what will become of you? I tremble to think how many words of mine will be brought up against you on that day. What will you say, what will you answer, how will you excuse yourselves? Oh, sirs, if you will not be prevailed upon, you will, with eternal self-reproach, curse the day that you knew me, or heard one word from my mouth. Why, why will ye die with so aggravated a destruction? May the Lord incline you to think ! May he cause this word to sink deep into your hearts ! May he show you all your dangers, and with an outstretched arm bring you out of the hands of the devil, and translate you into the kingdom of his dear Son."

The letters which Mr. Sidney has collected in his biography of Walker are all interesting, especially those addressed to the two Wesleys, and to Mr. Adam of Winteringham, author of " Private Thoughts upon Religion." Indeed, the whole book is valuable. I only regret that the author should have thought it necessary to elaborate so carefully his favourite idea, that Mr. Walker was a sound Churchman and not a Dissenter. It may be perfectly true, no doubt. But it is too often pressed and thrust upon our notice. Walker lived in a day when the very existence of Christianity in England was at stake, and when the main business of true-hearted Christians was to preserve the very foundations of revealed religion from being swept away. To my eyes, Walker's thorough Christianity is a far more conspicuous object than his Churchmanship.

After all, I leave the subject of this chapter with a very deep conviction that we know comparatively very little about Walker. The half of his work, I suspect, has never yet been recorded. He lived near the Land's End. He seldom left his own parish. His life was never fully written till fifty or sixty years after he was dead. What wonder, then, if we know but little of the man! Yet I venture the surmise that in the last day, when the secrets of all ministries shall be disclosed, few will be found to have done better work for Christ in their day and generation than Walker of Truro.

XI

James Herbey of Weston Favell, and his Ministry.

Born near Northampton, 1713—Educated at Lincoln College, Oxford—Intimacy with John Wesley—Ordained, 1736—Curate of Dummer, 1738; of Bideford, 1740; and of Weston Favell, 1743—Early Religious History—Correspondence with Whitefield—Studious Habit at Weston Favell—Literary Remains Analyzed—Correspondence—Humour—Private Life—Charity—Self-denial—Died, 1758—Testimony of Romaine, Venn, Cowper, Cecil, Bickersteth, and Daniel Wilson.

HERE is a striking chapter in the Book of Judges, in which Deborah and Barak sing a triumphal hymn after the defeat of the hosts of Sisera. In one part of this hymn they recount the names of the tribes who came forward most readily to do battle for the freedom of Israel. Some of the tribes are mentioned in high praise. Others are dismissed with expressions of reproach. None are so much commended as Zebulun and Naphtali. They were "a people who jeoparded their lives unto the death in the high places of the field." But a sentence is used in the account of Zebulun, which deserves special notice: "Out of Zebulun," it is said, "came down they that handle the pen of the writer" (Judges v. 14).

The expression is a strange one. It cannot be denied that the meaning of it is involved in some obscurity. There is some probability in the conjecture of those who think it signifies scribes, who mustered the levies of Zebulun, and wrote down the names of those who went to war (compare Jer.

lii. 25). But be the precise meaning what it may, one thing is abundantly clear. The zeal of Zebulun in God's cause was such that, among her warriors in the day of battle, there were some who were more accustomed to wield the pen than the sword. When God's work was to be done, the soldier and the writer stood shoulder to shoulder, and side by side.

The expression has often recurred to my mind of late, in studying the history of English religion a hundred years ago. I am struck with the variety of instruments which God employed in carrying on the great revival of Christianity which then took place. I see some men who were mighty with the tongue, and bowed the hearts of assemblies by their preaching, as the trees of the wood are bowed by the wind. I see others who were mighty in government, and skilful in organizing, directing, methodizing, and administering. But, besides these, I see others who were mighty with the pen, and did work for Christ as real and lasting as any of their contemporaries. They made no public show. They did not cry, or strive, or let their voice be heard in the street. But they laboured in their way most effectually for the advancement of pure evangelical religion. They reached minds which were never brought under the influence of Whitefield, Wesley, or Romaine. They produced results in many quarters which will never be fully known till the judgment day. Foremost, perhaps, in this class of men in the last century, was the subject of my present paper, James Hervey of Weston Favell, the author of "Theron and Aspasio."

James Hervey was born on February 26, 1713, at Hardingstone, near Northampton. His father was rector of the neighbouring parishes of Collingtree and Weston Favell, but appears for some reason to have resided out of his parish. About his parents I can find no certain information, either as to their religious opinions or their practice. The parishes of which his father was rector are small rural places, very near the town of Northampton, on the south-eastern side. The date of his birth deserves notice on one account. It shows that he was one of the little band whom God sent into the world at a special time, to do a special work together in England. Whitefield, Wesley, Grimshaw, Berridge, Rowlands, Romaine, Venn, Walker, and Hervey, were all born in the first twenty years of the eighteenth century, between 1700 and 1720.

The facts and events of Hervey's life are singularly few. He was educated at the Grammar School of Northampton, and remained there from the time he was seven years old till he was seventeen. Two things only are recorded about his school-boy life. One is, that he was very skilful and dexterous in all games and recreations. The other is, that he made great progress in Latin and Greek, and would have got on even faster than he did, if his schoolmaster had allowed him. But it appears that this worthy pedagogue made it a rule never to allow any of his pupils to learn quicker than his own son! The fiction of "Do-the-boys Hall," it may be feared, is built on a very broad foundation of facts. Obscure Yorkshire schools are not the only academies where little boys are victimized and unfairly used.

In the year 1731, Hervey was sent to Oxford, and entered at Lincoln College. The first two years of his University life appear to have been spent in idleness. Like many young men, he suffered much from the want of some wise friend to advise and direct him in his studies. In 1733, however, he became acquainted with the two Wesleys, Whitefield, Ingham, and other steady young men, and derived great benefit from their society. Under their influence and example, he began a steady course of reading, and made himself master of such books as "Derham's Astro-Theology," "Ray's Wisdom of God in Creation," and other works of a similar kind. He also commenced the study of the Hebrew language. Nor was this all. He began to follow his new companions in their efforts to attain and promote a high standard of religion. Like them, he began to live by method, received the communion every Sabbath, visited the sick and the prisoners in jail, and read to poor people. The last three years of his Oxford life were thus use-fully employed, and the result was that he left the University, in 1736, with a good foundation of steady habits of living, and with a very fair amount of knowledge and scholarship. His literary remains, indeed, supply abundant proof that, consider-ing the times he lived in, he was a well-read and well-educated man.

No one seems to have been more useful to Hervey, at this period of his life, than John Wesley. At a later date, after doctrinal differences had separated the two men, the Rector of Weston Favell bore grateful and honourable testimony to this fact. He says, in one of his letters : "I heartily thank you, as for all other favours, so especially for teaching me Hebrew. I have cultivated this study, according to your advice. I can never forget that tender-hearted and generous Fellow of Lincoln, who condescended to take such compassionate notice of a poor undergraduate, whom almost everybody contemned, and whose soul no man cared for." Happy is that college where Fellows show kindness to undergraduates, and do not neglect them ! Attentions of this kind cost little ; but they are worth much, gain influence, and bear fruit after many days.

In the year 1736, Hervey was ordained a minister by Dr. Potter, Bishop of Oxford, and in 1736 became curate to his father at Weston Favell. He seems to have filled this position for a very short time. In 1738, we find him Curate of Dum-mer, near Basingstoke, in Hampshire, a position, singularly enough, which Whitefield had also occupied about the same year. In 1740, he removed to Bideford, in North Devonshire, and remained there till August 1743. He then returned to Weston Favell, and became once more curate to his father. This was his last move. On the death of his father, in 1752, he succeeded him as Rector of Weston Favell and Collingtree.

but only survived him six years. He finally died, at Weston Favell, on Christmas-day 1758, of pulmonary consumption, at the comparatively early age of forty-five. Unlike most ministers, he preached the gospel amongst the people who had known him from his earliest infancy, and was buried within a very few miles from the place where he had been born. In life and death he "dwelt among his own people."

The spiritual history of Hervey presents several interesting features. I can find no evidence that he knew anything of vital religion when he was a boy or a young man. Though mercifully kept from the excess of riot and immorality into which the young frequently run, he seems to have been utterly careless and thoughtless about his soul. The beginning of a work of grace in his heart may undoubtedly be traced to his residence at Oxford, and his intercourse with Wesley and Whitefield, which he commenced at the age of twenty. Yet even then he seems to have been much in the dark for some years, and to have been comparatively ignorant of the distinctive doctrines of real Christianity. His college friends, it must be admitted, knew little more than he did. Their early struggles after light were made through a fog of mysticism and asceticism which impeded their course for years. The freeness and simplicity of the gospel, the finished work of Christ on the cross, the real meaning of justification by faith without the deeds of the law, the folly of putting doing before believing, all these were subjects which this little band of young men at Oxford were very slow to understand. Each and all in their turns struggled through their mental difficulties, and came out on the right side. But one of the last to reach "terra firma," and grasp the whole truth as it is in Jesus, undoubtedly was James Hervey. In fact, it was not till the year 1741, five years after he had been ordained, that he thoroughly received the whole gospel into his heart, and embraced the whole system of evangelical doctrine. Two sermons preached by Hervey at Bideford about the year 1741, in which he plainly avowed his change of sentiments, were commonly called his "Recantation" sermons.

The state of Hervey's heart during the seven years preceding 1741 must have been one of continual conflict and inward dissatisfaction. Enlightened enough to feel the value of his soul, and to see something of the sinfulness of sin, he was still unacquainted with the way of peace. His letters written at this period, both before and after ordination, exhibit a mind full of pious thoughts, holy desires, and high aspirations, but with everything out of proportion and out of place. The writer says excellent things about the soul, and sin, and God, and the Bible, and the world, and duty, and even says much about Christ. You cannot help admiring his evident sincerity, purity of mind, and zeal to do good. But you cannot help feeling that he has not got hold of things by the right end, and does not see the whole of religion. He is like an excellent and well-formed ship without a compass and rudder. He has not yet got his feet upon the Rock. He is incessantly putting things in their wrong places. The last are too often first, and the first are too often last. He does not say things that are not true,. but he does not say them in the right way, and at the same time leaves out much that ought to be said.

The unsatisfactory character of Hervey's theology at the beginning of his ministry is well illustrated by the following anecdote. In one of the Northamptonshire parishes where he preached before 1741, there lived a ploughman who usually attended the ministry of Dr. Doddridge, and was well-informed in the doctrines of grace. Hervey being ordered by his physicians, for the benefit of his health, to follow the plough, in order to smell the fresh earth, frequently accompanied this ploughman when he was working. Knowing that he was a serious man, he said to him one morning, "What do you think is the hardest thing in religion?"—The ploughman replied;

" Sir, I am a poor man, and you are a minister; I beg leave to return the question."—Then said Mr. Hervey: "I think the hardest thing is to deny *sinful* self;" grounding his opinion on our Lord's admonition, "If any man will come after me, let him deny himself." "I argued," said Mr. Hervey, "upon the import and extent of the duty, showing that merely to forbear sinful actions is little, and that we must deny admittance and entertainment to evil imaginations and quench irregular desires. In this way I shot my random bolt."—The ploughman quietly replied : " Sir, there is another instance of self-denial to which the injunction of Christ equally extends, which is the hardest thing in religion, and that is, to deny *righteous* self. You know I do not come to hear you preach, but go every Sunday with my family to hear Dr. Doddridge at Northampton. We rise early in the morning, and have prayer before we set out, in which I find pleasure. Walking there and back I find pleasure. Under the sermon I find pleasure. When at the Lord's Table I find pleasure. We return, read a portion of Scripture, and go to prayer in the evening, and I find pleasure. But yet, to this moment, I find it the hardest thing to deny righteous self, I mean to renounce my own strength and righteousness, and not to lean on that for holiness or rely on this for justification." In repeating this story to a friend, Mr. Hervey observed, " I then hated the righteousness of Christ. I looked at the man with astonishment and disdain, and thought him an old fool, and wondered at what I fancied the motley mixture of piety and oddity in his notions. I have since seen clearly who was the fool; not the wise old ploughman, but the proud James Hervey. I now discern sense, solidity, and truth in his observations."

During this period of Hervey's life, his old Oxford friend, the famous George Whitefield, frequently corresponded with him. That mighty man of God had been brought into the full light of the gospel, and, like the Samaritan woman, burned with desire to bring all whom he knew and loved into the same glorious liberty. The following letter, while it shows Whitefield's deep concern for his friend's salvation, makes Hervey's defective religious principles at this period very evident: " I long to have my dear friend come forth and preach the truth as it is in Jesus; not a righteousness or holiness of our own, whereby we make ourselves meet, but the righteousness of another, even the Lord our righteousness; upon the imputation and apprehending of which by faith we shall be made meet by his Holy Spirit to live with and enjoy God. Dear Mr. Hervey, it is an excellent thing to be convinced of the freeness and riches of God's grace in Christ Jesus. It is sweet to know and preach that Christ justifies the ungodly, and that all good works are not so much as partly the cause, but the effect of our justification. Till convinced of these truths, you must own free will is in man, which is directly contrary to the Holy Scriptures and to the Articles of our Church. Let me advise dear Mr. Hervey, laying aside all prejudices, to read and pray over St. Paul's Epistles to the Romans and Galatians, and then to tell me what he thinks of this doctrine. Most of our old friends are now happily enlightened. God sets his seal to such preaching in an extraordinary manner, and I am persuaded the gates of hell will never be able to prevail against it. O that dear Mr. Hervey would also join with us! O that the Lord would open his eyes to behold aright this mystery of godliness? How would it rejoice my heart! How would it comfort his own soul! He would no longer groan under a spirit of bondage; no, he would be brought into the glorious liberty of the children of God." This letter was dated Philadelphia, November 10, 1739.

Hervey's excellent biographer, John Brown of Whitburn, gives the following clear account of his state of mind at this period: " It is evident that he was seeking salvation; but he sought it, as it were, by the works of the law. One of his leading errors was, that he had low, scanty, inadequate apprehensions of the love of God. From this unavoidably followed a disesteem of imputed righteousness, a conceit of personal qualifications, a spirit of legal bondage, and a tincture of Pharisaical pride. He conceived faith to be no more than a mere believing of promises if he did well, and of threatenings if he did ill. He wished for a salvation to be bestowed upon some sincere, pious, and worthy persons, and was distress'd because he could not find himself of that number. To use his own words, when he felt he was deplorably deficient in duty, he would comfort himself with saying, ' Soul, thy God only requires sincere obedience, and perhaps to-morrow may be more abundant in acts of holiness.' When overcome by sin, he would call to mind his righteous deeds, and so think to commute with divine justice, and quit scores for his offences by his duties. In order to be reconciled to God, and to ease his conscience, he would promise stricter watchfulness, more alms, and renewed fastings. Overlooking entirely the active obedience of our Redeemer, he fondly imagined that through the death of Christ he might have pardon of his sins, and could by his own doings secure eternal life."

" For some time," continues his biographer, " letters from Whitefield were disregarded, or answered with stubborn silence ; but at length, by this and other means, a saving change took place in Mr. Hervey's mind. Says he, The two great commandments—Thou shalt love the Lord thy God with all thy heart ; Thou shalt love thy neighbour as thyself—made the first awakening impression on my heart. Amazing ! thought I ; are these commands of God as obligatory as the prohibition of adultery or the observation of the Sabbath ? Then has my whole life been a continued act of disobedience ; not a day nor an hour in which I have performed my duty ! This conviction struck me as the handwriting upon the wall struck the presumptuous monarch. It pursued me, as Saul pursued the Christians, not only to my own house, but to distant cities ; nor even gave up the great controversy till, under the influence of the Spirit, it brought me, weary and heavy laden, to Jesus Christ. Then God, who commanded the light to shine out of darkness, shined into my heart, and gave me the light of the glory of God in the face of Jesus Christ."

After all, it would be difficult to give a more vivid and interesting account of the change which came over Hervey than that which he himself gives in a letter to his faithful friend, George Whitefield. He says: "You are pleased to ask how the Holy Ghost convinced me of self-righteousness, and drove me out of my false rest. Indeed, sir, I cannot tell. The light was not instantaneous; it did not flash upon my soul, but arose like the dawning of the day. A little book by Jenks, upon 'Submission to the Righteousness of God,' was made serviceable to me. Your journals, dear sir, and sermons, especially that sweet sermon on the text, 'What think ye of Christ?' were a means of bringing me to the knowledge of the truth. Another piece has been also like precious eye-salve to my dim and clouded understanding—I mean Marshall's 'Gospel Mystery of Sanctification.' These, blessed be He who is a light to them that sit in darkness, have in some degree convinced me of my former errors. I now begin to see I have been labouring in the fire, and wearying myself for very vanity, while I have attempted to establish my own righteousness. I trusted I knew not what, while I trusted in some imaginary good deeds of my own. These are no hiding-place from the storm; they are a refuge of lies. If I had the meekness of Moses and the patience of Job, the zeal of Paul and the love of John, I durst not advance the least plea to eternal life on this footing. As for my own beggarly performances, wretched righteousnesses, gracious Emmanuel! I am ashamed, I am grieved that I should thrust them into the plan of thy divine, thy inconceivably precious obedience! My schemes are altered. I now desire to work in my blessed Master's service, not for life, but from life and salvation. I would study to please him in righteousness and holiness all the days of my life."

In another letter to Whitefield, of about the same date, Hervey says: "I own, with shame and sorrow, I have been a blind leader of the blind. My tongue and my pen have perverted the good ways of the Lord, have darkened the glory of redeeming merit and sovereign grace. I have dared to invade the glories of an all-sufficient Saviour, and to pluck the crown off his head. My writings and discourses have derogated from the honour, the everlasting, incommunicable honour of Jesus. They presumed to give works a share in the redemption and recovery of a lost sinner. They have placed filthy rags on the throne of the Lamb, and by that means have debased the Saviour and exalted the sinner. But I trust the divine truth begins to dawn upon my soul. Oh, may it, like the rising sun, shine more and more till the day break in all its brightness, and the shadows flee away! Now, was I possessed of all the righteous acts that have made saints and martyrs famous in all generations, could they be transferred to me, and might I call them my own, I would renounce them all that I might win Christ."

I make no excuse for the length at which I have dwelt on this portion of Hervey's history. A mere worldly man may see nothing interesting in it; but a true Christian, unless I am greatly mistaken, will find it full of instruction. It is useful to mark the diversities of the operation of the Spirit. How slowly and gradually he carries on his work in some hearts, compared to the rapid progress he makes in others! It is useful to mark the extent of his operations. How thoroughly he can turn upside down a man's theological opinions! How little we know what a young self-righteous minister may one day, by God's grace, become! Well would it be for the Christian Church if there were more ministers in her pale taught of God, and brought to sit at the feet of Christ, like James Hervey.

The last seventeen years of Hervey's life were spent in comparative retirement at Weston Favell. "My house," he writes to a friend, "is quite retired. It faces the garden and the field, so that we hear none of the tumultuous din of the world, and see nothing but the wonderful and charming works of the Creator. Oh, that I may be enabled to improve this advantageous solitude!" Willing as he doubtless was to go forth into public and do the work of an evangelist, like his beloved friend Whitefield, his delicate health made it quite impossible. From his youth up he had shown a decided tendency to pulmonary consumption. He had neither voice nor physical strength to preach in the open air, address large congregations, and arrest the attention of multitudes, like many of his contemporaries. He saw this clearly, and wisely submitted to God's appointment. Those whom he could not reach with his voice, he resolved to approach by his pen. From his isolated study in his Northamptonshire parish he sent forth arrows which were sharp in the hearts of the King's enemies. In a word, he became a diligent writer on behalf of the gospel from the time of his conversion till he was laid in his grave. Ill health, no doubt, often stopped his labour, and laid him aside. But, though faint, he was always pursuing. Delicate and weak as he always was, his pen was very seldom idle, and he was always doing "what he could." The work to which he devoted himself required a large measure of faith and patience. He laboured on uncheered by admiring crowds, and unaided by the animal excitement which often carries forward the wearied preacher. But while health and strength lasted he never ceased to labour, and seldom laboured in vain. Hundreds were reached by Hervey's writings, who would never have condescended to listen to Whitefield's voice.

The very retirement of Weston Favell was not without its advantages. It gave the worthy rector unbroken leisure for writing. He could sit down in his study without fear of being disturbed by the endless petty interruptions which disturb the dweller in large towns, and make the continuous flow of thought almost impossible. Above all, it gave him plenty of time for reading and storing his mind. It has been well said that "reading maketh a full man," and no one can look through Hervey's literary remains without seeing abundant evidence that he was a great reader. With Greek and Roman classical writers he was familiar from his youth. The following theological writers are said to have been among his special favourites: Chrysostom, Gerhard, Alting, Owen, Manton, Goodwin, Reynolds, Hall, Beveridge, Bunyan, Hopkins, Howe, Bates, Flavel, Caryl, Poole, Charnock, Traill, Turretine, Witsius, Vitringa, Hurrion, Leighton, Polhill, Gill, Brine, Guyse, Boston, Rawlins, Coles, Jenks, Marshall, Erskine, Milton, Young, and Watts. The names of these authors speak for themselves. The man who was familiar with their works was likely to be full of matter, and when he wrote for the press he had a fair right to claim a patient hearing. The ways of God's providence are mysterious and truly instructive. If Hervey had not been kept at home by ill health, he would probably never have had time for much reading. If he had not had time to be a reader, he would never have written what he did.

The English Puritans appear to have been special favourites with Hervey. Again and again, in his biography, we find him speaking of them in terms of the highest commendation. For instance, he says in one place, " Be not ashamed of the name Puritan. The Puritans were the soundest preachers, and, I believe, the truest followers of Christ in their day." Again : " For my part I esteem the Puritans as some of the most zealous Christians that ever appeared in our land." Again : " The Puritans, one and all of them, glory in the righteousness of their great Mediator ; they extol his imputed righteousness in almost every page, and pour contempt on all other works compared with their Lord's. For my part I know no set of writers in the world so remarkable for this doctrine and diction. It quite distinguishes them from the generality of our modern treatises." I make no apology for these quotations. They throw broad, clear light on Hervey's theological opinions. Nothing brings out a man's distinctive religious views so thoroughly as his choice of books. Tell me what divines a minister loves to read, and I will soon tell you to what school of theology he belongs.

The principal literary works which Hervey published in his life-time, were two volumes of " Meditations and Contempla-tions," and three volumes of " Dialogues and Letters" between two fictitious persons, whom he named " Theron and Aspasio." The " Meditations" are soliloquies and thoughts arising out of such subjects as the tombs, a flower-garden, creation, night, and the starry heavens. The " Dialogues" touch on many points of theology, but especially upon the great doctrine of justifica-tion by faith in the imputed righteousness of Christ. If life had been continued, Hervey intended to have added a fourth volume of " Dialogues," of which the subject was to have been Chris-tian holiness. But his early death cut short the design, and he was only able to tell his friends that they must regard his favourite book, Marshall on Sanctification, as his deputy and representa-tive. His words were,—" I do, by these presents, depute Marshall to supply my lack of service. Marshall expresses my thoughts, prosecutes my schemes, and not only pursues the same end, but proceeds in the same way. I shall therefore rejoice in the prospect of having the ' Gospel Mystery of Sanctification' stand as a fourth volume to ' Theron and Aspasio.'"

Both the works above mentioned attained an extraordinary degree of popularity from the moment they were published, and procured for the author a world-wide reputation. They formed, in fact, the whole foundation of his fame. Thousands and tens of thousands of Christians have never known anything of Hervey except as " the author of Theron and Aspasio." His first work, the Meditations, ran through twenty editions in a very short time, and was translated into the Dutch language! Theron and Aspasio met with acceptance all over England and Scotland, and obliged even worldly critics to take notice of it. All these are plain facts which admit of no controversy. They are facts which arouse in our minds a little curiosity. We naturally want to know what kind of religious writing was popular in England a hundred years ago.

The first thought that will probably start up within us as we read Hervey's Meditations and Dialogues, will be unmixed surprise and amazement. The style is so peculiar, that we marvel how our forefathers could possibly have liked it. From first to last the author writes in such a florid, high flown, luxuriant, bombastic, stilted fashion, that he almost takes your breath away. You can hardly believe that he is in earnest, and that the whole thing is not an assumed mannerism and affectation. The long words, the grandiose mode of expressing thoughts, the starched and painted dress of the sentences—all, all is so utterly unlike the writing of the present century, that the reader stands dumbfounded, and hardly knows whether he ought to laugh or to cry. In the whole range of popular English books, I do not hesitate to say that I do not know a style of writing less to be admired than the style of " Theron and Aspasio." One cannot help inwardly feeling, What a strange standard of public taste must have prevailed, when such writing as this was deliberately published and universally admired !

However, first impressions are not always correct. We must not hastily condemn Hervey's writings as worthless, because their style is not to our mind. A little calm consideration will probably show us that there is far more to be said for them than at first sight appears. A second look at the rector of Weston Favell's writings will very likely modify our verdict about them. To those who are disposed to think lightly of Hervey's writings I venture to submit the following considerations.

For one thing, we must in common fairness remember the

times in which Hervey wrote. The middle of last century was an era in English literature, when no writing would go down with the public that was not somewhat stilted, classical, long-worded, and stiff. The short, plain, cut-and-thrust style of the present day would have been condemned as indicative of a vulgar, uneducated mind. Poor Hervey wrote in days when moral essays were framed on the model of the *Spectator*, the *Tatler*, and the *Rambler*, and fictions were written like " Sir Charles Grandison " and " Clarissa Harlow." If he wanted to get the ear of the public, he had no alternative but to write according to the public taste. Let us grant that his style of English composition is far too ornate and florid ; but let us not forget to lay the blame at the right door. His faults were the faults of his day. If he had written Theron and Aspasio in a plain unadorned style, it is probable that the book would have fallen unnoticed to the ground.

For another thing, we must do Hervey the justice to remember, that under all the gaudy ornamentation of his compositions his Master's business is never forgotten. The more we read his books the more we must admit, that although he may offend our tastes, he is always most faithful to Christ's truth. It is impossible not to admire the vein of piety which runs through every page, and the ability with which he defends doctrines which the heart of man naturally detests. The only wonder is that books containing so much scriptural truth should ever have become so extensively popular. Even Whitefield did not expect so much acceptance for them. "I foretell the fate of these volumes," he said in a letter ; " nothing but your scenery can screen you. Self will never consent to die, though slain in so genteel a manner, without showing some resentment against the artful murderer." In fact, I always feel that God gave a special blessing to Hervey's writings on account of his eminent faithfulness to the gospel in evil times. I look at them with reverence and respect as weapons which did good service in their day, though the fashion of them may not suit my taste. To use the author's own words, they were an " attempt to dress the good old truths of the Reformation in such drapery of language as to allure people of all conditions." God was pleased to honour the effort in its day, and we need not be ashamed to honour it also.

No well-informed Christian will be surprised to hear that Hervey's writings did not please everybody. Of course they were far too Scriptural to escape the enmity of the children of this world. But this unhappily was not all the enmity that the author of " Theron and Aspasio" had to endure. His clear and sharply cut statements about justification gave great offence to Christians of the Arminian school of theology. John Wesley openly assaulted his views of imputed righteousness. Sandeman, a Scotch Independent, fiercely attacked his views of faith. In short, the amiable rector of Weston Favell had to learn, like many other good men, that the most beautiful writing will not command universal acceptance. The way of accurate Scriptural divinity is a way which many will always call " heresy," and speak against.

I will not weary my readers by entering into the details of Hervey's controversial campaigns. Without pretending to endorse every sentence that he wrote, I feel no doubt that on the whole he was right, and his adversaries wrong. Cudworth, Ryland, and others, ably defended him. The only remark that I make is, that Hervey's spirit and temper, under the assaults made upon him, were beyond all praise. Never was there a divine so utterly free from " odium theologicum." Well would it have been for the credit of the Church of Christ, if the controversialists of the last century had all been as meek, and gentle, and amiable, and kind-tempered as the author of "Theron and Aspasio."

The *letters* which Hervey wrote, on a great variety of subjects, are exceedingly good, and will repay an attentive perusal. Sitting in his quiet country parsonage, he had time to think over all that he wrote ; and his correspondence, like his contemporary Venn's, is one of the best part of his literary remains. Those who read his letters will find their style, as a general rule, very different from that of " Theron and Aspasio." The writer seems to come down from his high horse, and to deal familiarly and easily with men. The following letter to a dying young lady is a beautiful specimen of his epistolary style, and is so good all through that my readers will probably not blame me if I give it to them whole and entire. A fac-simile of it faces the title-page of my copy of Brown's life of Hervey, and is a perfect specimen of small, delicate, finished, copper-plate handwriting :

" DEAR MISS SARAH,—So you are going to leave us, and will be at your eternal home before us ! I heartily wish you an easy, a comfortable, and a lightsome journey. Fear not. He that died for you on the cross will be with you when you walk through the valley of the shadow of death. (Ps. xxiii. 4.)

" People that travel often sing by the way, to render their journey more pleasant. Let me furnish you with a song most exactly and charmingly suited to your purpose : ' *Who shall lay anything to my charge ? It is God that justifieth me. Who is he that condemneth me ? It is Christ that died ; yea, rather, that is risen again, who is even at the right hand of God, who also maketh intercession for me.*' Shall the law lay anything to my charge ? That has been fully satisfied by the obedience and death of my divine Lord. Shall sin condemn me ? That has all been fully borne, all been abolished, by the Lamb of God which taketh away the sin of the world. Shall Satan accuse me ? What will that avail when the Judge himself justifies me, the Judge himself pronounces me righteous ! (See Rom. viii. 33, 34 ; Gal. iii. 13 ; 1 Pet. ii. 24 ; Daniel ix. 24 ; John i. 29.)

" But shall I be pronounced righteous who have been and am a poor sinner ? Hear what the Holy Ghost saith : ' *Christ loved the Church and gave himself for it, that he might present it to himself a glorious Church, not having spot or wrinkle, or any such thing.'* What reason have they to be afraid or ashamed who have neither spot nor wrinkle, nor any blemish? And such will be the appearance of those who are washed in Christ's blood, and clothed in Christ's righteousness. They will be presented faultless and with exceeding joy before the throne. (See Eph. v. 25, 27; Jude 24.)

"But what shall I do for my kind companions and dear friends? You will exchange them for better, far better. You will go to Mount Zion, to the city of the living God, the heavenly Jerusalem. You will go to an innumerable company of angels, to the general assembly and Church of the first-born which are written in heaven, and to the spirits of just men made perfect. You will go to God, your reconciled God, the Judge of all, and to Jesus the Mediator of the new covenant, and to the blood of sprinkling that speaketh better things for you than your heart can wish or your thoughts imagine. (See Heb. xii. 22–24.)

"Perhaps your spirits are weak. Therefore I will not tire you. The Lord Jesus make these sweet texts a cordial to your soul. I hope to follow you ere long, to find you in the mansions of peace and joy, and to join with you in singing praise, everlasting praise, to him who hath loved us, and washed us from our sins in his own blood. (Rev. i. 5.)

"Into his hands, his ever merciful and most compassionate hands, I commend your spirit.—Your truly affectionate friend,

" J. Hervey.

"Weston, *April* 26, 1755."

I make no comment on this letter; it needs none. There are not many such letters written in these days of universal hurry, under the influences of railway travelling, electric telegraphs, and penny post. The faculty of writing such letters is fast dying out of the world. But my readers will probably agree with me that the man who could write to his friends in this fashion was no common correspondent.

The published *sermons* of James Hervey are very few in number. It is much to be regretted that we have no more of them. The few published are so extremely good, both as to matter and composition, that one feels sorry he did not give the world a hundred more of the same sort. Of course, he could never be a popular preacher. His weak health, feeble voice, and delicate constitution, made this impossible. He often lamented his inability to serve his people better in the pulpit, comparing himself to a soldier wounded, bleeding, and disabled, and only not slain. He would frequently say, " My preaching is not like sending an arrow from a bow, for which some strength of arm is necessary, but like pulling the trigger of a gun ready charged, which the feeblest finger can do." This remark was most true. No doubt, his want of a striking action and delivery robbed his sermons of effectiveness. But they were always full of excellent stuff, excellently put together.

The reader of Hervey's Sermons will discover at once that they are written in a style very unlike that of "Theron and Aspasio." He will find comparatively little of that luxuriancy and ornamentation to which I have already alluded. He will see, to his surprise, a mode of address eminently simple, perspicuous, pointed, and direct, though never degenerating into rant and vulgarity. The rector of Weston Favell had evidently most just and wise views of the wants of a mixed country congregation. He knew that, next to proclaiming sound doctrine, a minister's first aim should be to be understood. When, therefore, he got up into his Northamptonshire pulpit, he deliberately left behind his flowers and feathers, his paint and his gilding, his fine words and long sentences, his classical allusions and elaborate arguments. Usefulness was the one thing that he desired to obtain, and to obtain it he was not ashamed to speak very plain English to plain men. The following paragraphs from a sermon preached by him in 1757, on "The Means of Safety," from Hebrews xi. 28, will probably be read with interest, as conveying a fair idea of his style of preaching :—

"Let me give a word of direction. Fly to Christ, alarmed sinners? Come under the covert of his blood. Appropriate the blessed Jesus ; look unto him, and his merits are your own. Thus sprinkle his blood : sprinkle it upon your lintel and door-posts ; upon all you are, upon all you have, and all you do ; upon your consciences, that they may be purged ; upon your souls, that they may be sanctified ; upon your works, that they may be accepted. Say, every one of you, I am a poor, guilty, helpless creature ; but in Jesus Christ, who is full of grace and truth, I have righteousness and strength. I am a poor, polluted, loathsome creature ; but Jesus Christ, who is the image of the invisible God and the brightness of his Father's glory, has loved me and washed me from my filthiness in his own blood. I am by nature a perverse, depraved creature, and by evil practices a lost, damnable sinner ; but Jesus Christ who made the world, Jesus Christ whom heaven and earth adore, Jesus Christ himself came from the mansions of bliss on purpose to save me, to give himself for me. And how can I perish who have such a ransom ?

"Should you say, Have I a warrant for such a trust? I reply, You have the best of warrants, our Lord's express permission, 'Whosoever will let him take the water of life freely.' It is not said, this or that person only, but *whosoever*, including you and me, excluding no individual man or woman. It is not said, whosoever is worthy, but whosoever is *willing*. Wilt thou be made whole? was our Lord's question to the impotent man at the pool of Bethesda. Wilt thou, all terms and conditions apart, inherit grace and glory? is his most benevolent address to sinful men in all ages.

"You have our Lord's most gracious invitation ; 'Come unto me.' And whom does he call? The righteous? No.

The excellent? Quite the reverse. He calls sinners, miserable sinners, even the most miserable of sinners. Those who are weary and heavy-laden, overwhelmed with iniquities, bowed down to the brink of hell, and ready to think, 'There is no hope.' Yet them he encourages, them he invites; to them he declares, 'I will give you rest,' rest in the enjoyment of peace with God, and peace in your own consciences. Observe and admire the riches of your Redeemer's grace. He says not, Ye are vile, wretched, polluted by sin, and enslaved to the devil, therefore keep at a distance; but therefore come. Come, and be cleansed by my blood; come, and be made free by my Spirit. He says not, Furnish yourselves with this or that or the other recommending accomplishment; but only come. Come just as you are, poor, undone, guilty creatures. Yea, come to me for pardon and recovery; to me, who have given myself, my life, my all for your ransom.

"Should you still question whether these inestimable blessings are free for you? Remember, brethren, they are free for sinners. Is this your character? Then they are as free for your acceptance as for any person in the world. To us eternal life is given—not to us who had deserved it by our goodness, but us who had forfeited it by our sins. To you is preached the forgiveness of sins—not to you whose transgressions are inconsiderable, but you whose iniquities are more in number than the hairs of your head. Even to you who are the lost and perishing sinner of Adam's family, is the word of this salvation sent. And by God's commission we publish it, that as sinners you may receive it, that receiving it you may commence believing, and that believing you may have life through his name.

" Come then, fellow-sinners, believe the record of heaven. Set to your seal that God is true. Honour his word, which cannot lie. Honour his grace, which is absolutely free. Honour his dear Son, who has obtained eternal redemption for such unworthy creatures as you and I.

I have only two remarks to make on the above extract before I pass on. If any reader of Hervey's works has imbibed the idea that he could only write English after the model of "Theron and Aspasio," I advise him to alter his estimate of the good man's powers. The rector of Weston Favell could be plain enough to suit the humblest intellect, when he pleased. If any one thinks that the English pulpit of the present day is greatly in advance of the last century, I venture to think that he has something yet to learn. My own deliberate opinion is, that it would be a great blessing to this country, if we had more of such direct preaching as some parishes in Northamptonshire heard a hundred years ago.

The *private life* of Hervey was in thorough harmony with his writing and preaching. It is the universal testimony of all who knew him, that he was an eminently holy man. Even the clergy of the neighbourhood, who disliked his theology, and had no sympathy with his ways and opinions, could find no fault in his daily walk. In fact, they used to call him "Saint James." He never married, and by reason of ill health seldom left home, and was confined to the house. But in-doors or out-of-doors, he was always full of his Master's business, always redeeming the time, always reading, writing, or speaking about Christ, and always behaving like a man who had recently come from his Lord's presence to say something, and was soon going back again.

His *humility* was eminent. He never considered himself as James Hervey, the celebrated writer, but as a poor guilty sinner, equally indebted to divine grace with the lowest day-labourer in his parish. To two malefactors condemned to be hanged, he said: "You have just the same foundation for hope as I must have when I shall depart this life. When I shall be summoned to the great tribunal, what will be my plea, and what my dependence? Nothing but Christ. I am a poor unworthy sinner; but worthy is the Lamb that was slain. This is my only hope, and this is as free for you as it is for your friend and fellow-sinner James Hervey." On publishing his famous Fast-day Sermons, he observes: "May the Lord Jesus himself, who was crucified in weakness, vouchsafe to work by weakness, or, in other words, by James Hervey!"—When near his death he wrote to a friend: "I beseech Mr. —— to unite his supplication with yours, for I am fearful lest I should disgrace the gospel in my languishing moments. Pray for me, the weakest of ministers and the weakest of Christians."

His *charity and self-denial* were most eminent. He literally gave away almost all that he had, and lived on a mere fraction of his income. In his giving he was always discreet. "I am God's steward," he said, "for his poor, and I must husband the little pittance I have to bestow on them, and make it go as far as possible." But when money was likely to be particularly serviceable, as in the case of long sickness or sudden losses, he would give away five, ten, or fifteen guineas at a time, taking care it should not be known from whom the money came. His income was never large, and it might be wondered how he managed to spare such sums for charitable uses. But he saved up nothing, and gave away all the profits arising from his books —which were sometimes large sums—in doing good. In fact, this was his bank for the poor. "I have devoted this fund," he said, "to God. I will, on no account, apply it to any worldly uses. I write, not for profit or fame, but to serve the cause of God; and, as he has blessed my attempt, I think myself bound to relieve the distresses of my fellow-creatures with the profit that comes from that quarter." He carried out this principle to the very last. Even after his death, he was found to have ordered all profits arising from any future sale of his books to be constantly applied to charitable uses.

But space would fail me if I were to dwell particularly on all the leading features of Hervey's private character. The picture is far too large to go into the frame of a short memoir like this.

His spirit of Catholic love to all God's people of every denomination—his delight in the society and conversation of godly people—his faithfulness in reproving sin—his singular love to Christ, and delight in his finished work and atonement—his devotional diligence—his veneration for the Scriptures—his meekness, gentleness, and tenderness of spirit—all these are points on which much might be written, and much will be found in the pages of his biography. So far as I can judge, he appears to have been a man of as eminently saintly character as any that this country can point to, and one worthy to be ranked by the side of Bradford, Baxter, and George Herbert. Few evangelical men, at any rate, in the last century, can be named, who seem to have had so few enemies, and to have lost so few friends. None, certainly, were so universally lamented.

The closing scene of James Hervey's life was curiously beautiful. He died, as he had lived for seventeen years, in the full faith and peace of Christ's gospel. His life had long been a continual struggle with disease; and when his last illness came upon him, it found him thoroughly prepared. Invalids have one great advantage over strong people, at any rate—a sudden accession of pains and ailments does not startle them, and they are seldom taken by surprise. The holy rector of Weston Favell had looked death in the face so long that he was no stranger to him; and when he went down into the cold waters of the great river, he walked calmly, quietly, and undisturbed. Those glorious evangelical doctrines which he had proclaimed and defended as truths while he lived, he found to be strong consolations when he died.

His last attack of illness began in October 1758, and carried him off on Christmas day. Disease of the lungs, with all its distressing accompaniments, was the agent employed to take down his earthly tabernacle; and he seems to have gone through even more than the ordinary suffering which such disease entails. But nothing shook the dying sufferer's faith. He had his days of conflict and inward struggle, like most of Christ's faithful soldiers; but he always came out more than conqueror, through Him that loved him. An abundant entrance into rest was ministered to him. He entered harbour at last, not like a shipwrecked sailor clinging to a broken plank, but like a stately ship, with all her sails expanded, and wafted forward by a prosperous gale.

The dying sayings of eminent saints, when God permits them to say much, are always instructive. It was eminently the case with James Hervey. Like dying Jacob, he was enabled to speak to all around him, and to testify his deep sense of the value of Christ's great salvation. Like Christiana, in "Pilgrim's Progress," he was enabled to speak comfortably to those who stood near him, and followed him to the river-side. To his doctor he wrote, at an early period of his last illness: "I now spend almost all my whole time in reading and praying over the Bible. Indeed, you cannot conceive how the springs of life in me are relaxed, and relaxing. 'What thou doest, do quickly,' is a proper admonition for me as I approach dissolution. My dear friend, attend to the one thing needful. I have no heart to take any medicine; all but Christ is to me unprofitable. Blessed be God for pardon and salvation through his blood! Let me prescribe this for my dear friend. My cough is very troublesome; I can get little rest; but my never-failing remedy is the love of Christ."

On the 15th of December—the month that he died—he spoke very strongly to his curate, Mr. Maddock, about the assurance of faith, and the great love of God in Christ. "Oh!" said he, "how much has Christ done for me, and how little have I done for so loving a Saviour! If I preached even once a week it was but a burden to me. I have not visited the people of my parish as I ought to have done, and thus preached from house to house. I have not taken every opportunity of speaking for Christ. Do not think I am afraid to die. I assure you I am not. I know what my Saviour has done for me. I want to be gone. But I wonder and lament to think of the love of Christ in doing so much for me, and how little I have done for him ! "

On the 25th of December—the day that he died—his loving friend and physician, Dr. Stonehouse, came to see him about three hours before he expired. Hervey seized the opportunity, spoke strongly and affectionately to him about his soul's concerns, and entreated him not to be overcharged with the cares of this life. Seeing his great weakness and prostration, the doctor begged him to spare himself. " No, doctor," replied the dying man, with ardour, "no! You tell me I have but a few minutes to live ; let me spend them in adoring our great Redeemer." He then repeated the words, " Though my heart and my flesh fail, God is the strength of my heart, and my portion for ever ;" and also dwelt, in a delightful manner, on St. Paul's words, " All things are yours ; whether life, or things present, or things to come." " Here," he exclaimed, " here is the treasury of a Christian ! Death is reckoned among this inventory ; and a noble treasure it is. How thankful I am for death, as it is the passage through which I go to the Lord and Giver of eternal life, and as it frees me from all the misery which you see me now endure, and which I am willing to endure as long as God thinks fit ! I know that he will by-and-by, in his own good time, dismiss me from the body. These light afflictions are but for a moment, and then comes an eternal weight of glory. Oh, welcome, welcome death ! Thou mayst well be reckoned among the treasures of the Christian ! To live is Christ, and to die is gain !" After this he lay for a considerable time without seeming to breathe, and his friends thought he was gone. But he revived a little, and, being raised in his chair, said :—" Lord, now lettest thou thy servant depart in peace, according to thy most holy and comfortable words ;

for mine eyes have seen thy most holy and comfortable salvation! Here, doctor, is my cordial. What are all the cordials given to support the dying, in comparison of that which arises from the promises of salvation by Christ? This, this supports me!"

He said little after this, and was rapidly drawing near his end. About three o'clock in the afternoon he said: "The conflict is over; now all is done." After that time he scarcely spoke anything intelligible, except the words, "Precious salvation!" At last, about four o'clock, without a sigh or a groan, he shut his eyes and departed, on Christmas-day 1758, in the forty-fifth year of his age. Never, perhaps, was there a more triumphant illustration of the saying of a great spiritual champion of the last century,—"The world may not like our methodists and evangelical people, but the world cannot deny that they die well!"

I leave James Hervey here, having traced his history from his cradle to his grave. He was a man of whom the world was not worthy, and one to whom even the Church of God has never given his due measure of honour. I am well aware that he was not perfect. I do not pretend to say that I can subscribe *entirely* to everything he wrote, either about the nature of faith or about assurance; but whatever his faults and defects, I do believe that he was one of the holiest and best ministers in England a hundred years ago, and that he did a work in his time which will be seen to have borne good fruit in the last great day.

I know well that Hervey was only a writer, and nothing but a writer. I know well that the value of his works has almost passed away. Like our old wooden three-deckers, they did good service in their time, but are now comparatively obsolete and laid aside. But I believe the day will never come when the Church will not require pens as well as tongues, able writers as well as able preachers; and I venture to think it would be well for the Church of our day, if we had a few more hard students and careful writers of the stamp of James Hervey. I therefore boldly claim for him a high place among the spiritual heroes of the last century. Let us admire Whitefield and Wesley; but let us not grudge Hervey his crown. He deserves to be had in remembrance.

I now conclude this sketch with a few testimonies to Hervey's merits, which, to say the least, demand serious attention. The witnesses are all men of mark, and men who had many opportunities of weighing the merits of preachers and writers. Let us hear what they thought of the subject before us, the rector of Weston Favell.

My first witness shall be William Romaine. He says: "I never saw one who came up so near to the Scripture character of a Christian, as Mr. Hervey. God enriched him with great gifts and great graces. He had a fine understanding and a great memory. He was very well skilled in Hebrew, and an excellent critic in Greek.—There was great experience of heart-love upon his tongue. He used to speak of the love of the adorable Redeemer like one who had seen him face to face in the fulness of his glory. As to his writings, I leave them to speak for themselves. They stand in no need of my praises."

My next witness shall be Henry Venn. He says: "Mr. Hervey was the most extraordinary man I ever saw in my life, as much beyond most of the excellent as the swan for whiteness and stately figure is beyond the common fowl. His Meditations and Contemplations deserve your most sincere regard. You may look upon them as you would upon Aaron's rod, by which such wonders were wrought. These Thoughts have been the means of giving sight to the blind, life to souls dead in trespasses and sins, and winning the young, the gay, and the rich, to see greater charms in a crucified Saviour than in all that dazzles vain minds."

My next witness shall be Cowper the poet. He says: " Perhaps I may be partial to Hervey; but I think him one of the most Scriptural writers in the world."

My next witness shall be Richard Cecil. He says: " Let us do the world justice. It has seldom found considerate, gentle, but earnest, heavenly, and enlightened teachers. When it has found such, truth has received a very general attention. Such a man was Hervey, and his works have met their reward."

My next witness shall be the late Edward Bickersteth. He says: " Few books have been so useful as Hervey's 'Theron and Aspasio;' though like every human writing, it is not free from error. But, with a few exceptions, the clear statements or divine truth in the book, and the Christian addresses of the author, full of kindness and affection, gentleness and sweetness of spirit, draw out your best feelings, and win you over to evangelical principles."

My last witness shall be Daniel Wilson, Bishop of Calcutta. He says in his Journal, July 24, 1846: " I have been reading tranquilly and pleasantly a volume of Hervey's Letters, full of that thorough devotedness of heart, deadness to all earthly things, and longings after grace and holiness, which characterized the leaders of the revival in our church.—Oh! that the spirit of Hervey might pervade our younger clergy and myself. To walk with God is the only spring of happiness and usefulness."

Testimonies like these deserve serious attention. My firm belief is, that they are well deserved.

XII.

Toplady and his Ministry.

 PERFECT orchestra contains many various instruments of music. Each of these instruments has its
own merit and value; but some of them are curiously
unlike others. Some of them are dependent on a player's
breath, and some on his skill of hand. Some of them are large,
and some of them are small. Some of them produce very
gentle sounds, and some of them very loud. But all of them
are useful in their place and way. Composers like Handel, and
Mozart, and Mendelssohn, find work for all. There is work
for the flageolet as well as for the trumpet, and work for the
violoncello as well as for the organ. Separately and alone,
some of the instruments may appear harsh and unpleasant.
Combined together and properly played, they fill the ear with
one mighty volume of harmonious sounds.

Thoughts such as these come across my mind when I survey
the spiritual champions of England a hundred years ago. I see
among the leaders of religious revival in that day men of singularly varied characteristics. They were each in their way eminent instruments for good in the hands of the Holy Ghost.
From each of them sounded forth the word of God throughout
the land with no uncertain sound. Yet some of these good
men were strangely compounded, peculiarly constituted, and

oddly framed. And to none, perhaps, does the remark apply more thoroughly than to the subject of these remarks, the well-known hymn-writer, Augustus Toplady.

I should think no account of English religion in the last century complete which did not supply some information about this remarkable man. In some respects, I am bold to say, not one of his contemporaries surpassed him, and hardly any equalled him. He was a man of rare grace and gifts, and one who left his mark very deeply on his own generation. For soundness in the faith, singleness of eye, and devotedness of life, he deserves to be ranked with Whitefield, or Grimshaw, or Romaine. Yet with all this, he was a man in whom there was a most extraordinary mixture of grace and infirmity. Hundreds, unhappily, know much of his infirmities who know little of his graces. I shall endeavour in the following pages to supply a few materials for forming a just estimate of his character.

Augustus Montague Toplady was born at Farnham, in Surrey, on the 4th of November 1740. He was the only son of Major Richard Toplady, who died at the siege of Carthagena shortly after his birth, so that he never saw his father. His mother's maiden name was Catherine Bates, of whom nothing is known except that she had a brother who was rector of St. Paul's, Deptford. About the history of his family I can discover nothing. I only conjecture that some of them must have been natives of Ireland. Who his parents were, and what they were doing at Farnham, when he was born, and what kind of people they were, are all matters about which no record seems to exist.

Few spiritual heroes of the last century, I must freely confess, have suffered more from the want of a good biographer than Toplady. Be the cause what it may, a real life of the man was never written. The only memoir of him is as meagre a production as can possibly be conceived. It is perhaps only fair to remember that he was an only child, and that he died

unmarried; so that he had neither brother, sister, son nor
daughter, to gather up his remains.   Moreover, he was one
who lived much in his study and among his books, spent
much time in private communion with God, and went very
little into society.   Like Romaine, he was not what the world
would call a *genial* man—had very few intimate friends—and
was, probably, more feared and admired than loved.   But be
the reasons what they may, the fact is undeniable that there
is no good biography of Toplady.   The result is, that there is
hardly any man of his calibre in the last century of whom so
very little is known.

The principal facts of Toplady's life are few, and soon told.
He was brought up by his widowed mother with the utmost
care and tenderness, and retained throughout life a deep and
grateful sense of his obligations to her.   For some reason,
which we do not know now, she appears to have settled at
Exeter after her husband's death; and to this circumstance
we may probably trace her son's subsequent appointment to
cures of souls in Devonshire.   Young Toplady was sent at an
early age to Westminster School, and showed considerable
ability there.   After passing through Westminster, he was
entered as a student of Trinity College, Dublin, and took his
degree there as Bachelor of Arts.   He was ordained a clergyman in the year 1762; but I am unable to ascertain where, or
by what bishop he was ordained.   Shortly after his ordination
he was appointed to the living of Blagdon, in Somersetshire,
but did not hold it long.   He was then appointed to Venn-
Ottery, with Harpford, in Devonshire, a small parish near Sid-
mouth.   This post he finally exchanged, in 1768, for the rural
parish of Broad Hembury, near Honiton, in Devonshire, a
cure which he retained until his death.   In the year 1775 he
was compelled, by the state of his health, to remove from
Devonshire to London, and became for a short time preacher
at a Chapel in Orange Street, Leicester Square.   He seems,

however, to have derived no material benefit from the change of climate; and at last died of decline, like Walker and Hervey, in the year 1778, at the early age of thirty-eight.

The story of Toplady's inner life and religious history is simple and short; but it presents some features of great interest. The work of God seems to have begun in his heart, when he was only sixteen years old, under the following circumstances. He was staying at a place called Codymain, in Ireland, and was there led by God's providence to hear a layman named Morris preach in a barn. The text—Ephesians ii. 13, "Ye who sometimes were far off are made nigh by the blood of Christ"—and the address founded on it, came home to young Toplady's conscience with such power, that from that time he became a new man, and a thorough-going professor of vital Christianity. This was in August 1756.

He himself in after-life referred frequently to the circumstance of his conversion with special thankfulness. He says in 1768: "Strange that I, who had so long sat under the means of grace in England, should be brought nigh to God in an obscure part of Ireland, amidst a handful of God's people met together in a barn, and under the ministry of one who could hardly spell his name! Surely it was the Lord's doing, and is marvellous! The excellency of such power must be of God, and cannot be of man. The regenerating Spirit breathes not only on whom, but likewise when, where, and as he listeth."

Although converted and made a new creature in Christ Jesus, Toplady does not seem to have come to a full knowledge of the gospel in all its perfection for at least two years. Like most of God's children, he had to fight his way into full light through many defective opinions, and was only by slow degrees brought to complete establishment in the faith. His experience in this matter, be it remembered, is only that of the vast majority of true Christians. Like infants, when they are born into the world, God's children are not born again in the full possession of all their spiritual faculties; and it is well and wisely ordered that it is so. What we win easily, we seldom value sufficiently. The very fact that believers have to struggle and fight hard before they get hold of real soundness in the faith, helps to make them prize it more when they have attained it. The truths that cost us a battle are precisely those which we grasp most firmly, and never let go.

Toplady's own account of his early experience on this point is distinct and explicit. He says : " Though awakened in 1756, I was not led into a clear and full view of all the doctrines of grace till the year 1758, when, through the great goodness of God, my Arminian prejudices received an effectual shock in reading Dr. Manton's sermons on the seventeenth chapter of St. John. I shall remember the years 1756 and 1758 with gratitude and joy in the heaven of heavens to all eternity."

In the year 1774, Toplady gave the following curious account of his experience at this period of his life :—" It pleased God to deliver me from the Arminian snare before I was quite eighteen. Up to that period there was not (I confess it with abasement) a more haughty and violent free-willer within the compass of the four seas. One instance of my warm and ignorant zeal occurs now to my memory. About a year before divine goodness gave me eyes to discern and a heart to embrace the truth, I was haranguing one day in company on the universality of grace and the power of free agency. A good old gentleman, now with God, rose from his chair, and coming to me, held me by one of my coat-buttons, while he mildly said :—' My dear sir, there are marks of spirituality in your conversation, though tinged with an unhappy mixture of pride and self-righteousness. You have been speaking largely in favour of free-will ; but from arguments let us come to experience. Do let me ask you one question, How was it with you when the Lord laid hold on you in effectual calling? Had you any hand in obtaining that grace? Nay, would you not have resisted and baffled it, if

God's Spirit had left you alone in the hand of your own counsel?'
—I felt the conclusiveness of these simple but forcible interrogations more strongly than I was then willing to acknowledge. But, blessed be God, I have since been enabled to acknowledge the freeness of his grace, and to sing, what I trust will be my everlasting song, '*Not unto me, Lord, not unto me; but unto thy name give the glory.*'"

From this time to the end of his life, a period of twenty years, Toplady held right onward in his Christian course, and never seems to have swerved or turned aside for a single day. His attachment to Calvinistic views of theology grew with his growth, and strengthened with his strength, and undoubtedly made him think too hardly of all who favoured Arminianism. It is more than probable, too, that it gave him the reputation of being a narrow-minded and sour divine, and made many keep aloof from him, and depreciate him. But no one ever pretended to doubt his extraordinary devotedness and singleness of eye, or to question his purity and holiness of life. From one cause or another, however, he appears always to have stood alone, and to have had little intercourse with his fellow-men. The result was, that throughout life he appears to have been little known and little understood, but most loved where he was most known.

One would like much to hear what young Toplady was doing between the date of his conversion in 1756, and his ordination in 1762. We can only guess, from the fact that he studied Manton on the seventeenth of John before he was eighteen, that he was probably reading hard, and storing his mind with knowledge, which he turned to good account in after-life. But there is an utter dearth of all information about our hero at this period of his life. We only know that he took upon himself the office of a minister, not only as scholar, and as an outward professor of religion, but as an honest man. He says himself, that " he subscribed the articles and liturgy from principle ; and that he did not believe them merely because he subscribed them, but subscribed them because he believed them."

One would like, furthermore, to know exactly where he began his ministry, and in what parish he was first heard as a preacher of the gospel. But I can find out nothing about these points. One interesting fact about his early preaching I gather from a curious letter which he wrote to Lady Huntingdon in 1774. In that letter he says: "As to the doctrines of special and discriminating grace, I have thus much to observe. For the first four years after I was in orders, I dwelt chiefly on the general outlines of the gospel in this remote corner of my public ministry. I preached of little else but of justification by faith only, in the righteousness and atonement of Christ, and of that personal holiness without which no man shall see the Lord. My reasons for thus narrowing the truths of God were these two (I speak it with humiliation and repentance):—1. I thought these points were sufficient to convey as clear an idea as was absolutely necessary of salvation; 2. And secondly, I was partly afraid to go any further.

" God himself (for none but he could do it) gradually freed me from that fear. And as he never at any time permitted me to deliver, or even to insinuate anything contradictory to his truth, so has he been graciously pleased, for seven or eight years past, to open my mouth to make known the entire mystery of the gospel, as far as his Spirit has enlightened me into it. The consequence of my first plan of operations was, that the generality of my hearers were pleased, but only few were converted. The result of my latter deliverance from worldly wisdom and worldly fear is, that multitudes have been very angry; but the conversions which God has given me reason to hope he has wrought, have been at least three for one before. Thus I can testify, so far as I have been concerned, the usefulness of preaching predestination; or, in other words, of tracing salvation and redemption to their first source."

An anecdote related by Toplady himself deserves repetition, as a curious illustration of the habits of clergymen at the time when he was ordained, and his superiority to the habits of his contemporaries. He says: " I was buying some books in the spring of 1762, a month or two before I was ordained, from a very respectable London bookseller. After the business was over, he took me to the furthest end of his long shop, and said in a low voice, ' Sir, you will soon be ordained, and I suppose you have not laid in a very great stock of sermons. I can supply you with as many sets as you please, all original, very excellent ones, and they will come for a trifle.' My answer was : ' I certainly shall never be a customer to you in that way; for I am of opinion that the man who cannot, or will not make his own sermons, is quite unfit to wear the gown. How could you think of my buying ready-made sermons? I would much sooner buy ready-made clothes." His answer shocked me. ' Nay, young gentleman, do not be surprised at my offering you ready-made sermons, for I assure you I have sold ready-made sermons to many a bishop in my time.' My reply was : ' My good sir, if you have any concern for the credit of the Church of England, never tell that news to anybody else henceforward for ever.' "

The manner of Toplady's life, during the fifteen or sixteen years of his short ministry may be gathered from a diary which he wrote in 1768, and kept up for about a year. This diary is a far more interesting record of a good man's life than such documents ordinarily are, and gives a very favourable impression of the writer's character and habits. It leaves the impression that he was eminently a man of one thing, and entirely engrossed with his Master's business—much alone, keeping little company, and always either preaching, visiting his people, reading, writing, or praying. If it had been kept up for a few years longer, it would have thrown immense light on many things in Toplady's ministerial history. But even in its present state it is the most valuable record we possess about him, and there seems no reason to doubt that it is a tolerably accurate picture of his mode of living from the time of his ordination to his death.

So little is known of the particular events of the last fifteen years of Toplady's life, that it is impossible to do more than give a general sketch of his proceedings. He seems to have attained a high reputation at a very early date as a thorough-going supporter of Calvinistic opinions, and a leading opponent of Arminianism. His correspondence shows that he was on intimate terms with Lady Huntingdon, Sir R. Hill, Whitefield, Romaine, Berridge, Dr. Gill, Ambrose Serle, and other eminent Christians of those times. But how and when he formed acquaintance with them, we have no information. His pen was constantly employed in defence of evangelical religion from the time of his removal to Broad Hembury in 1768. His early habits of study were kept up with unabated diligence. No man among the spiritual heroes of last century seems to have read more than he did, or to have had a more extensive knowledge of divinity. His bitterest adversaries in controversy could never deny that he was a scholar, and a ripe one. Indeed, it admits of grave question whether he did not shorten his life by his habits of constant study. He says himself, in a letter to a relative, dated March 19, 1775:—"Though I cannot entirely agree with you in supposing that extreme study has been the cause of my late indisposition, I must yet confess that the hill of science, like that of virtue, is in some instances climbed with labour. But when we get a little way up, the lovely prospects which open to the eye make infinite amends for the steepness of the ascent. In short, I am wedded to these pursuits, as a man stipulates to take his wife; viz., for better, for worse, until death us do part. My thirst for knowledge is literally inextinguishable. And if I thus drink myself into a superior world, I cannot help it."

One feature in Toplady's character, I may here remark, can

hardly fail to strike an attentive reader of his remains. That feature is the eminent spirituality of the tone of his religion. There can be no greater mistake than to regard him as a mere student and deep reader, or as a hard and dry controversial divine. Such an estimate of him is thoroughly unjust. His letters and remains supply abundant evidence that he was one who lived in very close communion with God, and had very deep experience of divine things. Living much alone, seldom going into society, and possessing few friends, he was a man little understood by many, who only knew him by his controversial writings, and specially by his unflinching advocacy of Calvinism. Yet really, if the truth be spoken, I hardly find any man of the last century who seems to have soared so high and aimed so loftily, in his personal dealings with his Saviour, as Toplady. There is an unction and savour about some of his remains which few of his contemporaries equalled, and none surpassed. I grant freely that he left behind him many things which cannot be much commended. But he left behind him some things which will live, as long as English is spoken, in the hearts of all true Christians. His writings contain " thoughts that breathe and words that burn," if any writings of his age. And it never ought to be forgotten, that the man who penned them was lying in his grave before he was thirty-nine !

The last three years of Toplady's life were spent in London. He removed there by medical advice in the year 1775, under the idea that the moist air of Broad Hembury was injurious to his health. Whether the advice was sound or not may now, perhaps, admit of question. At any rate, the change of climate did him no good. Little by little the insidious disease of the chest, under which he laboured, made progress, and wasted his strength. He was certainly able to preach at Orange Street Chapel in the years 1776 and 1777 ; but it is equally certain that throughout this period he was gradually drawing near to his end. He was never, perhaps, more thoroughly appreciated than he was during these last three years of his ministry. A picked London congregation, such as he had, was able to value gifts and powers which were completely thrown away on a rural parish in Devonshire. His stores of theological reading and distinct doctrinal statement were rightly appraised by his metropolitan hearers. In short, if he had lived longer he might, humanly speaking, have done a mighty work in London. But He who holds the stars in his right hand, and knows best what is good for his Church, saw fit to withdraw him soon from his new sphere of usefulness. He seemed as if he came to London only to be known and highly valued, and then to die.

The closing scene of the good man's life was singularly beautiful, and at the same time singularly characteristic. He died as he had lived, in the full hope and peace of the gospel, and with an unwavering confidence in the truth of the doctrines which he had for fifteen years advocated both with his tongue and with his pen. About two months before his death he was greatly pained by hearing that he was reported to have receded from his Calvinistic opinions, and to have expressed a desire to recant them in the presence of Mr. John Wesley. So much was he moved by this rumour, that he resolved to appear before his congregation once more, and to give a public denial to it before he died. His physician in vain remonstrated with him. He was told that it would be dangerous to make the attempt, and that he might probably die in the pulpit. But the vicar of Broad Hembury was not a man to be influenced by such considerations. He replied that " he would rather die in the harness than die in the stall." He actually carried his resolution into effect. On Sunday, June the 14th, in the last stage of consumption, and only two months before he died, he ascended his pulpit in Orange Street Chapel, after his assistant had preached, to the astonishment of his people, and gave a short but affecting exhortation founded on 2 Pet. i. 13, 14: "I think it meet, as long as I am in this tabernacle, to stir you up by putting you in remembrance." He then closed his address with the following remarkable declaration :—

"It having been industriously circulated by some malicious and unprincipled persons that during my present long and severe illness I expressed a strong desire of seeing Mr. John Wesley before I die, and revoking some particulars relative to him which occur in my writings,—Now I do publicly and most solemnly aver that I have not nor ever had any such intention or desire ; and that I most sincerely hope my last hours will be much better employed than in communing with such a man. So certain and so satisfied am I of the truth of all that I have ever written, that were I now sitting up in my dying bed with a pen and ink in my hand, and all the religious and controversial writings I ever published, especially those relating to Mr. John Wesley and the Arminian controversy, whether respecting fact or doctrine, could be at once displayed to my view, I should not strike out a single line relative to him or them."

The last days of Toplady's life were spent in great peace. He went down the valley of the shadow of death with abounding consolations, and was enabled to say many edifying things to all around him. The following recollections, jotted down by friends who ministered to him, and communicated to his biographer, can hardly fail to be interesting to a Christian reader.

One friend observes :—"A remarkable jealousy was apparent in his whole conduct as he drew near his end, for fear of receiving any part of that honour which is due to Christ alone. He desired to be nothing, and that Jesus might be all and in all. His feelings were so very tender upon this subject, that I once undesignedly put him almost in an agony by remarking the great loss which the Church of Christ would sustain by his death at this particular juncture. The utmost distress was immediately visible in his countenance, and he exclaimed, 'What! by my death? No, no! Jesus Christ is able, and will, by proper instruments, defend his own truths. And with regard to what little I have been enabled to do in this way, not to me, not to me, but to his own name, and to that only, be the glory.'

" The more his bodily strength was impaired the more vigorous, lively, and rejoicing his mind seemed to be. From the whole turn of his conversation during our interview, he appeared not merely placid and serene, but he evidently possessed the fullest assurance of the most triumphant faith. He repeatedly told me that he had not had the least shadow of a doubt respecting his eternal salvation for near two years past. It is no wonder, therefore, that he so earnestly longed to be dissolved and to be with Christ. His soul seemed to be constantly panting heavenward, and his desire increased the nearer his dissolution approached. A short time before his death, at his request, I felt his pulse, and he desired to know what I thought of it. I told him that his heart and arteries evidently beat almost every day weaker and weaker. He replied immediately, with the sweetest smile on his countenance, ' Why, that is a good sign that my death is fast approaching ; and, blessed be God, I can add that my heart beats every day stronger and stronger for glory.'

"A few days before his dissolution I found him sitting up in his arm-chair, but scarcely able to move or speak. I addressed him very softly, and asked if his consolations continued to abound as they had hitherto done. He quickly replied, ' O my dear sir, it is impossible to describe how good God is to me. Since I have been sitting in this chair this afternoon I have enjoyed such a season, such sweet communion with God, and such delightful manifestation of his presence with and love to my soul, that it is impossible for words or any language to express them. I have had peace and joy unutterable, and I fear not but that God's consolation and support will continue.' But he immediately recollected himself, and added, ' What have I said ? God may, to be sure, as a sovereign, hide his face and his smiles from me ; however, I believe he will not ; and if he should, yet will I trust him. I know I am safe and secure, for his love and his covenant are everlasting!'"

To another friend, speaking about his dying avowal in the pulpit of his church in Orange Street, he said : " My dear friend, these great and glorious truths which the Lord in rich mercy has given me to believe, and which he has enabled me (though very feebly) to defend, are not, as those who oppose them say, dry doctrines or mere speculative points. No! being brought into practical and heartfelt experience, they are the very joy and support of my soul ; and the consolations flowing from them carry me far above the things of time and sense. So far as I know my own heart, I have no desire but to be entirely passive, to live, to die, to be, to do, to suffer whatever is God's blessed will concerning me, being perfectly satisfied that as he ever has, so he ever will do that which is best concerning me, and that he deals out in number, weight, and measure, whatever will conduce most to his own glory and to the good of his people."

Another of his friends mentioning the report that was spread abroad of his recanting his former principles, he said with some vehemence and emotion, " I recant my former principles! God forbid that I should be so vile an apostate!" To which he presently added, with great apparent humility, " And yet that apostate I should soon be, if I were left to myself."

Within an hour of his death, he called his friends and his servant to him, and asked them if they could give him up. Upon their answering that they could, since it pleased the Lord to be so gracious to him, he replied : " Oh, what a blessing it is that you are made willing to give me up into the hands of my dear Redeemer, and to part with me! It will not be long before God takes me ; for no mortal man can live, after the glories which God has manifested to my soul." Soon after this he closed his eyes, and quietly fell asleep in Christ on Tuesday, August 11, 1778, in the thirty-eighth year of his age.

He was buried in Tottenham Court Chapel, under the gal-
lery, opposite the pulpit, in the presence of thousands of people,
who came together from all parts of London to do him honour.
His high reputation as a champion of truth, the unjust misre-
presentations circulated about his change of opinion, his effectiveness as a preacher, and his comparative youthfulness,
combined to draw forth a more than ordinary expression of
sympathy. "Devout men carried him to his burial, and made
great lamentation over him." Foremost among the mourners
was one at that time young in the ministry, who lived long
enough to be a connecting link between the last century
and the present—the well-known and eccentric Rowland Hill.
Before the burial-service commenced, he could not refrain from
transgressing one of Toplady's last requests, that no funeral-
sermon should be preached for him, and affectionately declared
to the vast assembly the love and veneration he felt for the
deceased, and the high sense he entertained of his graces, gifts,
and usefulness. And thus, amidst the tears and thanksgivings
of true-hearted mourners, the much-abused vicar of Broad Hembury was gathered to his people.*

The following passage from Toplady's last will, made and
signed six months before his decease, is so remarkable and
characteristic, that I cannot refrain from giving it to my readers:
"I most humbly commit my soul to Almighty God, whom I
honour, and have long experienced to be my ever gracious and
infinitely merciful Father. Nor have I the least doubt of my
election, justification, and eternal happiness, through the riches
of his everlasting and unchangeable kindness to me in Christ
Jesus, his co-equal Son, my only, my assured, and my all-sufficient Saviour ; washed in whose propitiatory blood, and clothed
with whose imputed righteousness, I trust to stand perfect,

---

* It is a curious fact that Toplady expressly desired that he might be buried at least
nine feet, and, if possible, twelve feet, under ground ! He assigned no reason. Perhaps
it was because he wished to be buried inside his church.

sinless, and complete; and do verily believe that I most certainly shall so stand, in the hour of death, and in the kingdom of heaven, and at the last judgment, and in the ultimate state of endless glory. Neither can I write this my last will without rendering the deepest, the most solemn, and the most ardent thanks to the adorable Trinity in Unity, for their eternal, unmerited, irreversible, and inexhaustible love to me a sinner. I bless God the Father for having written from everlasting my unworthy name in the book of life—even for appointing me to obtain salvation through Jesus Christ my Lord. I adore God the Son for having vouchsafed to redeem me by his own most precious death, and for having obeyed the whole law for my justification. I admire and revere the gracious benignity of God the Holy Ghost, who converted me to the saving knowledge 'of Christ more than twenty-two years ago, and whose enlightening, supporting, comforting, and sanctifying agency is, and (I doubt not) will be my strength and song in the hours of my earthly pilgrimage."

Having now traced Toplady's history from his cradle to his grave, it only remains for me to offer some general estimate of his worth and attainments. To do this, I frankly confess, is no easy task. Not only is his biography a miserably deficient one —this alone is bad enough—but his literary remains have been edited in such a slovenly, careless, ignorant manner, without order or arrangement, that they do not fairly represent the author's merits. Certainly the reputation of great writers and ministers may suffer sadly from the treatment of injudicious friends. If ever there was a man who fell into the hands of the Philistines after his death, that man, so far as I can judge, was Augustus Toplady. I shall do the best I can with the materials at my disposal; but I trust my readers will remember that they are exceedingly scanty.

1. As a *preacher*, I should be disposed to assign to Toplady a very high place among the second class men of the last cen-

tur, His constitutional delicacy and weakness of lungs, in all probability, made it impossible for him to do the things that Whitefield and Berridge did. Constant open-air addresses, impassioned extempore appeals to thousands of hearers, were a style of thing entirely out of his line. Yet there is pretty good evidence that he had no mean reputation as a pulpit orator, and possessed no mean powers. The mere fact that Lady Huntingdon occasionally selected him to preach in her chapels at Bath and Brighton, of itself speaks volumes. The additional fact that at one of the great Methodist gatherings at Trevecca he was put forward as one of the leading preachers, is enough to show that his sermons possessed high merit. The following notes about preaching, which he records in his diary, as having received them from an old friend, will probably throw much light on the general turn of his ministrations :—(1.) Preach Christ crucified, and dwell chiefly on the blessings resulting from his righteousness, atonement, and intercession. (2.) Avoid all needless controversies in the pulpit ; except it be when your subject necessarily requires it, or when the truths of God are likely to suffer by your silence. (3.) When you ascend the pulpit, leave your learning behind you : endeavour to preach more to the hearts of your people than to their heads. (4.) Do not affect much oratory. Seek rather to profit than to be admired.

Specimens of Toplady's ordinary preaching are unfortunately very rare. There are but ten sermons in the collection of his works, and out of these the great majority were preached on special occasions, and cannot, therefore, be regarded as fair samples of his pulpit work. In all of them there is a certain absence of fire, animation, and directness. But in all there is abundance of excellent matter, and a quiet, decided, knock-down, sledge-hammer style of putting things which, I can well believe, would be extremely effective, and especially with educated congregations. The three following extracts may perhaps give some idea of what Toplady was in the pulpit of Orange Street Chapel. Of his ministry in Broad Hembury, I suspect we know next to nothing at all.

The first extract forms the conclusion of a sermon preached in 1774 at the Lock Chapel, entitled " Good News from Heaven :"—" I perceive the elements are upon the sacramental table. And I doubt not many of you mean to present yourselves at that throne of grace which God has mercifully erected through the righteousness and sufferings of his co-equal Son. Oh, beware of coming with one sentiment on your lips and another in your hearts ! Take heed of saying with your mouths, ' We do not come to this thy table, O Lord, trusting in our own righteousness,' while perhaps you have in reality some secret reserves in favour of that very self-righteousness which you profess to renounce, and are thinking that Christ's merits alone will not save you unless you add something or other to make it effectual. Oh, be not so deceived ! God will not thus be mocked, nor will Christ thus be insulted with impunity. Call your works what you will—whether terms, causes, conditions, or supplements—the matter comes to the same point, and Christ is equally thrust out of his mediatorial throne by these or any similar views of human obedience. If you do not wholly depend on Jesus as the Lord your righteousness—if you mix your faith in him with anything else—if the finished work of the crucified God be not alone your acknowledged anchor and foundation of acceptance with the Father, both here and ever—come to his table and receive the symbols of his body and blood at your peril ! Leave your own righteousness behind you, or you have no business here. You are without the wedding garment, and God will say to you, ' Friend, how camest thou here ?' If you go on, moreover, to live and die in this state of unbelief, you will be found speechless and excuseless in the day of judgment ; and the slighted Saviour will say to his angels concerning you, ' Bind him hand and foot, and cast him into outer darkness, ... for many are called, but few are chosen."

My second extract is from a sermon on " Free Will," preached at St. Anne's, Blackfriars, in 1774:—"I know it is growing very fashionable to talk against spiritual feelings. But I dare not join the cry. On the contrary, I adopt the apostle's prayer that our love to God and the manifestation of his love to us may abound yet more and more in knowledge and in all feeling. And it is no enthusiastic wish in behalf of you and myself, that we may be of the number of those godly persons who, as our Church justly expresses it, ' feel in themselves the workings of the Spirit of Christ, mortifying the works of the flesh, and drawing up their minds to high and heavenly things.' Indeed, the great business of God's Spirit is to draw up and to bring down—to draw up our affections to Christ, and to bring down the unsearchable riches of grace into our hearts. The knowledge of this, and earnest desire for it, are all the feelings I plead for ; and for these feelings I wish ever to plead, satisfied as I am that without some experience and enjoyment of them we cannot be happy living or dying.

" Let me ask you, as it were one by one, has the Holy Spirit begun to reveal these deep things of God in your soul? If so, give him the glory of it. And as you prize communion with him, as ever you value the comforts of the Holy Ghost, endeavour to be found in God's way, even the highway of humble faith and obedient love, sitting at the feet of Christ, and imbibing those sweet sanctifying communications of grace which are at once an earnest of and a preparation for complete heaven when you die. God forbid that we should ever think lightly of religious feelings. If we do not in some measure feel ourselves sinners, and feel that Christ is precious, I doubt the Spirit of God has never been savingly at work upon our souls."

My last extract shall be from a sermon preached at St. Anne's, Blackfriars (Romaine's church, be it remembered), in 1770, entitled, " A Caveat against Unsound Doctrine :"—" Faith is the eye of the soul, and the eye is said to see almost every object but itself; so that you may have real faith without being able to discern it. God will not despise the day of small things. Little faith goes to heaven no less than great faith ; though not so comfortably, yet altogether as surely. If you come merely as a sinner to Jesus, and throw yourself, at all events, for salvation on his alone blood and righteousness, and the grace and promise of God in him, thou art as truly a believer as the most triumphant saint that ever lived. Amidst all your weakness, distresses, and temptations, remember that God will not cast out nor cast off the meanest and unworthiest soul that seeks salvation only in the name of Jesus Christ the righteous. When you cannot follow the Rock, the Rock shall follow you, nor ever leave you for a single moment on this side the heavenly Canaan. If you feel your absolute want of Christ, you may on all occasions and in every exigence betake yourself to the covenant-love and faithfulness of God for pardon, sanctification, and safety, and with the same fulness of right and title as a traveller leans upon his own staff, or as a weary labourer throws himself upon his own bed, or as an opulent nobleman draws upon his own banker for whatsoever sum he wants."

I make no comment on these extracts. They speak for themselves. Most Christians, I suspect, will agree with me, that the man who could speak to congregations in this fashion was no ordinary preacher. The hearers of such sermons could never say, " The hungry sheep look up, and are not fed." I am bold to say that the Church of the nineteenth century would be in a far more healthy condition if it had more preaching like Toplady's.

2. As a *writer of miscellaneous papers on religious subjects*, I do not think Toplady has ever been duly appreciated. His pen seems to have been never idle, and his collected works contain a large number of short useful essays on a great variety of sub-

jects. Any one who takes the trouble to look at them will be surprised to find that the worthy vicar of Broad Hembury was conversant with many things beside the Calvinistic controversy, and could write about them in a very interesting manner. He will find short and well-written biographies of Bishop Jewell, Bishop Carleton, Bishop Wilson, John Knox, Fox the Martyrologist, Lord Harrington, Witsius, Allsop, and Dr. Watts. He will find a very valuable collection of extracts from the works of eminent Christians, and of anecdotes, incidents, and historical passages, gathered by Toplady himself. He will find a sketch of natural history, and some curious observations on birds, meteors, animal sagacity, and the solar system. These papers, no doubt, are of various merit; but they all show the singular activity and fertility of the author's mind, and are certainly far more deserving of republication than many of the reprints of modern days. Of Toplady's "Family Prayers" I shall say nothing. They are probably so well known that I need not commend them. Of his seventy-eight letters to friends, I will only say that they are excellent specimens of the correspondence of the last century—sensible, well composed, full of thought and matter, and supplying abundant proof that their writer was a Christian, a scholar, and a gentleman. I cannot, however, do more than refer to all these productions of Toplady's pen. Those who wish to know more must examine his works for themselves. If they do, I venture to predict that they will agree with me that his miscellaneous writings are neither sufficiently known nor valued.

3. As a *controversialist*, I find it rather difficult to give a right estimate of Toplady. In fact, the subject is a painful one, and one which I would gladly avoid. But I feel that I should not be dealing fairly and honestly with my readers, if I did not say something about it. In fact, the vicar of Broad Hembury took such a very prominent part in the doctrinal controversies of last century, and was so thoroughly recognized as the champion

and standard-bearer of Calvinistic theology, that no memoir of him could be regarded as complete, which did not take up this part of his character.

I begin by saying that, on the whole, Toplady's controversial writings appear to me to be in principle scriptural, sound, and true. I do not, for a moment, mean that I can endorse all he says. I consider that his statements are often extreme, and that he is frequently more systematic and narrow than the Bible. He often seems to me, in fact, to go further than Scripture, and to draw conclusions which Scripture has not drawn, and to settle points which for some wise reason Scripture has not settled. Still, for all this, I will never shrink from saying that the cause for which Toplady contended all his life was decidedly the cause of God's truth. He was a bold defender of Calvinistic views about election, predestination, perseverance, human impotency, and irresistible grace. On all these subjects I hold firmly that Calvin's theology is much more scriptural than the theology of Arminius. In a word, I believe that Calvinistic divinity is the divinity of the Bible, of Augustine, and of the Thirty-nine Articles of my own Church, and of the Scotch Confession of Faith. While, therefore, I repeat that I cannot endorse all the sentiments of Toplady's controversial writings, I do claim for them the merit of being in principle scriptural, sound, and true. Well would it be for the Churches, if we had a good deal more of clear, distinct, sharply-cut doctrine in the present day! Vagueness and indistinctness are marks of our degenerate condition.

But I go further than this. I do not hesitate to say that Toplady's controversial works display extraordinary ability. For example, his " Historic Proof of the Doctrinal Calvinism of the Church of England" is a treatise that displays a prodigious amount of research and reading. It is a book that no one could have written who had not studied much, thought much, and thoroughly investigated an enormous mass of theological literature. You see at once that the author has completely digested what he has read, and is able to concentrate all his reading on every point which he handles. The best proof of the book's ability is the simple fact that down to the present day it has never been really answered. It has been reviled, sneered at, abused, and held up to scorn. But abuse is not argument. The book remains to this hour unanswered, and that for the simplest of all reasons, that it is unanswerable. It proves irrefragably, whether men like it or not, that Calvinism is the doctrine of the Church of England, and that all her leading divines, until Laud's time, were Calvinists. All this is done logically, clearly, and powerfully. No one, I venture to think, could read the book through, and not feel obliged to admit that the author was an able man.

While, however, I claim for Toplady's controversial writings the merit of soundness and ability, I must with sorrow admit that I cannot praise his spirit and language when speaking of his opponents. I am obliged to confess that he often uses expressions about them so violent and so bitter, that one feels perfectly ashamed. Never, I regret to say, did an advocate of truth appear to me so entirely to forget the text, " In meekness instructing those that oppose themselves," as the vicar of Broad Hembury. Arminianism seems to have precisely the same effect on him that a scarlet cloak has on a bull. He appears to think it impossible that an Arminian can be saved, and never shrinks with classing Arminians with Pelagians, Socinians, Papists, and heretics. He says things about Wesley and Sellon which never ought to have been said. All this is melancholy work indeed ! But those who are familiar with Toplady's controversial writings know well that I am stating simple truths.

I will not stain my paper nor waste my readers' time by supplying proofs of Toplady's controversial bitterness. It would be very unprofitable to do so. The epithets he applies to his adversaries are perfectly amazing and astonishing. It must in fairness be remembered that the language of his opponents was exceedingly violent, and was enough to provoke any man. It must not be forgotten, moreover, that a hundred years ago men said things in controversy that were not considered so bad as they are now, from the different standard of taste that prevailed. Men were perhaps more honest and outspoken than they are now, and their bark was worse than their bite. But all these considerations only palliate the case. The fact remains, that as a controversialist Toplady was extremely bitter and intemperate, and caused his good to be evil spoken of. He carried the principle, " Rebuke them sharply, that they may be sound in the faith," to an absurd extreme. He forgot the example of his Master, who " when he was reviled, reviled not again ;" and he entirely marred the value of his arguments by the violence and uncharitableness with which he maintained them. Thousands who neither cared nor understood anything about his favourite cause, could understand that no cause ought to be defended in such a spirit and temper.

I leave this painful subject with the general remark, that Toplady is a standing beacon to the Church, to show us the evils of controversy. " The beginning of strife is like letting out water." " In the multitude of words there wanteth not sin." We must never shrink from controversy, if need be, in defence of Christ's gospel, but we must never take it up without jealous watchfulness over our own hearts, and over the manner in which we carry it on. Above all, we must strive to think as charitably as possible of our opponent. It was Calvin himself who said of Luther, " He may call me a devil if he will ; but I shall always call him a good servant of Jesus Christ." Well would it have been for Toplady's reputation, if he had been more like Calvin ! Perhaps when we open our eyes in heaven we shall be amazed to find how many things there were which both Calvinists and Arminians did not thoroughly understand.

4. There is only one point about Toplady on which I wish

to say something, and that is his character as a *hymn-writer*.
This is a point, I am thankful to say, on which I find no difficulty at all. I give it as my decided opinion that he was one
of the best hymn-writers in the English language.   I am
quite aware that this may seem extravagant praise; but I
speak deliberately.   I hold that there are no hymns better than
his.

Good hymns are an immense blessing to the Church of
Christ. I believe the last day alone will show the world the
real amount of good they have done.   They suit all, both rich
and poor.   There is an elevating, stirring, soothing, spiritualizing,
effect about a thoroughly good hymn, which nothing else can
produce.   It sticks in men's memories when texts are forgotten.
It trains men for heaven, where praise is one of the principal
occupations.   Preaching and praying shall one day cease for
ever; but praise shall never die.   The makers of good ballads
are said to sway national opinion.   The writers of good hymns,
in like manner, are those who leave the deepest marks on the
face of the Church.   Thousands of Christians rejoice in the
" Te Deum," and " Just as I am," who neither prize the Thirty-
nine Articles, nor know anything about the first four councils,
nor understand the Athanasian Creed.

But really good hymns are exceedingly rare.   There are only
a few men in any age who can write them.   You may name
hundreds of first-rate preachers for one first-rate writer of hymns.
Hundreds of so-called hymns fill up our collections of congre-
gational psalmody, which are really not hymns at all.   They
are very sound, very scriptural, very proper, very correct, very
tolerably rhymed; but they are not real, live, genuine hymns.
There is no life about them.   At best they are tame, pointless,
weak, and milk-and-watery.   In many cases, if written out
straight, without respect of lines, they would make excellent
prose.   But poetry they are not.   It may be a startling assertion to some ears to say that there are not more than two

hundred first-rate hymns in the English language; but startling as it may sound, I believe it is true.

Of all English hymn-writers, none, perhaps, have succeeded so thoroughly in combining truth, poetry, life, warmth, fire, depth, solemnity, and unction, as Toplady has. I pity the man who does not know, or, knowing, does not admire those glorious hymns of his beginning, "Rock of Ages, cleft for me;" or, "Holy Ghost, dispel our sadness;" or, "A debtor to mercy alone;" or, "Your harps, ye trembling saints;" or, "Christ, whose glory fills the skies;" or, "When languor and disease invade;" or, "Deathless principle, arise." The writer of these seven hymns alone has laid the Church under perpetual obligations to him. Heretics have been heard in absent moments whispering over "Rock of Ages," as if they clung to it when they had let slip all things beside. Great statesmen have been known to turn it into Latin, as if to perpetuate its fame. The only matter of regret is, that the writer of such excellent hymns should have written so few. If he had lived longer, written more hymns, and handled fewer controversies, his memory would have been had in greater honour, and men would have been better pleased.

That hymns of such singular beauty and pathos should have come from the same pen which indited such bitter controversial writings, is certainly a strange anomaly. I do not pretend to explain it, or to offer any solution. I only lay it before my readers as a naked fact. To say the least, it should teach us not to be hasty in censuring a man before we know all sides of his character. The best saints of God are neither so very good, nor the faultiest so very faulty, as they appear. He that only reads Toplady's hymns will find it hard to believe that he could compose his controversial writings. He that only reads his controversial writings will hardly believe that he composed his hymns. Yet the fact remains, that the same man composed both. Alas! the holiest among us all is a very poor mixed creature!

I now leave the subject of this chapter here. I ask my readers to put a favourable construction on Toplady's life, and to judge him with righteous judgment. I fear he is a man who has never been fairly estimated, and has never had many friends. Ministers of his decided, sharply-cut, doctrinal opinions are never very popular. But I plead strongly that Toplady's undeniable faults should never make us forget his equally undeniable excellencies. With all his infirmities, I firmly believe that he was a good man and a great man, and did a work for Christ a hundred years ago, which will never be overthrown. He will stand in his lot at the last day in a high place, when many, perhaps, whom the world liked better shall be put to shame.

XIII

Fletcher of Madeley and his Ministry.

CHAPTER I.

Born in Switzerland, 1729—Educated at Geneva and Leutzburg—Wishes to be a Soldier— Becomes a Tutor in England, 1750—Private Tutor in Mr. Hill's Family, 1752—Becomes Acquainted with Methodists — Inward Conflict — Ordained 1757 — Vicar of Madeley, 1760—Correspondence with Charles Wesley and Lady Huntingdon.

 BELIEVE that no one ever reads his Bible with attention without being struck with the deep beauty of the fourteenth chapter of St. John's gospel. I suspect that few readers of that marvellous chapter fail to notice the wondrous saying of our Lord, " In my Father's house are many mansions : if it were not so, I would have told you." Cold and dull must be the heart that is not roused and stirred by these words.

This beautiful saying, of late years, has been painfully wrested from its true meaning. Men of whom better things might have been expected, have misapplied it sadly, and imposed a false sense on it. They have dared to say that men of all faiths and creeds will find a place in heaven at last ; and that " every man shall be saved by the law or sect which he professeth, so that he be diligent to frame his mind according to that law and the light of nature." They would fain have us believe that the inhabitants of heaven will be a mixed body, including heathen idolaters and Mohammedans as well as Christians, and compris-

ing members of every religious denomination in the world, however opposite and antagonistic their respective opinions may be.
Miserable indeed is such theology ! Wretched is the prospect
which it holds out to us of eternity ! Small could be the harmony in such a heterogeneous assembly ! At this rate, heaven
would be no heaven at all.

But we must not allow human misinterpretations to make us
overlook great truths. It is true, in a most comfortable sense,
that " in our Father's house there are many mansions," and that
all who are washed in Christ's blood, and renewed by Christ's
Spirit, will find a place in heaven, though they may not see eye
to eye upon earth. There is room in our Father's house for all
who hold the Head, however much they may differ on points
of minor importance. There is room for Calvinists and room
for Arminians, room for Episcopalians and room for Presby-
terians, room for Thomas Cranmer and room for John Knox,
room for John Bunyan and room for George Herbert, room for
Henry Martyn and room for Dr. Judson, room for Edward
Bickersteth and room for Robert M'Cheyne, room for Chalmers
of Edinburgh, and room for Daniel Wilson of Calcutta. Yes !
thank God, our Father's house is a very wide one. There is
room in it for all who are true-hearted believers in the Lord
Jesus Christ.

Thoughts such as these come crowding over my mind as I
take up my pen to write an account of the eleventh spiritual
hero of the eighteenth century, whom I want to introduce to my
readers. The man whom I mean is the well-known Fletcher,
vicar of Madeley. I cannot forget that there was a doctrinal
gulf between him and my last hero, Toplady, and that while one
was a Calvinist of Calvinists, the other was an Arminian of
Arminians. But I will never shut my eyes to the fact that
Fletcher was a Christian as well as an Arminian. Mistaken, as
I think he was, on some points, he was certainly thoroughly
right on others. He was a man of rare grace, and a minister of

rare usefulness. In short, I think that no account of English religion a hundred years ago could be considered just, fair, and complete, which did not supply some information about Fletcher of Madeley.

John William Fletcher was a native of Switzerland, and was born at Nyon, in that country, on the 12th of September 1729. His real name was De La Flechiere, and he is probably known by that name among his own countrymen to this day. In England, however, he was always called Fletcher, and, for convenience' sake, I shall only speak of him by that name. His father was first an officer in the French army, and afterwards a colonel in the militia of his own country. The family is said to have been one of the most respectable in the canton of Berne, and a branch of an earldom of Savoy.

Fletcher appears to have been remarkable for cleverness even when a boy. At the first school which he went to at Geneva, he carried away all the prizes, and was complimented by the teachers and managers in a very flattering manner. During his residence at Geneva, his biographer records that " he allowed himself but little time either for recreation, refreshment, or rest. After studying hard all day, he would often consume the greater part of the night in writing down whatever had occurred in the course of his reading which seemed worthy of observation. Here he acquired that true classical taste which was so frequently and justly admired by his friends, and which all his studied plainness could never entirely conceal. Here, also, he laid the foundation of that extensive and accurate knowledge for which he was afterwards distinguished, both in philosophy and theology."

From Geneva his father sent him to a small Swiss town called Leutzburg, where he not only acquired the German language, but also diligently prosecuted his former studies. On leaving Leutzburg, he continued some time at home, studying the Hebrew language, and perfecting his acquaintance with mathematics. Such was Fletcher's early training and education. I ask the reader's special attention to it. It supplies one among many proofs that those who call the leaders of the English revival of religion in the last century " poor, ignorant, illiterate fanatics," are only exposing their own ignorance. They know neither what they say, nor whereof they affirm. In the mere matter of learning, Wesley, Romaine, Berridge, Hervey, Top-lady, and Fletcher, were second to few men in their day.

Young Fletcher's education being completed, his parents hoped that he would at once turn his attention to the ministry, a profession for which they considered him to be eminently well fitted. In this expectation, however, they were at first curiously disappointed. Partly from a sense of unfitness, partly from scruples about the doctrine of predestination, young Fletcher announced that he had given up all idea of being ordained, and wished to go into the army. His theological studies were laid aside for the military works of Vauban and Cohorn, and, in spite of all the remonstrances of his friends, he seemed determined to become a soldier.

This strange determination, however, was frustrated by a singular train of providences. The same overruling hand which would not allow Jonah to go to Tarshish, and sent him to Nineveh in spite of himself, was able to prevent the young Swiss student carrying out his military intentions. At first, it seems, on his parents flatly refusing their consent to his entering the army, young Fletcher went away to Lisbon, and, like many of his countrymen, offered his services to a foreign flag. At Lisbon, on his offer being accepted, he soon gathered a company of Swiss recruits, and engaged a passage on board a Portuguese man-of-war which was about to sail for Brazil. He then wrote to his parents, asking them to send him money, but met with a decided refusal. Unmoved by this, he determined to go without the money, as soon as the ship sailed. But, on the morning that he ought to have put to sea, the servant at breakfast let the kettle fall and scalded his leg so severely that he had to keep his bed for a considerable time. In the meanwhile the ship sailed for Brazil, and, curiously enough, was never heard of any more !

Fletcher returned to Switzerland, in no wise shaken or deterred by his Lisbon disappointment. Being informed that his uncle, then a colonel in the Dutch service, had procured a commission for him, he joyfully set out for Flanders. But just at that time a peace was concluded, and the continental armies were reduced; and his uncle dying shortly after, his expectations were completely blasted, and he gave up all thought of being a soldier.

Being now disengaged from business, and all military prospects seeming completely at an end, young Fletcher thought it would not be amiss to spend a little time in England. He arrived in this country, almost totally ignorant of our language, sometime in the year 1750, and began at once to inquire for some one who could instruct him in the English tongue. For this purpose he was recommended to a boarding-school, kept by a Mr. Burchell, at South Mimms, and afterwards at Hatfield, in Hertfordshire. With this gentleman he remained eighteen months, and not only acquired a complete mastery of English, but also became exceedingly popular as a clever, amiable, and agreeable man, both in his tutor's family and throughout the neighbourhood in which he resided. While staying at Mr. Burchell's, Mr. Dechamps, a French minister to whom he had been recommended, procured him the situation of private tutor in the family of Mr. Hill of Tern Hall, in Shropshire. His acceptance of this post in the year 1752, in the twenty-second year of his age, was the turning-point in his life, and affected his whole course, both spiritually and temporally, to the very end of his days.

Up to this time, there is not the slightest evidence that Fletcher knew anything of spiritual and experimental religion. As a well-educated man, he was of course acquainted with the facts and evidences of Christianity. But he appears to have been profoundly ignorant of the inward work of the Holy Ghost, and of the distinctive doctrines of the gospel of Christ. Happily for him, he seems to have been carefully and morally brought up, and to have had a good deal of religion of a certain sort when he was a boy. From an early period of life, he was familiar with the letter of Scripture, and to this circumstance he traced his preservation from infidelity, and from many vices into which young men too often fall. Beside this, a succession of providential escapes from death, which his biographers have carefully recorded, undoubtedly had a restraining effect upon him. Nevertheless, there is no reason to think that he really experienced a work of grace in his heart until he had been some time an inmate of Mr. Hill's house. Up to this time he had, after a fashion, believed in God and feared God; but he had never felt his love in Christ Jesus shed abroad in his heart by the Holy Ghost. He had never really seen his own sinfulness, nor the preciousness of Christ's atoning blood.

The first thing which awakened Fletcher to a right conviction of his fallen state, was the simple remark of a servant in Mr. Hill's household. This man, coming up into his room one Sunday evening, in order to make up the fire, found him writing some music, and, looking at him with concern, said, "Sir, I am sorry to see you so employed on the Lord's day." At first his pride was aroused and his resentment moved, to hear a reproof given by a servant. But, upon reflection, he felt the reproof was just, put away his music, and from that very hour became a strict observer of the Lord's day. How true is that word of Solomon, "Reproofs of instruction are the way of life!" (Prov. vi. 23.)

The next step in his spiritual history was his becoming acquainted with the people called Methodists. The way in which this was brought about he afterwards related to John Wesley, in the following words:—"When Mr. Hill went to London to attend Parliament, he took his family and me with him. On one occasion, while they stopped at St. Alban's, I walked out into the town, and did not return till they were set out for London. A horse being left for me, I rode after them and overtook them in the evening. Mr. Hill asked me why I stayed behind. I said, 'As I was walking I met with a poor old woman, who talked so sweetly of Jesus Christ, that I knew not how the time passed away.' Said Mrs. Hill, 'I shall wonder if our tutor does not turn Methodist by-and-by.' 'Methodist, madam,' said I; 'pray what is that?' She replied, 'Why, the Methodists are a people that do nothing but pray; they are praying all day and all night.' 'Are they?' said I; 'then, by the help of God, I will find them out, if they be above ground.' I did find them out not long after, and was admitted into the society."

The third important step in Fletcher's spiritual history was hearing those clergymen who were called Methodists preach about *faith*. Under the influence of newly awakened feelings, he had begun to strive diligently to make himself acceptable to God by his doings. But hearing a sermon one day preached by a clergyman named Green, he became convinced that he did not understand the nature of saving faith. This conviction was only attained through much humiliation of soul. "Is it possible," he thought, "that I, who have always been accounted so religious, who have made divinity my study, and received the premium of *piety* (so-called) from a Swiss university for my writings on divine subjects—is it possible that I should yet be so ignorant as not to know what faith is?" But the more he examined himself and considered the subject, the more he was convinced of the momentous truth. The more he saw his sinfulness, and the entire corruption and depravity of his whole nature, the more his hope of being able to reconcile himself to God by his own works began to die away. He still sought, by the most rigorous austerities, to conquer this evil nature, and to bring into his soul a heaven-born peace. But alas! the more he strove the more he saw and felt that all his soul was sinful. In short, like Bunyan's Christian, before he saw the way to the wicket-gate, he felt his imminent danger, and yet knew not which way to flee.

How long this inward struggle continued in Fletcher's mind is not quite clear. It seems probable that it was at least two years before his soul found peace and was set at liberty, and his burden rolled away. Evangelists were rare in these days, and there were few to help an anxious conscience into the light. His diary shows that he went through an immense amount of inward conflict. At one time we find him saying, " I almost gave up all hope, and resolved to sin on and go to hell." At another time he says, "If I go to hell, I will serve God even there; and since I cannot be an instance of his mercy in heaven, I will be a monument of his justice in hell; and if I show forth his glory one way or the other, I am content." At another time he says, " I have recovered my ground. I thought Christ died for all, and therefore he died for me. He died to pluck such sinners as I am as brands out of the burning. And as I sincerely desire to be his, he will surely take me." At another time he records, " I heard a sermon on justification by faith, but my heart was not moved in the least. I was only still more convinced that I was an unbeliever, that I am not justified by faith, and that till I am, I shall never have peace with God." At another time he says, " I have found relief in Mr. Wesley's journal, when I heard that we should not build on what we feel, but go to Christ with all our sins and all our hardness of heart."

Mental struggles like these are no strange things to many of God's people. They are deep waters through which some of the best and holiest saints have had to pass, in the beginning of their journey towards heaven. John Bunyan's little book called " Grace Abounding," is a striking account of the inward agony which the author of " Pilgrim's Progress " had to endure before he found peace. There are many points of resemblance between his experience and that of Fletcher. It is a pleasant thought, however, that sooner or later these painful struggles end in solid peace. The greater the conflict at first, the greater sometimes is the peace at the last. The men that God intends to use most as instruments to do his work, are often tempered for his service by being frequently put into the fire. The truths that we have got hold of by tremendous exertion are precisely the truths which we afterwards grasp most firmly, and proclaim most positively and powerfully. The man who has embraced the doctrine of justification by faith alone, through a hand-to-hand fight with Satan, and a contest even unto death, is precisely the man to preach the doctrine to his fellow-men with unction, with demonstration of the Spirit, and with crushing power. This was the experience of that mighty evangelist, George Whitefield. This was the experience of Fletcher of Madeley.

Once set free from the burden of sin unforgiven, and feeling the blessedness of peace with God, we need not wonder that Fletcher longed to tell others of the way to life. Long before he was ordained a minister, he began to speak to others about their souls, according as he had opportunity. Both in London, when he accompanied Mr. Hill, and even during the sitting of Parliament, and in the neighbourhood of Tern Hall, he seized every occasion of trying to do spiritual good. And even at this early period his labours were not in vain. His biographer says: " Though he was at present by no means perfect in the English tongue, particularly in the pronunciation of it, yet the earnestness with which he spoke, then seldom to be found in English preaching, and the unspeakably tender affection to poor, undone sinners, which breathed in every word and question, drew multitudes of people to hear him, and few went empty away."

We can easily understand that Fletcher's views about taking orders now went through a complete change. Little by little

his doubts, and fears, and scruples as to his fitness for the
ministerial office melted away.   Correspondence with John
Wesley encouraged him to go forward with the idea of being
ordained.   Difficulties which seemed likely at one time to put
an insuperable barrier in his way, were unexpectedly removed.
A gentleman whom he hardly knew offered him a living which
was likely to be soon vacant.   A clergyman whom he had never
even spoken to, of his own accord offered him a title to orders;
and at length, in the year 1757, he was ordained deacon on
Sunday the 6th of March, and priest on the following Sunday,
by the Bishop of Bangor, in the Chapel Royal at St. James's.
How Fletcher got over the difficulty of being a foreigner, and
of not having taken an University degree, I am unable to explain.   I can only suppose that the influence of the family of
the Hills, in which he was still tutor, made a bishop of those
days ready to ordain him as a "literate person."   On what
title he was ordained, I am also unable to say.   But, putting
things together, I conjecture that he was nominated curate
of Madeley, the parish of which he afterwards became vicar.
The whole matter of his ordination seems to have been attended
with strange irregularities, judged by the standard of the present
day.   But things were strangely managed in the Church of
England a hundred years ago.

With characteristic energy, Fletcher lost no time in beginning
the work of the ministry.   The very day that he was ordained
priest, he came straight from the Chapel Royal to West Street
Chapel, and assisted John Wesley in the administration of the
Lord's Supper.   Throughout the next two months, until Mr.
Hill's family left London for Shropshire, he preached in many
London pulpits both in the English and French language,
according as he had opportunity.   Labouring in this way, he
soon became well known as a fellow-labourer of the leading evangelists of the day, and rapidly attained a very high reputation.

In the month of May 1757 he went down into Shropshire

with Mr. Hill's family, and found comparatively few openings for the exercise of his ministry. In fact, a friend says that he did not preach more than six times in six months; partly, no doubt, from his time being occupied with the education of his young pupils, and partly, in all probability, because the Shropshire clergy were afraid of him, and would not admit him into their pulpits. The only churches in which he preached were Atcham, Wroxeter, Madeley, and St. Alkmunds, and the Abbey Church, Shrewsbury.

Whatever the cause may have been, I cannot discover that Fletcher had any regular stated ministerial work for the first three years after his ordination. From March 1757 to the latter part of 1760, he seems to have retained his position as tutor in Mr. Hill's family, and in that capacity to have gone regularly to London for one part of the year, and to have been generally in Shropshire for the other. Wherever he was, he appears to have found time for itinerating and preaching a good deal, and it is only natural to suppose that he was not required to devote himself entirely to the superintendence of Mr. Hill's sons.

I must confess my inability to trace out Fletcher's history very accurately during the first three years of his ministry. The memoirs of men of that day are so often written with a reckless neglect of dates, that at this distance of time it is impossible to follow their movements. Sometimes I read of his being at Bristol, preaching for John Wesley at Kingswood; sometimes I find him in London, preaching in Lady Huntingdon's drawing-room; sometimes he is at Brighton, occupying the pulpit of Lady Huntingdon's Chapel; sometimes he is at Tunbridge, preaching to French prisoners; sometimes he is itinerating about the country, and appearing in all sorts of strange and unexpected places. But the order and reasons of his movements during these three years are matters which I cannot pretend to explain. One thing only is very clear. He became notorious as a public supporter of the great religious revival of which Lady Huntingdon was the mainspring, and formed friendships with all its leading agents which lasted till death.

It was about this period of his life that Fletcher became acquainted with the famous Berridge of Everton. This took place under such singular circumstances that I shall give them at length in the words of Lady Huntingdon's biographer. It appears that he went to Everton vicarage uninvited and unexpectedly, and "introduced himself as a raw convert who had taken the liberty to wait on Berridge for the benefit of his instruction and advice. From his accent and manner the shrewd vicar of Everton perceived at once that he was a foreigner, and inquired from what country he came. 'I am a Swiss, from the canton of Berne,' was the reply. 'From Berne!' said Berridge; 'then probably you can give me some account of a young fellow-countryman of yours, one John Fletcher, who has lately preached a few times for Mr. Wesley, and of whose talents, learning, and piety, he speaks in high terms. Do you know him?' 'Yes, sir,' said Fletcher; 'I know him intimately; and did the Messrs. Wesley know him as well as I do, they would not speak of him in such terms, for which he is more obliged to their partial friendship than to his own merits.' 'You surprise me,' said Berridge, 'by speaking so coldly of a countryman in whose praise they are so warm.' 'I have the best reason,' he rejoined, 'for speaking as I do, for I am myself John Fletcher.' 'If you are John Fletcher,' said his host, 'you must do me the favour to take my pulpit to-morrow, and when we are better acquainted, without implicitly receiving either your statement or that of your friends, I shall be able to judge for myself.' Thus commenced an intimacy between Fletcher and Berridge, which no subsequent controversy could ever entirely interrupt."

The turning-point in Fletcher's ministerial history was his appointment to the vicarage of Madeley, in October 1760.

Madeley is a large and unattractive parish near Wellington, in Shropshire, containing at this time between eight and nine thousand inhabitants, employed almost entirely in collieries and ironworks. There is no reason to suppose that it was very different a hundred years ago from what it is now, though the population has probably increased. The circumstances under which he obtained the living were very remarkable, and are well described in his own letters.

The first link in the chain of providence which took him to Madeley, was the offer of the living of Dunham in Cheshire by his friend Mr. Hill. He told Fletcher that the parish was small, the duty light, and the income good—£400 a-year— and that it was situated in a fine sporting country. After thanking Mr. Hill most cordially for his kindness, Fletcher replied, "Alas, sir! Dunham will not suit me. There is too much money, and too little work." "Few clergymen make such objections," said Mr. Hill; "it is a pity to resign such a living, as I do not know that I can find you another. What shall we do? Would you like Madeley?" "That, sir, would be the very place for me." "My object, Mr. Fletcher, is to make you comfortable in your own way. If you prefer Madeley, I shall find no difficulty in persuading Chambers, the present vicar, to exchange it for Dunham, which is worth twice as much, and in getting Madeley for you." In this way, curious as it now appears, John Fletcher, in the month of October 1760, found himself in the strange position of an English incumbent, and vicar of a large parish in Shropshire.

He did not go to Madeley without many doubts and misgivings. Not a few of his best friends thought it a move of very questionable wisdom. Even now, one cannot help fancying that his valuable life would have been longer, and his extraparochial usefulness greatly increased, if he had been content with the lighter work and smaller population of Dunham. But we must not forget that the "steps of a good man are ordered by the Lord." It is place that often draws out grace. For anything we know, Fletcher might have sunk into comparative indolence and obscurity, if he had not been planted at Madeley. His letters, however, at this period, show plainly that the move was not made without great anxiety and exercise of soul.

To Charles Wesley he writes : " My heart revolts at the idea of being at Madeley alone—opposed by my superiors, hated by my neighbours, and despised by all the world ; without piety, without talents, without resolution, how shall I repel the assaults and surmount the obstacles which I foresee if I discharge my duty at Madeley with fidelity ? On the other hand, to reject this presentation, burn the certificate, and leave in the desert these sheep whom the Lord has evidently brought me into the world to feed, appears to me nothing but obstinacy and refined self-love. I will hold a middle course between these extremes. I will be wholly passive in the steps I must take, and yet active in praying the Lord to deliver me from the evil one, and to conduct me in the way that he would have me go. If you can see anything better, inform me of it speedily ; and at the same time remember me in all your prayers, that if this matter be not of the Lord, the enmity of the Bishop of Lichfield—who must countersign my testimonials, the threats of the Bishop of Hereford's chaplain who was a witness to my preaching at West Street Chapel, the objections drawn from my not being naturalized, or some other obstacle, may prevent the kind intention of Mr. Hill."

It is written that " when a man's ways please the Lord, he maketh his enemies to be at peace with him." This text was eminently illustrated in the matter of Fletcher's appointment to Madeley. Obstacles which at one time seemed insuperable, melted away in a most extraordinary manner, and, almost in spite of himself, he was instituted into possession of the living. In a letter to Lady Huntingdon, on the 3rd of October, he says, " I seem to be the prisoner of God's providence, who is going, in all probability, to cast my lot for life among the colliers and forgemen of Madeley. The two thousand souls of that parish, for whom I was called into the ministry, are many sheep in the wilderness, which, after all, I cannot sacrifice to my own private choice. When I was once suffered to attend them for a few days, some began to return to the Shepherd of their souls, and I found it in my heart to spend and be spent for them. When I was afterwards sent away from them, that zeal, it is true, cooled to such a degree that I have wished a thousand times they might never be committed to my charge. But the impression of the tears of those who, when I left them, ran after me crying, 'Who shall now show us the way to heaven?' never quite wore off from the bottom of my heart; and, upon second thoughts, I always concluded that if the Lord made my way plain to this church, I could not run away from it without disobeying the order of providence. That time is come, the church is vacated, the presentation to it brought unasked into my hands; the difficulty of getting proper testimonials, which I looked upon as insurmountable, vanishes at once; the three clergymen who had opposed me with most bitterness signed them;—the Bishop of Lichfield countersigns them without the least objection; the lord of the manor, my great opponent, leaves the parish; and the very man, the vicar, who told me I should never preach in that church, now recommends me to it, and tells me he will induct me himself. Are not these intimations of the will of God?"

On the 28th of October 1760, he writes to Lady Huntingdon as follows:—" Since I had the honour to write last, all the little circumstances of my institution and induction have taken such an easy turn that I question whether any clergyman noted for good fellowship ever got over them with less trouble. I preached last Sunday, for the first time, in my church, and shall continue to do so, though I propose staying with Mr. Hill till he leaves the country, partly to comply with him to the last, and partly to avoid falling out with my predecessor, who is still at Madeley, but who will remove about the same time. If I know anything of myself, I shall be much more ready to resign my benefice, when I have had a fair trial of my unprofitableness to the people committed to my care, than I was to accept it. Mr. John Wesley bids me do it without a trial. He will have me see in this appointment to Madeley 'the snare of the devil, and fly from it at the peril of my soul.' I answer, I cannot see it in that light. He says, 'Others may do well in a living; you cannot, for it is not your calling.' I tell him I readily own I am not fit either to plant or water any part of the Lord's vineyard, but that if I am called at all, I am called to preach at Madeley, where I was first sent into the ministry, and where a chain of providences I could not break has again fastened me. I tell him, that though I should be as unsuccessful as Noah before the flood, yet I am determined to try to be to them a preacher of Christ's righteousness; and that, notwithstanding my universal inability, I am not quite without hope that he who reproved a prophet's madness by the mouth of an ass, may reprove a collier's profaneness even by my mouth."

The doubts and misgivings with which Fletcher accepted the living of Madeley, appear to have clung to him for several months after he entered on the duties of his parish. Great allowance must, of course, be made for the natural ignorance of a young Swiss about the habits and customs of a neglected mining population in England. But, judging from the three following letters, he seems for some time to have gone through great exercise of mind after commencing his residence at Madeley. I make no excuse for inserting these letters at length.

On the 19th of November 1760, he writes to Lady Huntingdon as follows:—" I have hitherto written my sermons, but I am carried so far beyond my notes when in the pulpit, that I propose preaching with only my sermon-cover in my hand next

Friday, when I shall venture on an evening lecture for the first time. I question whether I shall have half-a-dozen hearers, as the god of a busy world is doubly the god of this part of the world; but I am resolved to try. The weather and the roads are so bad, that the way to church is almost impracticable; nevertheless, all the seats were full last Sunday. Some begin to come from the adjacent parishes, and some more, as they say, *threaten* to come when the season permits. I cannot yet discern any deep work, or, indeed, anything but what will always attend the crying down man's righteousness and exalting Christ's—I mean a general liking among the poor, and offence and ridicule and opposition among the respectable and rich people. Should the Lord vouchsafe to plant the gospel in this country, my parish seems to be the best centre of a work, as it lies just among the most populous, profane, and ignorant parts. But it is well if, after all, there is any work in my parish. I despair of this when I look at myself, and fall in with Mr. John Wesley's opinion about me. Yet sometimes, too, I hope the Lord has not sent me here for nothing; and I beg for strength to stand still and see the salvation of the Lord. Nevertheless, I am still fully determined to resign my living after a while, if the Lord does not think me worthy to be his instrument. If your Ladyship could at any time spare me a minute, I should be glad to know whether you do not think I should then be at full liberty to do it before God. I abhor the title of a living for a living's sake. It is death to me.

" There are three meetings in my parish—a Papist, Quaker, and Baptist ; and they begin to call the fourth the Methodist one—I mean the church. But the bulk of the inhabitants are stupid heathens, who seem past all curiosity, as well as all sense of godliness. I am ready to run after them into their pits and forges, and I only wait for God's providence to show me the way. I am often reduced to great perplexity, but the end of it is sweet. I am driven to the Lord, and he comforts, encourages, and teaches me. I sometimes feel that zeal which forced Paul to wish to be accursed for his brethren's sakes, but I want to feel it without interruption. The devil, my friends, and my heart, have pushed hard at me to make me fall into worldly cares, and creature snares—first by the thought of marrying, then by the offer of several boarders, one of whom offered me sixty pounds a-year; but I have been enabled to cry, 'Nothing but Jesus, and the service of his people;' and I trust the Lord will keep me in the same mind."

On the 6th of January 1761, he writes to Lady Huntingdon again, even in a lower key and a more depressed frame of mind. He says:—"I had a secret expectation to be the instrument of a work in this part of our Church, and I did not despair of soon becoming a little Berridge! Thus warmed with sparks of my own kindling, I looked out to see the rocks broken in pieces and the water flowing out; but, to the great disappointment of my hopes, I am now forced to look within, and to see the need I have of being broken, and of repenting myself. If my being stationed in this howling wilderness is to answer no public end as to the gospel of Christ, I will not give up the hope that it may answer a private end as to myself, in humbling me under a sense of universal unprofitableness. If I preach the gospel ten years here, and see no fruit of my labours, in either case I promise to bless God, if I can only say from my heart, 'I am nothing, I have nothing, I can do nothing.'

"As to my parish, all that I see hitherto in it is nothing but what one may expect from speaking plainly, and with some degree of earnestness. Many cry out, 'He is a Methodist, a downright Methodist;' while some of the poorer sort say, 'Nay, but he speaketh the truth.' Some of the best farmers and most respectable tradesmen talk often among themselves, I hear, about turning me out of my living as a Methodist or a Baptist, and spread about such stories as your Ladyship may guess at without my writing them. My Friday lecture took better than I expected, and I propose to continue it till the congregation desert me. The number of hearers then is larger than that which my predecessor had on Sunday. The number of communicants is increased from thirty to above a hundred, and a few seem to seek grace in the means. May they do it in sincerity !"

The last letter which I shall quote in this memoir was addressed to Lady Huntingdon on the 27th of April 1761. He says:— "I learn by slow experience, that in me dwelleth no good thing. This I find cannot be learned of man, nor by man. It is a lesson that grace alone teaches effectually in the furnace of affliction. I am still at the first line; but I think I read it and understand it in a manner quite different from what I did before. Surely the Saviour speaks as no man ever spake; and he teaches with authority, not as the scribes. His words are recorded in the heart, while those of men only graze the surface of the understanding. I have met with several trials since Providence cast me, I shall not say into this part of the Lord's vineyard, but into this part of our spiritual Sodom. Nevertheless, they did not work upon me as they ought to have done. I stood out against them in a kind of self-resolution, supported by human fortitude rather than divine humility; and so they did not bring down the pride of nature, but rather increased it. The old man, if he cannot have his own food, will live quietly and comfortably on spiritual food; yea, he is often pampered by what the natural mind supposes will poison him.

"Of late I have met with a trial that, by God's infinite mercy, has found its way to my heart. Oh, may the wound be deep enough to let in the mind of Jesus! A young woman, daughter of one of my most substantial parishioners, giving place to Satan by pride and impatience, is driven in her convictions into a kind of madness. I could not bear patiently enough, before this, the reports that went about that I drove people mad; but the fear of having this laid to my charge, backed with so glaring an instance, has thrown me into some agonies of soul.

"Why God permits these offences to arise, has not a little staggered me. Once I was for taking to my heels, and hireling-like, flying at the first approach of the wolf. But, thanks to divine grace, I now try to commit to the Lord the keeping of his own work, and pray for a blind faith in him who calls light out of darkness. Had not this trial staggered me, I should have great hopes that a few living stones may be gathered here for the temple of the Lord. There is a considerable stir about religion in the neighbourhood; and though most people rise up against it, yet some begin to inquire in earnest what they must do to be saved; and some get a sight of the way. My church is full, notwithstanding the oaths that some of my parishioners have sworn never to hear me preach again. I am insensibly led into exhorting sometimes in my house and elsewhere. I preach on Sunday morning and Friday evening; and on Sunday evening, after catechising or preaching to the children, I read one of the Homilies, or a sermon of Archbishop Usher, insisting on all that confirms what I advanced in the morning, which greatly stops the mouth of the gainsayers, till God shall turn their hearts."

Such were the beginnings of Fletcher's ministry of Madeley. His subsequent history would occupy far more room than can be assigned to it in this chapter. How he persevered in his evangelistic work at Madeley for twenty-five years—how he became the principal of Lady Huntingdon's College at Trevecca—how his health broke down under the abundance of his labours—how he lived on through evil report and good report—how he married—how he died—how he preached and how he wrote,—all these are matters which I think it best to reserve for another distinct chapter.

CHAPTER II.

Ministerial Labours at Madeley—Superintendent of Trevecca College, 1768—Resigns Trevecca, 1771—Laid aside by ill health, 1776—Goes to Clifton, Newington, and Switzerland—Returns to Madeley, 1781—Marries—Dies, 1785—His Preaching—Writing—Private Character—Testimony of Wesley and Venn.

THE position of a parish clergyman in the Church of England who does his duty, is one of peculiar difficulties and discouragements. He has not to deal with a voluntary congregation, whose members have no connection with him beyond that of free choice and inclination. He has the nominal charge of all who reside within certain territorial boundaries, and, whether they like him or not, in the eye of the law he is bound to do what he can for their souls.

The larger the population of an English parish, the greater are the English clergyman's difficulties. Many a clergyman finds himself placed in the midst of dense masses of people whose spiritual necessities he is utterly unable to overtake. He sees around him hundreds of immortal souls continually passing out of time into eternity—ignorant, immoral, without God, without Christ, and without hope—and yet has neither time nor strength to get at half of them! A position like this is dreadfully trying and crushing to the spirit of a conscientious man. Yet this is the position in which Fletcher found himself at Madeley. Who can wonder that at first he felt sorely cast down, and half inclined to think, with Wesley, that he had mistaken his calling?

These first feelings of discouragement, however, gradually passed away. Little by little he became fitted to his post, and saw clearly that he was where God would have him be. Once settled down in his work at Madeley, he never gave it up, and for twenty-five years did the work of an evangelist among his semi-heathen parishioners in a way that few have ever equalled, and none probably have surpassed. No other cure ever tempted him away. Where he began his ministry, there he ended it. Madeley was his first charge, and Madeley was his last.

The machinery which Fletcher used in doing his work at Madeley was very simple and apostolic. He was instant in season and out of season, always "preaching the Word." Publicly in church, privately from house to house, by the road-side, in the fields, at the coal-pit mouth, he was continually lifting up his voice, and "teaching and preaching Jesus Christ." He counted the day lost in which he was not actually employed in doing his Master's business. A warfare of holy aggression on sin and Satan's kingdom was constantly kept up throughout the district, and no one was let alone. So great indeed was his zeal, that people who were determined to have their sins agreed to lock their doors, and refuse him admission. Like Ahab, they hated him because he did not speak good of their condi-tion, but evil. Even John Wesley, who thought him wrong in going to Madeley, bore this testimony to his work: "From the beginning of his settling there, he was a laborious workman in the Lord's vineyard, endeavouring to spread the truth of the gospel and to suppress vice in every possible way. Those sin-ners who tried to hide themselves from him he pursued to every corner of his parish, by all sorts of means, public and private, early and late, in season and out of season, entreating and warning them to flee from the wrath to come. Some made it an excuse for not attending the church service on a Sunday morning, that they could not awake early enough to get their families ready. He provided for this also. Taking a bell in his hand, he set out every Sunday for some months at five in the morning, and went round the most distant parts of the parish inviting all the inhabitants to the house of God."

He found abundance of organized wickedness in his neglected, overgrown parish. It was a common thing for young men and women to meet in large bodies on stated evenings for what they called "recreation." This recreation usually consisted in dancing, drinking, revelling, and immorality, and continued all night. Against these licentious assemblies Fletcher resolutely set his face, and used every exertion to put them down. He would often burst suddenly into the room where the disorderly company were assembled, rebuke the thoughtless revellers with a holy indignation, and beard Satan in his high places. Nor was his labour altogether in vain in this unpromising field. After standing the first outbursts of rudeness and brutality, he generally found his exhortations received with silent submission; and in some cases he had the comfort of seeing a reformation in the behaviour of the revellers.

Cases of sickness in a mining district like Madeley were necessarily very frequent, and coal-pit accidents, we need not doubt, were very many and often fatal. In attending such cases Fletcher was peculiarly zealous and indefatigable. "It was a work," says Wesley, "for which he was always ready. If he heard a knock at his door in the coldest winter night, his window was thrown open in a moment. And when he understood that some one was hurt in a pit, or that a neighbour was likely to die, no consideration was ever had of the darkness of the night or the severity of the weather. One answer was always given: 'I will attend you immediately.'"

"In all labour there is profit." It will not surprise any Christian to hear that Fletcher's labours at Madeley produced an immense effect on many souls. At first, indeed, he seemed to labour in vain, and to spend his strength for nothing. People were not converted in masses, and all at once. But gradually a large number of hearers were led by the Spirit to Christ, and became witnesses for God in the midst of the sin and darkness around them. With success, no doubt, came opposition and persecution of no common kind. This, however, will not surprise any Bible-reading Christian. Satan will never allow his kingdom to be pulled down without a mighty struggle, and never is his wrath so great as when he sees he has but "a short time." Let a great and effectual door be opened to the gospel, and there will never fail to be "many adversaries." It is an invariable mark of a real work of God, that it is carried on "through much persecution."

One Sunday, for instance, after doing his usual duty at Madeley, Fletcher was on the point of going to a place called Madeley Wood, to preach and catechise. But, just as he was setting out, he received a sudden notice that a child was to be buried, and had to wait for the funeral. This waiting till the child was brought prevented his going to the Wood till some time after the appointed hour. Herein the providence of God appeared in a very remarkable manner. At the hour originally appointed for his preaching, some colliers, who neither feared God nor man, were baiting a bull just by the place where he was expected. Having had plenty to drink, they had all agreed, as soon as he came, to "bait the parson." Part of them were then appointed to pull him off his horse, and the rest to set the dogs upon him. But in the meantime the bull broke loose, and threw down the booth in which the ring-leaders were drinking, and the people were dispersed. The result was that the godly people who had come together to hear him preach were enabled to hold their meeting in quietness and safety.

To enter into all the details of Fletcher's history during the twenty-five years of his ministry at Madeley, would be clearly impossible in the narrow limits of a brief and condensed memoir. In fact, to attempt it would be only telling the same story over and over again. Throughout this whole period, with little intermission, he was always doing one and the same thing— always preaching, always teaching, always trying to awaken sinners, always trying to build up saints; but always one and the same man, giving himself up wholly to his Master's business. Sometimes he found time to take a few Sundays at Lady

Huntingdon's chapel at Bath. Sometimes he exchanged duties for a little season with friends, such as Mr. Sellon, at Bredon, in Leicestershire. Sometimes he wrote long controversial treatises, in defence of what he believed was Christ's truth, against what he called Calvinism and Antinomianism. Sometimes he was entirely laid aside from work by ill health. But wherever he was, and in whatever condition, John Fletcher was unmistakably the " man of God," always the minister of Christ, always delighting in work, always insatiably desirous to do good to souls. I find no man of the last century, whatever his defects may have been in doctrine, to whom the scriptural motto might be so justly applied, " One thing I do."

About the year 1768 Fletcher was invited by Lady Huntingdon to become superintendent of her Training College for young ministers at Trevecca, in Wales. He accepted this important post with the distinct understanding that he was not to be generally resident there. He felt strongly that his duty to his flock at Madeley would not admit of this. But it was settled that he should attend as often as he could, should give advice about the appointment of masters and the admission or exclusion of students, should oversee their studies and conduct, and should judge of their fitness for the work of the ministry.

Whether a native of Switzerland, who had never seen England or spoken the English language till he was twenty-one, was exactly the man to be head of a training college, may admit of some doubt. In all probability, however, Fletcher was the best man among the evangelists of the day whom Lady Huntingdon could find. His reputation as tutor to Mr. Hill's son was probably a strong recommendation. His learning and scholarship were undeniable. His character as a holy, decided man stood very high. In short, if he were not the fittest person in the world to be principal of a college, it would not be very easy to say who, in that day, was more fit.

Fletcher, at any rate, appears to have done what he could to give the new Institution success. A letter to Lady Huntingdon, dated January 1768, gives a very favourable idea of his sound judgment. He evidently sees the materials he had to work upon, and wisely resolves not to pitch the standard of attainments required too high. He proposes to instruct all the students in grammar, logic, rhetoric, ecclesiastical history, geography, a little natural philosophy, and a great deal of practical divinity. The books he specially wishes to have in the library are,—Henry's and Gill's Commentaries on the Bible, Baxter's Works, Keach on Metaphors, Taylor on Types, Gurnall's Christian Armoury, Edwards on Preaching, Wesley's Christian Library, Usher's Body of Divinity, Scapula's Greek Lexicon, Lyttleton's Latin Dictionary, and Johnson's English Dictionary. Short and scanty as this list may appear for the beginning of a college library, it cannot be denied that it was well selected, considering the times. The mention of Gill's Commentary is also an interesting fact. It is enough to show that Fletcher's Arminianism did not prevent him valuing the works of a thoroughly Calvinistic writer.

The best account of Fletcher's proceedings as Principal of Trevecca is to be found in the writings of one of the under-masters; and it is so interesting, that I shall make no apology for giving it entire. He says :—" I went to reside at Trevecca in 1770. The young men whom I found there were serious, and made considerable progress in learning, and many of them seemed to have talents for the ministry. Mr. Fletcher visited us frequently, and was received as an angel of God. It is not possible for me to describe the veneration in which we all held him. Like Elijah in the school of the prophets, he was revered, he was loved, he was almost adored; and that not only by every student, but by every member of the family. And indeed he was worthy. Prayer, praise, love, and zeal, all-ardent, elevated above what we would think attainable in this state of frailty, was the element in which he continually lived. And as to others, his one employment was to call, entreat, and urge them to ascend with him to the glorious source of being and blessedness. He had leisure, comparatively, for nothing else. Languages, art, sciences, grammar, electricity, logic, even divinity itself, so-called, were all laid aside when he appeared in the school-room among the students. His full heart would not suffer him to be silent; he must speak. The students were readier to hearken to this servant and minister of Christ than to attend to Sallust, Virgil, Cicero, or any Latin or Greek historian, poet, or philosopher they had been engaged in reading. And they seldom hearkened long before they were all in tears, and every heart caught fire from the flame which burned in his soul. Such seasons generally terminated in this. Being convinced that to be filled with the Holy Ghost was a better qualification for the ministry of the gospel than any classical learning, after speaking awhile in the school-room he used often to say, 'As many of you as are athirst for the fulness of the Spirit, follow me into my room.' On this many of us have instantly followed him, and there continued for two or three hours, wrestling, like Jacob, for the blessing; and praying one after another, till we could not bear to kneel any longer." I make no comment on this curious account. I dare not say that I think it would be well to be incessantly converting college-lectures into prayer-meetings. But I will not shrink from saying, that a few more head-masters of schools and principals of colleges as spiritual-minded and prayerful as the Vicar of Madeley, would be an immense blessing to the Church of Christ. Head-masters and principals too often go into the very opposite extreme from that into which Fletcher went. Too often they are cold, dry, hard, and unsympathizing, and seem to forget entirely that young men have hearts, and consciences, and souls.

Fletcher's connection with Trevecca College only lasted three years. It came to an end in 1771, in consequence of his steady adherence to Arminian principles, and his firm determination to stand by John Wesley in matters of doctrine. He parted from the Institution on good terms with Lady Huntingdon, and without any bitterness or asperity on either side. Whether, in point of fact, there was so very much difference in doctrinal views between him and Lady Huntingdon's party, as he supposed, is a matter on which I feel considerable doubt. At any rate, I suspect it was greatly exaggerated. There is no getting over the remarkable fact that for three years he took a leading part in the great anniversary gatherings at the college, and preached side by side with men like Whitefield, Rowlands, Berridge, and Venn. That simple fact speaks volumes. In days of controversy, bystanders are fond of exaggerating differences, and blowing up the fire of division. When men can preach and pray together with freedom, we may rest assured that in heart they do not greatly differ. Let us try to believe that all was ordered for good. It is pretty certain that Fletcher could not long have retained his double position as Principal of Trevecca and Vicar of Madeley. The double responsibility would have killed him. It is far from improbable that he saw this himself, and was not sorry to have a door opened for retiring.

About the year 1776, Fletcher's health failed so much that he was completely laid aside from public work, and obliged to leave Madeley entirely for the long space of five years. He had never been very strong at any time, and for some years before 1776 he had many premonitory symptoms of consumption. Like many unmarried ministers, he had lived alone and taken no care of himself, and at the age of forty-seven he seemed to be breaking down entirely under the abundance of his labours. He felt himself that he had often been imprudent, and taxed his constitution too much. But it is just one of those lessons which ministers generally find out too late, when the mischief is done. Over-laziness is so much more a besetting sin than over-zeal, that a conscientious man may well be excused if he turns a deaf ear to the suggestion, "Spare thyself," and suspects it to be a temptation of the devil. Such, I have little doubt, was the case with Fletcher.

The first two years of Fletcher's forced retirement from work was spent in England,—partly at Brislington, near Bristol; partly at Newington, near London; and partly at other places, —but always at the house of loving friends. His one employment was that most wearing and depressing one, the search for health; and many, strange, and various were the remedies he seems to have tried in order to obtain it. At no time of his life, perhaps, did his graces shine more than they did a this. He gave full proof that he could bear God's will as well as do it, suffer patiently as well as work actively, sit still and do nothing as well as run about and do a great deal. Let me here express my own firm conviction, that this is the highest point of excellence in a Christian. Self-conceit, and the love of the praise of men, will often help us to preach, and speak, and write, and make a great noise in the world. Nothing but great grace will enable us to be content to do nothing, and to sit still and wait. No wonder that one who came to visit him at Newington, when he was thought to be dying, said afterwards, "I went to see a man that had one foot in the grave, but I found a man that had one foot in heaven."

The last three years of Fletcher's period of ill health were spent on the Continent,—partly in the south of France, and partly in Switzerland. This Continental tour was a wisely-devised plan, and answered perfectly. The return to his native air, the entire change of scene and occupation, the freedom from a thousand causes of care and anxiety in England, the society of his valued and kind travelling companion, Mr. Ireland of Brislington,—all these things acted with mighty power on Fletcher's shattered constitution. Little by little he began to rally. Little by little he lost the many unfavourable symptoms with which he had left England. At last, to his own great delight, he was able to preach without difficulty; and at length, in the month of June 1781, like one miraculously raised from the dead, he found himself once more in his vicarage at Madeley.

In the latter end of 1781, the same year that he returned to Madeley, Fletcher was married. He was now in the decline of life, a man of broken health, in the fifty-second year of his age, and the step probably took his friends by surprise. But it seems to have been a wise and well-ordered step, and one that added much to the comfort of his latter days. The lady of his choice, a Miss Bosanquet, was one whom he had known well as a decided Christian for at least twenty years, and she appears in every respect, both in age and character, to have been eminently calculated to be a help-meet for him. The account of the wedding, which is given at great length by Fletcher's biographer, Mr. Benson, is very curious indeed, and deserves an attentive perusal. Seldom, perhaps, was a marriage ever celebrated in a fashion so utterly unlike the fashion of this world. But Fletcher was no common man, and his wedding was no common wedding.

The Vicar of Madeley's letter to a friend, written shortly after his marriage, is interesting; and the more so as it throws some light on his motives for changing his state. He says: " I am married in my old age, and have a new opportunity of considering a great mystery, in the most perfect type of our Lord's mystical union with his Church. I have now a new call to pray for a fulness of Christ's holy, gentle, meek, loving spirit, that I may love my wife as he loved his spouse the Church. But the emblem is greatly deficient. The Lamb is worthy of his spouse, and more than worthy: whereas I must acknowledge myself unworthy of the yoke-fellow whom Heaven has reserved for me. She is a person after my own heart; and I make no doubt we shall increase the number of the happy marriages in the Church militant. Indeed, they are not so many but it may be worth a Christian's while to add one more to the number. God declared that it was 'not good for man,' a social being, 'to live alone;' and therefore he gave him a help-meet for him. For the same reason our Lord sent forth his disciples two and two. Had I searched the three kingdoms, I could not have found one brother willing to share, gratis, my weal, woe, and labour, and complaisant enough to unite his fortune to mine. But God has found me a partner, 'a sister, a wife,' to use St. Paul's language, who is not afraid to face with me the colliers and bargemen of my parish, until death part us. Buried together in our country village, we shall help one another to trim our lamps, and to wait, as I trust you do continually, for the coming of the heavenly Bridegroom."

In another letter, written in the beginning of 1782, he says: "Strangely restored to health and strength, considering my years, by the good nursing of my dear partner, I ventured to preach of late as often as I did formerly : and, after having read prayers, I preached twice on Christmas-day. I did last Sunday what I had never done : I continued doing duty from ten till past four in the afternoon, owing to christenings, churchings, and the sacrament, which I administered to a churchful of people ; so that I was obliged to go from the communion-table to begin the evening service, and then to visit some sick. This has brought back upon me one of my old dangerous symptoms, so that I had flattered myself in vain to do the whole duty of my parish. But my dear wife nurses me with the tenderest care, gives me up to God with the greatest resignation, and helps me to rejoice that life and death, health and sickness, work all for our good, and are all sure, as blessed instruments, to forward us in our journey to heaven."

Fletcher's most useful ministry did not last long after his return to Madeley. He died on Saturday the 14th of August 1785, after a short illness of only ten days' duration—appa·

rently a typhus fever—in the fifty-sixth year of his age. His constitution was probably broken down by his long-continued labours in Christ's cause, and a constant tendency to consumption; and when the last enemy came, he had no strength or stamina to enable him to resist disease. Even to the last he was the same man that he had been for twenty-five years, and his obstinate determination to work on to the uttermost in all probability made his attack of fever terminate fatally. Though taken ill on Thursday the 4th of August, he persisted in taking the full morning duty on the following Sunday in his church. He read prayers, preached, and administered the Lord's Supper, though he nearly fainted several times in the service. From the church he was supported into his bedroom, where he lay for some time in a swoon, and from that time he never left his house alive. Never, perhaps, was there a more striking instance of the "ruling passion being strong in death." Like Whitefield, he almost died in harness.

All through the early part of the week he lay very ill, able to speak little, but full of joy and peace, and delighting greatly in hearing his wife read hymns and treatises on faith and love. On Thursday and Friday he spoke very little, but seemed to take peculiar pleasure in the text, "God is love," and in the verse of a hymn containing these words,—

> " The blood of Christ through earth and skies,
> Mercy—free, boundless mercy cries;
> Mercy's full power I soon shall prove—
> Loved with an everlasting love."

On Saturday afternoon the fever seemed to leave him for a little time, and he became so much more like himself that a friend said, " Do you think the Lord will raise you up?" He strove to answer, but could only just pronounce the words, " Raise me up in the resurrection." To another who asked the same question, he said, " I leave it all to God."

On Saturday evening the fever returned again, and with

greater violence than ever. It became evident that he was dying very fast. His wife then said, " My dear creature, I ask not for myself—I know thy soul—but I ask for the sake of others :—If Jesus be very present with thee, lift up thy right hand." Immediately he did so. " If the prospect of glory sweetly open before thee, repeat the sign." He instantly raised his hand again, and in half a minute raised it a second time. He then threw it up, as if he would reach the top of the bed. After this he moved and spoke no more, excepting when Mrs. Fletcher said, " Art thou in pain ?" when he answered, " No." From that time he lay in a kind of sleep, though with his eyes open and fixed, sitting upright in his bed, with his head leaning on pillows. Eighteen hours he continued in this position, breathing quietly like a person in common sleep, and with a countenance so calm and composed that not a trace of death could be seen on it. During this period many of his mourning parishioners, who had assembled for Sunday service, were permitted to walk through the house, and past the open door of his bedroom, and to see his much-loved face once more. At length, at half-past ten on Sunday night, August 14th, he fell asleep in Christ, without a struggle or groan, and entered into the joy of his Lord. On the 17th, he was buried in Madeley churchyard, amidst the tears and lamentations of thousands, of whom many never knew the true value of their vicar until they had lost him.

I have now followed Fletcher from his cradle to his grave. It only remains for me to offer some estimate of his real worth as a preacher, a writer, and a man.

As a *preacher*, I am disposed to assign Fletcher a very high rank. Even in the last century, when there were " giants of pulpit power on the earth," I suspect there were not half-a-dozen men superior to the Vicar of Madeley. He was naturally an eloquent man. He had a mind well trained and stored with scriptural matter. He was eminently direct, bold, and conscience-stirring, in his way of putting things. Not least, he had a very fine voice, and a singularly fervent and attractive manner. It is recorded that many English people used to go to hear him preach in French to the French congregations in London, though they could not understand a word that he said. "We go," they used to say, "to look at him, for heaven seems to beam from his countenance." A minister possessing such qualifications as these must have been a man of no common power in the pulpit. John Wesley, who was no mean judge, used to say, that if Fletcher had had more physical strength, he would have been the first preacher in England. This is probably saying too much. Nothing, I suspect, would ever have made Fletcher equal Whitefield or Rowlands. But we need not hesitate to place him in the first class among the Christian orators of England a hundred years ago.

The following passage will probably convey a pretty correct idea of what Fletcher was as a preacher. I have taken it from his "Address to a serious reader who inquires what must he do to be saved." The address was certainly not published in the form of a sermon; but if it had not been preached, I am greatly mistaken. Ministers who spend their whole life in preaching, as Fletcher did, have seldom time to think and compose in more than one style. To that rule Henry Venn was perhaps the only exception among the great men of the last century. But that Fletcher had preached the following passage in Madeley pulpit before he committed it to the press, I feel thoroughly persuaded in my own mind. After quoting a long list of encouraging promises and invitations in Scripture, he goes on,—

"Are these, O sinner, the gracious sayings of God to thee? the compassionate expostulations of God, become incarnate for thee? Did God so love thee as to set forth his only-begotten Son, as a propitiation through faith in his blood, thus to declare his righteousness for the remission of sins that are past? May the Almighty now be just, and yet the justifier of him that believeth in Jesus? Is there no difference, no respect of persons, with him? And is the same Lord over all rich unto all that call upon him? Then shout, ye heavens! triumph, thou earth! and thou, happy sinner, know the day of thy visitation; be wise, ponder these things, and thou shalt understand the loving-kindness of the Lord.

"Be no longer afraid that it will be presumption in thee to believe, and that God will be offended with thee if thou makest so free with Jesus as to wash instantly in the fountain of his atoning blood. He not only gives thee leave to believe, but he invites thee to do it freely. Nay, he commands thee to believe; for 'this is his commandment, that we should believe on the name of his Son Jesus Christ.' He even enforces the precept by a double promise, that if thou believest thou 'shalt not perish, but have everlasting life.' And that nothing may be wanting to stir thee up to this important business, he is gracious enough to threaten the neglect of it with the most dreadful punishment; for 'he that believeth not shall not enter into his rest,' and 'shall be damned;' and he that to the end remains 'fearful and unbelieving' 'shall be cast into the lake that burneth with fire and brimstone, which is the second death.' How canst thou doubt, then, whether thou art welcome to receive the Son by believing on his name?

"Come to him just as thou art, and he will make thee what thou shouldst be. When he counsels thee to buy of him the gold of faith, and the garment of salvation, take him at his gospel-word. Come without regarding thy stuff—the poorer thou art the better—the oil of his grace flows most abundantly into empty vessels—his charity is most glorified in the relief of the most miserable objects—his royal bounty scorns the vile compensation of thy wretched merits—he sells like a king, like the King of kings, 'without money and without price.'

"'Ask and have,' and 'take freely,' are the encouraging

mottoes written upon all the unsearchable treasures of his grace.

"Be of good comfort, then; rise, he calleth thee—stretch out thy withered hand, and he will restore it—open thy mouth wide, and he will fill it—bring an empty vessel, a poor hungry heart, and he will give into thy bosom good measure, pressed down, shaken together and running over.

"And now, what meanest thou, sleeper? Why tarriest thou? Arise, and wash away thy sins, calling on the name of the Lord. Lose not time in conferring with flesh and blood; much less in parleying with Satan, or consulting thy unbelieving heart. These delays lead to ruin; the Philistines are upon thee, instantly shake thyself; if thou art not altogether blinded by the god of this world, and led captive by him at his will, this moment, in the powerful name of Jesus, burst the bonds of spiritual sloth—break, like a desperate soul, out of the prison of unbelief—escape for thy life—look not behind thee—stay not in all the plain. This one thing do; leaving the things that are behind—Sodom and her ways—press forwards towards Zoar, and escape to the mount of God, lest thou be consumed. By the new and living way consecrated for us, in full assurance of faith, fly to the Father of mercies, pass through the crowd of Laodicean professors, press through the opening door of hope, take the kingdom of heaven by violence.

"With halting, yet wrestling, Jacob, say to the Friend of sinners, 'I will not let thee go unless thou bless me.' If he makes as if he would go farther, with the two mournful disciples, 'constrain him to stay;' or rather, with the distressed women of Canaan, 'follow him whithersoever he goeth,' take no denial. Through the veil, that is to say, his flesh, torn from the crown of his head to the sole of his feet—through this mysterious veil, rent from the top to the bottom, rush into the blood-besprinkled sanctuary; embrace the horns of the golden altar; lay all thy guilt on the head of the sin-atoning victim; read thy name on the breast of thy merciful high-priest. Claim the safety, demand the blessings, receive the consolations bestowed on all that fly to him for refuge, and begin a new, delightful life, under the healing and peaceful shadow of his wings."

As *a writer*, Fletcher's reputation will never perhaps stand so high as it deserves. Unfortunately, a very large portion of his literary remains consists of controversial treatises against Calvinism, and in defence of Arminianism. In these treatises I must plainly say the worthy Vicar of Madeley says many things with which I cannot agree, because I cannot reconcile them with the statements of Scripture. Yet, even when I do not agree with him, I feel bound as an honest man to admit that Fletcher is a very able adversary, and makes the best that can be made of a bad cause, and writes with courtesy. Indeed, I never can help suspecting that he was not nearly so much an Arminian in his heart as he thought he was, and that he was pushed into saying things, in the heat of controversy, which he afterwards regretted.

The following passage, from Fletcher's "Checks to Antinomianism," will convey a very fair idea of his power as a writer, and will show how thoroughly his mind was saturated and imbued with Scripture. It is almost needless to remark that, like many controversialists, he was constantly fighting shadows of his own creation, and that his Calvinistic antagonists hated Antinomianism and unholy living quite as much as he did. But the passage is a good specimen of his style of writing. He is giving a long catalogue of the melancholy inconsistencies of professors of religion, and says :—

"Who can number the 'adulterers and adulteresses' who know not that the friendship of the world is enmity against God?—the concealed idolaters, who have their 'chambers of imagery' within, and 'set up their idols in their hearts?'—the envious Cains, who carry murder in their breast?'—the profane Esaus, who give up their birthright for a sensual gratification; and

covetous Judases, who ' sell the truth' which they should ' buy,'
and part with Christ ' for filthy lucre's sake ?'—' the sons of God,
who look at the fair daughters of men, and take to themselves
wives of all which they choose ?'—the gay Dinahs, who ' visit
the daughters of the land,' and come home polluted in body or
in soul ?—the prophets of Bethel, ' who deceive the prophets of
Judah,' entice them out of the way of self-denial, and bring the
roaring lion and death upon them ?—the fickle Marcuses, who
depart when they should ' go to the work ?'—the self-made
prophets, who ' run before they are sent,' and scatter instead of
' profiting the people ?'—the spiritual Absaloms, who rise against
their fathers in the gospel, and, in order to ' reign without them,'
raise a rebellion against them ?—the furious Zedekiahs, who
' make themselves horns of iron to push' the true servants of
the Lord, because they will not ' prophesy smooth things and
deceit' as they do ? Who can count the fretful Jonahs, who
are ' angry to death' when the ' worm' of disappointment
' smites the gourd' of their creature-happiness ?—the weak Aarons,
who dare not resist a multitude, and are carried by the stream
into the greatest absurdities ?—the jealous Miriams, who rise
against the ministers that God honours ?—the crafty Zibas, who
calumniate and supplant their brethren ?—the treacherous Joabs,
who ' kiss' them to get an opportunity of ' stabbing them under
the fifth rib ?'—the busy sons of Zeruiah, who perpetually stir
up resentment and wrath ?—the mischievous Doegs, who carry
about poisonous scandal, and blow up the fire of discord ?—the
hypocritical Gehazis, who look like saints before their masters
and ministers, and yet can impudently lie and impiously cheat ?
—the Gibeonites, always busy in hewing wood and drawing
water, in going through the drudgery of outward services, without ever aspiring at the adoption of sons ?—the halting Naamans,
who serve the Lord and bow to Rimmon ?—the backsliding
Solomons, who once ' chose wisdom,' but now pursue folly
in her most extravagant and impious forms ?—the apostatizing

Alexanders, who 'tread under foot the Son of God, and count the blood of the covenant, wherewith they are sanctified, an unholy thing?'—and, to include multitudes in one class, the Samaritans, who, by a common mixture of truth and error, of heavenly and earthly mindedness, 'worship the Lord and serve their gods;' are one day for God, and the next for mammon?—or the thousands in Israel who 'halt between two opinions,' crying out, when Elijah prevails, 'The Lord he is the God!' and when Jezebel triumphs, returning to the old song, 'O Baal, save us!' O trinity of the world, money, pleasure, and honour, make us happy!"

But it really is not fair to judge Fletcher, as a writer, by his controversial treatises alone. Out of the eight volumes of his works, at least four contain many admirable things, which are far less known than they ought to be. His admirable "Letter to Mr. Prothero in Defence of Experimental Religion;" his "Critical Vindication of the Catholic Faith, in reply to Priestley;" his "Portrait of St. Paul;" his "Pastoral Epistles" to his flock at Madeley, are, generally speaking, all worthy of high praise. Last, but not least, his letters to friends, like most of the letters of the spiritual heroes of last century, are often most excellent. If a volume of letters by Whitefield, Venn, and their contemporaries, could be compiled and published— and I have long regretted that the thing has not been done—I am bold to say that Fletcher's letters would occupy a very prominent place among them.

As *a man*, Fletcher's character stands above all praise. I can find very few men of a hundred years ago about whom there is so striking an agreement on all sides that he was pre-eminently and peculiarly a most holy man, a saint indeed, a living epistle of Christ. His deep humility, his extraordinary self-denial, his unwearied diligence, his courage in Christ's cause, his constant spirituality of tone, his fervent love to God and man, his singleness of eye, are features in his character so strongly marked and

developed, that even his adversaries never pretended to deny
them.   Wrong as he was in some of his views of doctrine, his
worst foes never ventured to doubt his singular holiness of life.
In this respect, at any rate, the Vicar of Madeley ranked high
among his contemporaries.   Like every earthen vessel, he had
his cracks and flaws, no doubt, and no one knew it better than
himself; but they were cracks and flaws which were far less
visible than, unhappily, they are in many of God's saints.

Let us hear what John Wesley thought of Fletcher.   No
doubt he was an Arminian, like Fletcher, and likely to think
well of him.   But Wesley was a calm, cool-blooded man, and
not one to speak strongly in any one's praise without good
reason.   This is his testimony :—

"I was intimately acquainted with Mr. Fletcher for thirty
years.   I conversed with him morning, noon, and night, without the least reserve, during a journey of many hundred miles;
and in all that time I never heard him speak an improper word,
or do an improper action.   To conclude, within fourscore years
I have known many excellent men, holy in heart and life; but
one equal to him I have not known, one so uniformly devoted
to God.   So unblamable a man, in every respect, I have not
found, either in Europe or America, nor do I expect to find
another such on this side eternity."

Let us hear, finally, what Henry Venn thought of Fletcher.
His testimony, at any rate, is unexceptionable.   Though not an
extreme Calvinist, he certainly was not in the least an Arminian.
He had little or no direct connection with the Vicar of Madeley, and did not move in the same path.   Above all, he was a
man of rare good sense as well as grace, and one whose gift of
sound judgment was great and extraordinary.

His testimony was as follows :—"Mr. Fletcher was a luminary.   A luminary, did I say ?   He was a sun.   I have known
all the great men for these fifty years, but I have known none
like him.   I was intimately acquainted with him, and was under

the same roof with him once for six weeks, during which I never heard him say a single word which was not proper to be spoken, and which had not a tendency to minister grace to the hearers. One time meeting him when he was very ill with a hectic fever, which he had brought on himself by excessive labour, I said, ' I am sorry to find you so ill.' Mr. Fletcher answered with great sweetness and energy, ' Sorry, sir ! Why are you sorry ? It is the chastisement of my heavenly Father, and I rejoice in it. I love the rod of my God, and rejoice therein, as an expression of his love and affection towards me.' "

With John Fletcher I now close my biographical accounts of the ministers who were prime movers in the revival of English religion a hundred years ago. I have shown, I think, that in the best sense " there were giants in those days." The Vicar of Madeley, my readers will probably agree with me, was not the least of them.

XIV.

Conclusion.

Y contribution to the religious history of England a hundred years ago is now concluded. I have fairly exhausted the list of leading ministers who were the spiritual reformers of our land in the last century. That there were other great and good men beside the eleven whom I have selected, I do not for a moment deny. I only say that there were none equal to them in public usefulness. There were other labourers in the gospel-field of England whose record is on high. But they "attained not to the first" eleven.

In compiling these biographies I am very sensible of many deficiencies. I know they might have been made larger. But I cannot forget that we do not live in a reading age, and that "great books are great evils." I know they might have been better written. But I hope the reader will remember that their preparation has been carried on under immense difficulties, and under the daily pressure of other ministerial duties. I have, at any rate, the satisfaction of feeling that this volume contains a mass of facts which have never been brought together before, and throws light on some points in English Church history which have never yet been rightly understood.

There are a few general statistics about my eleven heroes which deserve notice. Reading their lives singly and one by one, we may possibly overlook them. Viewed altogether and in combination, they will probably be thought interesting.

For one thing, every one of the eleven leading ministers in

the revival of last century was an ordained clergyman of the Church of England. This is a fact which ought not to be overlooked. I am not what is called a High Churchman. I do not hold the divine right of Episcopacy. I desire to regard all ministers who love Christ and preach the truth as my brethren. But still, honour should be given where honour is due. It is a total mistake to suppose, as many do, that English religion a hundred years ago was revived by Dissenters. Nothing of the kind! The men who did the mighty work of that day, and plucked Christianity out of the dust, were all clergymen of the Church of England—clergymen of whom the Church was unworthy, but still clergymen as really and truly as George Herbert, or Andrews, or Bull. Let that fact never be forgotten. Well would it have been for the Church of England if she had more children like Rowlands and Berridge, and fewer like Laud.

For another thing, the greater part of the leaders of the revival of English religion last century were University men. Five of them—namely, Wesley, Whitefield, Romaine, Hervey, and Walker—took their degrees at Oxford. Three of them—namely, Grimshaw, Berridge, and Venn—took their degrees at Cambridge. Toplady was educated at Trinity College, Dublin. Rowlands and Fletcher alone were at no University at all. Let this fact also be carefully remembered. The common notion that the men who turned England upside down last century were mere common-place, illiterate, ignorant, uneducated fanatics, is a stupid mistake. So far from this being the case, the eleven clergymen described in this volume were in all probability better read and more furnished with knowledge than most ministers of their day.

For another thing, the majority of the eleven clergymen who led the revival of last century were married men. Of the four who never married, three died at a comparatively early age, of consumption, namely, Hervey, Toplady, and Walker. The most eminent one of the eleven who died unmarried was Berridge, and he, we have seen, was so quaint, that he was always unlike other men. This fact is one that ought not to be overlooked. In a day when celibacy is held up to admiration as the grand secret of exalted spirituality, it is worth remembering that devoted servants of God like Grimshaw, Rowlands, Venn, and Romaine, could walk with God like Enoch, and yet, like Enoch, " live according to God's ordinance in the holy estate of matrimony." The minister who has no sons and daughters of his own, suffers immense loss in the study of human nature.

It only remains for me now to point out a few practical lessons which appear to flow naturally from the biographies which fill the pages of this book. They are lessons which are strongly impressed on my own mind. Thankful should I be if I could impress them on the minds of others !

1. In the first place, would we know the right instrumentality for doing good in the present day ? Evil is about us and upon us on every side, evil from Romanism, evil from infidelity, evil from tractarianism, evil from neologianism, evil amidst the working classes, evil amidst the educated bodies. What is the true remedy for the disease ? What is the weapon to be wielded if we would meet the foe ? Can anything be done ? Is there no hope ?

I answer boldly that the true remedy for all the evils of our day is the same remedy that proved effectual a hundred years ago — the same pure unadulterated doctrine that the men of whom I have been writing used to preach, and the same kind of preachers. I am bold to say that we want nothing new — no new systems, no new school of teaching, no new theology, no new ceremonial, no new gospel. We want nothing but the old truths rightly preached and rightly brought home to consciences, minds, and wills. The evangelical system of theology revived England a hundred years ago, and I have faith to believe that it could revive it again.

There never has been good done in the world excepting by the faithful preaching of evangelical truth. From the days of the apostles down to this time, there have been no victories won, no spiritual successes obtained, except by the doctrines which wrought deliverance a hundred years ago. Where are the conquests of neologianism and tractarianism over heathenism, irreligion, immorality? Where are the nations they have Christianized, the parishes they have evangelized, the towns they have turned from darkness to light? You may well ask where? You will get no answer. The good that has been done in the world, however small, has always been done by evangelical doctrines; and if men who are not called "evangelical" have had successes, they have had them by using evangelical weapons. They have ploughed with our heifer, or they would never have had any harvest to show at all.

I repeat it emphatically, for I believe it sincerely. The first want of our day is a return to the old, simple, and sharply-cut doctrines of our fathers in the last century; and the second want is a generation of like-minded and like-gifted men to preach them. Give me in any county of England and Wales a man like Grimshaw or Rowlands or Whitefield, and there is nothing in the present day which would make me afraid. I confidently believe that in the face of such men and such preaching ritualism, neologianism, and infidelity would be paralyzed and wither away.

2. Would we know, in the next place, why the ministers who profess to follow the evangelical fathers of last century are so much less successful than they were? The question is a delicate and interesting one, and ought not to be shelved. The suspicion naturally crosses some minds, that the doctrines which won victories a hundred years ago are worn out, and have lost their power. I believe that theory to be an entire mistake. The answer which I give to the inquiry is one of a very different kind.

I am obliged then to say plainly, that, in my judgment, we have among us neither the men nor the doctrines of the days gone by. We have none who preach with such peculiar power as Whitefield or Rowlands. We have none who in self-denial, singleness of eye, diligence, holy boldness, and unworldliness, come up to the level of Grimshaw, Walker, Venn, and Fletcher. It is a humbling conclusion; but I have long felt that it is the truth. We lack both the men and the message of the last century. What wonder if we do not see the last century's results. Give us like men and a like message, and I have no fear that the Holy Ghost would grant us like results.

Wherein do evangelical Churchmen fall short of their great predecessors in the last century? Let us look this question fairly in the face. Let us come to particulars. They fall short *in doctrine.* They are neither so full nor so distinct, nor so bold, nor so uncompromising. They are afraid of strong statements. They are too ready to fence, and guard, and qualify all their teaching, as if Christ's gospel was a little baby, and could not be trusted to walk alone. They fall short *as preachers.* They have neither the fervour, nor fire, nor thought, nor illustration, nor directness, nor holy boldness, nor grand simplicity of language which characterized the last century. Above all, they fall short *in life.* They are not men of one thing, separate from the world, unmistakable men of God, ministers of Christ everywhere, indifferent to man's opinion, regardless who is offended, if they only preach truth, always about their Father's business, as Grimshaw and Fletcher used to be. They do not make the world feel that a prophet is among them, and carry about with them their Master's presence, as Moses when he came down from the mount. I write these things with sorrow. I desire to take my full share of blame. But I do believe I am speaking the truth.

It is no use trying to evade the truth on this subject. I fear that, as a general rule, the evangelical ministry in England has fallen far below the standard of the last century, and that the simple account of the want of success to which so many point is, the low standard both of doctrine and life which prevails. Ease and popularity, and the absence of persecution, are ruinous to some. Political questions eat out the vitality of others. An extravagant and excessive attention to the petty details of parish machinery withers up the ministry of others. An absurd straining after the reputation of being "intellectual" and original is the curse of others. A desire to seem charitable and liberal, and keep in with everybody, paralyzes the ministry of others. The plague is abroad. We want a revival among evangelical ministers. Once let the evangelical ministry of England return to the ways of the last century, and I firmly believe we should have as much success as before. We are where we are, because we have come short of our fathers.

3. Last of all comes the all-important question, What ought we to do? I answer confidently, There are three things which we shall do well to remember, if we wish our work to prosper.

First, let us resolve to cast in our lot boldly on the side of what I must call "evangelical" religion in England. Let us not be moved by the sneers and contempt which are poured on it in some quarters. Let us cleave to it, hold it fast, and never let it go. Let us beware of the plausible charity which says, "All earnest men hold the truth. No earnest man can err." Let us beware of the idolatry of intellect, which says, "A man cannot make mistakes in doctrine if he is a clever man." Of both these dangers let us beware. Let us lay hold firmly on evangelical religion as the truth of God, and never be ashamed to confess it. Let us stand by it, and it will stand by us in the hour of sickness and on the bed of death, in the swellings of Jordan, and in the day of judgment.

Next, let us resolve to work heartily for evangelical truth, each in his own place. There is always work for every one before his own door. Let us never stand still because we are in a minority. What though we stand alone in a house of business, alone in the banking-house, alone in a regiment, alone in a ship, alone in a family! What of it? Let us think of the little company who shook England one hundred years ago, and work on. It is truth, not numbers, which shall always in the end prevail. The three hundred at Thermopylæ were better than the million of Persians. A small minority of evangelical Christians with the gospel in their hearts are stronger than a host of servants of the Pope, the devil, and the world.

And let us pray, last of all, as well as work. Let us pray night and day that God would revive his work in England, and raise up many more instruments to do his will. Let us pray with the abiding thought that God's arm is not shortened, that what he has done he can do again, and that the same God who wrought so mightily for England one hundred years ago can do greater things still. Let us ask Him who holds the stars in his right hand to revive his work among our ministers, and to raise up men for our times. He can do it. He is willing to do it. He waits to be entreated. Then let all who pray cry night and day to the Lord of the harvest, " Lord, send forth more labourers into thy harvest."